PISTOLS AND POLITICS

Pistols and Politics

Feuds, Factions, and the Struggle for Order
in Louisiana's Florida Parishes, 1810–1935

Second Edition

Samuel C. Hyde, Jr.

Louisiana State University Press
Baton Rouge

Published with the assistance of the V. Ray Cardozier Fund

Published by Louisiana State University Press
Copyright © 2018 by Louisiana State University Press
This volume is an expanded and updated second edition of *Pistols and Politics: The Di-
lemma of Democracy in Louisiana's Florida Parishes, 1810–1899*, copyright © 1996 by
Louisiana State University Press.
All rights reserved
Manufactured in the United States of America
First printing

Designer: Michele Myatt Quinn
Typeface: Goudy Old Style
Printer and binder: Sheridan Books, Inc.

Library of Congress Cataloging-in-Publication Data

Names: Hyde, Samuel C., 1958– author.
Title: Pistols and politics : feuds, factions, and the struggle for order in Louisiana's Florida Parishes, 1810–1935 / Samuel C. Hyde, Jr.
Description: Second edition. | Baton Rouge : Louisiana State University Press, [2018]
   | Includes bibliographical references and index.
Identifiers: LCCN 2017040482 | ISBN 978-0-8071-6927-8 (pbk. : alk. paper)
Subjects: LCSH: Florida Parishes (La.)—History—19th century. | Florida Parishes
   (La.)—History—20th century. | Florida Parishes (La.)—Politics and government.
   | Florida Parishes (La.) —Social conditions. | Violence—Louisiana—Florida Par-
   ishes—History—19th century. |Violence—Louisiana—Florida Parishes—Histo-
   ry—20th century.
Classification: LCC F377.F6 H93 2018 | DDC 976.3/18—dc23
LC record available at https://lccn.loc.gov/2017040482

The paper in this book meets the guidelines for permanence and durability of the
Committee on Production Guidelines for Book Longevity of the Council on Library
Resources. ∞

For my parents, Sammie and Allie—you made it all possible!

CONTENTS

Illustrations

Tables

Preface to the Second Edition

Growing up in southeast Louisiana, I was regularly exposed to stories of feuds, lynchings, "Bloody Tangipahoa," and the chronic instability that historically plagued the region. Surprisingly, little scholarly interest focused on a region whose troubled past seemed intrinsically connected to an extraordinary pattern of development that included governance by every major European power that intruded into the North American wilderness, an armed insurrection that arguably initiated the process of hemispheric freedom from Spanish colonialism, and, among other curiosities, chronic episodes of violence that dwarfed many of the Wild West stories common to American folklore.

My active interest in the turbulent history of Louisiana's Florida parishes began during my undergraduate years at Tulane University. In the course of my studies there, it became apparent that the level of violence that convulsed southeastern Louisiana in the late nineteenth and early twentieth centuries was truly peculiar. The incredible level of brutality involved much more than scores of personal difficulties and an ineffective legal system. The violence proved merely a product of much larger circumstances—circumstances that remained central to the development of the region from the colonial period into the early twentieth century.

Though intrigued by the conditions, I remained dismayed that so little had been written on the subject. As I continued my research, a sense of understanding emerged; the stories were not pleasant, some were outright painful. The names of families involved and the locations of horrific acts of violence were well-known to scores of regional residents. Perhaps less had been written because many preferred to forget, while others never fully understood their peculiar past and thus avoided the topic. What I regarded as a study designed to detail how justice and/or democracy had failed the people of southeast Louisiana could not be separated from the human stories that revealed the dilemma. I hesitated to take on a challenge that demanded personal detachment from a subject to which I was historically attached.

Several years later while studying on a Fulbright fellowship in Germany, I advised one of my professors about the subject and the challenge it presented for me. Equally intrigued by the course of development in the Florida parishes, he forthrightly encouraged me to become coldly indifferent to my subject or get out of the profession. In other words, professionally confront the challenge or make way for someone who could. I returned home determined to relentlessly pursue the subject from every possible angle in an effort to form a comprehensive understanding of why the region endured and, perhaps more importantly, why the people tolerated such a troubled pattern of development.

Not surprisingly, the centrality of racism to the violence was readily apparent, though it took a somewhat unusual form. Like the South as a whole, the Florida parishes witnessed abundant white-on-black brutality during the nineteenth century, yet the violence that destabilized the region remained overwhelmingly white-on-white. Of the two primary white factions that emerged in the late nineteenth century, one sought to exploit African Americans for its own self-serving interests, while the other sought rigidly to exclude them from politics and sources of economic development. The dilemma of which course racism would take, and hence an important component of the violence, centered on the conflict between the so-called cooperationists and those committed to the absolute exclusion of blacks.

The intricacies of the racial dilemma revealed an even larger basis for the violence, one that proved to be the very determinant of social stability. The direction provided by powerful river-parish planters delivered the territory from a condition of near chaos, promoting economic prosperity and political stability. However, planter leadership frequently stifled the ambitions of the plain folk, and in the aftermath of war and Reconstruction the common folk rejected the dominance of the planter class. Lacking firm leadership, the region declined into anarchy.

The original edition of *Pistols and Politics* accordingly revealed elements of both continuity and change. The heavy-handed direction of the slaveholding elite produced stability in a chaotic territory emerging from an armed insurrection, and maintained it through the close of the antebellum period. The planter leaders emerged from the destruction of the war and, with the enthusiastic support of the common folk, directed resistance to federal Reconstruction efforts. Change came in the immediate aftermath of Reconstruction, when the plain folk rejected the governance of their former leaders and turned to new men schooled in the effectiveness and finality of violence.

The result was a return to the near anarchy of the colonial period amid an astonishing level of human cruelty. In short, the chaotic circumstances characterizing development in the Florida parishes demonstrated that democracy in southeastern Louisiana worked best under oligarchic supervision and that even then, if it was dominated by a self-serving elite, the subsequent failings of democracy could be dramatically amplified.

Such were the conclusions of the first edition of this study. I came under deserved criticism from some scholars and general readers alike for failing to finish the story. When asked why I had not taken the study to some level of resolution, I gave the easy answer that my major professor advised me to stop writing at 450 pages when I had just passed page 511. More accurately, I did believe that by 1899 the violence had climaxed and that all indicators suggested the region was entering a more normal pattern of development—a conclusion that I personally, along with some others, found unsatisfying.

In 2010, following the successful hosting of the bicentennial of the West Florida Revolt, I was approached by three prominent regional history buffs who urged me to "finish the story." I was initially reluctant. I had long since moved on to other topics and believed I had done all I could with the original subject. But after some sustained prodding, I agreed to take another look at the region and its troubled past. I assumed the new project would finally allow me to answer how peace was restored. As the region entered the twentieth century, vast technological changes including communication and transportation networks along with new sources of employment and entertainment seemed certain to facilitate a more modern, accountable way of life. Yet in one key critical sense, little if any change proved evident. Despite the new opportunities and improving conditions of life, the residents, or enough of them to determine the course of regional identity, remained rooted in a frontier mentality—a kill-or-be-killed perspective that compromised law enforcement's efforts and rendered the system of justice ineffective. To my dismay, the violence actually accelerated in the new millennium among a people who Dr. Clark Forrest, longtime director of the Edward Livingston Historical Society, declared held to "an Old Testament view of the world, where the notion of an eye for an eye governed interpersonal relations."

Accordingly, the purpose of the new project changed. The elusive peace required more than just a recounting of what happened; indeed, it demanded an explanation for why things occurred as they had. This second edition of *Pistols and Politics* employs the tragic history of southeastern Louisiana to offer an accounting of the adverse components that, when combined, may create a society in undesirable equilibrium, one where the system of justice is ineffective, the people cowed, and seemingly primordial relations govern a society on the brink of utter chaos. Through this explanation of the past, it also offers a possible formulation for confronting such undesirable social equilibrium today in the hope that the demise of those victimized by the region's tragic history may find purpose in helping others to avoid similar circumstances in the future.

Many individuals and institutions have provided valuable assistance during the course of my research and writing. The T. Harry Williams Fellowship, awarded by the History Department at Louisiana State University, and a Newberry Library Fellowship provided crucial funding in the early stages of my research, as did a series of travel grants from Louisiana State University and Southeastern Louisiana University. The Leon Ford Endowed Chair in Regional Studies, awarded by Southeastern Louisiana University, has proven crucial to my continuing efforts to advance understanding of the Florida parishes and surrounding regions of the South.

The staff at Louisiana State University Press proved exceptionally helpful through the course of the publication process. Leslie Phillabaum, Margaret Dalrymple, John Easterly, and freelance editor Christine Cowan gave freely of their time and expertise to produce the first edition, just as MaryKatherine Callaway, Rand Dotson, Catherine L. Kadair, and Laura Gleason helped make possible the second edition. I am indeed grateful for their assistance.

It is always a pleasure to locate a library or archival collection maintained by a helpful and friendly staff, and in this regard I was particularly fortunate. The staffs at the Newberry Library, Mississippi Department of Archives and History, the Middleton Library at Louisiana State University, and the Department of Manuscripts and Rare Books at Tulane University proved particularly helpful. Numerous staff members in the clerk of court offices in Livingston, St. Tammany, Tangipahoa, and Washington Parishes, as well as Pike County, Mississippi, patiently endured my obsessive searches through records and files long assigned to the back shelves of their archives, frequently assisting by lifting boxes, holding flashlights, or finding ways to make a nonventilated back room cooler. I am most thankful for their help.

To the staff of the Louisiana and Lower Mississippi Valley Collection at Louisiana State University I owe a particular word of thanks, for their research expertise, courteous attentiveness, and exceptional resourcefulness. Their patience and help as I implored them to open early every morning month after month, dominated their time during operating hours, and begged to see "just one more item" as the clock ticked past closing time exemplified the true spirit of professionalism. Collectively, they remain very special to me, and their assistance ensured that the idea would become a book.

No group of research assistants bore the brunt of my relentless pursuit of evidence better than the staff at the Center for Southeast Louisiana Studies at Southeastern Louisiana University. Burdened by my near constant presence, they cheerily retrieved collections, made scans, reproduced photographs, and the like, all the while tolerating my obsession with the project, computer naïveté, need for quiet, and hopeless distraction. I am deeply grateful to Faith Allen, Megan Arledge, Sarah Chauppette, Nick Heyd, Sarah Pardue, Blake Constant, Chase Tomlin, and Christian White for their patience and assistance.

Numerous friends and colleagues also contributed significantly to the completion of this project. Robert Becker, Gale Carrithers, John Henderson, Richard Kilbourne, Ed Muir, Larry Powell, Miles Richardson, and Karl Roider all read and provided substantive criticism of early drafts. One of my colleagues at Southeastern Louisiana University, Michael Kurtz, kindly read portions of the first edition and has consistently responded to my calls for assistance, as have Margaret and Murray Quin. Keith Finley not only read and critiqued multiple drafts of the second edition, but in his capacity as assistant director at the Center for Southeast Louisiana Studies made vital suggestions concerning the location of evidence and useful photos, among other contributions. Finally, two of my fellow graduate students at Louisiana State University, Jay Peacock and especially Brad Bond, made useful suggestions and gave constant encouragement during times of both jubilation and distress. The contributions of these individuals are apparent in my book, and to each, I am deeply grateful.

I owe a deep debt of gratitude to William J. Cooper, Jr. I feel blessed to have had the opportunity to work with a man of Bill's character and professionalism. He freely gave of his time to inspire confidence in my purpose, to calm this often panicky student, and diligently to critique every passage of the manuscript. Similarly, Gaines Foster not only provided insightful criticism of the first edition of the book, but he selflessly gave of his time to provide key suggestions for the new edition that dramatically advanced delivery of the message it is designed to offer.

The new edition of the book necessitated my entrance into regions of thought previously outside my consideration. Economists Jay Johnson and Sang Lee kindly, and patiently, refined my understanding of game theory and critiqued my application of equilibrium in this study. Gavin Wright likewise critiqued relevant portions of the study and suggested improvements for my application model. Clark Forrest reminded me that southern culture is not monolithic and that efforts at immersive appreciation of microcultures can offer enhanced awareness of subjects that may challenge normal understanding. District Attorney Scott Perrilloux provided visible insight into the challenges confronting the system of justice in a region where some recalcitrant individuals seem reluctant to decouple from the past. The new edition could not have been possible without the contributions of these individuals.

Finally, during the course of this project my immediate family contributed in profoundly important ways. My eldest son, Clay, through his continuing immersion in the study of both law and international economics, has offered an emerging outlet for scholarly discourse that included his suggestion to consider game theory as a method for interpretation. Whether on the football field, basketball court, or in a violin concert, my son Andrew's growing accomplishments have offered moments of boundless pride and relaxation. My youngest son Sammie's out-of-the-gates success excites me with anticipation for the future, just as our precious Sophie's obsession with ballet and all manner of dance makes me smile at the thought of our expanding horizons. The life I enjoy with my wife Sarah transcends my expectations for this world. Despite raising our children, holding multiple jobs, and editing her own manuscript, she graciously read every passage of this study, offering critical help and support. The traditional marital vows, "for better or for worse, in sickness and in health," summarize our bond. She has been with me through the toughest times of life and has shared with me many of its greatest joys. For me there is no other, "till death do us part!"

Years ago, just after the first edition of *Pistols and Politics* came out, I arrived at a book signing only to have the bookstore owner rush out to meet me in the parking lot. As he escorted me past a line of people waiting to get their books signed, he remarked that he wanted to speak to me before we began. "I wanted you to know that your book is a funeral," he said. "A funeral?" I responded somewhat incredulously. He explained that many people who bought the book told him that it finally revealed the story of what had happened to an ancestor or close family relation. He added, "it has offered them closure." It was an observation I had not considered, but one that I fully understood. Few of the older Florida parish families were untouched by the events discussed in this study. And many of them, particularly those prominent in the later chapters, including the Amackers, McMichaels, Kemps, and of course the Hydes, I call family. No effort has been made to justify the cause of any faction or family. I have concentrated merely on reporting the events as demonstrated by the evidence in an effort to seek the source of the troubles. Whatever failings have resulted in that effort are exclusively my responsibility.

Pistols and Politics

Introduction

Thomas Green Davidson was surprised when he heard of the brutal murder in neighboring East Feliciana Parish. Homicide was not unknown in the area, but a killing of this nature was certainly unusual. The reports told of a farmer shot in the back by an apparent lone gunman from ambush—a "bushwhacking." Although it was a peculiar occurrence in 1854, Davidson would live to see a day when such acts of violence would overwhelm the region, serving as a primary means of settling differences.

Davidson's dismay concerned the state of relative peace and prosperity temporarily prevailing in his home territory—a state of community equilibrium associated with the mutually beneficial relationship that existed between the ruling elite and the common folk. Although the current conditions proved advantageous to both planter and commoner, such had not always been the case in Davidson's region, nor would it remain that way. This variable relationship between southern planters and plain folk has long been the focus of scholarly research, in large measure because the deferential social and political system erected by the planters shaped the character of the antebellum South. The basis of planter power remained a brutal system of human bondage. To most planters and many other whites, all other social and political concerns proved secondary to the maintenance of slavery. The planters' determination to preserve the practice that guaranteed their power created a dilemma for the mass of southern commoners. They either aspired to enter the ranks of the slaveholding elite, accepted a system often antagonistic to their own economic and political livelihood, or agitated for democratic reform. The plain folk's response to planter dominance proved central to the maintenance or absence of social stability in many regions of the South.

The implications of the planter-plain folk relationship proved exceptionally significant in Louisiana. The lower Mississippi valley boasted some of the richest plantation country in the nation, whereas the piney woods of

north-central and eastern Louisiana represented some of the poorest territory in the state. Since soil quality went far in determining economic activity in each region, it influenced the nature of the people and, correspondingly, local politics. Within Louisiana, however, one region, the Florida
parishes, provides an even clearer statement on the implications of the
planter-plain folk relationship.

The seven parishes comprising that territory within the top of the "toe" of
Louisiana, between the Pearl and Mississippi Rivers and above Lakes Maurepas and Pontchartrain—East Baton Rouge, East and West Feliciana, Livingston, St. Helena, St. Tammany, and Washington Parishes (Tangipahoa
Parish was not formed until 1869)—shared the statewide dichotomy between
wealthy plantation country and poorer piney woods. The Felicianas and East
Baton Rouge remained among the wealthiest and most politically powerful
parishes in the state, while the eastern piney-woods parishes were far less developed. Even so, the region endured a peculiar pattern of development. An
extended period of territorial ambiguity, which included interims of French,
British, and Spanish overlordship, climaxed with an insurrection and the
short-lived Republic of West Florida. Prior to its incorporation with the rest
of the state in 1812, the region served as a haven for Tories, army deserters,
and desperadoes, all of whom exploited the prevailing instability and absence
of American control.

Typically, Louisiana has been divided into three general areas. The first,
New Orleans and its urban environs, has been traditionally considered
unique not only to Louisiana but to the nineteenth-century South in general.
Second, Acadiana, or the bayou country, also emerged as a peculiar region to
both the state and the South. Settled primarily by French Catholics, Acadiana has been regarded as unique both for its population and for its topography. These two areas of the state tend to dominate the popular perception of
Louisiana. The third region may best be called upstate Louisiana, encompass-
ing the remaining portion of the state north of Alexandria, as well as the region along the Sabine River and the Florida parishes. More typical of the
South as a whole, this region contained considerable numbers of Protestant
yeoman farmers. By 1850, the white population of upstate Louisiana consisted largely of immigrants of Scotch-Irish ancestry from Georgia and the
Carolinas. Even though upstate farmers maintained significant herds of livestock, particularly in the north-central region, cotton farming dominated.[1]

1. Milton B. Newton, *Atlas of Louisiana: A Guide for Students* (Baton Rouge, 1972).

The Florida parishes share many of the characteristics of upstate Louisiana, but they also differ in fundamental ways. First, though large numbers of Scotch-Irish settlers called this area home, immigrants of English descent predominated within the Anglo-Celtic group. After the American Revolution, significant numbers from the Tidewater region of Virginia and the Carolinas, many of them Tories fleeing persecution, migrated to the Florida parishes.[2] The relative isolation and the abundance of cheap available land in eastern Louisiana inspired major migrations in the first decade of the nineteenth century. Additionally, many Tories seem to have considered the territory a refuge from the lingering persecution they faced in many American-controlled areas.

Cultural distinctions separated the Florida parishes from upstate Louisiana in other ways. Unlike upstate, the southeastern parishes attracted considerable numbers of a variety of ethnic groups. Spanish efforts in the late eighteenth century to build a barrier against the encroaching Americans led to a scattering of small yet significant settlements in lower Livingston and St. Tammany Parishes. Under the direction of Governor Bernardo de Gálvez, immigrants from the Canary Islands, known as Isleños, located along the Amite River and its environs, with their primary settlement appropriately named Galvez-Town. In their effort to increase the Catholic population in the region, Spanish authorities at New Orleans also directed German Catholic immigrants and recently displaced Acadians to the Florida parishes. In 1785, over two hundred Acadians settled at Manchac on the south pass connecting Lakes Maurepas and Pontchartrain. In the same year another group of Acadians located at Thompson's Creek, in the Feliciana district above Baton Rouge. French immigrants continued to trickle into the Florida parishes in the first few decades of the nineteenth century. By 1810, French-speaking communities flourished at Port Vincent and French Settlement in Livingston Parish. Other French-speaking peoples colonized the lakeshore in St. Tammany Parish, where they participated in the shipping of goods to and from the markets of New Orleans. The presence of French, German, and Isleño settlers distinguished the Florida parishes from the more homogeneous

2. Amite City *News Digest*, March 13, April 17, and May 1, 1959; Stanley C. Arthur, *The Story of the West Florida Rebellion* (St. Francisville, La., 1935), 14–15; Alvin L. Bertrand, *The Many Louisianas: Rural Social Areas and Cultural Islands* (Baton Rouge, 1955), 19; John Hawkins Napier, III, *Lower Pearl River's Piney Woods: Its Land and People* (Oxford, Miss., 1985), 28; Louisiana Folklife Program, *Folklife in the Florida Parishes* (Baton Rouge, 1989), 15.

pattern of settlement occurring in upstate Louisiana and provided the region with a strong Catholic minority.[3]

In the late nineteenth century, other immigrant groups came to southeast Louisiana. Like their predecessors, the new settlers had a significant social and political impact on the region. Principal among these were the Sicilians, who by the late 1880s had established numerous truck farms along the Illinois Central Railroad. By 1920, Independence, in present-day Tangipahoa Parish, emerged as the largest rural Italian community in the United States. Likewise, Hungarians, though far fewer than the Sicilians, migrated to Livingston Parish in such numbers in the early 1890s that they established the largest rural Hungarian settlement in the United States.[4]

Despite these differences, the Florida parishes and upstate Louisiana shared many similarities, particularly in terms of topography and relative wealth. Both contained wealthy plantation parishes bordered by less affluent piney-woods parishes. Farming patterns were similar: farmers in each area invested heavily in cotton and livestock, though those in the Florida parishes devoted far more resources to the cultivation of rice. Five of the seven Florida parishes appeared among the top fifteen rice-producing parishes in the state, with Washington, St. Tammany, and Livingston each producing about 100,000 pounds annually.

Yet the Florida parishes clearly constituted a unique region of Louisiana. As late as the middle of the 1830s, the territory remained a distinctive region in the eyes of the state legislature. The constitution adopted in 1812 did not include the Florida parishes as a part of Louisiana. Over twenty years later, in apportioning representation and other issues, the legislature continued to treat the area known as West Florida as a separate, seemingly ambiguous portion of the state.[5] Since the southeastern parishes exhibited characteristics

3. New Orleans *Daily Picayune*, February 21, 1892; Gilbert Din, "Early Spanish Colonization Efforts in Louisiana," *Louisiana Studies*, XI (1972), 31–49; Louisiana Folklife Program, *Folklife in the Florida Parishes*, 39; H. M. Brackenridge, *Views of Louisiana: Together with a Journal of a Voyage up the Missouri River, in 1811* (Pittsburgh, 1814), 281; Timothy Flint, *Recollections of the Last Ten Years in the Valley of the Mississippi* (Carbondale, Ill., 1968), 216–17.

4. John V. Baiamonte, *Immigrants in Rural America: A Study of the Italians of Tangipahoa Parish, Louisiana* (New York, 1990); Bertrand, *Many Louisianas*, 23–25; Ginger Romero, "Hungarian Folklife: The Sweet Taste of Yesterday," *Florida Parishes of Southeast Louisiana Series*, III (1987), 1–26.

5. For a good example of the legislature's treatment of the Florida parishes as a distinctive region of the state, see *Louisiana House Journal*, 2nd Sess., 1833, pp. 15–19.

similar to both upstate Louisiana and Acadiana, as well as some of the ethnic mix of New Orleans, they might best be regarded as a blending of the diverse regions of Louisiana, sharing similarities and differences with each. By delineating this area as a separate, or fourth, region of the state, we can more easily identify the specifics of its development.

Although a few plantations operated in the piney woods of eastern Louisiana, family farming dominated. And in the Florida parishes, the social and political interaction between the planters and the piney-woods dwellers played a central role in the region's peculiar pattern of development. The primary differences between the people in the plantation and those in the piney-woods sections revolved around economic wealth and political philosophy, characteristics initially influenced by geography. As in many other regions, land served as the originating source of wealth and power.

The fertile bluffs along the Mississippi attracted the earliest settlers to West Florida. Boasting some of the best farmland in the Gulf South and a ready access to market, West Feliciana and East Baton Rouge Parishes, like their neighbors across the river, soon supported huge plantations. Several villages arose along the Mississippi. Baton Rouge, with a population of 3,905 in 1850, emerged as the largest town. As cotton prices soared in the 1830s, the plantation culture expanded outward into the pine hills. The completion of a railroad in 1840 from Port Hudson, on the Mississippi above Baton Rouge, to Clinton, in East Feliciana Parish, provided that territory with the direct link to the Mississippi it needed to prosper. East Feliciana became an extension of the delta plantation culture and the trading center for the piney-woods regions to the north and east. Small-scale industries, such as engine repair shops, developed in conjunction with railroad and shipping interests at Baton Rouge and Clinton, as well as at Bayou Sara and St. Francisville in West Feliciana Parish. A few brickyards and sawmills arose to facilitate construction of the emerging villages and farms.[6]

The plantation culture of the Felicianas and rural East Baton Rouge differed significantly from the eastern Florida parishes. The Felicianas in partic-

6. *Seventh Census, 1850; Compendium,* 246; *Louisiana House Journal,* 2nd Sess., 1833, pp. 24–25, 32; Eli J. Capell Diary, November 21–24, December 24, 1842, in Eli J. Capell Papers, Louisiana and Lower Mississippi Valley Collections, Louisiana State University, Baton Rouge, hereinafter referred to as LLMVC; Diary of William Y. Dixon, August 14, 1860, LLMVC; Duncan W. Taylor to Eugene Hunter, September 13, 1856, in Hunter-Taylor Family Papers, LLMVC; James Peacock, "Historical and Statistical Sketches of Louisiana," *De Bow's Review,* XI (1851), 265; Louisiana Folklife Program, *Folklife in the Florida Parishes,* 46.

ular ranked among the wealthiest and most powerful parishes in the state both economically and politically. Clinton and the nearby village of Jackson boasted well-established banking and commercial centers. Sophisticated theatrical productions were commonplace, as were society balls and gatherings. Clinton alone supported two theatrical troupes, a Shakespearean society, several poetry-reading circles, and a thespian orchestra.[7] Noted American and European actors and musicians frequently performed. Religious tolerance, which typically existed between Catholics and Protestants in the Florida parishes, was extended to Jews in the Felicianas, where small but influential Jewish communities developed at St. Francisville and Clinton. A comparatively generous system of poor relief, by Louisiana standards, extended to both destitute whites and free blacks.[8]

Perhaps most important, by 1850 East Feliciana supported educational institutions, including Centenary College at Jackson and the Silliman Female Institute at Clinton, unsurpassed by those in any other parish in the state. In short, a genteel attitude permeated a progressive society supported by a prosperous cotton economy. Writing in the fall of 1855, Mary E. Taylor, wife of a prominent Clinton minister and planter, summarized the comfortable existence of the planter class in the western Florida parishes by declining to attend a bountiful dinner in the country: "There was no inducement at all [to go]; for when people live as well as we do at home they never care about going elsewhere."[9]

Despite the grandeur of the western "aristocratic" parishes, the core of the Florida parishes lay in the eastern piney woods. Far less blessed with good soil and other natural resources, the eastern portion stood in sharp contrast to the plantation district of the western parishes. A different set of incentives and convictions shaped the life-style, labor, and outlook on life of the people in

---

7. Clinton *American Patriot*, November 3, December 15, 29, 1855; Clinton *Feliciana Democrat*, April 14, 21, June 2, 9, 30, October 20, 1855.

8. Clinton *Feliciana Democrat*, May 28, November 24, 1855; Clinton *American Patriot*, January 10, March 14, 21, 1855; F. Jay Taylor, ed., *Reluctant Rebel: The Secret Diary of Robert Patrick, 1861–1865* (Baton Rouge, 1959), 10; East Feliciana Parish Police Jury Minutes, VIII, Folder Group 1853–59, January 1, 1855, p. 134, in WPA Louisiana Parish Police Jury Minutes Collection, LLMVC.

9. F. Jay Taylor, ed., *Reluctant Rebel*, 10; *Seventh Census, 1850: Compendium*, 477–80; James William Mobley, "The Academy Movement in Louisiana," *Louisiana Historical Quarterly*, XXX (1947), 821; Mary E. Taylor to B. Hunter, October 19, 1855, in Hunter-Taylor Family Papers, LLMVC.

the region. In short, a different culture appeared. As late as 1852, this area remained virtually isolated from the outside world. Most of the few reliable roads crossing these parishes had served previously as military highways, many constructed by Andrew Jackson's troops and laborers nearly forty years earlier. Extremely shallow or otherwise unnavigable streams made gaining access to markets difficult.[10] Yet the majority of the piney-woods dwellers produced marketable goods. Whether they raised cattle, produced milk, harvested timber, or more likely grew cotton or rice, most of the plain folk required a ready access to market. A sample survey of heads of household demonstrates that farmers in the region produced far more goods than would be necessary for home use (see Table 1).[11] The limited number of towns and trading centers, however, inhibited local commercial development. The scarcity of retail stores also retarded economic advancement in the eastern parishes. Drummers, traveling salesmen who carried essential products such as coffee, pots, pans, and sugar through rural areas, frequently visited the piney woods, but they and other traveling merchants seldom purchased the goods produced in rural areas.[12]

The South's one great metropolis, New Orleans, less than fifty miles away across Lake Pontchartrain, fundamentally shaped the trade and transportation of the Florida parishes. Despite the isolation, economic development in the area depended directly on the great Mississippi River port. Farmers in the central parishes of Livingston and St. Helena found access to the New Orleans markets through the small river port of Springfield on the Tickfaw River. Steamers crossing Lakes Pontchartrain and Maurepas deposited and collected goods there, and oxen-pulled wagons provided the connection to the interior. The only other viable route, to Port Hudson on the Mississippi

10. Powell Casey, "Military Roads in the Florida Parishes of Louisiana," *Louisiana History,* XV (1974), 229–42; "Report of the Civil Engineer of the State," *Louisiana House Journal,* 2nd Sess., 1833, pp. 21–28.

11. *Louisiana Senate Journal,* 1st Sess., 1853, pp. 269–71; *Louisiana House Journal,* 1st Sess., 1852, pp. 163–65, 1st Sess., 1854, pp. 123–28, 1st Sess., 1856, p. 62, 1st Sess., 1857, p. 90; *Seventh Census, 1850,* Manuscript, and *Eighth Census, 1860,* Manuscript, Louisiana, Schedule 2, Agricultural Statistics, Microfilm.

12. "Address of Governor Robert C. Wickliffe, *Louisiana Legislative Documents,* 1st Sess., 1860, pp. 5–8; *Louisiana Senate Journal,* 7th Legis., 1st Sess., 1824, p. 15 (referring to a bill respecting peddlers); John Inscoe, *Mountain Masters, Slavery, and the Sectional Crisis in Western North Carolina* (Knoxville, 1989), 40; New Orleans *Daily Picayune,* November 9, 1897; Raleigh Suarez, "Bargains, Bills, and Bankruptcies: Business Activity in Rural Antebellum Louisiana," *Louisiana History,* VII (1966), 191–92.

TABLE 1. FARM PRODUCTION, 1850

Parish	Livestock						Crops					
	% Raising Cattle	Avg. No. of Cattle	% Raising Hogs	Avg. No. of Hogs	% Raising Sheep	Avg. No. of Sheep	% Raising Corn	Avg. Amount Raised (Bushels)	% Raising Rice	Avg. Amount Raised (Pounds)	% Raising Cotton	Avg. Amount Grown (Bales)
Plantation Parishes												
East Baton Rouge	77	33.8	71.4	79.0	14.2	25.0	100.0	417.8	11.0	220	56.0	13.3
East Feliciana	73	22.7	85.7	59.0	43.0	37.0	78.5	1695.0	14.0	1133	81.0	46.0
West Feliciana	85	51.0	71.0	59.2	33.0	36.0	85.7	2329.0	12.5	700	83.0	201.8
Piney-Woods Parishes												
Livingston	100	31.0	100.0	98.0	28.5	30.8	85.7	109.0	36.0	300	26.6	3.2
St. Helena	100	23.7	86.6	52.6	46.6	33.2	80.0	443.8	40.0	585	66.6	6.7
St. Tammany	75	65.0	82.0	53.0	30.0	4.0	66.6	280.0	33.0	1430	25.0	2.3
Washington	90	31.2	100.0	48.0	38.0	16.6	100.0	376.0	37.5	1100	75.0	2.8

Sources: Seventh Census, 1850, Manuscript, and Eighth Census, 1860, Manuscript, Louisiana, Schedule 2, Agricultural Statistics, Microfilm. Individual farm statistics were based on a 3 percent sample survey of heads of household of each parish.

via Clinton, consumed both more time and more resources. Both routes were tedious, demanding, and hazardous.[13]

Although less developed than the central region, the eastern parishes of Washington and St. Tammany fared a little better in terms of access to the markets of New Orleans. Some commercial traffic took place on the Pearl River, but the primary route remained the Jackson Military Road, which traversed the region from the Mississippi border to Madisonville on Lake Pontchartrain. Steamers then completed the connection with New Orleans. Yet this route also constituted a slow and tedious journey: oxen teams often took as long as six days to travel the ten miles between Madisonville and the St. Tammany Parish seat at Covington. Throughout the antebellum period, the need for market access served as a central element of the planter-plain folk relationship in the Florida parishes. Increasing planter control of the travel routes to market promoted their economic dominance of the territory.[14]

Recognizing the territory's relative isolation is central to understanding the residents' outlook on life. As late as 1852, the Florida parishes remained surrounded on the north and east by vast expanses of sparsely populated pine forest and on the south by virtually impenetrable swamps. Geographical isolation affected social as well as economic development. Like the life-styles of the residents of the pine flats of Mississippi, of hill-country Alabama, Georgia, and Kentucky, and even of the mountain regions of Tennessee and North Carolina, the life-style of the people in the eastern Florida parishes appeared rather peculiar to their more cosmopolitan neighbors. Planters and urbanites often referred to these regions as "backwoods," a term they employed as a synonym for "backwards." Many outsiders generally regarded these isolated rural dwellers as poor, neglectful, nonmaterialistic, and lazy. This description

13. "Report of the Civil Engineer of the State," *Louisiana House Journal*, 2nd Sess., 1833, pp. 21–22; Clinton-Port Hudson Railroad Flyer, 1850, in Henry W. Marston Family Papers, LLMVC; Capell Diary, November 21, 24, 1842, in Capell Papers; Amite Navigation Company Document, 1818, LLMVC; Amite City *News Digest*, October 2, 1959; William Darby, *Geographical Description of the State of Louisiana . . . with an Account of the Character and Manners of the Inhabitants* (Philadelphia, 1816), 174–75; F. Jay Taylor, ed., *Reluctant Rebel*, 9.

14. St. Francisville *Louisiana Journal*, June 16, 1825; P. L. Bonny to Lt. J. G. Robert, May 5, 1864, J. G. Robert to Cousins, Jones, and J. A. Leblanc, April 23, 1864, both in P. L. Bonny Papers, LLMVC; Brackenridge, *Views of Louisiana*, 285; Darby, *Geographical Description of Louisiana*, 175; Amite City *News Digest*, October 2, 1959; Casey, "Military Roads," 234; Amy Quick, "The History of Bogalusa, the Magic City of Louisiana," *Louisiana Historical Quarterly*, XXIX (1946), 74–79; Robert J. Baxter, "Cattle Raising in Early Mississippi," *Mississippi Folklore Register*, X (1976), 15.

doubtless could be applied to many piney-woods folk, yet this perception of them is as negative as the term *backwoods* is derogatory. It originated in the outlook of the planter class, who, having reached the top, either ridiculed or failed to understand those who did not appreciate their values or aspire to be like them. Their lack of understanding often bordered on contempt. Writing to his sister in July, 1856, concerning a political barbecue in the piney woods, Augustus Carpenter, a wealthy planter from Clinton, complained that he did not enjoy himself because he was "amongst the piney woods folks." Robert Patrick spent much of his youth in St. Helena Parish but aspired to join the planter elite. After his father moved the family to neighboring East Feliciana in 1842, Patrick described the piney-woods people as virtually without culture, claiming that his family had "blessed little to do with them."[15] A more balanced observation of these rural dwellers would combine the perspective of the elite with an understanding of how these people viewed themselves.

Historians of the piney woods typically assign a variety of other characteristics to these regions and their residents. They include relatively low agricultural production with an emphasis on sweet potatoes, endemic drinking and gambling, hospitality, ranging livestock, and violence. Others, though viewing the piney-woods inhabitants as proverbially poor, note more positive qualities, such as honesty, high moral standards, and a virtuous life-style. The editor of the Amite City *Democrat*, a rural newspaper, described the typical piney-woods home: "The piney woods home is often a log hut plastered with mud or boards enclosed by a rail fence, a general air of thriftless, careless management around the place, an ox wagon in front outside an insecure looking gate, three or four hungry looking dogs which bark and whelp at your entrance, a lean, woe begone looking horse grazing in the yard; a few flowers which tell of a womans [sic] presence, as the pipes and tobacco which lie upon the portice surely betoken the masculine element." The article continued with an idyllic description of the piney-woods existence.[16]

15. Frederick L. Olmsted, *A Journey in the Backcountry* (New York, 1863), 237, 297; Frank Lawrence Owsley, *Plain Folk of the Old South* (Baton Rouge, 1949), 1–3; Augustus Carpenter to his Sister, July 9, 1856, in George H. Carpenter Family Papers, LLMVC; F. Jay Taylor, ed., *Reluctant Rebel*, 9.

16. J. William Harris, *Plain Folk and Gentry in a Slave Society: White Liberty and Black Slavery in Augusta's Hinterlands* (Middletown, Conn., 1985); Grady McWhiney, "Antebellum Piney Woods Culture: Continuity over Time and Place," in *Mississippi's Piney Woods: A Human Perspective*, ed. Noel Polk (Jackson, Miss., 1986), 40–51; Owsley, *Plain Folk*, 1–5; Amite City *Democrat*, October 2, 1875.

Other contemporary observers noted that the piney woods consisted of many little communities bound together by kinship or long friendship. F. M. Kent, an antebellum immigrant from New England, marveled at how friendly the people seemed, noting that "as guests you are expected to make yourself at home and no one accepts payment even from strangers." He added that "hospitality is looked upon as a virtue and it generally extends to friend and stranger." Kent indicated that though the people appeared less educated than in New England, they possessed considerable "general information" and a keen interest in politics.[17]

In making perceptive observations of the region, Kent provided a basis for understanding many of the traits that characterized southerners in general. He noted that the law commanded less respect here than in New England and that a "service of honor" proved as binding as a written obligation. Religion, though significant, played less of a role in the daily lives of the residents than it did in the older states of the northeast, Kent surmised. Ministers exercised influence only if the people agreed with the clergyman's position. Also, he observed, the people seemed more independent in thought and action, and he speculated that a want of energy on their part resulted from the presence of slavery. Most ominous for the future development of eastern Louisiana, he noted, was a tendency to defy the legal system; he added that in the Florida parishes "public opinion will have its weight upon the jurors' seat."[18]

A significant body of evidence suggests that many among the piney-woods folk of the Florida parishes aspired to improve their own personal financial situation as well as the economy of their region. Numerous well-attended barbecues, the principal mechanism for social and political gatherings, took place in the piney woods to encourage the construction of railroads and plank roads. On an excursion through the piney woods in the summer of 1854, a reporter for the Baton Rouge *Daily Advocate* expressed shock at the number of people willing to sell land to the railroad and the number of opportunistic businessmen surveying possibilities along the proposed road.[19]

17. Daniel Dennett, *Louisiana as It Is: Its Topography and Material Resources . . . Climate and People of the State* (New Orleans, 1879), 31; F. M. Kent to Uncle Moody, February 19, June 2, 1857, in Amos Kent Papers, LLMVC.

18. Kent to Moody, February 19, June 2, 1857, in Kent Papers.

19. Amite City *Times*, July 27, 1867; Clinton *Feliciana Democrat*, May 5, July 28, August 18, 1855; William Pike to Henry Marston, September 10, 1852, in Marston Family Papers; New Orleans *Daily Delta*, December 14, 1854; *Louisiana House Journal*, 1st Sess., 1852, p. 164, 1st Sess.,

Despite the willingness of some to improve the transportation network as well as economic conditions, many more appeared ambivalent about change, and others, as railroad promoters would soon learn, would violently resist it. Efforts to assign specific traits to these people prove misleading. The piney-woods dwellers should not be regarded as uniform in thought and action: some were opportunistic, some lackadaisical; some were outspoken, others more reticent. Yet a unique piney-woods culture did exist. The piney-woods dwellers shared certain general qualities, the sum of which embodied their culture. Contrary to the stereotypical generalizations assigned to them by outsiders, the presence of these qualities prompted the emergence of a distinctive way of life. Words such as *laziness, hospitality,* and *violence* describe the symptoms of behavior, not the causes. To be true, any examination of the results of behavior should incorporate an understanding of the sources of that behavior. What separates the seemingly derogatory descriptive term *back-woods* from the potentially positive term *piney woods* is an understanding of the motivating forces that made these rural dwellers who they were. These inspirational qualities gave shape to their conception of the order of society, to their perceptions of the outside world, and to their understanding of the sources of wealth, happiness, and security.

Independence and honor served as the principal qualities motivating the piney-woods dwellers, or plain folk. Primarily yeoman farmers, they valued independence in a way that is difficult for us in our automated, regulated society to comprehend. In his introductory remarks preceding the *Seventh Census* of the United States in 1850, prominent New Orleans editor and promoter J. D. B. De Bow lamented that in 1840 in many regions of the South, objections loomed so strong to the searching nature of the census questions that several counties and parishes peremptorily refused to answer them. De Bow noted that though fewer such problems occurred in 1850, in several cases "it was necessary to call in the services of the district attorney to enforce the requisitions of the law." This mistrust of a meddling or energetic government remained central to the piney-woods existence. The Livingston Parish Police Jury solved the perennial problem of forcing rural farmers to

1854, pp. 121–29, 1st Sess., 1856, p. 63, 1st Sess., 1857, p. 89; St. Tammany Parish Police Jury Minutes, 2nd Sess., December, 1851, 1st Sess., January, 1852, in WPA Louisiana Parish Police Jury Minutes Collection; Harry H. Evans, "James Robb, Banker and Pioneer Railroad Builder," *Louisiana Historical Quarterly,* XXIII (1940), 199; Baton Rouge *Daily Advocate,* August 22, 1854; Greensburg *Imperial,* April 25, 1857.

honor their obligations to maintain public roads by appointing them over-seers with independent control over designated sections of the roads. Each specific section would theoretically belong to a farmer and typically would be named for him. Such a system relied on peer pressure rather than legal coercion to ensure road maintenance.[20]

The importance of personal independence involved not simply freedom from government interference but a desire to obtain productive resources and to escape subservience to outsiders. F. M. Kent noted that "the people here are more independent in thought and action than in New England," so "none of the isms can find a foothold here." The piney-woods folk readily resorted to violence if they deemed it necessary to maintain their independence, even from their neighbors.[21] Yet traditionally in the Florida parishes, the piney-woods dwellers, like the plain folk in many other regions of the South, appeared to see no inconsistency in their surrender of political control to the planters.[22]

Like the planters, the plain folk adhered to a rigid code of honor, albeit one peculiar to their circumstances. Unlike the planters, who often resolved affairs of honor in prearranged duels, however, the piney-woods dwellers usually settled affronts to honor spontaneously. Every man knew that he risked his life by insulting another. Upon learning in April, 1876, that his neighbor Francis Bardwell issued statements the previous evening that could be interpreted as insulting to his wife, Fayette Wells promptly tracked the man down and emptied his pistol into the unarmed and unsuspecting Bardwell. To have done any less would have called down shame and ridicule upon the Wells family. Just as they did with the elite, the consequences of such actions for the plain folk remained secondary to the fear of public and private humiliation.[23]

20. J. D. B. De Bow, Introductory Remarks, *Seventh Census, 1850: Compendium*, 12; Livingston Parish Police Jury Minutes, June Term, 1875, pp. 10–13, in WPA Louisiana Parish Police Jury Minutes Collection.

21. Amite City *Florida Parishes*, September 16, 1891; Clinton *American Patriot*, December 15, 1855; Edward Stewart to John Gurley, April 22, 1859, in John W. Gurley Papers, LLMVC; Kent to Moody, February 19, 1857, in Kent Papers; Steven Hahn, "The Yeomanry of the Non-Plantation South: Upper Piedmont Georgia, 1850–1860," in *Class, Conflict, and Consensus: Antebellum Southern Community Studies*, ed. Orville Burton and Robert C. McMath, Jr. (Westport, Conn., 1982), 29–48.

22. For a detailed discussion of the political interaction between the planters and plain folk, see Chapter 2.

23. Amite City *Democrat*, April 22, 1876; Kent to Moody, February 19, June 2, 1857, in Kent Papers; Clinton *Feliciana Whig*, December 15, 1842; Serrano Taylor to Adeline, November

The end result of these motivating qualities of independence and honor often appeared to outside observers as simple laziness, pointless violence, or some other misunderstood behavior. Without a proper understanding of the social mores of the plain folk, Wells's killing of Bardwell appears to be only a heinous, cold-blooded murder. That it certainly was, but it was also a culturally conditioned response condoned by the local populace. Appreciating that, under certain circumstances, murder served as not merely an accepted but an expected response remains central to understanding the course of events in the Florida parishes in the late nineteenth century. In short, in eastern Louisiana the qualities of independence and honor ultimately proved as dangerous as they were virtuous.

As the cotton economy spread from the plantation parishes into the piney woods during the 1820s and 1830s, it brought with it slaves, prosperity, and increasing planter control. The presence of slavery created an important bond between planters and plain folk in the Florida parishes where large numbers of commoners also owned slaves. The shared investment in slaves permitted the planters to achieve political dominance in the territory, but the pervasive presence of the slave system also reinforced an acute awareness that independence demanded constant vigilance.[24]

The shifting political patterns in mid-nineteenth-century Louisiana served to augment the necessity of vigilance and suspicion of government. The famous statement attributed to Jefferson, "I am not a friend to an energetic government; it is always oppressive," appeared to warn of political tendencies in late antebellum Louisiana. Although planter dominance brought stability to the traditional disorder of eastern Louisiana, it also subjected the plain folk to economic and political exploitation. The dilemma for piney-woods dwellers in the Florida parishes involved maintaining their independence while enjoying the prosperity associated with political stability. The transition to a more dynamic economy in the 1820s and 1830s challenged the fierce independence of piney-woods dwellers long accustomed to a virtual hermetic existence free of the demands of stable government. Through the 1830s the planter elite maintained their dominance through control of

27, 1857, in Hunter-Taylor Family Papers; Robert Barrow Letter, January 15, 1858, LLMVC; Edwin A. Davis, ed., *Diary of Bennett H. Barrow: Plantation Life in the Florida Parishes of Louisiana, 1836–1846, as Reflected in the Diary of Bennett Barrow* (New York, 1943), 253; Bertram Wyatt-Brown, *Honor and Violence in the Old South* (New York, 1986); Grady McWhiney, *Cracker Culture: Celtic Ways in the Old South* (Tuscaloosa, Ala., 1988), 160.

24. William J. Cooper, Jr., *Liberty and Slavery: Southern Politics to 1860* (New York, 1983).

the mechanisms of governance and the means of access to market—control that ultimately proved detrimental to plain-folk interests. During the 1840s, Jacksonian-inspired demands for greater democracy produced a brief revolt against planter power. Developments associated with the construction of a railroad through the piney woods in the early 1850s presented a further challenge to planter authority. In confronting the challenges to their power, the planters played on the fears of the plain folk. From the colonial period through the close of Reconstruction, they consistently employed a series of enemies common to white residents, successively Spanish authorities, abolitionists, Federal troops, carpetbaggers, and ever-present racial fears, to promote the necessity of white unity.

With the close of Reconstruction, the planters sought to reassert their power in the piney woods. The legacy of republican-inspired demands for independence emerged forcefully among the plain folk, however, and they rejected the authority of the antebellum elite. Unfortunately for the local residents, the brutal lessons of the war and Reconstruction had been well learned. In the aftermath of this education in violence, with the source of social and political stability the planters had previously provided now eliminated, the piney woods of the Florida parishes began a rapid descent into anarchy. Several factions aspiring to assert their authority emerged, but none commanded the deferential respect or so successfully manipulated the issues as the planters had. The collapse of white unity as some groups sought to manipulate black labor and votes while others sought to exclude them contributed to the acrimony between the factions. The legacy of colonial lawlessness and a fierce contempt for authority as a result of the war and Reconstruction combined to produce a warped impression of individual rights among the residents, one that permitted an aggressive response, such as shooting perceived agents of oppression in the back, to any effort to curtail individual liberty. What resulted were some of the most ferocious feuds in American history. From the close of Reconstruction to the end of the century, the piney-woods region of the Florida parishes consistently sustained some of the highest rural murder rates in the nation.

This study examines the composition of antebellum political power and the implications of its collapse. The story is one of controlled aspirations, political corruption, and human cruelty in a society long repressed and suddenly unfettered. It is a story primarily of white men oppressing other white men and of the consequences for society once the bonds binding the oppressed are removed. The rich contributions of black Americans to southern society do not figure significantly here. Excepting a brief period of meaningful assertive-

ness during Reconstruction, blacks in the Florida parishes remained so brutally repressed that it is a credit to their endurance that they survived such
callous persecution. Women, too, remained peripheral to the central focus of
this story.

Although this study is not an effort to write a definitive social statement
of the Florida parishes, it does seek to give the reader an understanding of the
nature of the region, identifying which qualities contributing to the violence
were common to the South and which were peculiar to the region. A brief
social history is included to demonstrate how the initial benefits that accompanied planter dominance in the early antebellum period gave way to exploitation of the commoners and climaxed with the violent rejection of
planter authority. Many aspects of the Florida parishes resemble other areas
of the state and the South. Among the differences, though, are a legacy of
multiple ethnic overlords, the impact of the West Florida Rebellion, and the
peculiar combination of initial settlers. Some of these factors are found in
other areas, but few can claim them all. In order more effectively to demonstrate specific attributes of the area's development that may have contributed
to the chaotic conditions of the late nineteenth century, data from other regions of Louisiana, as well as from other southern states, are frequently employed.

Fundamentally, this study examines the sources of the violence that overwhelmed the piney woods of the Florida parishes. Traditionally, many historians regard late-nineteenth-century southern violence as a legacy of the slave
system. Although there is certainly truth in the assumption that human
bondage conditioned southerners to brutality, much of the violence was concentrated in hill and piney-woods country, where slavery often remained at
most peripheral to social development. This study does not seek to challenge
the correlation between slavery and postbellum violence but instead highlights other contributing factors. In doing so, it underscores the significance
of planter power in less-developed regions of the South, while also enhancing
historians' understanding of the ideals and aspirations of the common folk
that ultimately contributed to the chaos.

· 1 ·

A Brief Moment of Stability

After traveling through the backcountry South in the early 1840s, the Mississippi historian and editor J. F. H. Claiborne described some of the subtle differences between the plantation and piney-woods regions of southwestern Mississippi. Finding it unnecessary to provide details on the evident contrasts of life in each section, Claiborne instead focused on less obvious yet significant differences, such as foods consumed and leisure activities pursued. In one instance he contrasted the "glorious supper" of oysters, chicken salad, turkeys, terrapin, and champagne he received in Wilkinson County, in the lower Mississippi delta, with a meal he was given in the piney woods. The latter, though abundant according to Claiborne, contained numerous dishes all composed of potatoes prepared in a variety of ways. He and his companion feasted on baked potatoes, fried potatoes, bacon and potatoes boiled together, a hash of wild turkey garnished with potatoes, potato biscuit, potato-based coffee ("strong and well flavored"), and, finally, potato pie and a tumbler of potato beer.[1] Claiborne appeared to prefer the finer dining found in Wilkinson County. As with many travelers in the rural South, he found the relative splendor of the plantation setting and the delicacies provided there overshadowed the comfortable but seemingly bland existence of the plain folk. Nonetheless, his observations provide important evidence concerning conditions in the antebellum rural South. The amount and quality of foods consumed indicate that in the late antebellum period prosperous times prevailed in both the plantation and piney-woods regions. Although the nature of the foods in each area differed, sustenance was abundant and in keeping with local crops and conditions.

The term *prosperity* often appears in conjunction with the term *stability* when historians discuss conditions in the antebellum South. In 1852, the re-

---

1. J. F. H. Claiborne, "A Trip Through the Piney Woods," *Publications of the Mississippi Historical Society*, IX (1906), 491, 533–34.

gion of the Florida parishes and environs was highly stable—a stability that resulted from economic prosperity and a corresponding mutual dependence existing between planters and plain folk. Shared interests based on similar agricultural pursuits and on political fears allowed for the prevailing, if temporary, conditions in the Florida parishes. Such a beneficial state of affairs is of particular significance, not only because it contributed directly to the secession appeal, but also because stability had proven inconsistent with the pattern of development in the Florida parishes.

Early instability resulted from the curious history of the area, which had passed from French to British to Spanish hands, placing different and opposing ethnic groups in the territory, many with conflicting land claims. Scores of army deserters and criminal elements exploited the absence of stable government, settled in the area, and exacerbated the prevailing instability. The successful introduction of a cotton-based economy, however, promoted prosperity and stability under the direction of the slaveholding elite. Shared agricultural pursuits, increasing prosperity, and, most important, the bond of slaveholding encouraged the plain folk to defer to the leadership of the planters. The planters nevertheless soon translated leadership into uncompromising power. By establishing themselves as the principal source for purchasing and processing the goods of the plain folk and by securing control of the means of access to market, the planters manipulated the economy to entrench their dominance.

Initial French efforts to colonize West Florida ended abruptly in 1763 with France's defeat at the hands of Britain in the French and Indian War. In 1764, British troops occupied the fort at Baton Rouge and established additional fortifications on Thompson's Creek in the Feliciana district and at Fort Bute at the mouth of Bayou Manchac south of Baton Rouge. In an effort to solidify their control of the territory, the British offered liberal land grants to retired soldiers. Officers received from three thousand to five thousand acres, while privates could claim up to three hundred acres. The beneficiaries of this land policy, supplemented by British Loyalists who migrated from the Atlantic Seaboard to the Florida parishes during the American Revolution, planted a strong pro-British element among the few scattered French settlers remaining in the area.[2]

2. Amite City *News Digest*, August 7, 1795; Arthur, *Story of the West Florida Rebellion*, 14–15; John Hebron Moore, *The Emergence of the Cotton Kingdom in the Old Southwest: Mississippi, 1770–1860* (Baton Rouge, 1988), 2.

Despite intensive colonization efforts, British control constituted only a brief interlude. In 1779, Spanish forces, under the direction of the governor of the Orleans Territory Bernardo de Gálvez, seized West Florida from the British in a military expedition designed to support the American revolutionaries. The new Spanish overlords graciously allowed the British to remain, with their land claims intact, provided they swore loyalty to the Spanish Crown and embraced Catholicism. These conditions, for some, proved a bitter pill, but the dismal prospect of losing one's homestead and being uprooted induced many to swallow the pill so as to stay.[3]

Like their British predecessors, the Spanish also offered large tracts of land to those who would settle in West Florida. In many cases, though, the Spanish grants conflicted with or overlapped the earlier British grants, which Spain had promised to honor. Further complicating the situation, both the British and Spanish grants were almost always vague and confusing. Illustrative of the imprecision inherent in the British titles is a 1776 grant on the Amite River: "Elihu Bay receives all that tract of land situated on the east side of the River Amit [sic] about four miles back from said river upon a creek called the Three Creeks butting and bounding southwesterly unto land surveyed out to Joseph Blackwell and on all other sides by vacant land." Similarly, an 1804 Spanish grant proclaimed that "Luke Collins claims four hundred superficial arpents nine leagues up the east bank of the Tickfaw River, bounded on one side by William George and by public land on the other two." Disputed land claims created tension between pro-British and pro-Spanish factions in West Florida.[4]

From the outset the Spanish government appeared weak and corrupt to the inhabitants of West Florida. Not only did the Spanish make little, if any, effort to resolve the conflicting land claims, but they also failed to appoint district courts to deal with growing criminal activity in the territory. In the first decade of the nineteenth century, large numbers of Americans, encouraged by the United States' claim to the region presumed in the Louisiana Purchase of 1803, augmented the smattering of French and Isleño settlers mi-

3. The stipulation requiring residents to convert to Catholicism appears to have been a token gesture rather than a realistic matter of policy. Little evidence exists to indicate that the Spanish made more than minimal efforts to enforce the decree.

4. Napier, *Lower Pearl River's Piney Woods*, 31; Henry Dart, ed., "Documents Covering a Royal Land Grant and Other Transactions on the Mississippi and Amite Rivers During the English Rule," *Louisiana Historical Quarterly*, XII (1929), 638; *Amite City News Digest*, August 7, 1975; Arthur, *Story of the West Florida Rebellion*, 16.

grating to West Florida. Many army deserters and criminals were among these Americans seeking a safe haven in West Florida. The territory quickly became infested with undesirables who disrupted settlement patterns and waylaid wagons and travelers on the trails and highways. In addition, considerable numbers of American filibusters, adventurers inciting revolution in Spanish-held areas, were also counted among these migrants. Spanish inability to control marauding, to resolve internal disputes, or to control seditious elements created a volatile mix in West Florida. Official communications and settler petitions demonstrate that a perception of neglect and vulnerability promoted a general feeling of discontent among the population.[5] Napoleon Bonaparte's manipulation of the Spanish Crown further exemplified Spain's weakness, heightening the belief among some elements that Spain could never adequately police and promote the territory.

An abortive attempt to overthrow Spanish control and to bring stability to West Florida in 1804 originated with Reuben Kemper of Pinckneyville, Mississippi, and his brothers. The Kempers, like many of their neighbors just across the border in the Mississippi Territory, acted to secure their property rights in West Florida out of a belief that increasing instability in West Florida could eventually destabilize their own region. The brief Kemper Rebellion failed because its leaders miscalculated the strength of pro-French, pro-British, and pro-Spanish elements, all of whom felt threatened by the pro-American faction the Kempers represented.[6]

By 1810, virtual chaos prevailed in West Florida. Spanish authority rarely extended beyond the fort at Baton Rouge and the nearby river towns of Bayou Sara and St. Francisville. Rising criminal activity in the absence of district courts and increasing turmoil resulting from disputed land claims propelled the territory to the brink of anarchy. The chaotic conditions intensified as increasing numbers of army deserters and other fugitives exploited West Florida's weakness, settled in the eastern parishes, and added to the factional tension. William C. C. Claiborne, who would later become the first American governor of Louisiana, observed that many desirables were coming

5. Peacock, "Historical and Statistical Sketches," 265; Thomas D. Clark, "The Piney Woods and the Cutting Edge of the Lingering Southern Frontier," in *Mississippi's Piney Woods*, ed. Polk, 64; Amite City *News Digest*, August 7, 14, 1975; James A. Padgett, "The Constitution of the West Florida Republic," *Louisiana Historical Quarterly*, XX (1937), 881–94.

6. Peacock, "Historical and Statistical Sketches," 264; Arthur, *Story of the West Florida Rebellion*, 29; Amite City *Progress*, July 12, 1945; Amite City *News Digest*, August 7, 1975; St. Francisville *Louisianian*, November 6, 1819.

to the territory but added that "among them are many adventurers of desperate fortunes and characters." By the fall of 1810, contempt for the ineffectiveness of the "pukes," a derogatory name applied to Spanish officials, exploded in the West Florida Rebellion.[7]

Calls for armed rebellion came from large numbers of American settlers, concentrated primarily in the Feliciana district, and others contemptuous of Spanish authority. Following a surprise raid that led to the capture of the fort at Baton Rouge, the rebels moved rapidly to consolidate their control of West Florida. Two groups of citizen militia forming in support of the Spanish in the Springfield and Tangipahoa areas dispersed before rebel contingents arrived. Their hasty retreat allowed the rebels to proclaim the territory independent. The Republic of West Florida endured for seventy-four days before its president, Fulwar Skipwith, reluctantly allowed William C. C. Claiborne to take control of the territory for the United States.

American control, however, failed to bring immediate stability to West Florida. Claiborne reorganized the territory into four parishes but neglected to address aggressively the disorder in the less populated eastern region. He defended his failure to appoint judges for the two eastern parishes, St. Helena and St. Tammany, by arguing that "there is in that quarter a great scarcity of talent, and the number of virtuous men (I fear) is not as great as I could wish." The state legislature intensified the chaotic conditions in the Florida parishes by delaying six years before moving to organize the judicial system effectively there. Additionally, the new American officials aggravated the dispute over land claims by conferring a blanket recognition of existing claims while issuing new land grants themselves.[8]

Moreover, the seemingly ambiguous status of the territory created further problems. An 1811 bill providing for the attachment of West Florida to the Mississippi Territory failed in Congress. When in the same year Congress made provisions to admit the Orleans Territory as a state without including West Florida, rebellion flared anew. On March 11, 1811, rebellious elements again raised the lone star flag of the West Florida Republic, forcing Claiborne

7. Dunbar Rowland, ed., *Official Letter Books of W. C. C. Claiborne, 1801–1816* (6 vols.; Jackson, Miss., 1917) V, 56–57; *House Documents*, 25th Cong., 2nd Sess., No. 463; *Amite City Progress*, July 12, 1945; *Amite City News Digest*, April 10, 1959, August 14, 21, 1975; Arthur, *Story of the West Florida Rebellion*, 29.

8. *Amite City News Digest*, September 11, 1975; Arthur, *Story of the West Florida Rebellion*, 141; *Louisiana House Journal*, 2nd Sess., 1818, pp. 10–12; William C. C. Claiborne to Secretary of State Smith, December 2, 1810, in Dunbar Rowland, ed., *Official Letter Books*, V, 56–57.

to dispatch troops to enforce his authority. On April 12, 1812, Congress admitted Louisiana to the Union. Nearly four months later, on August 4, 1812, the state assented to the inclusion of West Florida, from the Mississippi to the Pearl River, as part of the new state.[9]

Despite lingering legal problems concerning the status of West Florida, statehood introduced a degree of territorial certainty but not internal stability in the Florida parishes.[10] Disputed land claims, resulting from the conflicting grants of the various governing powers, continued to create difficulties. As late as 1844 the state legislature implored Congress to resolve the disputed land claims that persisted in impeding settlement. The primary problem, however, continued to lie with the people themselves. Composed of various antagonistic ethnic groups, many containing hostile internal social and political factions, the Florida parishes constituted a volatile melting pot. Lingering British, French, and Spanish loyalties, coupled with land disputes and rampant criminal activity, inhibited the establishment of an effective American system of justice. Addressing Congress concerning complaints he had received regarding the turbulent conditions in the Florida parishes, Governor Claiborne asserted that "civil authority has become weak and lax in West Florida particularly in the parish of St. Tammany in which the influence of laws is scarcely felt."[11] Claiborne's dilemma seemed compounded by his awareness that many of the residents came to the territory specifically because no effective legal authority existed there. These migrants aggressively resisted the implementation of American authority.

Regional patterns of settlement illustrate the significance of the continuing disorder in the Florida parishes. Although the number of settlers coming

9. Clinton *Patriot-Democrat*, August 28, 1880; William C. C. Claiborne to Secretary of State Smith, December 16, 1810, in *House Documents*, 25th Cong., 2nd Sess., No. 463; "Report of the Select Committee Making an Apportionment of Representation in the House of Representatives," *Louisiana House Journal*, 2nd Sess., 1833, pp. 17–18; Arthur, *Story of the West Florida Rebellion*, 141; Amite City *News Digest*, September 18, 1975.

10. As noted in the Introduction, the Constitution of 1812 did not include West Florida as a portion of Louisiana. This omission continued to create problems for the legislature, which persisted in treating the region as distinctive into the 1830s (*Louisiana House Journal*, 2nd Sess., 1833, pp. 15–19).

11. *American State Papers: Legislative Documents of the Congress of the United States in Relation to Public Lands*, 19th Cong., 1st Sess., Nos. 455–57, pp. 336–38, and 22nd Cong., 1st Sess., No. 1072, pp. 506–509; "Annual Message of Governor Alfred Mouton," *Louisiana House Journal*, 2nd Sess., 1844, pp. 2–5; St. Francisville *Louisiana Journal*, February 5, 1824; Dunbar Rowland, ed., *Official Letter Books*, VI, 161–62.

to West Florida increased significantly in the first fifteen years of the nineteenth century, the population remained relatively sparse. By contrast, in the Mississippi Territory, the counties bordering the Florida parishes typically contained populations three or four times the number in West Florida. Likewise, the parishes to the west and south had considerably larger populations. These regions, particularly the southwestern counties of Mississippi, had benefited from the disorder in West Florida. Many planters, such as William Dunbar, removed their operations from West Florida to southwestern Mississippi either to avoid the instability and legal confusion prevailing in West Florida or simply to live in territory under American control.[12] Since the Florida parishes comprised the area just north of the largest market in the South and possessed soil and natural resources very similar to those in the adjacent counties in the Mississippi Territory, clearly the region's instability served to inhibit settlement. This situation continued until the 1830s, when an intricate combination of politics and economics ushered in a new era in West Florida. The virgin pine forests, numerous clear running streams, and the expanding and increasingly profitable market for staple crops virtually necessitated the advent of stability in the Florida parishes. Agricultural prosperity, coupled with the introduction of the political dominance of delta planters, led to a state of equilibrium in West Florida.

The residents' seeming inability to find a profitable crop in the first decades of development retarded progress in the Florida parishes nearly as much as did territorial instability. French, British, and Spanish efforts to promote tobacco and indigo farming proved at best marginally successful. In the first decade of the nineteenth century, however, good fortune finally arrived for the delta planters of West Florida. Facing financial ruin as a result of their failure to market tobacco and indigo profitably, they turned to cotton. The introduction of the cotton gin into the lower Mississippi valley around the turn of the century stimulated this transformation. Planters in the Feliciana district and East Baton Rouge experimented with an upland cotton of the Siamese black seed variety, which proved adaptable to the Louisiana environment. Fortunately for these planters, the slave rebellion in Saint Domingue, occurring at virtually the same time, deprived European manufacturers of one of their principal sources of the fiber. Cotton prices skyrocketed to unprecedented levels, creat-

12. *Third Census, 1810: Compendium*, 82–84; Darby, *Geographical Description of Louisiana*, 175; Eron Rowland, ed., *Life, Letters, and Papers of William Dunbar of Elgin, Morayshire, Scotland, and Natchez, Mississippi: Pioneer Scientist of the Southern United States* (Jackson, Miss., 1930), 10.

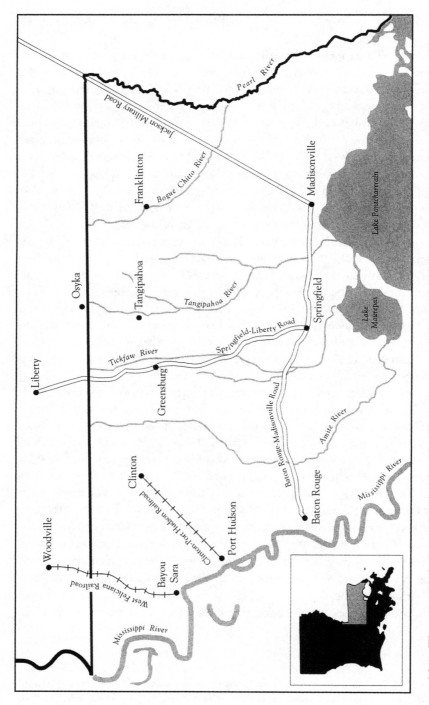

Major Waterways, Highways, and Railroads in the Florida Parishes, *ca.* 1852

ing an economic boom for the emerging cotton planters of West Florida. By the 1830s, the delta region of Louisiana and Mississippi had surpassed Georgia and South Carolina in the production of cotton.[13]

High prices encouraged the expansion of the cotton economy, but the piney woods of the eastern Florida parishes appeared unfit for cotton farming. Typically, the piney-woods regions of the Gulf South contained a sandy soil, deposited when the area comprised a part of the Gulf of Mexico. Moreover, pine needles, unlike the remains of rotting hardwood leaves, did not produce the deep, rich, loessial covering above the soil conducive to intensive farming. The eastern parishes, though, like most of Louisiana and southwestern Mississippi, contained numerous rivers and streams. By the late 1830s, industrious farmers had demonstrated that cotton could be profitably raised in the river bottoms and creek beds of the piney woods.[14]

The introduction of successful commercial agricultural pursuits in the piney woods encouraged farmers in the Florida parishes to experiment with crops other than cotton. Rice cultivation began as early as the second decade of the nineteenth century. By the middle of the 1830s, enterprising farmers demonstrated that the marshland along the north shore of Lakes Maurepas and Pontchartrain, as well as the abundant swampland along the Pearl, Amite, and other rivers, proved conducive to rice farming. Rice required minimal capital in its cultivation, making it a viable alternative crop for middling and poorer farmers. By 1840, rice farming constituted a popular and profitable business in the eastern Florida parishes, as well as in the southwestern counties of Mississippi. Amite and Pike Counties in Mississippi, for instance, each produced about 150,000 pounds of rice annually. Marion, Hancock, and Wilkinson Counties also cultivated rice, though to a far lesser extent. Despite the presence of a few sugarcane fields, located primarily in East Baton Rouge Parish, the Florida parishes remained outside the sugar-producing region.[15]

13. Gavin Wright, *The Political Economy of the Cotton South: Households, Markets, and Wealth in the Nineteenth Century* (New York, 1978), 13–22; Moore, *Emergence of the Cotton Kingdom*, 6; Lewis C. Gray, *History of Agriculture in the Southern United States to 1860* (2 vols.; New York, 1941–58), I, 687–89.

14. *Sixth Census, 1840: Compendium*, 240; Moore, *Emergence of the Cotton Kingdom*, 7; *Amite City Progress*, June 25, 1937; Robert J. Baxter, "Cattle Raising in Early Mississippi," *Mississippi Folklore Register*, X (1976), 3.

15. *House Documents*, "Report of the Commissioner of Agriculture," 40th Cong., 2nd Sess., Exec. Doc., 1867, 174–75; J. D. B. De Bow, *The Industrial Resources, Etc., of the Southern and*

The pattern of growing cotton along fertile stream beds and rice in swampland continued in the piney-woods parishes through the end of the antebellum period. A 3 percent sample survey of farmers gathered from the 1850 and 1860 census returns demonstrates the significance of staple-crop farming in the piney woods. In 1850, 36.6 percent of farmers produced rice while 48.3 percent grew cotton. Ten years later, though only 20.0 percent continued to raise rice, cotton production had soared, involving 72.2 percent of piney-woods farmers. The increasing emphasis on cotton reflects the rising profitability and expanding availability of machinery to process that staple. Table 2, based on the 3 percent census sample, demonstrates aggregate totals of cotton and rice production in the Florida parishes and confirms increasing productivity in the late antebellum period.[16]

Among the heads of household in the piney-woods parishes who listed their occupations, 72 percent in Livingston, 73 percent in St. Helena, 36 percent in St. Tammany, and fully 86 percent of the respondents in Washington declared themselves farmers or planters. As the vast majority of these farmers planted staple crops, the piney-woods parishes seemed to be fully incorporated into the cotton economy. However, unlike the plantation parishes, East and West Feliciana and East Baton Rouge, where typically larger farms averaged between fifty and two hundred bales of cotton annually, farms in the piney-woods parishes usually averaged ten bales or less. In the planter parishes the figures ranged from a low average of nearly fifty bales in East Baton Rouge to a high of almost two hundred bales in West Feliciana. By contrast, in the piney woods figures ranged from a low average of less than three bales in Livingston to a high of almost forty bales in St. Helena. Land holdings also contrasted widely. Holdings in the wealthiest planter parish, West Feliciana, averaged about 1,800 acres; in the wealthiest piney-woods parish,

Western States: Embracing a View of their Commerce, Agriculture, Manufactures . . . with an Appendix (2 vols.; New Orleans, 1853), II, 426–27; Brackenridge, Views of Louisiana, 285; Darby, Geographical Description of Louisiana, 141–42; Sixth Census, 1840: Compendium, 244–46, 240; F. F. Hansell, ed., Commercial and Statistical Almanac: Containing a History of the Epidemic of 1878 (New Orleans, 1879), 22.

16. For specific data from each individual parish in 1850, see Table 1. The percentages of farmers in each piney-woods parish producing cotton in 1860 were: Washington, 91; St. Tammany, 33; Livingston, 75; St. Helena, 90. The percentages of farmers producing rice in the same period were: Washington, 25; St. Tammany, 33; Livingston, 12; St. Helena, 10. All figures were based on a 3 percent sample survey of heads of households (Eighth Census, 1860, Manuscript, Louisiana, Schedule 2, Agricultural Statistics, Microfilm).

TABLE 2. AGRICULTURAL PRODUCTION AS A MEASURE OF PROSPERITY, 1850–1860

Parish	Cotton Produced (Bales) 1850	Cotton Produced (Bales) 1860	Rice Produced (Pounds) 1850	Rice Produced (Pounds) 1860	% Who Increased Cotton Production 1850–60	% Who Increased Livestock Holdings 1850–60	% Cotton Farmers Who Increased Landholding 1850–60
Plantation Parishes							
East Baton Rouge	1,346	11,621	4,009	0	Insuff. Data	50	50
East Feliciana	9,967	23,332	4,675	17	75	25	66
West Feliciana	18,291	21,331	8,000	0	33	66	33
Piney-Woods Parishes							
Livingston	265	1,563	83,480	1,060	91	50	50
St. Helena	1,284	6,484	54,868	11,772	80	60	40
St. Tammany	41	200	97,793	22,049	Insuff. Data	—	—
Washington	693	2,735	159,750	27,340	90	60	80

Sources: Seventh Census, 1850, Manuscript, and Eighth Census, 1860, Manuscript, Louisiana, Schedule 2, Agricultural Statistics, Microfilm

St. Helena, about 1,350 acres. Holdings in the remaining piney-woods parishes averaged notably less: 390 acres in Livingston, 294 in St. Tammany, and 400 in Washington.[17] Nevertheless, shared investments and a mutual dependence on the success of the cotton crop emerged as important bonds between the planters and piney-woods dwellers. Cotton, corollary agricultural pursuits, and the politics of slavery would serve as the cornerstones for stability in the Florida parishes.

Despite strong ties to the cotton economy, other factors such as lower crop yields, the limited availability of quality land, and the ravages of the army worm and rot encouraged a diversified economy in the piney-woods parishes. A passion for self-sufficiency prompted most farmers in the eastern parishes to devote considerable portions of their land to foodstuffs.[18] Sample surveys of individual households demonstrate that virtually all piney-woods farmers raised significant amounts of corn; some produced a considerable surplus. The ubiquitous cultivation of sweet potatoes made them a mainstay of the piney-woods diet, whereas Irish potatoes, peas, and beans appear to have been of lesser significance. This pattern of cultivation typified the piney-woods parishes. Delta planters usually directed their resources exclusively toward the production of staple crops and corn, though some, particularly in East Feliciana Parish, raised considerable quantities of potatoes and beans.[19] Planters who failed to produce adequate amounts of foodstuffs either relied on the New Orleans markets or purchased vegetables directly from the plain folk.

Row-crop farming played an undeniably important role in the piney woods, yet perhaps the more important resource of the piney-woods farmer, as it was a significant asset of many planters, could be found roaming in the thickets of their unimproved land. The importance of livestock herding to the southern economy has long been established. The piney woods of eastern Louisiana and southern Mississippi produced huge amounts of beef and pork in the antebellum period. Visitors to the region frequently expressed surprise at the number of cattle and hogs they observed roaming through the forests.

17. All figures were based on a 3 percent sample survey of heads of households (*Eighth Census, 1860*, Manuscript, Louisiana, Schedule 2, Agricultural Statistics, Microfilm).

18. Greensburg *Imperial*, October 10, 1857; Clinton *Feliciana Democrat*, September 15, 1855; New Orleans *Daily Picayune*, September 28, 1852; Baxter, "Cattle Raising in Early Mississippi," 3; Clinton *East Feliciana Patriot*, April 27, 1867.

19. Figures were based on a 3 percent sample survey of heads of households in each individual parish (*Seventh Census, 1850*, Manuscript, and *Eighth Census, 1860*, Manuscript, Louisiana, Schedule 2, Agricultural Statistics, Microfilm).

Following a tour of the region in 1813, Dr. James Perry, a United States naval inspector, concluded that "cattle are reared here to as great a perfection, and to perhaps as great an extent, on the waters of the Pearl River . . . as in any part of the United States."[20]

In both the plantation region and the piney woods, livestock, made identifiable by branding or ear cropping, usually roamed free in the forests. Fences served only to protect crops from foraging animals. Opposition to the fencing of livestock rested not only on a strong tradition of open grazing rights but also on the lingering problem of disputed land claims. As prosperity in the territory increased, most residents appeared willing to accept vague property lines in the woodlands in order to preserve the peace. Efforts to further the emerging pattern of stability necessitated a compromising attitude on the part of local farmers. Establishing fences along supposed property lines could have reignited old disputes concerning land claims, a situation the tumult-weary residents seemed eager to avoid.

During the period 1850 to 1860, livestock holdings in the Florida parishes dramatically increased. By 1860, the Florida parishes and the southeastern counties of Mississippi contained some of the heaviest concentrations of livestock, particularly cattle, in the South. The increasing popularity and profitability of livestock farming in the late antebellum period resulted primarily from both the shortfall in food production affecting many local planters and the accessibility of the New Orleans markets. In their zeal to maximize their yield of profitable staple crops, many planters failed to produce enough food for their families and slaves. Considerable numbers of them consequently relied on piney-woods herders to compensate for their deficiency in meat production, particularly beef. This situation provided the piney-woods cattlemen with a steady localized demand for their product. Acute shortages in food production often occurred on the plantations when cotton prices remained high for an extended period.[21] As a result, cotton prices had a direct impact on the profitability of livestock herding. In 1860, approximately 65 percent of farmers in the piney-woods parishes possessed levels of livestock large enough to indi-

20. Owsley, *Plain Folk*, 21–36; Forrest McDonald and Grady McWhiney, "The Antebellum Southern Herdsman: A Reinterpretation," *Journal of Southern History*, XLI (1975), 147–66; Inscoe, *Mountain Masters*, 45–52; Timothy Flint, *Recollections of the Last Ten Years*, 236–37; Claiborne, "A Trip Through the Piney Woods," 514–15.

21. *Seventh Census, 1850: Compendium*, 250; *Eighth Census, 1860: Agriculture*, 66–67; Gray, *History of Agriculture*, II, 836–37; Sam B. Hilliard, *Hog Meat and Hoecake: Food Supply in the Old South, 1840–1860* (Carbondale, Ill., 1972), 191–92.

cate herding. A sample survey of piney-woods farmers indicates average hold-ings of 40.6 cattle.[22] Thus, whether they farmed a few acres of the major staple or not, piney-woods herders also participated in an industry directly affected by the cotton economy.

The vast expanses of pine forests provided a natural habitat for livestock farming. Herding proved central to regional prosperity and to the piney-woods residents' ability to maintain their independent life-style. But the stands of virgin long-leaf pine contributed to the developing prosperity in a more fundamental way. By the 1840s, timber harvesting emerged as a locally controlled industry with seemingly unlimited potential. Planters as well as plain folk engaged in this profitable enterprise. Numerous small, family-owned sawmills arose across the piney-woods parishes and East Feliciana. In 1860, twenty-eight sawmills employing 187 laborers, with a total capital in-vestment of $289,900, operated in St. Helena, St. Tammany, and Washing-ton Parishes. Another four, valued at $20,200, employed 28 workers in West Feliciana Parish. By 1880, thirty water-powered sawmills operated in St. He-lena Parish alone.[23] From the early 1880s through the close of the nineteenth century, timber harvesting assumed an importance in the eastern Florida parishes that placed it at the center of both the piney-woods economy and the violence that consumed the region.

As it did with livestock herding, the cotton economy also influenced the fortunes of the timber industry. The temporary decline in cotton prices in the early 1850s dramatically affected the timber industry, which already suf-fered from waning demand in New Orleans. Although demand remained high in the northeast, exorbitant freight charges forced woodcutters to rely more exclusively on regional purchasers. Local planters had always ac-counted for a significant proportion of purchased lumber. Andrew McCol-lam, a wealthy planter who owned a sawmill near Donaldsonville below Ba-

22. Hilliard, *Hog Meat and Hoe Cake,* 113–17. Figure was based on a 3 percent sample of farmers (*Eighth Census, 1860,* Manuscript, Louisiana, Schedule 2, Agricultural Statistics, Mi-crofilm). Average cattle holdings for each of the piney-woods parishes were: Washington, 39.7; St. Helena, 53.6; St. Tammany, 32.5; and Livingston, 34.8.

23. Map of the Line of the New Orleans-Jackson Railroad from Canton, Mississippi, to New Orleans, circa 1861, in Illinois Central Railroad Collection, Newberry Library, Chicago; *Eighth Census, 1860; Manufactures,* 197, 201 (no figures were provided for the parishes of East Baton Rouge, East Feliciana, and Livingston); Amite City *News Digest,* September 18, 1959; Gray, *His-tory of Agriculture,* II, 936; Milton B. Newton, Jr., "Water-Powered Sawmills and Related Struc-tures in the Piney Woods," in *Mississippi's Piney Woods,* ed. Polk, 156, 164.

ton Rouge in Ascension Parish, sold virtually all of his processed lumber to regional planters. McCollam considered the trade so lucrative that he abandoned plans to buy an additional plantation and instead determined to erect a second sawmill in the belief that "it [would] bring more money than planting." John W. Gurley, absentee owner of Oak Lawn Plantation in lower Livingston Parish, instructed his overseer to purchase all of his lumber from local mills, in some transactions bartering with tobacco purchased in New Orleans. Timber purchases by local planters stimulated the industry, allowing for the hiring of more laborers, which in turn further cemented the economic bonds between planter and commoner. In the winter of 1831, the Baton Rouge *Gazette* called for the construction of a railroad into the piney woods to supply the city with turpentine, charcoal, and the "thousand cords of wood" that could be sold there annually. If they encouraged some local timber production, low cotton prices also discouraged many planters and other local residents from buying wood products for personal use or as an investment. When cotton prices recovered in the middle of the 1850s, timber prices also rebounded.[24]

As the prosperous economic conditions that had characterized the delta parishes for decades spread into the eastern Florida parishes, the need for labor also increased dramatically.[25] Cotton and rice farming, livestock herding, and activities associated with the timber industry all depended on large numbers of reliable laborers to ensure the levels of production necessary to turn a profit. The sparse pattern of settlement in Louisiana necessitated the impor-

24. R. E. Foster to Asa Hursey, September 1, 1849, October 23, 1853, John Henderson to Asa Hursey, August 19, 1850, all in Asa H. Hursey Family Papers, LLMVC; Diary and Plantation Record of Ellen McCollam, Vol. III, 237, 245, 247, 262a, 266, and 268, in Andrew and Ellen E. McCollam Papers, LLMVC; Edward Stewart to John Gurley, March 27, 1859, March 5, 1860, and undated letter [1858?] (see folder 1), all in Gurley Papers; receipt for lumber purchased by Lewis Stirling, December, 1850, in Lewis Stirling Family Papers, LLMVC; Duncan W. Taylor to Eugene Hunter, September 13, 1856 (about cost differentials in lumber operations in piney-woods parishes and plantation parishes), in Hunter-Taylor Family Papers; Baton Rouge *Gazette*, January 29, 1831; E. J. Donnell, *Chronological and Statistical History of Cotton* (New York, 1872), 388, 425, 447; Moore, *Emergence of the Cotton Kingdom*, 153; John Eisterhold, "Lumber and Trade in the Lower Mississippi Valley and New Orleans, 1800–1860," *Louisiana History*, XIII (1972), 77.

25. Throughout this study I have frequently employed *delta* as a term to distinguish the plantation parishes from the piney-woods parishes. For the purposes of description and easy identification, I have used *delta* as associated with the banks of the Mississippi River, as in the ancient buildup of the lower Mississippi delta.

tation of foreign laborers. As a result, chattel slavery emerged as central to increasing prosperity in the piney woods.

By the time large numbers of African bondsmen were introduced to the piney woods, slavery had long been established in Louisiana. With the successful introduction of cotton to the region, the number of slaves increased dramatically. By 1820, the slave population of East Baton Rouge and the combined Feliciana parishes slightly outnumbered the total white population there; in the remaining Florida parishes, the white population outnumbered the slaves by a ratio of 5 to 1. As cotton production expanded into the piney-woods parishes, so did the slave system. In 1850, the slave population of the Florida parishes reached 32,969, greatly exceeding the white population, which totaled 22,767. The proportion of slaves in the population ranged from a high of almost 80 percent in West Feliciana to a low of 24 percent in Livingston.[26]

During the 1850s slavery flourished in the Florida parishes. As cotton prices climbed in the middle of the decade and emphasis on cotton production increased, the advantages of the slave system increased as well. Nor did slaveholding remain limited to cotton farmers. Slaves served as lumbermen felling trees and working in sawmills; they also functioned as herdsmen rounding up livestock and participating in drives, often mounted on horseback.[27] As a result, high rates of slaveholding existed in all the piney-woods parishes. In 1850, the number of piney-woods heads of household owning slaves ranged from a high of 66 percent in St. Helena to a low of 28 percent in Livingston Parish (see Table 3).

The slave system increased the contact and reduced the divergence in lifestyle between planters and plain folk. Despite the vast difference in mean number of slaves between the plantation and piney-woods parishes, ranging from a high of 88.0 slaves per household in West Feliciana to a low of 5.8 in Livingston, slaveholding emerged as an important bond between planter and commoner. Slave transactions facilitated development of that relationship. Several slave auctions, such as the one at Bayou Sara, operated on a regular

26. *Fourth Census, 1820: Compendium*, 31; *Seventh Census, 1850: Compendium*, 246–49.

27. Diary of Eli Capell, January 13, 1850, and second week of September, 1850, in Capell Papers; Edward Stewart to John Gurley, April 22, 1859, March 5, 25, 1860, all in Gurley Papers; Eisterhold, "Lumber and Trade," 79; Newton, "Water-Powered Sawmills," in *Mississippi's Piney Woods*, ed. Polk, 165–66; Roger W. Shugg, *Origins of Class Struggle in Louisiana: A Social History of White Farmers and Laborers During Slavery and After, 1840–1875* (Baton Rouge, 1939), 157–63; Moore, *Emergence of the Cotton Kingdom*, 152; Gray, *History of Agriculture*, II, 936.

TABLE 3. SLAVEHOLDING, 1850–1860

Parish	% Heads of Households Owning Slaves 1850	% Heads of Households Owning Slaves 1860	% Owning Slaves in 1850 Who Increased Holding 1850–60	% of Slaves in Population 1850	% of Slaves in Population 1860
Plantation Parishes					
East Baton Rouge	29	17	50	53.0	53.4
East Feliciana	76	68	66	69.9	72.0
West Feliciana	55	57	60	80.5	82.0
Piney-Woods Parishes					
Livingston	28	16	50	24.8	29.5
St. Helena	66	58	80	48.0	52.0
St. Tammany	37	22	66	37.0	34.0
Washington	50	31	90	30.4	35.8

Sources: Seventh Census, 1850, Manuscript, and *Eighth Census, 1860,* Manuscript, Heads of Household and Slave Schedules. Columns 1–3 were based on a 3 percent sample survey of each parish. Columns 4–5 come from *Seventh Census, 1850: Compendium* and *Eighth Census, 1860: Compendium.*

basis in the Florida parishes, and the markets in New Orleans certainly attracted piney-woods farmers, but the principal mechanism for purchasing slaves involved personal transactions between planters and farmers.[28] After purchasing the Roncal Plantation in northeastern St. Helena Parish, Charles Gayarre, a prominent New Orleans attorney and historian, secured the bulk of his slaves from local farmers and planters. Absentee owner John Gurley consistently endorsed his overseer's slave transactions with local farmers in the Livingston Parish area, though in at least one instance he complained that the sale price had been too low. Taking advantage of the state's indebtedness, Amos Kent purchased two slaves from the Louisiana Department of Internal Improvements, later selling one at a profit to a local farmer. In April, 1856, Jefferson McKinney wrote his brother Jeptha, a physician and farmer at Greensburg, that after saving for years he had finally purchased a prime Negro girl from a local planter. He noted that the cost incurred would put him into debt and force him to do without many things but would eventually serve to raise his status in life.[29]

With the rising importance of the cotton economy in the piney woods, slaveholding increasingly came to be seen as the key to success. To accommodate farmers of little means, planters also leased slaves to their less wealthy neighbors. William Warren agreed to lease a female slave to D. L. McGehee, who farmed a modest tract near Greensburg in St. Helena Parish, for $100 a year, stipulating only that McGehee himself would have to persuade the girl

28. H. J. Noble to his Aunt Maria, May 20, 1853, in W. M. Barrow Family Papers, LLMVC; Edward Stewart to John W. Gurley, January 24, 1858, in Gurley Papers; Jefferson McKinney to Jeptha McKinney, April 21, 1856, in Jeptha McKinney Papers, LLMVC; receipt of sale for two slaves purchased by Amos Kent, June 11, 1860, in Kent Papers; Davis, ed., *Diary of Bennett H. Barrow*, 39; William Warren to D. L. McGehee, September 20, 1863, in D. L. McGehee Papers, LLMVC; two receipts of sale for slaves in 1846 and receipt of sale for slave, Joseph Bruin to Charles Gayarre, February 20, 1862, all in Charles Gayarre Collection, LLMVC; Amite City *News Digest*, August 14, 1975.

29. Receipt for sale of six slaves, Joseph Bruin to Charles Gayarre, February 20, 1862, also notes on purchases of slaves in 1859, box 16, all in Gayarre Collection; Edward Stewart to John Gurley, January 24, 1858, March 5, 1860, both in Gurley Papers; receipt for sale of slaves to Amos Kent, June 11, 1860, in miscellaneous file box, Kent Papers; Jefferson McKinney to Jeptha McKinney, April 21, 1856, in McKinney Papers; official recording of sale of slaves between St. Helena Parish farmers and planters by S. B. Draughon, notary public, May–October, 1838, in S. B. Draughon and Company Account Book, LLMVC; slave sale broadside, listing eleven slaves to be sold at the plantation of Mr. Griffith, credit terms offered to potential purchasers, 1820, in Miscellaneous File, LLMVC.

to accept the arrangement. In other cases, some planters assisted poorer friends' rise to the rank of slaveholder by selling them chattel at surprisingly low prices. St. Tammany Parish records contain numerous instances of planters selling prime field hands for considerably less than the prevailing market price. Thomas Green Davidson, the wealthiest planter in Livingston Parish, frequently sold slaves to farmers at barely half their market value.[30]

As the slave system expanded in the piney woods, the influence of the delta planters increased among the plain folk. Many piney-woods farmers incurred debts to the planters by purchasing or leasing slaves. What is more important, as with cotton production, when the plain folk's involvement escalated, they increasingly looked to their powerful neighbors for guidance and leadership. The shared commitment to slavery facilitated planter dominance in the piney woods.

Economic development advanced planter power in other ways. Whether piney-woods farmers raised surplus vegetables, herded livestock, or cut timber, large planters had always constituted a significant market for their goods. The relationship between planters and plain folk, though beneficial to both, gave the former a degree of economic leadership over the latter. Planters frequently allowed farmers to grind corn in their mills and transported goods to market for their less wealthy neighbors. The growing emphasis on cotton during the 1840s and early 1850s, however, provided the planters with an unprecedented opportunity to increase their influence in the piney-woods parishes.

To be profitable, cotton production required both capital and machinery. As farmers invested their limited resources in land and labor, most lacked the means to purchase gins, oxen, and other equipment necessary to process and transport the precious fiber to market. As a result, a system developed whereby farmers, lacking sufficient resources, would sell their cotton to a nearby planter to be ginned and carried to market. This process allowed the planters a direct influence over the economic fortunes of the smaller cotton farmers. Planters either purchased the farmers' cotton outright or charged a fee to gin the cotton and an additional amount to transport it to market. Such an arrangement,

30. Warren to McGehee, September 20, 1863, in D. L. McGehee Papers; Edward Stewart to John Gurley, February 19, March 5, 1860, both in Gurley Papers; Diary of Capell, esp. leases of slaves to local farmers in second week of September, 1850, in Capell Papers. In December, 1844, Davidson sold a twenty-two-year-old male with a market value of $1,000 for barely $600; see January 31, May 1, 18, December 18, 1844, February 25, April 12, May 6, 1845, March 19, 1849, all in Notarial Records of Parris Childress, 1843–51, St. Tammany Parish, Clerk of Court Archives, Covington, La.

allowing the planter to act as factor for the small farmer, benefited both parties. The farmer profited from the immediate cash payment he usually received for his crop, though the payment he accepted typically remained below the premium market value. The planter, in turn, benefited from the markup on the farmer's cotton or from fees charged for ginning and transporting it. Despite the give and take, the advantage clearly lay with the planter, not only in terms of profit, but in the increasing level of control he exercised over the farmer. Planters, however, were not alone in procuring cotton from the smaller farmers. Many country merchants also purchased the raw fiber. In larger towns such as Clinton, numerous store owners and commercial agents such as the firms of Abraham Levi and R. H. Draughon actively participated in the cotton trade. Most of these small-town merchants, though, had direct connections to planter interests and in most cases complemented rather than competed with the trade carried on by the planters.[31]

Abel John Norwood, a prominent planter and politician in East Feliciana Parish, epitomized the planter who served as factor for local farmers. Norwood's operations involved processing and transporting cotton for local farmers as well as buying crops outright that he later sold in the New Orleans markets. By the late 1840s his extensive purchases of the crops of local farmers and of those in neighboring parishes and counties gained him a partnership in a major New Orleans factorage firm. Norwood also translated his economic power into political fortune by securing election to a judicial post in East Feliciana Parish.[32]

31. S. M. Gafsarray to A. J. Norwood, December 5, 1870, in Abel John Norwood Papers, LLMVC; list of five purchases of cotton, ranging from five to seventy bales, by Robert Barrow, October, 1834, to February, 1835, in James P. Bowman Family Papers, LLMVC; receipt for $53.50, Joseph Embree to Daniel Tousinau, July 10, 1851, in Joseph Embree Papers, LLMVC; R. H. Draughon Record Book, 1860, winter and spring, 1860, East Feliciana Parish Archives Collection; Ralph Haskins, "Planter and Cotton Factor in the Old South: Some Areas of Friction," Agricultural History, XXIX (1955), 1–14; Moore, Emergence of the Cotton Kingdom, 234–35; Harold D. Woodman, King Cotton & His Retainers: Financing & Marketing the Cotton Crop of the South, 1800–1925 (Lexington, 1968), 68; Lacy Ford, Origins of Southern Radicalism: The South Carolina Upcountry, 1800–1860 (New York, 1988), 65–66; Steven Hahn, The Roots of Southern Populism: Yeoman Farmers and the Transformation of the Georgia Upcountry, 1850–1890 (New York, 1983), 33.

32. Receipts for purchase of cotton from C. Morgan, September 1, 1849, and J. D. Nettles, February, 1854, list of cotton shipped for John L. Lee, J. Robinson, John Pritchard, and Henry Scott, August, 1855, to March, 1856, in A. J. Norwood Account Books, ledgers 3 and 4, Norwood Papers.

As the demand for cotton increased, so, too, did the need for reliable routes to the markets at New Orleans. Dependable avenues of market access required the construction of new roads into isolated areas and the clearing of obstructions from numerous streams and rivers. These necessary improvements created additional opportunities for the capital-rich planter elite. Control of the routes of market access proved vital to their ability to dominate the economy and, concomitantly, regional politics.

In the first decades after statehood and into the early 1840s, the planters consented to the construction and improvement of numerous avenues of market access. On January 23, 1827, the state legislature approved, virtually without opposition, a bill appropriating state funds "to improve the road leading from Covington through Washington Parish to Holmesville, Mississippi." This measure marked one of the first state appropriations to improve roads in the piney-woods region of the Florida parishes. The substance of this bill also demonstrated the growing importance of the north shore of Lake Pontchartrain as a collecting and transporting center for the markets of New Orleans.[33]

During the 1830s, the state legislature appropriated large sums to promote the growth of the cotton economy in the piney woods. Following a report by the state engineer in December, 1833, indicating that the wealth of the eastern Florida parishes remained virtually untouched owing to the absence of reliable roads and obstructed streams, a flurry of activity produced a number of bills of improvement for the legislature to debate. In January, 1834, the legislature overwhelmingly approved a bill appropriating substantial funds to "improve navigation on the Tangipahoa, Bogue Falaya, and West Pearl rivers," all major streams in the eastern Florida parishes. This bill constituted a major state appropriation, for clearing the waterways of obstructions involved employing significant labor on snag boats in an expensive and time-consuming process. In addition to this major appropriation, the House, in the same session, approved by voice vote a bill earmarking funds "to improve the road from Springfield to the line of St. Helena on the way to Mississippi." Each of these bills was specifically designed to improve market access and to stimulate the growing cotton economy in the piney woods, and each passed with overwhelming support from the planters. In February, 1846, State Engineer P. O. Hebert reported that as a result of state appropriations, the West Pearl River and other regional streams had been cleared of their obstructions. Hebert continued: "These streams should remain so as they go through some

33. *Louisiana Senate Journal*, 1st Sess., 1827, pp. 16, 22.

of the richest cotton territory and best and most valuable timber regions. Steamboats can now carry 600 to 800 bales of cotton safely and receipts at New Orleans have demonstrated this."[34]

By the 1840s, the rapidly increasing volume of trade on the market trails and waterways in the Florida parishes inspired some enterprising individuals to seek a means to tap this lucrative source of profit. In antebellum Louisiana, as in much of the South, individuals had frequently opened privately operated bridges, ferryboats, or roads to the general public for a small user's fee. In the decade prior to secession, private ownership of the routes of travel dramatically increased. Moreover, actions of the state legislature and local police juries made possible the transformation of public travel routes into private ones. For the piney-woods farmers, the privatization process increasingly encumbered the means of access to market, creating further economic burdens and sources of dependency.

Essentially, privatization involved the selling of transportation improvements to wealthy individuals. Under the guise of relieving the state of major financial burdens, the legislature and most police juries typically assented to the privatization of roads, bridges, and ferryboats. Those wealthy enough to construct bridges and ferries or to maintain roads petitioned their representatives with promises of support, and possibly offered bribes, to seek legislative sanction for their endeavors. The privatization process relieved state and local governments of a major source of indebtedness. It also freed local residents and slaves from the necessity of maintaining public roads. Despite these obvious benefits, on the darker side privatization allowed wealthy individuals to secure greater control over the means of access to market. In the Florida parishes private control of the roads and bridges furthered the growing economic power of the planters.

The legislature proved quite willing to accommodate the privatization process. On February 1, 1850, Senator John P. Waddill, representing Rapides and Avoyelles Parishes, introduced a bill granting Michael and Joseph Tarras "exclusive privilege of keeping a ferry across the Mississippi at Shreve's Cut Off in Pointe Coupee and West Feliciana parishes." Six days later, Waddill

34. "Report of the State Engineer," pp. 21–30, and other transportation improvements, pp. 61–63, 69, both in *Louisiana House Journal*, 2nd Sess., 1833; "Report of the State Engineer," *Louisiana House Journal*, 1st Sess., 1835, p. 103; "Report of the State Engineer," *Louisiana State Legislative Documents*, 1st Sess., 1860, pp. 5–6; "Report of State Engineer P. O. Hebert," *Louisiana Senate Journal*, 1st Sess., 1846, pp. 16–20.

introduced another bill, this one granting "Joseph Kirk and his heirs exclusive privilege of operating a ferry across the Atchafalaya at the mouth of Bayou Des Glaize." By these measures and with the overwhelming assent of the legislature, Waddill placed into private hands the most direct connection between West Feliciana Parish and north-central Louisiana. This stratagem served not only to increase his own personal patronage but also to enrich the few at the expense of the many.[35]

The disposition of the legislature to support privatization became readily apparent in the first session of 1852. Legislative committees defeated efforts of privatization opponents to strengthen an act that provided for the policing of public roads. This measure would have ensured the standard of quality on public roads, thereby reducing the chance for individuals to argue the need for private endeavors. In addition, proponents of privatization sought to strip from the various police juries the exclusive right to establish and regulate ferries and toll bridges, thus expanding and streamlining privatization efforts. The bill to strip the police juries naturally faced tough opposition from supporters of local government, yet this measure demonstrated the aggressive nature of the proponents of privatization. In the same session, the Committee on Internal Improvements reversed a measure allowing for the construction of a public road in Catahoula Parish at the urging of several influential residents of that area.[36]

Perhaps most significant, privatization, rather than improving the means of transportation, often resulted in inferior roads, bridges, and ferryboat service. In the winter of 1850, the state legislature succumbed to public pressure and revoked the privilege of maintaining a private road in Jefferson Parish, granted three years earlier to Soloman Cohn, because of the inferior condition of the turnpike. In September, 1850, the West Feliciana Parish Police Jury received a petition from residents of the Fifth Ward requesting an appropriation to improve access to their primary market at Jackson, in East Feliciana Parish. The petition noted the significance of Jackson to the residents of the Fifth Ward in terms of business, religion, and education. The petitioners begged for relief, arguing that "the only way of travel to said town is by

35. *Louisiana Senate Journal*, 1st Sess., February 1, 7, 1850, pp. 34, 42; *Louisiana House Journal*, 1st Sess., 1852, pp. 39–41, 45–48, 61–64; *Louisiana House Journal*, 2nd Sess., 1844, p. 31. For an example of the problems associated with securing labor to work on public roads, see James Turnbull to William S. Hamilton, August 27, 1823, in William S. Hamilton Papers, LLMVC.
36. *Louisiana House Journal*, 1st Sess., 1852, pp. 39–41, 44–48, 71.

means of some paths and badly made private roads which are often difficult and **Dangerous** to travel." A similar petition presented to the West Feliciana Parish Police Jury requesting the construction of a public road from Bayou Tunica to the Mississippi state line below Pinckneyville pleaded, "we respectfully represent that it is with utmost difficulty that they [residents] can now pass over on horseback and have no power to force hands to work on any of the roads."[37] This petition highlighted another problem inherent in privatization: the absence of state quality control over private endeavors.

Although they entertained requests for relief, local government also contributed to the privatization of the means of access to market. In the spring of 1846, the St. Tammany Parish Police Jury granted to Abraham Penn and C. H. Allemand the right to build "a toll bridge across the Bogue Falaya River near Covington." In the spring of 1849, Allemand was granted the "exclusive right to a toll bridge across the Tchefuncte River near Covington." Penn and Allemand each possessed considerable resources. Penn not only remained one of the largest slaveholders in the parish but had also served as state representative from St. Tammany. By its action the police jury had awarded two of the wealthiest planters in the parish exclusive control of the most available means of access to the all-important north shore of Lake Pontchartrain. This pattern continued through the end of the antebellum period in St. Tammany, though the financial crisis prompted by the war caused the police jury to place a ceiling on the amount that could be charged for the use of roads, bridges, and ferries.[38]

Privatization also inhibited government appropriations for public internal improvements. Public projects that frequently served to antagonize as many voters as they pleased were often delayed or permanently tabled in favor of private endeavors that carried rewards of patronage and political support. In the summer of 1847, the East Baton Rouge Parish Police Jury appointed a

---

37. *Louisiana House Journal*, 1st Sess., 1850, pp. 19–21; West Feliciana Parish Police Jury Minutes, September Sess., 1850, June Sess., 1847, in WPA Louisiana Parish Police Jury Minutes Collection.

38. St. Tammany Parish Police Jury Minutes, May Sess., 1846, May Sess., 1849, December Sess., 1845, July Sess., 1847, and January Sess., 1852, all in WPA Louisiana Parish Police Jury Minutes Collection; *Police Jury Code for the Parish of East Feliciana, Louisiana, Containing a Digest of the State Laws Relative to Police Juries, and also a Digest of the Ordinances of East Feliciana Having the Force of Laws up to May 1, 1859* (Clinton, La., 1859), 63–84. A good description of the price ceiling enacted during the war can be found in the St. Tammany Parish Police Jury Minutes for March 17, 1862, in WPA Louisiana Parish Police Jury Minutes Collection.

committee to change the direction of the Comite River Road so that it would
intersect with a new private bridge being constructed across that stream. In
approving this privatization measure, which directly benefited several powerful planters in the region, the jurors altered the course of the road to serve
special interests on the upper Comite to the detriment of those in the more
populous lower Comite area. With the measure approved, a separate motion
to build a public bridge across the Comite was defeated by a margin of more
than two to one. Moreover, in the same session the police jury proceeded to
reject at least two motions to provide funding for bridges over lesser streams
that would have improved market trails other than the one proceeding to the
proposed private bridge. Similarly, the St. Tammany Parish Police Jury rejected a proposal to construct a new public road to Covington that would
necessarily compete with the existing private toll road.[39]

The privatization of transportation routes did not involve a calculated
plan on the part of the moneyed elite. The trend emerged as both a money-
making scheme and as a way planters could assure themselves the most direct
access to market. As a result, the argument can be made that privatization actually benefited the state. Private endeavors resulted in roads, bridges, and
ferries that might otherwise never have existed, particularly in a state notoriously deficient in the scope of its internal improvements. Like Louisiana's political system, however, privatization clearly served the interests of the elite.
More often than not, private roads and bridges proved inferior to state-
funded and -maintained ones. Furthermore, because politicians granted individuals the right to build private toll roads and bridges, they were naturally
reluctant to appropriate money to fund competing public endeavors. Although this issue underscored the power of patronage wielded by elected
officials, its results also often deprived the plain folk of adequate, inexpensive
means of travel. Poorer farmers thereby became increasingly dependent upon
the interests of planters who possessed the political clout and the resources to
develop and maintain roads, bridges, and ferries.

In sharp contrast to the trend evident in the 1830s, by the 1850s the state
legislature repeatedly denied requests to improve or expand means of access

39. East Baton Rouge Parish Police Jury Minutes, June Sess., 1847, esp. June 7–8, and the
scattered, largely undated sheets following, and St. Tammany Parish Police Jury Minutes, January
5, 1860, both in WPA Louisiana Parish Police Jury Minutes Collection. The issue of the Comite
River Road and bridge, which had long been debated, was one of the first major privatization efforts in the Felicianas and East Baton Rouge (*Louisiana House Journal*, 2nd Sess., January 5, 12,
1832).

to market. Planter interests, which increasingly controlled the routes to markets, aggressively sought to protect their investments by encouraging the legislature to defeat bills designed to improve existing public market trails or to create new ones. Powerful local figures such as Henry Marston, a prominent planter and commercial agent in East Feliciana Parish, exerted great effort to promote their own private ventures and to discredit public ones. Marston, a major stockholder in the Clinton-Port Hudson Railroad Company and the Baton Rouge-Clinton Plank Road Company, tirelessly advocated state support for these businesses. One of Marston's biggest rivals, William Elder, a wealthy Clinton merchant and slaveholder, promoted his own line of stages and transport wagon teams with equal vigor. Both men were types of the influential figure who encouraged state support for his own and his peers' private endeavors. By the early 1850s, efforts to create new market roads or improve old ones routinely failed in the legislature. An 1852 bill to provide funds to improve the market roads in Washington and St. Tammany Parishes failed by a large margin. These roads, the same ones the legislature overwhelmingly approved in the 1830s, consistently failed to secure any state funds for maintenance, which in part demonstrated the shift away from public support for market trails. Throughout the 1850s, efforts to improve existing public roads or to provide funds to develop new ones into isolated areas of the piney woods usually either died in committee or faced defeat on the floor of the legislature.[40]

By encouraging the restriction of funding for developing new public roads and for maintaining existing market trails and bridges, privatization had a financial impact on the region in another obvious sense. Tolls assessed for travel cut into a farmer's income. With the price of cotton at eleven cents per pound in 1860, a poor farmer independently attempting to haul a four-hundred-pound bale of cotton across Washington and St. Tammany Parishes had little to be optimistic about. The forty-cent toll he paid to cross the Bogue Falaya River bridge on the military road to Madisonville, both coming and going, cut significantly into his profit. The St. Tammany Parish Police Jury's inclination to privatize indicates that several tolls likely encumbered

40. William Pike to Henry Marston, September 10, 1852, Clinton-Port Hudson Railroad Flyer, 1850, and numerous scattered receipts for transport of goods on railroad, all in Marston Family Papers; Clinton-Port Hudson Railroad Company Records, Minute Book, 1852–79, p. 4, LLMVC; Clinton *American Patriot*, September 8, 1855; *Louisiana House Journal*, 1st Sess., 1852, pp. 27–28, 164–70, 1st Sess., 1856, pp. 62–70, 1st Sess., 1857, pp. 89–91.

travelers on the road to the vital collecting and transporting center at Madisonville. The cost incurred encouraged smaller farmers to sell their cotton to local planters at a reduced price so as to avoid the trouble and expense involved in transporting their own goods to market. This condition necessarily threatened the traditional life-style and independence of many piney-woods farmers.[41]

The privatization process contributed directly to a trend emerging in the Florida parishes in the last decade before secession. Even though economic development created substantial ties between planters and plain folk, the system worked primarily to the advantage of the planters. Prosperity continued, but farmers found it increasingly difficult to break class lines and improve their socioeconomic position. Parish tax assessment rolls demonstrate that, excepting an unusual pattern of development in St. Tammany Parish, all of the Florida parishes flourished in the last decade before secession.[42] Although the exact reasons for St. Tammany's separate pattern of development remain unclear, it was likely related to environmental conditions. Following the virtual collapse of rice production in the piney-woods parishes during the 1850s, St. Tammany alone among the eastern parishes proved to have soil inconsistent with the needs of cotton production (see Table 2).

Following the boom years of the early 1850s, the relative wealth of each parish leveled off by the close of the decade. In addition, livestock and land holdings of the freeholders generally increased in the same period. Yet as the relative wealth of the region increased, economic mobility actually stagnated. Despite the generally prosperous times, real wealth remained concentrated in the hands of the few.[43] In the midst of abundance, aspiring farmers found it in-

41. Figures for Bogue Falaya Bridge toll were based on St. Tammany Parish Police Jury Minutes, March 17, 1862, in WPA Louisiana Parish Police Jury Minutes Collection. See also December 1, 1845, and January Sess., 1852, for further evidence of privatization in that parish, in WPA Louisiana Parish Police Jury Minutes Collection. *Louisiana House Journal*, 1st Sess., 1835, p. 93 [i.e., 97], indicates that an exclusive right to operate a toll ferry across the Bogue Chitto River in Washington and St. Tammany Parishes was also in place. On the price and transport of cotton, see Donnell, *Chronological and Statistical History of Cotton*, 498. The New Orleans *Price Current and Commercial Intelligencer* lists the price of good middling cotton in 1860 at eleven cents per pound, middling at ten and a half cents (see December 31, 1859, and January 1, 1860).

42. For a good description of the prevailing prosperity of the period, see Governor Alfred Mouton's farewell address in *Senate Journal*, 1st Sess., 1846, pp. 3–6.

43. Statistics were based on a 3 percent sample survey of heads of households (*Seventh Census, 1850, Manuscript*, and *Eighth Census, 1860, Manuscript*, Louisiana, Schedule 2, Agricultural Statistics, Microfilm).

creasingly difficult to improve their financial position. In effect, the planters' growing economic power, which depended in some measure on their exploitation of common folk, in turn stimulated an emerging disaffection with planter leadership in the piney woods. According to one disgruntled piney-woods farmer, the labor of the poor sustained the life-style of the rich.[44]

Employing slaveholding as a measure of wealth, statistics indicate that, excepting West Feliciana Parish, each of the Florida parishes experienced a decline in the number of freeholders owning slaves. Among those owning slaves in 1850, though, the vast majority in each parish increased their holdings during the course of the decade (see Table 3). If we consider the popularity and profitability of slavery in the Florida parishes and the virtual necessity of slave labor in a cotton-dominated economy, the evidence indicates a sharp contraction in social mobility in the decade before secession. In short, as the rich got richer, the plain folk found it increasingly difficult to get ahead.

Economic development in the Florida parishes allowed for increasing stability under the direction of the slaveholding elite. The economic power commanded by the planters allowed them to exploit the commoners and to advance their increasing political dominance in the territory, activities that ultimately worked to the detriment of plain folk's interests.[45] Although piney-woods residents pugnaciously retained their traditional values, the increasing prosperity and stability of the last decades before secession, coupled with increasing agricultural ties and shared fears, strengthened the appeal of the planter as a political and economic leader. The sum of these circumstances combined to produce a brief moment of security in the Florida parishes. But beneath the placid appearance, destabilizing forces were also present. Decreasing opportunities for commoners in the late 1840s and 1850s created the possibility for a substantive challenge to this system that primarily served the interests of the elite. Confronted by this internal challenge in the face of a serious external threat to their very way of life, planters would employ politics and a shrewd manipulation of the sectional crisis to protect their dominant position. In suppressing the popular call for greater democracy and economic opportunity, however, the elite stirred up a simmering

44. J. W. Courtney to his Brothers and Sisters, February 7, 1864, in Joel A. Stokes Papers, LLMVC; P. K. Wagner to William Hamilton, July 30, 1826, in Hamilton Papers.

45. This interpretation conflicts with the one presented by Steven Hahn in *Roots of Southern Populism*. Hahn argues that though planters increased their contacts and political influence in the upcountry during the 1850s, their role in the economic life of the region actually receded.

contempt for their dominance—a contempt that ultimately resulted in the violent rejection of their leadership and authority in general. Unprecedented stability, prosperity, and governance by less-than-benevolent masters characterized all of the Florida parishes on the eve of disaster.

· 2 ·

GOVERNMENT FAR BEHIND THE TIMES: THE SEEDS OF CHAOS

It would be a degrading reverence for the darkness of antiquity, to adhere to government far behind the times in which we live.
—Governor Alfred Mouton, 1844 Address to Louisiana Legislature

As the residents of the Florida parishes struggled with the enormous problems facing them in the early years of the nineteenth century, a political system that would shape the destiny of the state through the end of the antebellum period emerged in Louisiana. A coalition of planters and their commercial allies in New Orleans created a constitution that ensured for decades their dominance of state government. With increasing stability in West Florida, planters in the delta parishes became a vital component of the ruling coalition; the plain folk essentially remained outside the political realm. Substantive politics remained behind closed doors, while the campaigns themselves constituted quiet affairs with limited participation. The Creole-American struggle that characterized Louisiana politics in the first decades of the nineteenth century stimulated delta planters to expand their political control into the piney-woods parishes. In particular, the planters' command of regional newspapers and government patronage facilitated an alliance with the piney-woods slaveholding elite, who served as spokesmen for the mass of commoners in the eastern parishes. Increasingly dynamic politics in the early 1840s encouraged among the plain folk an assertiveness that produced the relatively liberal Constitution of 1845. The forthright expressions of the common people, in turn, produced a reaction from the planters, as manifested in the more restrictive Constitution of 1852. The new constitution, coupled with the associated consequences of the "sellout" election of 1855 and the construction of a railroad through the piney woods, exasperated the plain folk, creating conditions conducive to substantive reform. On the threshold of a more democratic society, planters manipulated growing sectional hostility to their advantage. Plain-folk aspirations were sacrificed to the necessity of unity in the face of an external threat, which, for the planters, ensured continuing political dominance through the close of the antebellum period.

Initially, the chaotic conditions of the first two decades of the nineteenth century inhibited the development of a competitive political system in the Florida parishes. Unrestrained criminal activity, disputed land claims, and later the emerging prosperity accompanying agricultural success interested the residents more than politics did. The absence of effective means of communication and transportation in the sparsely populated parishes also contributed to the prevailing circumstances. What was more important, the popular perception of the role and nature of politics created by the restrictions inherent in the Louisiana Constitution of 1812 determined the course of political development.

The 1812 document, like many state constitutions of the period, served the interests of the elite. The right to vote extended only to white males, twenty-one years of age, who had resided in the state at least one year prior to the election and who had paid state taxes in the six months preceding the election. The suffrage law, particularly the clause concerning the payment of taxes, prevented large numbers of residents from voting.[1]

Yet the limited interest in politics did not result solely from the constitutional restrictions on the franchise. Despite the limitations, most Louisianians, through the early 1840s, exhibited little enthusiasm for politics. In 1822, 47.9 percent of white males over twenty-one qualified as electors statewide, but barely 50.0 percent of those eligible typically voted. Over twenty years later, interest remained low. Of the 50,110 males twenty-one years and older statewide in 1844, 32,508, or 64.8 percent, qualified to vote, yet only 43.0 percent of those actually cast their ballots. The smaller later figure reflects the impact of low voter turnout in Orleans Parish, where ethnic hostility and other sources of division consistently reduced electoral participation. During the same period, a similar pattern prevailed in the Florida parishes. Whereas approximately 54.6 percent of white males met the qualifications as electors in 1822, slightly less than 53.0 percent voted. By contrast, though the pattern in the Florida parishes resembled the statewide trend, the percentage of electors voting improved by 1844, indicating a regional inclination toward increasing political awareness in the mid-1840s. Of the slightly more than

1. *Constitution or Form of Government of the State of Louisiana* (New Orleans, 1812), Art. II, Sect. 8, pp. 6–7.

66.0 percent of white Florida parish males who enjoyed the privilege of voting, approximately 58 percent did so.[2]

Although these figures indicate a pattern of expanding political participation in the Florida parishes, the region, like the state as a whole, consistently suffered from political apathy, and the trend persisted through the middle of the 1840s. Electoral turnout in Louisiana regularly paled in comparison with voting in Alabama, Mississippi, and other neighboring states. In the 1840 presidential election, the turnout reached a high of 89.7 percent in Alabama and 88.2 percent in Mississippi, while the 39.4 percent of Louisiana voters who cast their ballots included a 56.8 percent return in the Florida parishes, exceeding the statewide ratio primarily again because of notoriously depressed returns from New Orleans. Louisiana voting patterns remained highly erratic from the 1820s through the early 1840s: electoral participation sometimes dropped as low as 20.0 percent and seldom exceeded 50.0 percent statewide and regionally. By the mid-1840s, however, political participation had improved statewide, and the greatest increase occurred in the Florida parishes. From the close of the 1840s through the 1850s, the 55.0 percent average turnout statewide trailed the 64.0 percent average recorded in the Florida parishes. Increasing political assertiveness among piney-woods voters in the Florida parishes emerged as both a response and a challenge to the mechanisms of planter dominance.[3]

The isolated condition of much of Louisiana, particularly the bayou and piney-woods parishes, certainly contributed to voting patterns. No newspapers existed in the piney woods until the late 1830s. Their absence made it difficult to advertise elections, and travel to the polls could be both arduous and dangerous. During the 1820s and 1830s virtually all of the southern states contained isolated regions facing similar problems. Moreover, voter

2. *Louisiana House Journal*, 2nd Sess., 1822, pp. 26–27, 2nd Sess., 1844, p. 11; *Fourth Census, 1820: Compendium*, 31; *Fourth Census, 1820*, Manuscript, and *Sixth Census, 1840*, Manuscript, Louisiana, Schedule 1, Free Population, Microfilm; St. Francisville *Asylum and Feliciana Advertiser*, July 3, 19, 1822; "Report of the Special Committee," *Journal of the Convention Called for the Purpose of Re-Adopting, Amending, or Changing the Constitution of the State of Louisiana* (New Orleans, 1845), 56; *Sixth Census, 1840: Compendium*, 60; *Historical Statistics of the United States, Colonial Times to 1970*, (2 vols.; Washington, D.C., 1975), II, 1072.

3. *Historical Statistics*, II, 1072; *Louisiana Senate Journal*, 1st Sess., 1853, pp. 9, 15; New Orleans *Bee*, November 10, 12, 1840; New Orleans *Daily Delta*, November 11, 27, 1845; Baton Rouge *Gazette*, November 13, 20, 1852; Clinton *American Patriot*, November 10, 24, 1855; Baton Rouge *Daily Advocate*, November 10, 1855; *Sixth Census, 1840: Compendium*, 240–46; *Seventh Census, 1850: Compendium*, 468–86.

turnout typically remained low in the plantation parishes as well, even though newspapers there regularly advertised for candidates and elections. Although the seeming lack of interest in politics reflected the national trend in this period, several issues particular to the state, as well as some peculiar to the region, contributed to the tendency in the Florida parishes.

The 1812 constitution and the government it produced denied the mass of Louisianians substantive political influence. The various branches of government, all dominated by planter interests, possessed exceptional power. As late as 1824, Louisiana remained one of only six states in which the legislature persisted in selecting presidential electors. The absence of popular participation in the selection of presidential electors so thoroughly exemplified the antidemocratic tendencies of Louisiana government that the St. Francisville *Asylum* urged its readers to follow the policy advocated in the *Journal*, another local newspaper, and write the name of their choice for president on their congressional ballot so that "a tolerably correct idea of the public sentiment may be obtained." In addition, the legislature enjoyed the privilege of selecting the governor from among the top two candidates in the general primary. Once installed, the governor exercised sweeping powers of appointment, increasing the possibilities for patronage and cronyism.[4] A strong executive contrasted with governmental structures in many other states where concentrations of power continued to be viewed with suspicion and rejected. By contrast, in Louisiana these features of the 1812 document not only denied voters the right to select statewide and national officials but also further entrenched the power of the governing elite.

Other safeguards erected to maintain the political dominance of the elite increased voter despondency, too. Strict property requirements ensured that only men of means would seek public office. Indeed, the entire political structure of Louisiana in the first half of the nineteenth century emerged as the exclusive domain of the privileged few. The coalition of delta planters and New Orleans commercial interests that initially developed as a result of the mutual economic pursuits of planters and their lawyers and factors in New Orleans dominated state government, jealously guarding power. Their combination, originally inaugurated to protect their economic positions, translated into unqualified political power that blocked reform efforts. An 1824 bill en-

---

4. *Constitution of Louisiana*, Art. III, Sects. 9, 10, pp. 13–14, Sect. 2, pp. 11–12; *Historical Statistics*, II, 1072; Emmett Asseff, *The History of the Government of Louisiana* (Baton Rouge, 1964), 53; St. Francisville *Asylum and Feliciana Advertiser*, July 3, 1824.

titled "An Act for Enlarging the Privilege of Voting" failed in the state senate by a nine-to-five vote. Excepting the vote cast by the senator from Lafourche, all affirmative votes came from piney-woods representatives from north Louisiana and the Florida parishes.[5]

The ruling politicians also secured and traded offices regularly, further entrenching their powers of patronage. In the fall of 1824, Thomas B. Robertson resigned as governor to accept a less demanding judicial position. Robertson's resignation occurred with the understanding that United States senator Henry Johnson would resign and be elected governor. A candidate endorsed by both Robertson and Johnson would, in turn, receive the Senate seat. The collusion between these two powerful political figures exemplified the restrictive nature of office holding in Louisiana and earned them the nickname "Willing Despots." In response to those critical of his seeming absolute power, Robertson asserted, "The people have no right to say who is to govern them—the constitution places the power in my hands." The arrogance of the ruling elite and their seeming misappropriation of power worked for a time but later served to erode their power in the years just preceding secession.[6]

Through the end of the antebellum period, despite efforts to the contrary, the eastern Florida parishes never secured the nomination of a local candidate for a statewide office, but the plantation parishes did. The plantation region of the Florida parishes exercised so much influence on state tickets that concerns about balance appeared. In the summer of 1855, G. W. Munday, state senator from East Feliciana Parish, declined the nomination for state treasurer, noting that the nominees for governor and state auditor lived less than twenty-five miles from his home and the ticket would therefore be "geographically imbalanced."[7] West Feliciana politicians, in particular, exercised immense power in state government. Two of the last four governors prior to secession, Isaac Johnson and Robert C. Wickliffe, hailed from West Feliciana. Their political fortunes and those of other West Feliciana native sons point to a correlation between financial success and political power.

Restrictive statewide political practices had an impact on voting patterns in the Florida parishes, but politics there also depended on attitudes unique

5. *Constitution of Louisiana*, Art. II, Sect. 4, p. 5, Sect. 12, p. 8, Art. III, Sect. 4, p. 12; *Louisiana Senate Journal*, 7th Legis., 1st Sess., 1824, p. 36.

6. *Louisiana House Journal*, 7th Legis., 1st Sess., 1824, pp. 2–8; John B. Dawson to William Hamilton, April 6, 1825, in Hamilton Papers.

7. Clinton *Feliciana Democrat*, April 21, June 23, 1855.

to the region. In the same way vague land claims gained their acceptance, emerging prosperity and stability encouraged the residents to avoid potentially divisive issues, politics being one of the most apparent. In sharp contrast to the boisterous campaigns of the late 1840s and 1850s, which witnessed the aggressive courting of voters through heated political meetings, barbecues, and other practices associated with mass political processes, local political contests from the beginnings into the early 1840s stimulated little public interest. In the first decades after statehood, politics followed a consistent pattern in eastern Louisiana. Gentlemen of means allowed their names to be placed before the voters with little, if any, indication of the candidates' positions on significant issues presented to the public. Regarding his decision to seek election to a local judicial post, West Feliciana planter and physician Thomas W. Chinn explained, "At first I thought it would be wrong for me to countenance the applications [to run for office] in my favor, but upon more mature reflection, I concluded to let the thing take such a course as the people thought proper to give it." Voters typically aligned themselves with the most powerful regional candidate, regardless of his political views. To avoid offending candidates, newspapers such as the St. Francisville *Louisianian* repeatedly asserted the neutral nature of their politics. In the summer of 1824, another West Feliciana newspaper, the *Asylum*, aggressively maintained its neutral position: "We shall not attempt, although in common with all thinking persons, we have our individual preferences, to draw any invidious comparisons between the candidates, or to bias the minds of our fellow citizens in their choice—the people have sufficient intelligence to choose for themselves." The failure to take a firm stand discouraged both commitment among the voters and interest in politics in general. Frustrated by the refusal of several planter candidates to campaign and the lack of voter interest in an 1824 election in the Florida parishes, a West Feliciana politician noted, "There seems to be a total absence of enthusiasm or even public spirit here . . . what indifference will not take at this moment."[8]

Throughout the 1820s, though they provided extensive coverage of congressional debates, local newspapers typically announced candidates and re-

8. Thomas W. Chinn to William S. Hamilton, August 9, 1823, in Hamilton Papers; St. Francisville *Louisianian*, October 2, 1819, March 23, 1820; St. Francisville *Louisiana Journal*, March 2, 1826; St. Francisville *Asylum and Feliciana Advertiser*, June 19, July 3, 1822; Moore, *Emergence of the Cotton Kingdom*, 145; John B. Dawson to Colonel Hamilton, July 3, 1824, in Hamilton Papers. Peacock, "Statistical and Historical Collections," 266, notes the neutral political stance always taken by the Jackson *Southern Mirror*.

sults but said little, if anything, regarding the candidate's position on the issues. On October 2, 1819, the *Louisianian* announced a special election to replace a local member of the state legislature who had resigned to accept the
parish judgeship. Not only did it fail to mention any specifics concerning the
candidates, but in the weeks that followed, the successful candidate was
never identified. Similarly, in reference to a coming municipal election in the
spring of 1826, the *Louisiana Journal* asserted, "Though we do not know who
the candidates are we hope good men will be chosen." To fill the blank spaces
created by their failure to stimulate public debate of significant issues, candidates often appealed to the baser emotions of the electorate. An 1822 election to the Louisiana House of Representatives in West Feliciana Parish focused exclusively on the honor of the candidates. The substance of the
contest centered on candidate Edward R. Chew's contention that his opponent, Charles Woodroof, had "refused after suitable application to render the
author such satisfaction as one gentleman ought to render another." During
the campaign, Chew distributed broadsides condemning Woodroof's alleged
cowardice and asking the voters if they could accept a man as representative
"whose pusillanimity of public spirit tamely [submitted] he [could] not be expected to be a bold defender of public rights." Chew's allegations obviously
carried weight with the voters as he led Woodroof in the polling by nearly
two to one.[9]

Actions of the state legislature also frequently received little, if any, special
notice in the local papers. In the spring of 1820, numerous editorials in the
Louisianian condemned the efforts in Congress to restrict the spread of slavery
into Missouri. Yet the same paper shrugged off the actions of the state legislature, noting that "little of general interest" had occurred. Another article in
the same issue acknowledged that a group of state representatives was visiting
St. Francisville but asserted that they had not revealed anything interesting
concerning the actions of the legislature.[10] Larger urban newspapers such as
the Baton Rouge *Gazette* did provide details on significant debates in the state
legislature. These papers, however, had few subscribers in rural areas.

As always, the absolute dominance of the rulers depended on the ignorance of the ruled. Precious few voices urged the legislature to grant more

---

9. St. Francisville *Asylum and Feliciana Advertiser*, June 19, 1822; Edward R. Chew broadside
"To The Public," June 25, 1822, A. Harralson to Colonel Hamilton, June 17, 1826, both in
Hamilton Papers.

10. St. Francisville *Louisianian*, October 2, 1819, March 23, 30, 1820; St. Francisville
Louisiana Journal, July 22, 1824, March 2, 9, 1826.

power to the people. In the winter of 1824, one such appeal read: "We have been anxiously looking for some effort to be made in our Legislature, to place in the hands of the people, the election of electors of President and Vice President. As yet we have seen nothing of the kind attempted. The people should receive this inestimable right." This entreaty, though extremely rare in the 1820s, foreshadowed the strategy of the planters in the 1850s.[11]

The nature and substance of newspaper reporting in the first three decades after statehood suggested the designs of the controlling elite. As always, newspapers played a fundamental role in shaping the inclinations of the public. The power of newspapers is particularly significant in regions with high rates of literacy. By 1850, fully 82 percent of the white population of the Florida parishes over twenty years of age could read and write. Literacy extended to almost 90 percent of white residents in the plantation parishes and to slightly more than 77 percent of the residents in the piney woods.[12] As a result, the planters, who usually either owned or exercised direct influence over local newspapers, skillfully employed the press to arouse the plain folk against the growing menace to their way of life presented by an increasingly aggressive North. Of the five primary newspapers published in the Florida parishes in this period, three belonged to planters. One of these, the *Louisianian*, belonged to G. W. Munday, who served repeatedly in the Louisiana legislature. The *Asylum* and the *Louisiana Journal* belonged to F. Bradford and William S. Hamilton, respectively, both prominent planter-politicians. Both of the remaining two papers were heavily influenced by planter interests.

In summarizing the role played by the newspapers in a congressional race in the Florida parishes, one disgruntled supporter of the defeated candidate concluded, "Thus you see what means the holders of power have adopted to prolong the reign of their masters and what dreadful odds we have had to contend against."[13] The planters, through newspapers, sought not only to limit commoners' participation in politics but also to contain their awareness of the actions of state government. The scarcity of reporting on state government and the minimum of election coverage contributed to the piney-woods dweller's disinterest. Not only did politics appear to be exclusively in the realm of the elite, but sparse coverage made it boring.

11. St. Francisville *Louisiana Journal*, February 5, 1824.

12. Figures were based on a 3 percent sample survey of each parish, (*Seventh Census, 1850*, Manuscript, Louisiana, Schedule 1, Free Population, Microfilm). Exact figures for each parish were: East Baton Rouge, 91 percent; East Feliciana, 94 percent; Livingston, 74 percent; St. Helena, 84 percent; St. Tammany, 74 percent; Washington, 76 percent; West Feliciana, 85 percent.

13. P. K. Wagner to William Hamilton, July 30, 1826, in Hamilton Papers.

The election process itself did little to stimulate voter interest. Unlike other states of the Gulf South, notably Alabama and Mississippi, where universal white male suffrage often contributed to a festive atmosphere at the polls on election day, the restrictive nature of Louisiana politics in the early antebellum period did not encourage a jovial mood at the voting precincts. Election guidelines, which varied slightly concerning the specifics in each parish, contained detailed regulations backed by stiff penalties to ensure that only those qualified voted. These regulations promoted a sense of separation between the haves and the have-nots on election day by encouraging those not qualified to avoid the polls entirely. The absence of large gatherings at the precincts, particularly in the rural parishes, contributed to the somber atmosphere surrounding elections.[14]

The voting procedure was set by statute and, in general, followed religiously. The parish judge, who served as the overseer of each election, appointed three commissioners for each precinct. At each precinct the judge himself or a justice of the peace acted as one of the commissioners so as to enhance the perception of legitimacy. Typically, three sites in each parish, usually public buildings, general stores, or the homes of prominent gentlemen, served as polling places. During an 1819 election in the Feliciana district, polling took place at "Wilson's Store in Bayou Sara, Evangelist Edward's house on the Comite, and at the Jackson Courthouse." Normally the sites selected as precincts were widely scattered to compensate for difficulties in travel. To give those qualified time to reach the polls, the election extended over a three-day period. On election days, voters cast a single ballot identifying the names of their preferences in each race. The ballots could be either printed or handwritten, with no apparent standard format required. Specific regulations, however, controlled the construction and maintenance of ballot boxes. The requirements stipulated that the boxes must contain a device that concealed the ballots cast from the eyes of the commissioners. Three separate locks secured the ballot box, with each commissioner given possession of one key. At 4:00 P.M. on the third day of voting, the commissioners would gather at the parish courthouse, open the boxes, and count the ballots in front of the observers gathered. Departures from the procedure constituted grounds to nullify the election. The use of a hat covered by a handkerchief, instead of the prescribed ballot box, at one precinct in St. Helena Parish during a leg-

14. A New Digest of the Statute Laws of the State of Louisiana, from the Change of Government to the Year 1841, Inclusive (New Orleans, 1842), 378–427.

islative race provoked weeks of bitter controversy in the legislature regarding the legality of the election.[15]

Elections for state legislators, as well as those for Congress, were held on the first Monday in July. The Creole politicians who had dominated the 1812 constitutional debates insisted on midsummer elections to take advantage of many American residents' tendency to absent themselves during Louisiana's sultry, plague-ridden, summer months. Upon arrival at the polls, voters typically encountered the most affluent and respected gentlemen each candidate could muster dispensing greetings and soliciting support.[16] The candidates dispatched carriages into the countryside to bring in supporters who might otherwise fail to vote. Inside the precincts, the commissioners sat at tables observing the process and guarding against irregularities. Voters entered the precinct, announced their names, and stated their qualifications to vote, which the commissioners verified by checking the tax rolls. Upon verification of eligibility, voters then placed their folded ballots in the box. Occasionally ballots were cast viva voce, particularly in the country parishes where paper ballots often proved scarce. Announcing one's choice vocally, though, increased the opportunity for intimidation, which always remained a problem, as did its complement, vote buying. In an effort to combat such illegal practices, the law dealt harshly with those who purchased votes with whiskey or monetary gifts. Despite these efforts, both intimidation and vote buying constituted a common aspect of Louisiana elections. Even more common was election trickery. Seldom did an election pass in which assessors did not omit known political opponents from the tax rolls or fabricated rumors of yellow fever did not keep dozens of voters away from the polls.[17]

In the first decades of the nineteenth century, voter apathy in Louisiana, and in the Florida parishes in particular, related directly to two additional and seemingly obvious aspects of the region's development. First, until

15. Ibid., 386–92; St. Francisville Asylum and Feliciana Advertiser, June 26, 1824; Louisiana House Journal, 1st Sess., 1856, pp. 32–34. The St. Francisville Louisianian, October 2, 1819, provides an example of the location of voting precincts.

16. A. M. Harralson to Colonel Hamilton, July 15, 1826, T. F. Hunt to Hamilton, July 30, 1826, both in Hamilton Papers, describe prominent gentlemen greeting voters at the polls.

17. New Digest of the Statute Laws, 386–92; St. Francisville Louisiana Journal, February 5, 1824; St. Francisville Louisianian, October 2, 1819; Joseph G. Tregle, "Louisiana in the Age of Jackson: A Study in Ego Politics" (Ph.D. dissertation, University of Pennsylvania, 1954), 99, 126; Clinton Feliciana Democrat, November 10, 1855.

Louisiana became a part of the United States, most of her citizens had no experience whatsoever with representative government. Unlike neighboring southern states, whose dominant American majorities contained many who had experienced this form of government, most Louisianians enjoyed no tradition of political representation. This problem proved particularly acute in the Florida parishes, where the suspect background of many of the American settlers had inhibited their participation in the political process. Louisiana residents therefore required time to acclimate themselves to the significance of representative government. The delay assisted the better-educated and more worldly planters to establish political dominance. Rather than seeing planter political dominance as a potential threat, the common folk, lacking experience in such matters, instead welcomed this authority because of the unprecedented stability that accompanied it. Furthermore, as the cotton economy expanded, bringing with it prosperity to the piney woods, the farmers there naturally sought economic security first. Full stomachs and a self-sufficient life-style free of the economic exploitation Jefferson had warned about, not politics, dominated the thinking of the plain folk.[18]

As the region stabilized and growing numbers of piney-woods farmers achieved that desired economic security, Louisiana's antiquated political system came under increasing attack. Jacksonian politics, which emphasized the threat to republican institutions posed by government-sanctioned sources of undemocratic privilege, stimulated many Louisiana farmers to reassess their fealty to the existing political order. The steady influx of settlers from other states already accustomed to democratic privilege furthered this transformation. As both Whigs and Democrats canvassed the state, each party insisting that its program constituted the best means to preserve republican ideals, increasing numbers came to recognize the restrictive nature of Louisiana's political system. The inconsistencies between the republican tradition they held so dear and their state's political structure became ever more apparent to many commoners. The removal of the state capital from Donaldsonville and its return to New Orleans in the early 1830s prompted one embittered farmer to write the Baton Rouge *Gazette:* "For many years the Aristocrats have given law to the state—they can not bear the idea of sharing the government with honest farmers and mechanics of the country. This may be emphatically termed the time for asserting the rights of the people—for laughing unto

18. Perry Howard, *Political Tendencies in Louisiana, 1812–1952* (Baton Rouge, 1957), 25, 49; Shugg, *Origins of Class Struggle in Louisiana*, 31.

scorn the machinations of those knots of Aristocrats who regard the working man as nothing."[19]

Increasing agitation for political change, led in part by Soloman W. Downs of Ouachita Parish, swept the northern part of the state. Initially, the representatives of the eastern parishes, including the piney-woods region of the Florida parishes, did not take part in this movement. The emerging cotton culture and the level of planter dominance there prompted these representatives to vote with the delta planters. On several crucial votes at the 1845 constitutional convention, the piney-woods delegates from the Florida parishes demonstrated their reluctance to support substantive reform. Most significantly, two of the four piney-woods representatives voted against the abolition of property requirements for office holding.[20]

The failure of the piney-woods representatives from the Florida parishes to vote as a bloc in support of democratic reform contrasted sharply with their position twenty years earlier. In the 1820s and 1830s the representatives from the eastern Florida parishes, along with those from north Louisiana, unanimously supported the few bills presented advocating democratic reform. Such a change of attitude exemplified the significance of the expansion of the plantation economy into the piney woods and its impact on political ideals. By the late 1840s, the representatives from the piney woods of the Florida parishes frequently voted with the planter representatives, often at the expense of the plain folk in their own region. An 1850 bill designed to exclude from seizure the property or home of a debtor whose total estate did not exceed $450 would have protected large numbers of Florida parish farmers from possible confiscation of their homesteads. The bill failed in the Louisiana House by a vote of fifty-eight to twenty-one. All of the piney-woods representatives from upstate Louisiana voted in favor of the bill, while their counterparts in the Florida parishes unanimously opposed it.[21]

19. Baton Rouge *Gazette*, January 1, 1831; Marvin Meyers, *The Jacksonian Persuasion: Politics and Belief* (Stanford, 1957), 8–9; James K. Greer, "Louisiana Politics, 1845–1861," *Louisiana Historical Quarterly*, XII (1929), 409.

20. *Journal of the Convention*, 63; Minnie Ruffin and Lilla McClure, "General Soloman Weathersby Downs, Democratic Leader of North Louisiana, 1840–1854," *Louisiana Historical Quarterly*, XVII (1934), 11, 14; Howard, *Political Tendencies in Louisiana*, 67.

21. *Louisiana Senate Journal*, 7th Legis., 1st Sess., 1824, p. 36; *Louisiana House Journal*, 1st Sess., 1831, pp. 62–64, 1st Sess., 1850, pp. 124–28; *Louisiana Senate Journal*, 1st Sess., 1850, pp. 54–55, 1st Sess., 1854, pp. 64–70, 1st Sess., 1848, pp. 88–89, 114–16; Milton Rickels, "Thomas Bangs Thorpe in the Felicianas, 1836–1842," *Louisiana Historical Quarterly*, XXXIX (1956), 175–76.

Despite the stiff opposition to change, the momentum for political reform increased. Twice in the late 1830s the senate rejected proposals made by the lower house authorizing the calling of a constitutional convention. By the early 1840s, the ruling elite could no longer ignore voices demanding political reform. In his annual message to the Louisiana legislature, Governor Alfred Mouton noted that "an entire revolution in public opinion" had occurred. Mouton continued: "It would be a degrading reverence for the darkness of antiquity, to adhere to government far behind the times in which we live. Let us organize a government for ourselves, adapted to the virtuous and enlightened state of society to which we are elevated, and framed by the high political wisdom to which we have attained."[22]

The 1844 election, called to determine popular support for a constitutional convention, resulted in a massive outpouring of support for proconvention forces. Nearly 80 percent of those voting cast their ballots in support of a new constitution. In the piney-woods region of the Florida parishes, support for the convention ranged from 100 percent in Livingston to 93 percent in St. Helena; the plantation parishes also provided large majorities in support of the convention. The vote in favor of the convention totaled 89 percent in East Baton Rouge, 95 percent in East Feliciana, and 86 percent in West Feliciana. The plantation parishes around New Orleans and the sugar-belt parishes returned the only significant anticonvention majorities.[23]

The resulting 1845 constitutional convention overcame bitter rivalries between New Orleans and the country parishes to make sweeping democratic reforms in the organic law of the state. The new constitution curtailed the power of the legislature and prohibited monopolies and special charters, long sources of abuse of legislative power. Other features provided for the establishment of free public education and for the protection of basic civil liberties. Perhaps most important, the changes made in the election laws created an unprecedented opportunity for the plain folk to vote and seek office. The new constitution forbade all property tests for voters and for candidates for public office. The preambles of the two constitutions demonstrate the democratization of state law. Whereas the 1812 document begins with "We the

22. "Annual Address of Governor Alfred Mouton," *Louisiana House Journal*, 2nd Sess., 1844, pp. 2–5; Greer, "Louisiana Politics," 409.

23. *Louisiana House Journal*, 2nd Sess., 1844, p. 11. Numbers in support of the convention from the remaining piney-woods parishes totalled 98.0 percent in Washington Parish and 95.8 percent in St. Tammany. Significant majorities against the convention were recorded in St. Charles, St. John, St. Bernard, Lafourche, Terrebonne, and Iberville Parishes.

representatives of the people" and ends with "do mutually agree with each other to form ourselves into a free and independent state," the new constitution exemplifies the democratic spirit that produced it. The preamble to the 1845 document reads, "We the people of the state of Louisiana do ordain and establish this Constitution."[24]

The new constitution fulfilled the democratic aspirations of the vast majority of Louisianians. Opposition to the new document, found primarily among Whig planter and commercial interests, received a devastating setback on February 18, 1845, when the convention voted thirty-eight to twenty-eight to remove property qualifications for office holding. Recognizing defeat, the opponents of the constitution found solace in the argument that their economic power could be translated into political power, thereby negating the need for property requirements. Senator Soloman Downs and other supporters of the new constitution repeatedly reminded the recalcitrants that property had always been capable of taking care of itself, regardless of who dominated government. Downs insisted that in his judgment poorer whites had always been and would continue to be the protectors of the property of the rich; therefore it remained for the ruling elite to grant plain folk the political rights they so earnestly desired. His comments foreshadowed developments in Louisiana, and especially those in the Florida parishes, through the end of the antebellum period. Although forced by popular demand to relinquish some political power, the planters' economic control in the piney woods kept the plain folk dependent on services they provided, thus sustaining their dominant position.[25]

Just as substantive wealth and economic power remained in the hands of the planters despite the preeminence of the cotton economy throughout the Florida parishes, political control also remained in their hands despite the liberalizing trend. The consummation of the planters' political dominance in the piney woods, and in the state in general, was realized in the Constitution of 1852. Even during the interim from 1845 to 1852, however, the interests of the planters, partially because of their economic power, continued to dominate politics in the piney woods of the Florida parishes, as they would through the end of the antebellum period.

24. *Constitution of Louisiana*, 1; "Constitution of Louisiana, 1845," in *Journal of the Convention*, 342.

25. *Journal of the Convention*, 63; *Louisiana Constitutional Convention, 1844–1845, Official Report of Constitutional Debates* (New Orleans, 1845), 116.

Initially, the restrictions inherent in the Constitution of 1812 limited office holding to only the wealthiest residents. As a result, planter interests had always dominated politics in the Florida parishes. Although the elite controlled their respective regions in both the eastern and western Florida parishes, the piney-woods representatives frequently remained independent of the delta-parish planter interests. The failure of the piney-woods legislators to follow the "natural leadership" of the planter representatives from the Felicianas and East Baton Rouge Parish frustrated the delta political leaders. Piney-woods opposition to bills of particular interest to large slaveholders, such as an 1818 measure entitled "An Act Respecting [the Ownership] of Slaves Imported into the State in Violation of the Act of Congress," deeply concerned the planter representatives. Many planter politicians, recognizing both the importance of piney-woods voters and their willingness "to take their opinions from powerful others," encouraged efforts to secure greater influence in the eastern parishes. Appeals to increase the authority of the planter region in the piney woods of the Florida parishes circulated among the delta planters.[26] Simple discussion of the issue ended in 1823, when a potential crisis served as the catalyst for the planters to assert their power aggressively in the piney woods.

As the increasing number of Americans migrating to north and central Louisiana steadily eroded their political strength, Creole politicians from the sugar parishes and New Orleans ventured a bold maneuver to preserve their power. Believing they had the votes necessary, and with the apparent support of Governor Robertson, on January 20, 1823, the members of this coalition introduced a bill to remove the Florida parish senators from the legislature. Essentially, the coalition sought, on a constitutional technicality, to eject a voting bloc often antagonistic to their interests. The bill asserted that the Florida parishes did not comprise a part of the state of Louisiana incorporated under the Constitution of 1812. Therefore, the senators from that region "had been unconstitutionally elected and [could] no longer retain their seats." The proposal failed by the narrowest of margins, seven senators in favor and seven opposed. Although the combination of senators voting to reject the bill sustained itself, heated debate continued in the Louisiana Senate for days.[27]

---

26. *Louisiana House Journal*, 2nd Sess., 1818, p. 53; Isaac Baker to William S. Hamilton, December 26, 1822, January 14, 21, 1823, Harralson to Hamilton, July 15, 1826, Wagner to Hamilton, July 30, 1826, F. H. Stackhouse to Maj. Joseph Johnson, June 3, 1822, all in Hamilton Papers.

27. *Senate Journal*, 1st Sess., 1823, pp. 13–14, 17–18.

Despite the failure of the effort, the motion exacerbated the bitter feelings between the American and Creole factions in the legislature. Moreover, it highlighted the centrality of ethnic rather than party divisions within the Louisiana political establishment. The outrage generated by this maneuver prompted one indignant planter to vent his anger: "An effort was made yesterday in the senate to exclude the Florida members from that body on a constitutional scruple. No measure since we became a state has been so mischievous or smelled so strongly of treason. We are all horrified about it here." Even more galling to planter interests in the Felicianas and East Baton Rouge was the fact that Elisha Clark, senator from the piney woods of the Florida parishes, failed to vote. In addition, Clark, after condemning the measure as "repugnant to the honor of state government," departed the capital on a brief leave of absence. This flagrant disregard for responsibility proved unbearable to some. The same planter continued:

> The measure was lost but it is to be revived today. Clark and [Isaac] McNutt are absent strolling around to some distant part of the state on private business—they deserve to be guillotined for it. After the dirt kicked up last fall every American at least in the legislature should have been at his post till he was certain that all was right. The conduct of some of the Florida folks in this particular was not right since nothing can justify the length to which the French seem disposed to go. Would to God you were here as a member of the lower house. Some leadership in Florida is greatly needed.

Clark's decision to avoid this crucial vote may have resulted from his desire to antagonize neither his American constituents nor the large bloc of Creole residents in his home parish of St. Tammany. It may also have been pure coincidence and poor timing of personal business. Obviously stung by the criticism, Clark returned to the senate to participate in the last debates concerning this issue. Regardless of his motives and despite his last-minute presence, Clark's earlier action and inconsistency remained a bitter memory and galvanized the planter politicians in the delta region of the Florida parishes to intensify their efforts in securing for themselves control of the politically strategic piney-woods parishes.[28]

---

28. *Ibid.*; Baker to Hamilton, January 21, 1823, Stackhouse to Johnson, June 3, 1822, Harralson to Hamilton, June 17, July 15, 1826, Wagner to Hamilton, July 30, 1826, Alex Barrow to

Throughout the 1820s and 1830s, planters in the Felicianas and East Baton Rouge endeavored to expand and secure their influence in the piney woods under the pretext of unifying American areas in opposition to their Creole antagonists. To achieve their goal, the planter politicians were forced to abandon their traditional distaste for electioneering and seeking favors. Prestigious Feliciana planters such as Alex Barrow and Daniel Turnbull abandoned customary scruples to promote their interests in the piney woods. Timidly asserting the need to engage in this displeasing necessity, prominent West Feliciana planter-politician F. H. Stackhouse advised, "I would recommend to no honorable man a course of electioneering servility and I know your friend Colonel [William] Hamilton would revolt at anything of the kind, but it will be highly important for him to visit immediately the parishes of St. Helena, Washington, and St. Tammany . . . and I do believe he may secure an interest in the eastern parishes that will render his election highly probable if not certain, by a proper exertion being made." To further this process, the river-parish planters compiled a list of gentlemen of influence in the piney-woods parishes who should be contacted to secure their support in each election.[29]

By the early 1830s such efforts had transformed politics in the piney woods. The delta planters boasted of their success in uniting the Americans of the eastern parishes behind their leadership. As political unity expanded among the Americans, the rivalry between the Whigs and the Jacksonian Democrats intensified, making party differences increasingly significant. The Jacksonians brushed off the John Quincy Adams-Henry Clay supporters and their Whig heirs as "Yankees." Although the Jacksonian appeal dominated, the Whigs attracted significant support throughout the Florida parishes. The delta planters' ability to secure backing across party lines in the piney woods exemplified the strength of their increasing power in the eastern parishes. In the spring of 1830, prominent anti-Jackson agitator William Winfree of St. Helena Parish, though maintaining his opposition to Jackson, acknowledged the necessity of unity in the Florida parishes and offered his support to the Jacksonian candidate for governor. Other Adams supporters, such as Mont-

William Hamilton, April 22, 1830, Robert Fluker to William Hamilton, June 30, 1830 (noting the power of Creole voters in St. Tammany Parish), all in Hamilton Papers.

29. Stackhouse to Johnson, June 3, 1822, A. M. Harralson to William S. Hamilton, May 13, 1822, both in Hamilton Papers. Among the planter politicians advocating a calculated aggressive political effort in the eastern parishes were Frank Hardesty, William Hamilton, A. M. Harralson, John Dawson, and William Boatner, in addition to Barrow and Turnbull.

gomery Sloan of East Baton Rouge, also sacrificed party solidarity in favor of ethnic unity.[30]

The burden of securing support across party lines was eased somewhat by the candidacy of native sons of the Florida parishes, such as perennial candidate William Hamilton of West Feliciana and John Dawson, both of whom enjoyed immense popularity in the piney woods. Drumming up support for regional candidates helped secure for the delta planters political dominance in the eastern parishes. In acknowledging the defection of Florida parish Whigs from the gubernatorial candidacy of the highly popular E. D. White to local favorite and Jacksonian John Dawson, the Whig Baton Rouge *Gazette* asserted, "This should not cause surprise when we reflect that General Dawson is personally acquainted and highly esteemed as a gentleman by three quarters of the residents, and in addition to this a large number of the Whig party voted for him through sectional feelings."[31]

The calculated effort to secure their political base in the piney woods, coupled with their control of the press and their growing economic control of the region, created conditions favorable for delta planters to achieve absolute dominance in the eastern parishes. The receptivity of local political figures, however, proved to be the most decisive factor allowing the delta planters to dominate the piney woods. Almost to a man, the brokers of political power in the piney woods were themselves planters and therefore natural allies of their counterparts in the delta parishes. Through the early 1850s, though planters constituted only a small fraction of the population in the piney woods, under the guidance of their delta allies they exercised virtually complete control of local politics.

If separated by regional, cultural, and in some cases religious differences, the political leaders in the delta and piney woods of the Florida parishes nevertheless shared two important determinants. In general, both sought to sustain American power in state government. The considerable numbers of Creole residents along the lakeshore in the eastern parishes did have a limited mitigating effect, but overall, American sympathizers dominated in the Florida parishes. Second, and more important, they shared the bond of slave-

30. Alex Barrow to William Hamilton, January 25, April 22, and June 4, 1830, William Boatner to William Hamilton, June 4, 1830, John McNeil to William Hamilton, January 25, 1830, William Winfree to William Hamilton, May 2, 1830, Montgomery Sloan to William Hamilton, February 10, 1830, all in Hamilton Papers. For patterns of voting and party support in this period, see Baton Rouge *Gazette*, July 3, 10, 1830, July 12, 1834.

31. Baton Rouge *Gazette*, July 12, 1834.

holding. In the decade preceding secession every representative and senator elected to the state legislature from the Florida parishes owned slaves. Recognizing that in this same period the number of slaveholders substantially declined (see Table 3) makes this detail of particular import. Significantly, virtually every piney-woods member of the state legislature in this period qualified as a planter.

In 1852 the legislative delegation from the Florida parishes exemplified the dominance of the slaveholding elite (see Table 4). Seventeen of the officials representing the Florida parishes in the early 1850s declared themselves to be planters or farmers. The remaining legislators who listed their occupations included six attorneys, one sawmill operator, two physicians, and one engineer. While most of those engaged in other occupations also owned farms, all were slaveholders. Excepting one attorney from Livingston and a

TABLE 4. STATE LEGISLATORS FROM FLORIDA PARISHES, 1852–1854

Parish	Name	Position	Value of Estate	No. of Slaves
East Baton Rouge	J. P. Chapman	Rep.	NA	2
	J. M. McCutchen	Rep.	$5,000	43
	G. S. Lacey	Sen.	NA	2
East Feliciana	G. W. Munday	Rep.	$23,380	32
	Wm. Patterson	Sen.	$42,500	19
Livingston	T. G. Davidson	Rep.	$88,500	60
	G. S. Lacey	Sen. (E.B.R.)	NA	2
St. Helena	H. Thompson	Rep.	$25,000	39
	P. H. Kemp	Sen.	$16,000	37
	Hardy Richardson	Sen. (Wash.)	$6,200	23
St. Tammany	A. F. Copper	Rep.	$10,550	21
	P. H. Kemp	Sen. (St. Hel.)	$16,000	37
	Hardy Richardson	Sen. (Wash.)	$6,200	23
Washington	J. F. Ard	Rep.	NA	21
	P. H. Kemp	Sen. (St. Hel.)	$16,000	37
	Hardy Richardson	Sen.	$6,200	23
West Feliciana	U. B. Phillips	Rep.	$9,000	5
	R. C. Wickliffe	Sen.	$2,100	5

Sources: *Louisiana House Journal* and *Louisiana Senate Journal*, 1852–54, and *Seventh Census*, 1850, Manuscript, Heads of Household and Slave Schedules

sawmill operator from St. Tammany, all of the piney-woods legislators declared themselves farmers or planters.[32]

The political dominance of the slaveholding elite also extended to local government. In Louisiana, the police jury or parish council served as the principal mechanism of local governance. Other parish officials, such as sheriffs, justices of the peace, clerks of court, and judges, also commanded influence, but during the antebellum period the police jury remained at the center both of the formulation of local policy initiatives and of provincial political intrigues. Courthouse fires and other destruction of records has limited a complete survey of local elected officials, but existing records indicate that though more occupationally diverse, those serving as parish officials further demonstrated the level of planter control of piney-woods politics.

In the initial years following statehood, slaveholders secured virtually all appointments to office. Among the piney-woods parishes, complete records are available only for St. Helena Parish. There, each of the initial officials, from parish judge to the police jury members, owned slaves and had significant landholdings. Partial records of other parishes indicate a similar pattern. By the middle of the 1830s, the power of the slaveholding elite was secure. In the plantation parishes slaveholders occupied nearly 88 percent of parish offices in East Baton Rouge, almost 80 percent in East Feliciana, and 83 percent in West Feliciana. Similarly, in the piney-woods parishes members of the slaveholding elite held slightly over 71 percent of elected positions in Livingston, 78 percent in St. Helena, and 70 percent in St. Tammany.[33]

32. *Seventh Census, 1850*, Manuscript, Louisiana, Schedule 1, Free Population, and Schedule 3, Slave Population, Microfilm. These statistics were based on the legislative delegation from the Florida parishes during the period 1850–54, the period surrounding the implementation of the 1852 constitution and the 1854 opening of the New Orleans-Jackson Railroad, which created an unprecedented challenge for the planters.

33. East Baton Rouge Parish Police Jury Minutes, June Sess., September Sess., 1828, June Sess., 1829, Summer Sess., 1845, West Feliciana Parish Police Jury Minutes, June Sess., 1840, East Feliciana Parish Police Jury Minutes, March Sess., 1839, St. Tammany Parish Police Jury Minutes, June Sess., 1833, May Sess., 1842, all in WPA Louisiana Parish Police Jury Minutes Collection. Livingston, St. Helena, and St. Tammany Elected Officials Collection, in possession of Clark Forrest, Holden, La.; Mortgage Book, 1825–31, Suit Docket Book No. 1, loose filed documents labeled "Criminal Bonds," 1815–60, Notarial Records of Parris Childress, 1843–51, all in St. Tammany Parish, Clerk of Court Archives; St. Helena Parish Records, folders 1822–40, LLMVC; Walter Prichard, ed., "Minutes of the Police Jury of St. Helena Parish, August 16–19, 1813," *Louisiana Historical Quarterly*, XXIII (1940), 405–27; *Fourth Census, 1820*, Manuscript,

By the mid-1840s existing records indicate that slaveholders occupied 68 percent of identified elected offices in West Feliciana, 75 percent in East Baton Rouge, and over 88 percent in East Feliciana Parish. Even though most slaveholders among the local elected officials in the piney woods did not possess the number of slaves necessary to characterize them as planters, they did belong to the slaveholding elite of the piney-woods parishes. Severe courthouse fires in Livingston in 1875 and Washington in 1897 damaged late antebellum records, rendering a complete survey of local elected officials in the piney-woods parishes impossible and necessitating Washington Parish's omission from the survey. However, surviving records for St. Helena and St. Tammany Parishes underscore the extent of planter power in the late antebellum period. Although the presence of a thriving shipping industry along the lakeshore region of St. Tammany served to diversify the economy there somewhat, in the mid-1850s slaveholders retained 62 percent of parish offices, whereas in St. Helena, 80 percent of elected parish officials owned slaves in the same period. The turnover among officeholders proved frequent, but substantial evidence indicates that many officials chose to serve only occasionally or, more commonly, simply rotated positions. In one such case Nicholas Gallatas began his political career as a St. Tammany Parish Police Jury member in the late 1830s. He then served periodically as justice of the peace and constable before closing the antebellum period with his election as sheriff in 1860.[34]

Fifth Census, 1830, Manuscript, and *Sixth Census, 1840,* Manuscript, Louisiana, Schedule 1, Free Population, and Schedule 3, Slave Population, Microfilm. Because of the lack of comprehensive tax assessment rolls and other indicators of financial status, slaveholding serves as the most reliable indicator of wealth in eastern Louisiana. Parish offices include police jury, justice of the peace, assessor, clerk of court, sheriff, and constable. Some parish statistics include other locally elected officials, such as recorder, whereas some are limited to only a few of the above-listed offices.

34. East Baton Rouge Parish Police Jury Minutes, Summer Sess., 1845, West Feliciana Parish Police Jury Minutes, January Sess., 1849, East Feliciana Parish Police Jury Minutes, March Sess., April Sess., 1844, St. Tammany Parish Police Jury Minutes, June Sess., 1833, May Sess., 1842, January Sess., 1860, all in WPA Louisiana Parish Police Jury Minutes Collection; St. Tammany Parish Officeholding Oath Book, 1852, 1854, 1855, in St. Tammany Parish, Clerk of Court Archives; St. Helena Parish Records, folders 1839–42; Greensburg *Imperial,* June 6, 1857, April 30, 1859; *Sixth Census, 1840,* Manuscript, *Seventh Census, 1850,* Manuscript, and *Eighth Census, 1860,* Manuscript, Louisiana, Schedule 1, Free Population, and Schedule 3, Slave Population, Microfilm. For statistics on the ratio of slaveholders to nonslaveholders in each parish, see Table 8.

But the sources of planter power on the local level were not limited simply to holding office. The slaveholding elite furthered their consequence in the territory through calculated use of the legal system. If the posting of bonds does not necessarily imply a political motive, it does indicate strong powers of influence. Members of the elite frequently posted office-holding bonds for local sheriffs, assessors, or other newly elected officials. Records from neighboring counties in Mississippi demonstrate that this practice was widespread. Similarly, wealthy members of the elite often posted criminal bonds, paid outstanding fines, or secured the property of commoners. In one notable instance in 1831, West Feliciana Parish planter-politician Charles Woodruff secured some property for St. Tammany Parish political aspirant Thomas Robertson.[35]

Increasing planter dominance on the state and local level redirected the emphasis of piney-woods politics. In the 1820s and early 1830s, piney-woods representatives supported efforts at democratic reform. The failure of these same legislators to take the lead in promoting the reform constitution of 1845 exemplified the growing power of the slaveholding elite in the piney woods. Recognizing the will of their constituents, the representatives from the eastern parishes did eventually support the new constitution. On key votes in the late 1840s and early 1850s, however, the position taken by the piney-woods legislators demonstrated the vacuous nature of their support for democratic reform and the excessive influence of planter interests.

Politically speaking, the control enjoyed by the coalition of delta and piney-woods planters served to injure the interests of the plain folk, who constituted the vast majority of the region's residents. This situation, in turn, contributed to the piney-woods dwellers' increasing alienation from government. The planter elite continued to present themselves as the defenders of

---

35. East Feliciana Parish Police Jury Minutes, March 4, 1844, in WPA Louisiana Parish Police Jury Minutes Collection; St. Tammany Parish Officeholding Oath Book, 1852, criminal bonds issued in St. Tammany Parish, March 10, 1815, March 14, 1820, August 6, 1860, filed as loose leaf pages under "Criminal Bonds," St. Tammany Suit Docket Book No. 1, 1846–59, esp. multiple bonds, 1846–47, April 4, 1857, and St. Tammany Parish Mortgage Book, 1825–31, esp. p. 238, all in St. Tammany Parish, Clerk of Court Archives; Amite County, Mississippi, Minutes of Board of Police (county supervisors) I and II, May 20, August 26, 1833, November 5, 1835, November 5, 1841, April 15, 1850, all in WPA Mississippi County Board of Police Minutes Collection, Mississippi State Archives, Jackson; *Fifth Census, 1830*, Manuscript, and *Sixth Census, 1840*, Manuscript, Louisiana, Schedule 1, Free Population, and Schedule 3, Slave Population, Microfilm.

southern rights against the threat posed by an increasingly hostile North, but their actions demonstrated that they took little interest in the basic needs of the commoners. Numerous bills exempting slave property from taxation and appropriating state funds as remuneration to owners of slaves convicted of crimes secured passage in the legislature and from local government. Although these measures assisted the small slaveholder, they benefited the planter far more. In supporting bills of this nature, the piney-woods legislators demonstrated their fealty to the planters and concomitantly reduced the state funds available to improve the quality of life of the plain folk. In February, 1850, the legislators from the piney woods voted against a bill to establish free public schools statewide. This measure would have substantially increased funding for existing public schools and would have provided for the creation of new ones at a time when parish superintendents of education relentlessly bemoaned the absence of state support for education. The annual report of Henry Duncan, Livingston Parish superintendent of education, illustrated the deplorable status of public education in Louisiana and the increasing tendency in the piney woods to see government as abusive rather than ameliorative. According to Duncan, "the funds apportioned to this parish will hardly keep a school three months, and parents think they are oppressed, that they have to pay their taxes and receive no benefit of any importance from it."[36]

In the same session the piney-woods representatives voted against a bill designed to protect the property of impoverished families from sheriffs' seizures. A similar bill dominated the first legislative session of 1853. This measure centered on swamp lands donated to the state by the federal government. The original 1850 bill allowed settlers to claim "not less than forty nor more than three hundred and twenty acres," provided the purpose of the claim remained cultivation, not speculation. The point of contention in the 1853 session involved the clause requiring that the land be paid for within one year of the claim. Failure to complete payment within the allotted year would result in state seizure of the claim, regardless of the improvements made. Supporters of a one-year extension on the time for payment argued that "a refusal to grant the indulgence contemplated in the bill, will be to

36. Baton Rouge *Daily Advocate*, February 3, 1854; *Louisiana House Journal*, 2nd Sess., 1859, pp. 3–7 (state treasury report delineating $10,000 paid out as refunds to owners of slaves convicted of criminal offenses); St. Tammany Parish Police Jury Minutes, May 5, 1842, in WPA Louisiana Parish Police Jury Minutes Collection; *Louisiana House Journal*, 1st Sess., 1850, pp. 89–91, 101–102, 126; "Report of the Superintendent of Livingston," *Louisiana Legislative Documents*, 1st Sess., 1852, p. 27.

take from the hardy, honest and industrious settler his home, and to turn it over to the hands of the public speculator." Sadly for those who supported the extension, Senator P. H. Kemp of St. Helena cast a crucial vote with the majority to limit that extension to only eight months rather than the requested twelve. These measures and others of a similar nature furthered the erosion of public confidence in government—the very confidence that increasing stability from the late 1820s to the early 1840s had promoted.[37]

Throughout the 1850s the pattern of neglecting the needs of the plain folk in the Louisiana legislature continued with the passage of bills unfriendly to their welfare. These bills ranged from the removal of restrictions on rates of interest money lenders could charge to conservative governor Robert Wickliffe's program to reduce the amount of state expenditures in support of "objects of an educational and charitable nature."[38] Collectively, these bills and others of a similar disposition served to make life more difficult for Louisiana's plain folk. In combination with the planters' increasing control over the economy in the piney woods, these measures frustrated the plain folk's efforts to enjoy their fair share of the prosperity occurring in this period. More important to the region's pattern of development, the exploitation of the less privileged impugned the very value system of the piney-woods dwellers, creating a potentially destabilizing force in the secure, yet planter-dominated society of the Florida parishes.

By the mid-1850s, three events of enormous consequence created a challenge to the planters' dominance over and exploitation of the plain folk. The watershed in planter-plain folk relations in the Florida parishes resulted primarily from the social and political fallout associated with the disillusionment created by the Constitution of 1852, the "sellout" election of 1855, and the construction of the New Orleans-Jackson Railroad.

Perhaps more so than any other single issue, the Constitution of 1852 testified to the presumptuous character of delta planters' efforts to dominate state politics. Frustrated by the expansion of the suffrage and the commercial restrictions that resulted from the Constitution of 1845, delta planters sought to compensate for the curtailment of their absolute power by creating a new constitution. In this effort they received strong support from Whig banking

---

37. *Louisiana House Journal*, 1st Sess., 1850, pp. 89–91, 126; *Louisiana Senate Journal*, 1st Sess., 1853, pp. 29–30, 72–74. In a compromise move, the legislature by voice vote later agreed to the full one-year extension.

38. Clinton *American Patriot*, February 28, 1855; *Louisiana House Journal*, 1st Sess., 1858, pp. 4–7.

and commercial interests in New Orleans and from railroad promoters. The principal sources of contention involved in the constitutional debates focused on the manner of apportioning legislative seats and on the granting of monopolies. When the debates ended, the planters had unquestionably obtained their goals. The new document allowed slaves to be counted as part of the population in the apportioning of seats in the legislature, a change that dramatically increased the power of delta planters at the expense of the piney woods.[39] The new constitution also allowed for the creation of certain monopolies, which pleased banking and railroad interests.

Opponents of the new constitution condemned what they perceived to be an attack on republican institutions inherent in the document. Many argued that the new apportionment put slaves on an equal footing with white men or that it essentially extended the franchise to slaves. The New Orleans *Daily Picayune*, which supported the commercial aspects of the new document, conceded its primary purpose: "[It] is to give the slaveholders the power to protect their own rights. This is a strong ground of defense for such a basis in a slaveholding state, but we still adhere to the opinion that the true, the just, and therefore the proper basis [of apportionment], is that of the present constitution." The Clinton *American Patriot* argued that the new constitution represented a calculated effort to reduce the political power of regions where the black population remained sparse, declaring, "This is beyond a doubt a glaring political injustice." Opponents railed against the "anti-republican elements" of the new document. A delegation of opposition legislators released a statement asserting that "the discrepancy in representation between the heavy slaveholding parishes and those where soil, locality, and atmosphere are more congenial to the laboring white man will not perpetuate the liberty of the yeoman and the people will not stand for it." Such appeals made a strong impression on many voters. Unlike the 1845 constitution, which easily secured approval by an overwhelming majority of Louisiana voters, the 1852 document passed by a narrow margin (see Table 5).[40]

---

39. Unlike the federal three-fifths basis of representation for slaves, the Constitution of 1852 allowed all slaves to be counted individually in apportioning representation ("Constitution of Louisiana, 1852," Title II, Art. 8, in *Journal of the State Convention to Form a New Constitution for Louisiana, 1852* [New Orleans, 1852], p. 91).

40. New Orleans *Daily Picayune*, October 24, 1852; Clinton *American Patriot*, February 7, 1855; "Report of the Committee on Amendments to the Constitution," in *Louisiana Legislative Documents*, 1852, pp. 1–2; "Annual Address of Governor Joseph Walker to the Louisiana Legislature," in *Louisiana House Journal*, 1st Sess., 1852, pp. 4–12, and *Louisiana Senate Journal*, 1st

TABLE 5. CONSTITUTIONAL RATIFICATION ELECTIONS

Parish	Constitution of 1845		Constitution of 1852	
	For	Against	For	Against
East Baton Rouge	402	29	504	480
East Feliciana	507	34	449	321
Livingston	222	2	73	320
St. Helena	312	1	246	191
St. Tammany	201	8	280	163
Washington	275	0	140	237
West Feliciana	280	34	294	248

Sources: Constitution of 1845: New Orleans Daily Delta, November 11, 27, 1845; Constitution of 1852: Baton Rouge Gazette, November 13, 20, 1852

The approval of the Constitution of 1852 underlined the power of the planters and their commercial allies in Louisiana. The permanence of their control of state government seemed assured when Governor Joseph Walker's effort to secure repeal of "anti-democratic" portions of the constitution failed in the legislature, but the large negative vote indicated that many electors opposed placing greater power in the hands of the planters. Large majorities against the constitution in the piney woods of upstate Louisiana were offset by strong support for the document in most of the delta parishes. The extremely close vote in the Florida parishes concerning a measure so obviously detrimental to the political power of the piney woods demonstrated the continuing strength of the planters in that region. The close vote, however, also indicated an erosion of the unqualified power of the planters. Excepting Washington and Livingston Parishes, which compiled large majorities against the constitution, the results proved very close in all of the other Florida parishes, including the Felicianas. The 1852 constitution secured some votes because it included a few democratic measures, such as making almost all state offices elective and shortening terms of office, but by far its most significant contribution involved the apportionment of political power to the planter class.[41]

Sess., 1853, pp. 3–7; New Orleans Daily Delta, November 11, 27, 1845; Baton Rouge Gazette, November 13, 20, 1852.

41. Baton Rouge Gazette, November 13, 20, 1852; "Annual Address of Governor Joseph Walker," Louisiana Senate Journal, 1st Sess., 1853, pp. 3–7; Roger Shugg, "Suffrage and Representation in Antebellum Louisiana," Louisiana Historical Quarterly, XIX (1936), 398–403.

The close vote returned in the Florida parishes in 1852 foreshadowed political contests in the area for the remainder of the decade. The once-passive political arena developed a reputation for fiercely contested elections. This change resulted in part from the increasing significance of party politics, especially as the Whigs gave way to the vitriolic politics of the Know-Nothings. Moreover, by the 1850s Americans dominated their Creole adversaries in state government, reducing the necessity of American unity behind a single regional candidate. The change also ensued from the political awakening of the masses. By the mid-nineteenth century, the vast majority of Louisiana's residents were acclimated to the dynamics of representative government, and since 1845 the vast majority of white males could vote. By this time, too, candidates had discovered they had a real flair for campaigning, which the voters had come to appreciate and enjoy. Writing home to his family in Massachusetts, F. M. Kent marveled at the extent and manner of electioneering in the Florida parishes in the late 1850s: "In political contests it is usual for men here who are prominent or well acquainted with the subject to *take the stump* and address the people, and as both sides of any question are argued men of good sense generally get very nearly correct ideas on any matter of public interest. This practice of stump speaking is pursued even by the parish / county candidates for every office."[42]

In the decade preceding secession, spirited politics characterized every local and statewide campaign. Perhaps no other single contest exemplified the tumultuous character of political campaigns in the mid-nineteenth-century Florida parishes as the 1855 election for statewide and congressional candidates did. The local newspapers focused on the congressional race pitting Democratic candidate Thomas Green Davidson against the Know-Nothing Preston Pond. This very bitter contest incorporated all of the pertinent political issues of the day, including national issues, such as which party best represented the needs of the South, and local issues, such as the railroad controversy. Furthermore, the election made evident the breakdown of planter unity and the growing political power of the masses in the Florida parishes. It also demonstrated that, despite the erosion of planter solidarity because of the decline of Creole power and the increasing significance of party politics, planters continued to dominate the region politically. Both Pond and Davidson represented the elite of planter-politicians in the Florida parishes.

42. F. M. Kent to his Uncle Moody, February 19, 1857, in Kent Papers.

Preston Pond, later to become Colonel Pond, epitomized the wealth and power of the political elite in the Felicianas. Although he was far from being one of the largest slaveholders in East Feliciana Parish, Pond came from a long line of politically prominent gentlemen. As with most of the affluent families in the Florida parishes, he dramatically increased his personal wealth in the last decade before secession. In 1860, Pond owned thirty-six slaves and placed the value of his plantation at $10,000. Like his father, Pond embraced the philosophy of the Whigs. Unlike many of the "old line Whigs," however, he enthusiastically made the switch to the Know-Nothings as the Whigs began to fade. Pond proved to be a brilliant orator, incorporating Whig ideas on internal improvements with the anti-immigrant bigotry of the Know-Nothings.[43]

His opponent symbolized the power of the piney-woods planter aristocracy. In 1855, fifty-year-old Thomas Green Davidson owned sixty slaves, making him the single largest slaveholder in Livingston Parish. With an estate valued at more than $88,000, Davidson remained one of the preeminent power brokers in the piney woods of the Florida parishes. A seasoned politician, he served in numerous elected positions both in the state legislature and Congress before his political career ended in the late 1870s. Throughout his long tenure of office, Davidson proved to be a political chameleon, changing parties and philosophies whenever necessary to secure election. In 1855, Davidson headed the Democratic ticket for Congress.[44]

The congressional election focused on the characters of the candidates, their positions concerning the New Orleans-Jackson Railroad and its proposed branch lines through the region, and the increasing obsession with the issue of which party more aggressively promoted southern rights. Each party attacked the opportunistic behavior of the opposing candidate and the lukewarm position the other had taken concerning support or opposition to the railroad. Democrats condemned the anti-Catholicism of the Know-Nothings and implied that in their secret circles the American party actually supported the abolitionists. Know-Nothings, in turn, argued that foreign elements uni-

43. *Eighth Census, 1860,* Manuscript, Louisiana, East Feliciana Parish, Schedule 1, Free Population, and Schedule 3, Slave Population, Microfilm; W. Wall to Tom Ellis, March, 1856, John Ellis to Tom Ellis, June 11, 1856, in Ellis Family Papers, LLMVC; Thomas G. Morgan to Henry Marston, October 23, 1859, in Marston Family Papers; Baton Rouge *Gazette,* October 23, 1852; Clinton *Feliciana Democrat,* October 13, 1855; New Orleans *Daily Picayune,* June 28, 1857.

44. *Seventh Census, 1850,* Manuscript, Louisiana, Livingston Parish, Schedule 1, Free Population, and Schedule 3, Slave Population, Microfilm; Clinton *American Patriot,* August 18, 1855; B. F. Jonas to Hardy Richardson, November 7, 1878, in Hardy Richardson Papers, LLMVC.

versally opposed slavery and suggested that many Democratic leaders lacked the intelligence to recognize this threat. Both sides hosted barbecues where prominent stump speakers praised the position taken by their favorite and condemned the opposition. In addition, several huge barbecues, attended by more than a thousand people, gave the masses an opportunity to hear both Davidson and Pond ramble on for nearly three hours about their own qualities and the opponent's faults. The campaign concluded with a week of almost explosive tension, a yellow fever panic concocted by the Know-Nothings to discourage voters, rampant accusations of fraud, and a narrow victory for Davidson.[45]

In itself, the 1855 campaign contributed to the sociopolitical transformation occurring in the Florida parishes. The incentive resulted in part from the acrimonious debate surrounding the congressional election but came primarily from a maneuver within the Democratic party that led the defeated faction to christen the election the "sellout of 1855." Believing the time had come to reward the piney-woods parishes for their loyal support of the Democratic party, politicians from upstate Louisiana and the Florida parishes determined that prominent men from their regions should head the state ticket in the 1855 gubernatorial election. Accordingly, in the two years preceding the state convention, supporters of this proposition lobbied to have Colonel John M. Sandidge, a powerful north Louisiana politician, and F. H. Hatch, state representative from St. Helena, nominated for governor and lieutenant governor, respectively. No apparent opposition to the proposal materialized, and only weeks before the convention most state Democratic newspapers took their nominations for granted. At the convention, however, the power brokers in the plantation parishes and New Orleans staged a coup and instead nominated Robert C. Wickliffe for governor and C. H. Mouton for lieutenant governor. Acknowledging the treachery of this maneuver, the Clinton *American Patriot* asserted that the results proved "adverse to the arrangement that north Louisiana was to have the Governor in the person of the late speaker Colonel Sandidge" and asked, "What must then be his disappointment and that of his section when they learn how they have been cheated?" Noting also that Hatch had been deprived of the nomination for lieutenant

45. Clinton *Feliciana Democrat*, May 5, 19, June 16, August 4, October 13, November 10, 1855; Clinton *American Patriot*, August 18, September 1, October 13, November 10, 24, 1855; Baton Rouge *Daily Advocate*, November 10, 1855; Baton Rouge *Weekly Advocate*, March 1, 1856.

governor, the same paper queried, "What will St. Helena and the other parishes which recommended him say and do? Grin and Bear it?" In attempting to minimize the damage to the party in the piney woods, the Democratic Baton Rouge *Weekly Advocate* expressed disappointment that the ticket was not more geographically balanced but still urged Democrats to unite to defeat the menace posed by Know-Nothingism. The same paper reported that after the election the delegates who remained nominated Wickliffe unanimously but failed to do the same for Mouton, further dramatizing the disappointment associated with Hatch's defeat.[46]

The absence of a unanimous mandate in support of the plantation-parish favorite C. H. Mouton may have resulted from the sense of betrayal felt by many piney-woods delegates from the Florida parishes. The level of disappointment with the Democratic state ticket in much of the region became evident in the general election when Wickliffe carried his home territory by only thirteen votes over the Creole Catholic Charles Derbigny. The damage to the Democratic party in St. Helena Parish continued through the end of the decade; in 1857 St. Helena elected the only Know-Nothing representative from the Florida parishes.[47] More so than any other single event, the 1855 political campaign manifested the lack of political influence wielded by the piney woods in state politics. After months of canvassing to secure the nomination of a favorite son for statewide office, piney-woods delegates were rebuffed by a powerful coalition that included many delta planters from their own region. Even more frustrating to piney-woods politicians from the Florida parishes, the sellout highlighted their decreasing power in state government.

By the 1850s, piney-woods residents of the Florida parishes had become among the least represented of Louisiana citizens in state government. Although each parish received at least one representative to the lower house, the method of apportionment allowing slaves to be counted as part of the population stipulated by the Constitution of 1852 created excessive representation from the plantation parishes. More significant was the result of the 1852 apportionment for the state senate: by the end of the decade the eastern parishes constituted the least represented region in that body.

46. Baton Rouge *Weekly Advocate*, June 7, 1855; Clinton *Feliciana Democrat*, April 21, June 2, 23, 1855; Clinton *American Patriot*, June 23, 1855; Baton Rouge *Weekly Advocate*, June 21, 28, 1855.

47. *Louisiana Senate Journal*, 1st Sess., 1856, p. 9; New Orleans *Daily Picayune*, November 15, 1857.

During the course of the first half of the nineteenth century, representation from the eastern parishes in the senate had steadily declined; the 1852 apportionment dramatically intensified this process. By 1854, the imbalance of senatorial representation proved painfully apparent to piney-woods politicians. Whereas two senators represented the piney woods of the Florida parishes as late as 1846, one senator represented the 10,405 free white residents of Livingston, St. Helena, St. Tammany, and Washington Parishes by 1854. One senator also represented the 2,299 white residents of Tensas and Concordia Parishes and the 3,670 citizens of St. Mary Parish. At the close of the decade, the eastern Florida parishes constituted by far the largest district, in terms of both territory and population, to have only one senator. The striking contrast between the levels of representation in the delta and in the piney woods created deep resentment in the eastern Florida parishes. The piney-woods representatives, led by F. H. Hatch of St. Helena, aggressively denounced this system of misrepresentation designed to secure the dominance of the delta planters.[48]

To many piney-woods dwellers, the refusal to heed the call for fairness in representation exemplified the level of planter arrogance and disregard for the needs of the common man in Louisiana. Increasing voices addressed the perceived exploitation of the plain folk. Attorney Thomas Ellis repeatedly condemned the lavish expenditures of a legislature that lacked all consideration for the wants of common people. Planter haughtiness had always been conspicuous in the Florida parishes, whether it appeared as Robert Barrow's obtrusive and unrepentant murder of a farmer who challenged the right of Barrow's slaves to cross his land or as George Lacey's securing election as senator from Livingston and East Baton Rouge and promptly returning to more comfortable environs at his home in New Orleans. Whatever the form of their arrogance, planters had frequently taxed the patience of the plain folk. But the Democratic refusal to allow a candidate from the piney woods a spot on the statewide ticket despite the region's traditional support for the party provoked surprise, disappointment, and frustration in the eastern parishes. This rebuff, coupled with their decreasing influence in state government and the intensifying economic control of the planters, promoted increasing disaffection among plain folk. With conditions favorable to change, a new ele-

48. *Louisiana House Journal*, 1st Sess., 1854, pp. 25–26, 2nd Sess., 1859, p. 28; *Senate Journal*, 1st Sess., 1846, pp. 8–36; Clinton *American Patriot*, January 24, 1855; "Minority Report of the Committee Appointed to Apportion the Representation of the State," *Louisiana Legislative Documents*, 1st Sess., 1853, pp. 3–4; Howard, *Political Tendencies in Louisiana*, 72.

ment, an implement of modernization, emerged in the early 1850s, providing the impetus to challenge the economic and political dominance of the planters and creating unprecedented opportunity in the Florida parishes. At the same time, it also produced a serious challenge to the value system of piney-woods dwellers. The new element, the railroad, thus provoked both adoration and condemnation and contributed directly to the chaotic conditions of the late nineteenth century.[49]

Debate concerning the feasibility of constructing a railroad to join New Orleans with the interior had been a staple of Louisiana politics since the 1830s. Commercial interests in New Orleans argued that the survival of the great river port depended on the construction of a transportation network to expedite the shipping of cotton and other commodities to the Crescent City. Failure to do so, the argument went, would result in the loss of cotton traffic to Mobile and other ports, just as the construction of railroads and canals had redirected shipments of midwestern foodstuffs to Atlantic ports. The success of small independent lines such as the West Feliciana and the Clinton-Port Hudson Railroads encouraged support for this argument. Unfortunately for railroad supporters, the initial, major, state-supported effort, the proposed New Orleans-Nashville line, failed after proceeding only eighteen miles north of New Orleans. Despite this setback, in his opening comments to the legislative session that would debate the wisdom of a new endeavor, Governor Walker declared his support for a another effort.[50]

The legislature removed a powerful obstacle to the construction of new railroads when in the early 1850s it approved the calling of a constitutional convention. The Constitution of 1845 had prohibited the pledging of state support for internal improvements of this nature, but the 1852 constitutional convention provided railroad supporters with an opportunity to reverse this prohibition. After a bitter debate, the Whigs secured approval of a measure allowing for state backing of railroads. The creation of the New Orleans-Jackson Railroad Company in response later that year opened a veritable Pandora's box of controversy.

49. Thomas Ellis to his Father, February 10, 1857, in Ellis Family Papers; Robert Barrow Letter, January 15, 1858; Davis, ed., *Diary of Bennett H. Barrow*, 253.

50. Clinton-Port Hudson Railroad Flyer, in Marston Family Papers; "Tangipahoa Parish," Typescript, n.d., in Velmarae Dunn Collection, Center for Regional Studies, Southeastern Louisiana University, Hammond; "Annual Address of Governor Joseph Walker," *Senate Journal*, 1st Sess., 1852, p. 11; Merl Reed, *New Orleans and the Railroads: The Struggle for Commercial Empire, 1830–1860* (Baton Rouge, 1966), 28–30.

Supporters of the New Orleans-Jackson line and the recently created New Orleans, Opelousas, and Great Western Railroad argued that railroads guaranteed future prosperity. Under the capable leadership of James Robb, the New Orleans-Jackson and Great Northern Railroad Company received strong support from the New Orleans business community. In 1852, legislative resolution of the controversy concerning the proposed route of the new railroad allowed plans to begin. The route finally agreed on would depart New Orleans, pass through the Manchac swamp, and cross the piney woods of the Florida parishes before arriving at the initial terminus at Canton, Mississippi.[51]

The primary motive for building the railroad remained the desire to increase commerce at New Orleans. Supporters also assumed that residents in the vicinity of the proposed line would recognize the prosperity it would create and thus would enthusiastically endorse the project. Considerable support did in fact materialize in the piney woods, but the primary supporters proved to be local merchants who hoped to tap the lucrative business prospects the railroad would bring and speculators who recognized the opportunities the sudden intrusion of a railroad into a semi-isolated society would create. Noticeably absent from the declared supporters of the railroad were the vast majority of Florida parish planters, and their absence constituted a major source of concern for proponents of the railroad. In the past, efforts to develop railroads in the Florida parishes had failed because of the opposition of powerful planters. In the 1830s several planters had initially prevented and then reluctantly permitted the construction of the West Feliciana Railroad.[52]

A small branch line dominated by local planter interests, however, lacked the far-reaching implications a major trunk railroad supported by northern capital and controlled by city interests necessarily included. In particular, a major railroad would threaten the planters' control of the regional economy. Many planters resented the high costs associated with a railroad, while others opposed the disruption to their plantations its construction would create. Yet by the early 1850s, much of the overt hostility exhibited by delta planters toward the railroads had abated. Throughout the controversy many planters re-

51. Henry L. Smith, "Southwestern Railroad Convention at New Orleans," *De Bow's Review*, X (1851), 690–94; New Orleans *Daily Picayune*, January 6, 1852.

52. C. R. Calvert, "History of the West Feliciana Railroad," Typescript, n.d., in James Stewart McGehee Papers, LLMVC. "Rules and Bylaws of the West Feliciana Railroad Company" demonstrates that local planters exercised absolute control over the branch railroads in the region (West Feliciana Railroad Collection, Newberry Library).

mained uncharacteristically silent, as if torn by their recognition of the benefits a railroad would bring but reluctant to support an endeavor they suspected would massively restructure their world. By their silence, they failed to provide the leadership expected of them at a critical moment when direction mattered most. The legislature did act, though. On a crucial vote to provide state aid to the proposed railroads, all of the senators from the Florida parishes voted yes with the majority, paving the way for construction of the line.[53]

The near unanimous support of the legislature indicated at least tacit approval on the part of delta planters, but strong opposition to the New Orleans-Jackson Railroad developed in the piney woods. Although the trunk railroad would pass through only the eastern parishes, the controversy extended to the entire region because of branch lines. With the advent of construction on the trunk line, railroad supporters issued numerous calls for the creation of branch lines to connect the Felicianas and East Baton Rouge to the mainline. The two most important of these proposals involved the connections to Clinton via Greensburg and to Baton Rouge via Springfield. Local newspapers relentlessly promoted the trunk line and the branch railroads, frequently listing prominent supporters who pledged funds. Those providing financial support included merchandising firms and factors such as Abraham Levi, Bloom and Company, Robert Germany, and Levi Spiller, as well as prominent gentlemen such as John Bach, Cade Strickland, and Eli Capell. The lists of prominent supporters demonstrate that the merchant community overwhelmingly supported the endeavor, but the same lists indicate that, excepting a few individuals, the planters either remained silent or opposed the railroad.[54]

Political rhetoric during this controversy also demonstrated the planters' lack of leadership. Pressed to take a position concerning a branch railroad during a hotly contested election in East Feliciana, prominent planter and state representative Bythell Haynes responded, "Should they [the people] be in favor of the road, and desire the state to subscribe for one fifth of the capital stock as provided for in the Constitution, and that knowledge is made known

53. New Orleans-Jackson and Great Northern Railroad Ledger, Vol. I, June, 1851–March, 1858, Illinois Central Railroad Collection; Senate Journal, 1st Sess., 1853, pp. 270–71. Smith, "Southwestern Railroad Convention," 690–94, demonstrates the virtual absence of Florida parish leaders among railroad promoters.

54. Clinton American Patriot, August 4, 11, 18, 1855; Clinton Feliciana Democrat, June 16, 1855; Greensburg Imperial, June 13, 1857; Baton Rouge Daily Advocate, August 22, 1854; Baton Rouge Weekly Advocate, May 10, 1856; New Orleans Daily Delta, December 14, 1854.

to me, in a tangible form, then I will support the measure; but on the contrary should the people be opposed to the road and against asking or receiving such assistance from the state, then I as their representative would oppose it and vote against it." Haynes further sidestepped the issue by adding that "the Democracy of the parish having as a party made nominations to be supported at the election in November next, by said party, it does not, in my opinion become those nominees to raise any side issues, on the railroad, or any other question, which may embarrass the voters in their choice." Haynes's position was indicative of the strength of opponents of the railroads. Even though he said he personally favored the proposed line, he cautiously avoided being publicly labeled either a supporter or an opponent of the railroad.[55]

Opposition to the railroad centered on different issues in different areas. Many planters feared that the power they exercised in a closed homogeneous society would decrease as a result of new opportunities created by the railroad. The fear that hordes of new residents unaccustomed to conditions in the Florida parishes would challenge their political power created alarm among some planter-politicians. Many resented the arrogance exhibited by outsiders linked with the railroad. Commenting disparagingly on the role of the company's leadership during the controversy, Charles Gayarre informed a piney-woods supporter, "The director is an utter stranger to Louisiana, and he ignores probably that there is a sensitiveness in this state which may not exist in the cooler atmosphere of Illinois, where he may have forgotten the habits, manners, and feelings of South Carolina which is said to be his native state."[56]

Others among the elite feared the challenge to their political and economic power posed by merchants and opportunists sure to follow in the wake of the railroad. Positions created by the rail line provided many laborers with a chance to work for a company free of the economic control of the planters. Moreover, like the plain folk, many planters resented the increasing taxation the railroad represented. From the beginning, it appeared certain that to secure construction of the line, taxes would have to be increased to fund the state subsidy. In the winter of 1853 the New Orleans *Daily Picayune* reported that a lawsuit challenging the legality and constitutionality of the railroad tax had been filed. Four months later, in an article urging people to demon-

55. "To the Voters of East Feliciana," Bythell Haynes Letter, LLMVC.

56. Charles Gayarre to N. R. Jennings, November 20, 1859, in Hennen-Jennings Papers, LLMVC; "Report of the New Orleans-Jackson Railroad," *Louisiana Legislative Documents*, 1853, pp. 11–20.

strate their support for the railroad, the same paper noted that opponents of the line "appear to have fearful strength at the polls." Attempting to contain the growing antirailroad agitation in the piney woods, Superintendent James Robb, in a series of letters to the New Orleans *Daily Crescent*, addressed the opposition resulting from the increasing tax burden. Robb expressed sympathy for the country residents who were "already taxed oppressively and loudly [objected] to it."[57]

The financial burden created by the railroad angered many plain folk as well as planters. In the piney woods, the core of the opposition rested not in economic issues but in an inherent suspicion of outside interference into their affairs. To many of the piney-woods dwellers, these suspicions proved well founded when their society and their value system came under immediate assault from the intrusion of the railroad. Although qualified by the planters' economic and political control of the region, an independent life-style remained the very essence of the piney-woods existence. This independence involved the freedom to travel, hunt, and fish wherever one pleased, unencumbered by legal or physical restraints. It meant a farmer could raise crops on unoccupied land or allow his livestock to graze wherever he pleased in a society that accepted these rights as fundamental. If their independent life-style had been redefined somewhat by modernization and the implications of a market intrinsically part of the cotton economy, their value system, based on the primacy of honor and independence, continued unchanged. The railroad threatened this manner of existence, for it brought government directly into the lives of the piney-woods dwellers in the form of increasing taxation, stock laws, and legal hassles involving land claims.

Trouble began with the surveys along the proposed route, as long-dormant land disputes came to the surface. Many residents deeply resented the en-

---

57. New Orleans *Daily Picayune*, January 6, October 12, 1852, May 22, December 15, 1853, April 21, 1854, April 22, 1856; Smith, "Southwestern Railroad Convention," 692; "Report of the New Orleans-Jackson Railroad," *Louisiana Legislative Documents*, 1853, pp. 11–20; Gayarre to Jennings, November 20, 1859, in Hennen-Jennings Family Papers; New Orleans *Daily Crescent*, March 6, 7, 8, 10, 1856; C. D. Strickland to John Calhoun, August 27, 1852, J. Y. Kilpatrick to A. Wang, March 10, 1857, both in New Orleans-Jackson and Great Northern Railroad Collection, Mississippi State Archives; E. D. Frost to H. S. McComb, November 3, 1875, in W. M. Francis and E. D. Frost Out Letters Collection, Newberry Library; Margaret L. Duval, "Legends of Wilkinson County and the Surrounding Area," *Louisiana Folklore Miscellany*, III (1975), 47; Hahn, *Roots of Southern Populism*, 34–37; J. Mills Thornton, III, *Politics and Power in a Slave Society: Alabama, 1800–1860* (Baton Rouge, 1978), 305–11.

croachment of an outside force certain to complicate an aspect of their lives that had long been resolved to the mutual satisfaction of all. Even more menacing, a federal act that donated to the railroad all public lands within six miles of both sides of the line threatened to uproot hundreds of homesteaders residing on those lands. Not only did the donation create outrage among the squatters, many of whom farmed the land in hopes of one day owning it, but it also disturbed nearby landowners who anxiously considered the prospect of scores of uprooted, landless families in their communities. The reaction to the measure proved so strong that Governor Wickliffe urged the state legislature to petition the company to reject the donation.[58]

Even more damaging to traditional piney-woods existence was the fencing of stock necessitated by the railroad. Promoters recognized the importance of the open range to piney-woods farmers, so in an effort to reduce opposition to the railroad, they initially rejected the use of legal coercion to force farmers to fence in their livestock. The earliest excursions along the road, however, demonstrated that it would be impossible to allow livestock to range in the vicinity of the railroad. An outing designed to demonstrate the partially completed railroad's cotton-carrying capacity in November, 1854, ended in disaster when the train hit a cow, overturning several cars and damaging much of the cotton. A few weeks later, a trip up the line attended by Governor P. O. Hebert and other state dignitaries proved less than satisfactory when the train again hit a cow, forcing the passengers to wait for hours until another train could be brought up from New Orleans. The resulting restrictions on the open range assaulted a central component of the piney-woods economy. The constraints placed on their traditional way of life and the resulting disruption of their economy, coupled with the increasing influx of immigrants, all constituted a direct attack on the piney-woods existence.[59]

In addition to the disruption of their traditional existence and economic livelihood, many residents of the Florida parishes and the southwestern counties of Mississippi considered the railroad a harbinger of death—death in the form of the plague of the period, yellow fever. Called by many names, "the fever," "yellow jack," or "the black vomit," this seemingly incurable disease

58. "Annual Message of Governor Robert C. Wickliffe," *Louisiana House Journal*, 1st Sess., 1857, pp. 4–8; New Orleans *Daily Picayune*, January 17, 1855, August 25, 1856.

59. New Orleans *Daily Picayune*, November 10, 1854; New Orleans *Daily Delta*, December 14, 1854; Shugg, *Origins of Class Struggle in Louisiana*, 46; Louisiana Folklife Program, *Folklife in the Florida Parishes*, 32; *Police Jury Code for the Parish of East Feliciana*, 56–62.

remained the most feared illness among Louisianians in the mid-nineteenth century. Unfortunately for railroad promoters, some of the most severe yellow fever epidemics occurred in the early 1850s.

Physicians experimenting with the disease at the time never determined the correct cause or treatment for the fever. Most believed that yellow fever was introduced into Louisiana from abroad, most likely from the Caribbean Islands, and that gases created by the swampy, often filthy conditions around New Orleans allowed it to gain a foothold and then spread. Despite the uncertainty surrounding its cause, there was no shortage of evidence on the panic that yellow fever created. An 1853 letter written by N. R. Jennings of St. Tammany Parish testifies to the horror associated with the fever. In the letter Jennings confides to his friend that a close associate of his wife recently died. The deceased woman's doctor assured his wife that her friend had died of dropsy; nevertheless, his wife and only one other woman attended this popular woman's funeral. While there, Mrs. Jennings was informed by the attending physician that her friend had indeed died of yellow fever. She reported to her husband that the physician appeared extremely agitated at his failure to determine the cause of the fever or to prescribe any effective treatment. Before they departed the funeral, the doctor urged Mrs. Jennings to remain silent so as to prevent a mass flight of suffering people who were likely to die anyway. A sense of hopelessness and despair permeates Jennings' words. He closed the letter with a note of near panic concerning the health of his wife.[60]

The epidemics of 1853, 1854, and 1855 killed thousands in Louisiana and proved especially severe in the Florida parishes. The epidemic of 1853, in particular, depopulated whole regions of the state. One-half the population of the villages of Port Hudson and Bayou Sara died from the fever. Panicked residents abandoned New Orleans and the surrounding parishes by the thousands, heading for drier, cooler environs to the north. Clinton, Jackson, Greensburg, and other towns in the Florida parishes were almost universally abandoned by their residents. The sheriff of East Feliciana Parish succumbed to the fever; his replacement died in the same manner four months later.

---

60. American Institute of Homeopathy, *Official Report of the Homeopathic Yellow Fever Commission* (New Orleans, 1879), 14–56; W. B. King to E. P. Skene, September 15, 1897, and J. B. Kemp to E. P. Skene, September 15, 1897, both in Illinois Central Railroad Overflow Reports, E. P. Skene Outletters, Newberry Library; "Report of the Joint Committee on Public Health," *Louisiana Legislative Documents*, 1853, pp. 3–8, 25–32; N. R. Jennings to Dimitry, n.d. [1853], in Hennen-Jennings Papers.

Work on the railroad came to a complete halt in the summer of 1853 when yellow fever decimated the labor force and most of the survivors fled for their lives. During each of the epidemics, all efforts to contain the disease failed. As late as the 1870s the primary defense against the fever remained repeated artillery discharges in the affected areas. Some physicians believed the concussion created by these discharges killed the yellow fever toxin, while others believed the ozone produced by the burnt powder cleaned the atmosphere. All agreed that the only means to contain the spread of yellow jack involved a rigid system of quarantine.[61]

Since most physicians agreed that the epidemics spread to the interior after first being introduced into New Orleans, quarantine attempted to prevent the arrival of plague-carrying ships at New Orleans. Once the fever was identified in New Orleans, the country parishes sought to repel travelers from the Crescent City. A typical quarantine station consisted of armed residents, frequently supported by crude breastworks, who were determined to prevent anyone having been in or having passed through an infected region from entering their locality. Quarantine usually remained in place for months until the threat of fever had passed. On the roads and trails crossing the Florida parishes, the guards could easily turn back any traveler attempting to enter their region. The railroad disrupted this arrangement, for it provided New Orleans with an unbreakable link to the piney woods. In January, 1854, Governor Hebert addressed this new menace: "The sanitary condition of New Orleans is no longer a question of local interest. When the meshes of railroads which must eventually connect every part of the state with its great emporium shall have been completed, the most distant villages on our frontiers shall be suburbs of New Orleans." Thus, Hebert concluded, the epidemics that always begin in great cities will easily spread statewide.[62]

61. "Annual Address of Governor P. O. Hebert," *Louisiana House Journal*, 2nd Sess., 1855, pp. 4–8; American Institute of Homeopathy, *Official Report of the Homeopathic Yellow Fever Commission*, 14–56; Mary E. Taylor to Stella Spence, August 14, 1855, Sereno Taylor to Eugene Hunter, May 26, 1855, both in Hunter-Taylor Family Papers; E. D. Frost to H. S. McComb, June 28, 1875, in Francis and Frost Out Letters Collection; "Report of the Joint Committee on Public Health," *Louisiana Legislative Documents*, 1853, pp. 3–8; Clinton *American Patriot*, August 25, September 15, November 17, 1855; Clinton *Feliciana Democrat*, September 1, 29, 1855; New Orleans *Daily Picayune*, October 6, 20, 22, November 10, 1853, September 6, 1855; John Ellis to Tom Ellis, August 20, 1855, in Ellis Family Papers; Baton Rouge *Daily Advocate*, October 10, 1854.

62. Hansell, ed., *Commercial and Statistical Almanac*, 45–53; E. D. Frost to H. S. McComb, September 4, 1875, in Francis and Frost Out Letters Collection; New Orleans *Daily Picayune*,

Based on the threat posed to their very manner of existence, and in some opinions to their very lives, much of the piney-woods dwellers' opposition to the railroad seemed justified. The perceived menace of yellow fever transported from New Orleans to the countryside broadened the appeal of railroad antagonists. Despite the ferocity of some opponents, though, the railroad could not be halted. By the summer of 1854, regular rail service traversed the Florida parishes. The power of New Orleans commercial interests, northern capital, and the silence of the planters guaranteed the construction of iron rails across the Florida parishes. In the spring of 1856, the New Orleans *Daily Picayune* reported an end to the dispute: "We hope we have now seen the last of the railroad controversy. With all deference to the parties engaged in this warfare with each other, we may be permitted to express the opinion that nothing is to be gained for themselves, or the public interest in prosecuting it further." The issues raised in the controversy surrounding the New Orleans-Jackson line did not die as hoped but instead stiffened opposition to the proposed branch railroads. Confronted by strong resistance and lacking the necessary capital, all of the branch railroad companies either failed or postponed their plans indefinitely.[63]

The New Orleans-Jackson Railroad transformed the territory along its route. In just a few years the railroad converted the thinly settled territory along the Tangipahoa River into the most densely populated and thriving region in the piney woods. Several new towns, including Ponchatoula, Tickfaw, Amite City, and Osyka, emerged at ten-mile intervals along the line in conjunction with the stations established by the railroad. Previously established villages such as Manchac and Tangipahoa also thrived as a result of the railroad.

In each of these villages, sawmills, cotton warehouses, stockyards, and, in many cases, brickyards arose to facilitate construction and traffic along the railroad. Hotels, restaurants, general stores, and saloons also emerged to serve travelers and the rapidly increasing local population. Real estate prices quickly escalated as speculators from New Orleans and other areas purchased all available property in the vicinity of the railroad. The region's rapid devel-

August 31, 1858, September 16, 1897; J. B. Kemp to E. P. Skene, September 15, 16, 17, 1897; King to Skene, September 15, 1897, all in Illinois Central Railroad Overflow Reports; "Report of the Joint Committee on Public Health," *Louisiana Legislative Documents*, 1853, pp. 3–8; Clinton *American Patriot*, August 25, 1855.

63. New Orleans *Daily Picayune*, April 25, July 9, 1856; Greensburg *Imperial*, April 30, 1859; Clinton *Feliciana Democrat*, July 21, 1855; Clinton *American Patriot*, February 21, 1855.

opment frustrated many of the older Florida-parish families. The contempt
that many of the established families felt for the hordes of speculators and opportunists who arrived in the wake of the railroad is evident in a letter from
Thomas Ellis to his brother John. Writing from the newly created Amite
City, Ellis underscored his disgust while expressing dismay at the level of
speculation occurring along the railroad. "One must get located here to have
an equal chance with those fresh water sharks and would be *large land holders*
who are trying to induce good natured people to give whole fortunes for a few
feet of *piney wood* land for the sake of the railroad, as if the New Orleans-
Jackson Railroad were the only communication in the state with New Orleans." The Ellises, natives of East Feliciana Parish, moved to Amite City
only upon the completion of the railroad.[64]

The masses of immigrants and city dwellers who established residences in
the piney woods in conjunction with the railroad changed the face of the territory along the Tangipahoa River and environs. Moreover, the rapidly increasing wealth and population of the region gradually shifted significant political power away from the delta parishes to the piney woods. Recognizing
the significance of this transformation, many delta-parish families, such as
the perennially political Ellises, relocated along the route of the railroad.
More important for the future development of the region, though, the railroad controversy contributed to the changing relationship between the area's
planters and plain folk. This relationship, based on the dominance of the
planters, had brought stability to an apparently perpetual state of chaos in the
Florida parishes. From the perspective of peace and security, planter dominance had been good for the region.

The relationship between the planters and plain folk had always been one
of patron and follower. Although this situation allowed the planters to dominate the region, both groups benefited in terms of the services each provided
the other and, more importantly, in terms of the security and stability that resulted. The railroad controversy jeopardized this relationship. While conditions associated with the railroad appeared likely to challenge the absolute
dominance of the planters, they also created an opportunity for the planters
to market their own crops more easily and raised the value of much of their

64. Map of the Line of the New Orleans-Jackson Railroad from Canton, Mississippi, to New
Orleans, circa 1861, in Illinois Central Railroad Collection; New Orleans *Daily Picayune*, July
19, August 1, 1854, September 16, 1855; Thomas Ellis to John Ellis, January 26, 1858, in Ellis
Family Papers.

land. This predicament provoked the vague and seemingly uncertain response of many planters to the controversy. The railroad also created many opportunities for the plain folk, but what was more significant, it challenged their value system, attacking their isolated, independent life-style. In what seemed to them a betrayal, the planters, to whom the piney-woods dwellers had surrendered their political power, failed to take control and protect their interests; the absence of leadership following the 1852 constitution and the sellout of 1855 threatened to unravel a time-tested arrangement in the Florida parishes. Yellow fever epidemics aggravated the prevailing anxiety. Additionally, the lack of a strong religious community denied the residents a fundamental avenue for venting their frustrations. As a result, by the close of the decade, on the eve of the crisis of the Union, the plain folk's fealty to the planters was in doubt.[65]

Much of the ruling elite's concern centered on the results of local political contests. Increasing sectional strife and the decline of two-party politics in the Deep South ensured the supremacy of the Democrats in statewide and national campaigns, but on the local level planter dominance seemed challenged. The 1856 legislative delegation from the piney woods contained no incumbents. More important, the social status and wealth of those elected demonstrated that though the power of the planters remained unbroken, it had been weakened. Some of the newly elected legislators, such as W. E. Walker of Livingston, had benefited from incumbents' failure to seek reelection. Others, such as J. B. Strickland of St. Helena, defeated powerful incumbents in extremely close races.[66]

Creating perhaps the most concern among the ruling hierarchy in the Florida parishes, the election of Steven Albitron in Washington Parish heralded the arrival of a new breed of politician in the piney woods. A highly

65. C. D. Strickland to John Calhoun, August 27, 1852, J. Y. Kilpatrick to A. Wang, March 10, 1857, both in New Orleans-Jackson and Great Northern Railroad Collection, provide examples of opportunities created for the plain folk by the railroad. For evidence of the limited nature of the regional religious community, see John Durnin to his Sister, January 11, 1868, in James and John Durnin Papers, LLMVC; Eugene Hunter to Stella Hunter, March 20, 1862, in Hunter-Taylor Family Papers; Abigail Amacker Diary, July 13, 1862, in O. P. Amacker Papers, LLMVC; S. F. Snell Letter, April 26, 1863, LLMVC; Kent to Moody, February 19, 1857, in Kent Papers; Hephzibah Church Books, May–September, 1863, LLMVC; Greensburg *Imperial*, August 6, 1859; Greensburg *Journal*, July 20, 1866; Clinton *American Patriot*, June 16, 1855; Davis, ed., *Diary of Bennett H. Barrow*, 66; Flint, *Recollections of the Last Ten Years*, 327.

66. *Louisiana House Journal*, 1st Sess., 1856, pp. 8, 45.

educated man, though of modest means, Albitron served as a school teacher in Franklinton. Unlike most of his predecessors, he owned no slaves, farmed no cotton, and possessed an estate valued at less than six hundred dollars.[67] Although Albitron played a minor role in the state legislature, his election symbolized the dawning political power of the masses in the piney woods and the deterioration of the absolute power of the planters.

Circumstances in the mid- and late 1850s in the Florida parishes combined to create a new political atmosphere in which the traditional power of the planters was qualified by the perception of failed leadership and an absence of concern for the plight of the plain folk. On the brink of their greatest opportunity, however, the increasing influence of the piney-woods dwellers was circumvented. The apparent chance for social and political change slipped away as a result of national issues that overwhelmed the local transformation occurring in eastern Louisiana. As the sectional crisis dramatically intensified at the close of the decade, it essentially negated the opportunity for choice among the plain folk. Just as the Creole-American conflict in state politics had necessitated unity and reduced the choices available to common voters, the reduction in the number of national political parties sympathetic to conditions in the South also reduced the choices available. The replacement of the Know-Nothings by a powerful Republican organization in the North negated the options open to southern voters. As a result, the growing sectional crisis allowed the planters to maintain their political dominance in the Florida parishes at the moment of greatest challenge.

As abolitionist agitation increased in the North, the large slaveholders sought to ensure southern unity at home. Planter propagandists relentlessly depicted themselves as the defenders of southern society in the face of increasingly hostile attacks. The New Orleans *Daily Picayune* emphatically argued that a natural unity of thought and conviction existed between planters and plain folk. Proslavery ideology increasingly stressed the connection between white freedom and black slavery, arguing that support for slavery was tantamount to support for southern republicanism. An 1856 article in *De Bow's Review* noted "the perfect spirit of equality so prevalent among the whites of all the slaveholding states," a condition the author found absent in the class-conscious North. The article continued: "It is this spirit of equality

---

67. *Ibid.*, 3; *Seventh Census, 1850*, Manuscript, Louisiana, Washington Parish, Schedule 1, Free Population, and Schedule 2, Agricultural Statistics, Microfilm.

which is both the generator and preserver of the genuine spirit of liberty."
Similar arguments could be found in local papers. The Greensburg *Imperial*
published articles praising North American slavery for liberating the blacks
from heathen oppression in Africa. Likewise, the *Feliciana Democrat* insisted
that if southerners did not present a united front against abolitionist agitation, then "our people are so dead to every feeling of independence and
manly courage as to suffer themselves to be absorbed after a faint, and reluctant struggle, into the North, and to become the ready and cringing slaves to
all its arrogant and unreasonable demands." Abolitionist attacks on slavery
were thus equated to attacks on the republican institutions of the South that
ensured white liberty. As a result, by the late 1840s the political rhetoric of
the planters, which equated support for slavery with support for republicanism, greatly influenced the political philosophy of the plain folk. According
to John Inscoe, slavery took on "a centrality in political rhetoric far out of
proportion to any commitment which the extent of slave ownership alone
would have justified."[68]

The propaganda blitz served two primary purposes. First, it helped convince the plain folk that their manner of living was under attack as a result of
the increasing assaults on slavery. Second, it encouraged the belief among
piney-woods dwellers that the great planters championed their cause against
their enemies. The history of the Florida parishes, which illustrated to them
the direct relationship between ineffective leadership and instability,
strengthened the appeal of determined leadership. In the legislative session
beginning in January, 1856, the messages of both outgoing governor Hebert
and incoming governor Wickliffe manifested the determined leadership presented by the planter aristocracy in the mid-1850s. In reference to the growing political friction with the North, Hebert argued that "the time for con-
cessions on our part and compromises has past [sic]." Similarly, Wickliffe
maintained that if southerners did not rise and present a united front to
northern aggression, "we shall have forfeited deservedly our heritage of freedom and the memory of our ancestors be but the brand of our own shame." In

68. New Orleans *Daily Picayune*, September 3, 1856; Drew Gilpin Faust, ed., *The Ideology of
Slavery: Proslavery Thought in the Antebellum South, 1830–1860* (Baton Rouge, 1981), 10–21;
Thornton, *Politics and Power in a Slave Society*, 18; C. [Charles?] B. Dew, ed., "Slavery in the Vir-
ginia Legislature," *De Bow's Review*, XX (1856), 474–75; Greensburg *Imperial*, June 6, 1857,
May 29, 1858; Clinton *Feliciana Democrat*, May 5, 1855; Inscoe, *Mountain Masters*, 9.

furtherance of this appeal, Wickliffe argued for the sanctity of political participation and demanded that laws to secure the suffrage "be stringent, stern,
and free from all ambiguity." The appearance of a strong reaction to external
threats and the seeming emphasis on securing the rights of the common man
played well with the piney-woods dwellers. Local newspapers condemned remote abolitionists and applauded the planter leadership that confronted enemies of white liberty. The *Feliciana Democrat* commended "the old patriarchs
of [St. Helena] Parish who are roused in opposition to this wild crusade
against the Constitution and liberties of the republic." The Greensburg *Imperial* relentlessly attacked the enemies of the South and urged unqualified support for the proponents of southern rights.[69]

The appeal to southern honor and the bond of slaveholding in response to
the growing northern threat served to dissuade the plain folk from continuing their challenge to planter dominance. In his farewell address to the legislature on January 17, 1860, Governor Wickliffe demonstrated the power of
this appeal: "The times that are upon us are rapidly precipitating a crisis
which must be met manfully. I know that the people of Louisiana will not be
found wanting in a practical vindication of their assailed rights, and a proper
defense of their honor. The character of Louisiana has not yet been stained
with the servility of dishonor, and I know her people in the present, like her
people in the past, would gladly accept any alternative which carries with it
honor and insures self respect."[70]

Following the election of Abraham Lincoln, Governor Thomas O.
Moore's call for a special session of the Louisiana legislature in December,
1860, resulted in the passage of a convention bill authorizing the governor to
call an election for delegates to a secession convention. If any doubted the
power of the appeals to honor and to defense of southern rights, the secession
convention must have convinced them. At the convention, the practice of
denying important positions to the favorite sons of the piney woods continued: despite strenuous efforts, the piney-woods representatives failed in their
efforts to secure election of one of their own to a position of leadership. In
spite of the constancy of this rebuff, when the vote to sever Louisiana's ties to

69. "Annual Message of Governor P. O. Hebert," "Inaugural Message of Governor Robert
Wickliffe," both in *Louisiana Senate Journal*, 1st Sess., 1856, pp. 6, 17–21; Clinton *Feliciana Democrat*, September 8, December 29, 1855; Greensburg *Imperial*, April 25, May 30, June 6, 13,
1857.

70. "Farewell Address of Governor Robert C. Wickliffe," *Louisiana House Journal*, 1st Sess.,
1860, pp. 9–10.

the old Union came, the piney-woods representatives stood beside their traditional leaders.[71]

On January 26, 1861, the Louisiana Secession Convention voted 113 to
17 to take the state out of the Union. Every representative from the Florida
parishes voted in support of the measure. The fear of the Yankee menace to
their peculiarly southern way of life and the assumed affronts to their honor
occasioned by the rhetoric of the abolitionists and Republicans proved more
important than challenging the power of the planters. Yet the seeds for the
chaos of the late nineteenth century had already been planted. If sectional
controversy had not derailed the increasing assertiveness of the plain folk,
the results of the breakdown of planter dominance in the postwar period
might have been softened, but the crisis Louisianians willingly threw themselves into would, for some, be enduring. The Florida parishes, and particularly the piney woods of that region, had commenced a journey of unmitigated catastrophe that would convulse the territory for the next fifty years. As
the celebrations in support of the independence of Louisiana echoed across
the state, perhaps a note of sadness should have sounded in the Florida
parishes, a sorrowful portent for the blood of the scores of her residents that
would stain the soil for decades and a sadness for lost opportunity as the
storm waxed near.

71. *Louisiana Senate Journal*, Extra Sess., 1860, pp. 4–6; *Journal of the Proceedings of the Convention of the State of Louisiana, 1861* (1862; microfilm rpr. New Haven, 1970), 7–18; Records of
the Louisiana State Government, 1850–1888, War Department Collection of Confederate
Records, Doc. F-75, pp. 1–3, National Archives, Washington, D.C. The secession convention
election in Louisiana returned eighty-four committed secessionists and forty-six cooperationists.
In the Florida parishes, East Baton Rouge elected straight cooperationist delegates, East Feliciana, St. Helena, and St. Tammany elected split delegations, and Livingston, Washington, and
West Feliciana elected straight secessionist delegations (Baton Rouge *Daily Advocate*, January
17, 1861).

Centenary College at Jackson, Louisiana, *ca.* 1858. The college was one of the most prestigious institutions of higher learning in the state during the antebellum period. War-related damage forced its closure and later removal to north Louisiana.
Courtesy Andrew D. Lytle Collection, Louisiana and Lower Mississippi Valley Collections, LSU Libraries, Louisiana State University

The Silliman Female Institute at Clinton, *ca.* 1858
Courtesy Andrew D. Lytle Collection, Louisiana and Lower Mississippi Valley Collections, LSU Libraries, Louisiana State University

Yellow Fever Quarantine Station in Rural East Baton Rouge Parish, *ca.* 1875. Such scenes were common across eastern Louisiana and southwestern Mississippi during yellow-jack epidemics. Armed guards forcibly turned back travelers from infected regions.

Photograph courtesy Andrew D. Lytle Collection, Louisiana and Lower Mississippi Valley Collections, LSU Libraries, Louisiana State University

Richland Plantation in East Feliciana Parish, *ca.* 1870. Constructed in the 1820s, the plantation symbolizes the wealth and power of the Feliciana planter aristocracy. *Courtesy Andrew D. Lytle Collection, Louisiana and Lower Mississippi Valley Collections, LSU Libraries, Louisiana State University*

Bonnie Burn Plantation in East Feliciana Parish. This home of the politically powerful Kilbourne family was indicative of the wealth concentrated in the Felicianas. *Courtesy Richard Kilbourne*

East Feliciana Courthouse, Clinton, *ca.* 1858. The courthouse was the site of presecession rallies and multiple episodes of Reconstruction-era violence.

Courtesy Andrew D. Lytle Collection, Louisiana and Lower Mississippi Valley Collections, LSU Libraries, Louisiana State University

Preston Pond, Jr., Colonel of the Sixteenth Louisiana Infantry Regiment. A prominent antebellum politician representing East Feliciana Parish, Pond went on to serve in the Confederate army.

Courtesy Center for Regional Studies, Southeastern Louisiana University

Silas T. White, Private in Company A, Fourth Louisiana Infantry Regiment. White was killed at Shiloh in the regiment's first major action.

Courtesy Center for Regional Studies, Southwestern Louisiana University

Vincent Scivique, *ca.* 1878. The son of immigrants, Scivique was a Confederate scout during the war and later the owner of the ferry across the Amite River and a Democratic party organizer.

Courtesy Katie Cambre Jenks

James G. Kilbourne (no date). Kilbourne served in the Fourth Louisiana Infantry Regiment of the Confederate army and was elected judge from East Feliciana Parish at the close of Reconstruction. He remained a leading figure in Democratic party strategy through Reconstruction and the late nineteenth century.
Courtesy Richard Kilbourne

Baton Rouge During the Civil War. In 1862, Federal troops damaged or destroyed large parts of the town.
Courtesy Andrew D. Lytle Collection, Louisiana and Lower Mississippi Valley Collections, LSU Libraries, Louisiana State University

Harvesting Corn in Livingston Parish, *ca.* 1870

Courtesy Andrew D. Lytle Collection, Louisiana and Lower Mississippi Valley Collection, LSU Libraries, Louisiana State University

Cattle Drive to New Orleans, *ca.* 1861. Shown here are long-horned cattle cross-ing the Amite River by ferry at Port Vincent in Livingston Parish to be driven along the market trail to Springfield, where they would be loaded on steamers bound for New Orleans.
Courtesy Katie Cambre Jenks

Transporting Goods to Market, *ca.* 1880. Dock workers are shown loading goods aboard a river steamer near French Settlement in Livingston Parish for transport to and from the markets at New Orleans.
Courtesy Katie Cambre Jenks

Downtown Baton Rouge, *ca.* 1880
   Courtesy Andrew D. Lytle Collection, Louisiana and Lower Mississippi Valley Collections, LSU Libraries, Louisiana State University

·3·

AN EDUCATION IN VIOLENCE

Liberty's what we're marchin' for, boys, but we ain't gettin' nearer to it.
—*Confederate soldier, Fourth Louisiana Infantry Regiment, marching to Liberty, Miss.*

On a cool spring morning in April, 1862, the Fourth Louisiana Infantry Regiment, C.S.A., received orders to abandon its encampment near Corinth, Mississippi, and move forward in support of the Confederate advance against Union positions in the vicinity of Pittsburg Landing, Tennessee. The rapid advance was occasioned by the Confederate high command's awareness that the evenly matched opponents would not remain that way for long. The approach of a second Union army would give the combined Federal forces the strength to overwhelm by sheer force of numbers the hastily assembled Confederate army. As the Fourth Louisiana approached the front, a Tennessee regiment mistakenly fired on them from the rear, creating temporary disorder in the ranks. Once reformed, the Louisianians, ranging in age from fifteen to forty-eight, received orders to assault a virtually impregnable Union position later named the "Hornets' Nest." Under orders from General Braxton Bragg, they gallantly launched three frontal attacks against the position, sustaining horrific losses. When the day ended, few among the regiment realized that for them this was only the beginning. Of the more than one thousand men who initially enlisted in the regiment, forty survived the war unscathed.[1]

The decimation of the Fourth Louisiana Regiment symbolized the implications of the war for the Florida parishes. Without an awareness of the un-

---

1. Eugene Hunter to Stella Hunter, March 15, 19, 1862, in Hunter-Taylor Family Papers; E. John Ellis Diary, 15–16, in Ellis Family Papers; John S. Kendall, "Recollections of a Confederate Officer," *Louisiana Historical Quarterly*, XXIX (1946), 1055–70; John S. Kendall, ed., "Muster Rolls of the Fourth Louisiana Regiment of Volunteers, Confederate States Army," *Louisiana Historical Quarterly*, XXX (1947), 481–82.

mitigated catastrophe the war represented in seemingly insignificant areas of the South, it is impossible to explain the tumultuous conditions that convulsed these regions in the late nineteenth century. The great struggle between North and South disrupted the process of societal transformation occurring in eastern Louisiana, destroyed the sources of stability, demonstrated the effectiveness of violence, and fostered chaos by creating a sociopolitical vacuum where order, however much the form it took was resented by most, once prevailed. During the course of the war, Federal raiders repeatedly visited the Florida parishes, devastating the area with increasing thoroughness as the combat persisted. In the later stages of the fighting, some Federal troops, frustrated by their inability to subjugate the region effectively, waged a war of terror on the civilian population. In response, exasperated residents initiated guerrilla operations against the Federals. The cruel tactics of the guerrillas proved exceptionally effective and, combined with the equally aggressive actions of the Yankees, served to intensify the horror for southerner and northerner alike. The Florida parishes shared the social and economic disorder the war occasioned in large areas of the South, but unlike many other regions that enjoyed the prompt return of a relative state of equilibrium, in eastern Louisiana the effects were enduring. In the Florida parishes the war promoted a determined contempt for authority and, more importantly, provided a lesson in the effectiveness of violence that would shape developments in eastern Louisiana for the remainder of the century.

The Fourth Louisiana Infantry Regiment, C.S.A., represented one of the first Confederate units recruited in the Florida parishes. Organized in the fall of 1860, this regiment embodied the jubilation that characterized the secession winter in the Florida parishes. The election of a presidential candidate whom many southerners regarded as hostile to their interests provoked the withdrawal of the states of the Deep South. In the same month that Abraham Lincoln secured election as president, the nucleus for the Fourth Louisiana emerged.[2]

Yet many Louisianians lamented the collapse of compromise and the triumph of fanaticism. Large numbers of voters in the Florida parishes had demonstrated their unionist sympathies by supporting the Constitutional Union party and the national Democrats. Headed by John Bell, the Constitutional Unionists carried East Baton Rouge and St. Tammany Parishes out-

2. Greensburg *Imperial*, February 2, 1861; Kendall, ed., "Muster Rolls of the Fourth Louisiana," 483–522.

right. In East Feliciana, the combined vote for Bell and the national Democrat Stephen Douglas exceeded that for southern Democratic candidate John C. Breckinridge. In Washington, West Feliciana, Livingston, and St. Helena, Breckinridge surpassed the combined total of the other candidates. Excepting Washington, the vote in each of these above-mentioned parishes proved close, particularly so in St. Helena, where Breckinridge outpolled the combined total of the other candidates by only twenty-one votes (see Table 6).[3]

The Republican victory stunned Florida parish Unionists, and a transformation of opinion, complete and immediate, occurred. Just days after the election, Charles Johnson noted that all party differences had been cast aside and that preparations were being made for a common defense: "The night after the election all partisanship was thrown away and nothing spoken of but the union. The spirit of disunion ran much higher here than I had supposed." Many equated the triumph of the Lincolnites with an endorsement of the bloody antics of John Brown and his followers, creating extreme fear and resentment among the former Unionists. Shortly after the election the Greensburg *Imperial* fanned the flames of panic with an article titled "A John Brown Raid Anticipated." The piece indicated that a schooner had recently departed Boston loaded with "Redpaths" and other John Brown followers and was presently lurking somewhere off the southern coast, awaiting the opportunity to strike.[4]

TABLE 6. ELECTION RESULTS, 1860

Parish	Bell	Breckinridge	Douglas
East Baton Rouge	569	490	136
East Feliciana	277	377	131
Livingston	249	425	117
St. Helena	292	331	18
St. Tammany	243	164	132
Washington	112	387	5
West Feliciana	188	272	33

Source: Baton Rouge *Daily Advocate*, November 18, 1860

3. Baton Rouge *Daily Advocate*, November 18, 1860; "Report of the Secretary of State on the Census of the State of Louisiana to the General Assembly," *Louisiana Legislative Documents*, 2nd Sess., 1859, pp. 5–7.

4. Charles Johnson to Lou, November 19, 1860, in Charles James Johnson Letters, LLMVC; Greensburg *Imperial*, February 2, 1861.

On January 7, 1861, Louisiana voters selected delegates to a secession convention. As in most other parishes and neighboring southern states, fewer voters in eastern Louisiana cast ballots in the secession election than did in the presidential election two months earlier. Barely 67.0 percent of the presidential vote total was recorded in the plantation parishes, while 65.7 percent of those voting in the piney-woods parishes in November did so during the second election. Although considerable excitement surrounded the vote on secession, no available evidence indicates voter intimidation. The decline in turnout, in fact, conforms to the normal pattern in nonpresidential elections. Many voters likely considered the secession election merely a question of procedure, finding it less critical than the implications associated with the November vote. Still others may have been confused by the complexity of the issue and failed to go to the polls. Except in St. Helena, where voters narrowly supported Breckinridge in November and then cast a majority for cooperation in the later election, the results in the Florida parishes demonstrate consistency between support for Breckinridge and support for immediate secession (see Tables 6 and 7). Moreover, the secession election provides evidence of the impact on piney-woods dwellers of the planters' political rhetoric equating secession with defense of southern honor. Whereas slightly less than 41 percent of voters in the plantation parishes supported immediate secession, a 53 percent majority in the piney woods voted to sever ties with the old Union immediately.[5]

TABLE 7. SECESSION ELECTION RESULTS

Parish	Secession	Cooperation
East Baton Rouge	227	550
East Feliciana	222	405
Livingston	197	140
St. Helena	192	288
St. Tammany	193	221
Washington	276	120
West Feliciana	233	32

Source: New Orleans Daily Delta, March 27–28, 1861

5. New Orleans Daily Delta, March 27, 28, 1861; Charles B. Dew, "Who Won the Secession Election in Louisiana?," Journal of Southern History, XXXVI (1970), 18–32; Baton Rouge Daily Advocate, January 1–7, 1861; Thornton, Politics and Power in a Slave Society, 407–408; Clement Eaton, A History of the Old South: The Emergence of a Reluctant Nation (New York, 1975), 499; Greensburg Imperial, February 2, 1861; Johnson to Lou, November 19, 1860, in Johnson Letters.

Fear, resentment, a sense of honor, and increasing southern nationalism combined to produce spirited celebrations in support of secession. The New Orleans *Daily Picayune* reported that "from every quarter of the state the same enthusiastic cry to arms resounds, and no one can remember the time when such a whirlwind of united patriotic feeling has swept over Louisiana." In one sense, the practically complete collapse of unionism could be traced to the absence of a strong unionist tradition in the Florida parishes. The legacy of their Tory forefathers and of other fugitives from the American system hindered the emergence of a commitment to the American Union among many of the original inhabitants. This tradition remained an issue for many older families into the mid-nineteenth century. A full year before the outbreak of war, the Greensburg *Imperial* noted the absence of patriotic sentiment in the region. The editor marveled at the complete lack of interest among the people for Fourth of July celebrations. Much of the enthusiasm for secession also likely related to the excitement over the process and the southern penchant for a good fight. Most important, though, was the perception created by southern statesmen and the press that northern politicians, speaking for the majority in their region, had insulted the South and now posed a direct threat to their very way of life. The perceived insult to their sense of honor and threat to their independence motivated Louisianians in a way nothing else could.[6]

During the initial months of the crisis, Louisianians flocked to the Confederate army. In the fall of 1861, the Bayou Sara *Ledger* announced that the West Feliciana Parish Court had been suspended as a result of the large numbers who had volunteered for Confederate service. Of 480 total voters, 300 had volunteered for the army, making it impossible to fill jury pools and summon plaintiffs and witnesses. In the same month the Greensburg *Imperial* noted that four companies had already been formed and outfitted from St. Helena alone. Many schools and colleges suspended operations for lack of male pupils. The faculty minutes of Centenary College on October 7, 1861, declared: "Students have all gone to war. College suspended and God help the right." On May 7, 1861, the *Daily Picayune* provided a list of the rates of enlistment for numerous parishes. The article noted that six full companies numbering more than 600 men had been outfitted in East Baton Rouge. Similarly, in East Feliciana 160 out of 400 voters had entered the ranks of the Confederate army.[7]

6. New Orleans *Daily Picayune*, May 7, 1861; Greensburg *Imperial*, June 23, 1860.

7. Bayou Sara *Ledger*, rpr. New Orleans *Daily Picayune*, October 3, 1861; Greensburg *Imperial*, October 12, 1861; Arthur Marvin Shaw, *Centenary College Goes to War in 1861* (Shreveport,

Volunteers for Confederate service continued to enlist at a high rate through the spring of 1862. By the fall of that year, the potential for a slave revolt and the increasing likelihood of a Union invasion in the absence of most of the region's white males dampened, though it did not destroy, the enthusiasm for volunteering. Throughout the war, recruiting rates in the Florida parishes slightly exceeded those of the state as a whole.[8]

Although some recruits complained of the harsh conditions of army life and many families bemoaned the absence of their men, the majority in the Florida parishes enthusiastically supported the war effort in its initial phase. Informed that his regiment would soon depart for the scene of fighting in Kentucky, John G. Smith advised his sister to shed no tears for him if he died, because his death would be "for one of the best causes we have ever experienced." Likewise, on the day he volunteered for Confederate service, young Willie Dixon vowed, "I am willing to shed the *last drop of my blood* on the altar of my *country*, if that could be the means of saving us from northern treachery."[9]

In spite of the celebrations in favor of the South's defiant response to the federal government, the preoccupation with death and the premonitions of suffering epitomized by Dixon's diary exposed another, darker side of the secession hysteria. Like the ancient Spartans who feared their Helots and maintained their society as an armed camp to discourage would-be invaders, the Confederates, handicapped by a potentially dangerous enemy within, now faced war with an immensely powerful foe. If slave rebellions never materialized, the very possibility remained a constant source of anxiety for soldiers in the field as well as for their families at home. The fear of invasion, however, constituted a realistic concern. As the South embarked on the struggle for independence, few residents of the Florida parishes could have dreamed of the horror that awaited them. The brutality of war struck quickly and with vengeance, providing the inhabitants with an unforgettable lesson

La., 1940), 3; New Orleans *Daily Picayune*, May 7, 1861; Howell Carter, *A Cavalryman's Reminiscences of the Civil War* (New Orleans, 1900), 9–10; Frank to Anne, April 13, 1863, in Anonymous Civil War Letters Collection, LLMVC.

8. "Report of the Adjutant General," *Louisiana Legislative Documents*, 1st Sess., 1862, pp. 1–14. The number of volunteer companies formed in the Florida parishes by the spring of 1862 were: East Baton Rouge, 7; East Feliciana, 4; St. Helena, 4; Livingston, 3; West Feliciana, 3; Washington, 2; St. Tammany, 0 (Baton Rouge *Weekly Advocate*, March 2, 1982).

9. John G. Smith to his Sister, March 12, 1862, in D. L. McGehee Papers; Alice Jennings to her Father, October 21, 1862, in Hennen-Jennings Papers; Willie Dixon Diary, March 1, 1862, November 30, December 31, 1861, in Dixon Papers.

in the effectiveness of cruelty and violence. Although far less publicized than events in more crucial theaters of the war, military operations in the Florida parishes left the region devastated and the residents with an enduring legacy of bitterness.[10]

Compared to the military significance of Richmond, Charleston, Wilmington, or New Orleans, the Florida parishes pale. Like many areas in the interior South, though, eastern Louisiana constituted a region that Union strategists considered essential to their plan of breaking both the South's ability and will to fight and that, unfortunately, the Confederacy's policy of cordon defense left vulnerable. The Florida parishes contained many diverse resources that collectively heightened its strategic significance. Most obvious was the region's proximity to New Orleans, which meant that any movement against the Crescent City would necessitate close observation of the north shore of Lake Pontchartrain. Throughout the war both armies would regard the area as a potential staging and collecting point for any effort designed to recapture the great river port. Eastern Louisiana's proximity to the Mississippi River also contributed to its military significance. Failure to gain command of the fertile bluffs along the Mississippi characterizing the Florida parishes would negate a central aspect of Union grand strategy. Baton Rouge, Louisiana's capital since 1849, and the Confederate bastion at Port Hudson guaranteed particular Union interest. As a result, constant fighting permeated the area throughout the war.

The river and the lakeshore region were not the only strategically significant territory in the Florida parishes. The vast herds of livestock and the hundreds of farms located in the piney woods remained important as a source of food production—an importance that increased as the war dragged on. As the blockade increasingly denied necessities to the residents, considerable industry emerged primarily along the railroad. Several machine shops, initially developed to maintain the railroad, also produced heavy industrial products for the Confederate army. At least two shoe factories arose to produce brogans for the local population and the army. Several tanneries and at least one gun factory also were established in the region.[11] In addition to food

10. Nannie C. to Cornelia Stewart, April, 1864, in Albert Batchelor Papers, LLMVC; Eugene Hunter to Stella Hunter, January 1, 1862, in Hunter-Taylor Family Papers; Mary Wilkinson to Micajah Wilkinson, August 1, November 9, 1862, in Micajah Wilkinson Papers, LLMVC; and Mrs. R. J. Causey to R. J. Causey, November 19, 1863, in R. J. Causey Correspondence, LLMVC, all provide examples of the lingering fear of a possible slave revolt.

11. Clinton-Port Hudson Railroad Company Records, Minute Book I, 1852–69, pp. 26–211; New Orleans Daily Picayune, February 11, 1862; J. G. Lea to Lemanda Lea, October 9,

and manufactured goods, the overwhelming support for the Confederacy demonstrated by the local residents made the piney woods an important source of reliable manpower. Most important, the New Orleans-Jackson Railroad underscored the importance of men and material by enabling both to be transported efficiently.

Finally, the presence of the largest training base in the Deep South dramatically increased the military significance of the piney woods of the Florida parishes. Initially, masses of volunteers traveled to Camp Walker near New Orleans to be mustered into Confederate service. In an effort to create a permanent training base in a more healthful region free of the problems associated with the immediate vicinity of New Orleans, the adjutant general's office selected a sight near Tangipahoa Station in St. Helena Parish. The new location contained abundant available land for training, plenty of fresh water, and easy access to the New Orleans-Jackson Railroad. In May, 1861, the first Confederate troops arrived at the newly established base, appropriately named Camp Moore in honor of Louisiana's secession governor. During the course of the war, thousands of troops from Louisiana, Mississippi, and Arkansas passed through the camp on their way to distant theaters of the war.[12]

Containing Union forces and protecting the residents and resources of the Florida parishes would be an overwhelming challenge for Confederate troops. Part of the difficulty involved defending a region surrounded by water and penetrated by numerous navigable streams without a navy. The effort to secure the region against an enemy possessing irresistible naval power and seemingly limitless assets eventually strained Confederate resources to the breaking point. In their hour of despair, though, the residents proved resourceful, learning to rely on themselves rather than government. This lesson, internalized by many, would contribute directly to popular attitudes in the late nineteenth century.

The celebration of independence and the excitement over the war continued unabated in the Florida parishes until the spring of 1862, when the consequences of their bold endeavor first became apparent. In April, 1862, a two-pronged catastrophe, from north and south, befell the western Confederacy. The feared invasion on the northern front necessitated the transfer of all

1862, in Lemanda Lea Papers, LLMVC; Map of the Line of the New Orleans-Jackson Railroad; circa 1861, in Illinois Central Railroad Collection.

12. Powell Casey, *The Story of Camp Moore* (New Orleans, 1985), 5–22; *The War of the Rebellion: A Compilation of the Official Records of the Union and Confederate Armies* (130 vols.; Washington, D.C., 1880–1901), Ser. I, Vol. VI, 594 (hereinafter cited as *OR*, and unless otherwise indicated, all citations are to Series I).

available manpower from the lower Mississippi northward in an effort to check the Union advance. The ensuing Battle of Shiloh resulted in heavy losses and particularly severe casualties for units recruited in the Florida parishes, which for the first time brought the bloody cost home. Despite the heavy casualties the Federal army remained unbroken and continued to menace the lower Mississippi valley from the north, giving residents no relief from the burdensome fear of invasion.

Unlike the northern threat, the menace from the south came unexpectedly. In late April, 1862, a powerful Federal fleet passed the forts on the lower Mississippi and forced the capitulation of New Orleans. The city's fall deprived Louisiana and southwestern Mississippi of their principal market and effectively sealed the region off from contact with the outside world. Suddenly the residents of the Florida parishes faced the threat of imminent invasion on two fronts and, for the first time, the threat of starvation. As the remnants of Confederate general Mansfield Lovell's tiny force streamed north from New Orleans to Camp Moore, they brought despair and apprehension with them. Watching the trains unload their melancholy cargoes near her home in Tangipahoa, Louisiana, Abigail Amacker described the depression prevailing in the area: "The Federals have taken New Orleans, the hour seems very dark for us, God grant we may have peace shortly. A great many soldiers have come and are coming into this neighborhood, we fear starvation just now more than the Lincolnites." A few days later she worried about the worsening conditions: "The suffering, the deaths in camp are awful, I pray God we may have peace speedily, on any terms. To be subjugated to be slaves would not be worse than this. Starvation stares us in the face and defeat too."[13]

Whether the Yankees realized that eastern Louisiana and southwestern Mississippi were virtually undefended remains unclear. What is certain is that in response to Richmond's call for troops to support operations in Virginia and Tennessee, the Florida parishes and environs had been literally denuded of regular Confederate forces. General Lovell, commander of the defenses about New Orleans, strenuously objected to the war department's neglect of Louisiana. He warned that to abandon Louisiana entirely "would have a very bad moral effect upon the state," promoting disaffection and encouraging residents to open a cotton trade with the enemy. Rebuffed in his pleas to the war department, Lovell proposed a solution that Governor Thomas Moore

---

13. OR, Vol. VI, 624; Abigail Means Kent Amacker Diary, April 26, May 9, 1862, in Amacker Papers; Sister to Edward, May 4, 1862, in John C. Burruss Papers, LLMVC.

heartily endorsed. The plan called for the creation of at least five regiments of partisan rangers to be armed and commissioned by the Confederate government. The purpose of this irregular force would be to "contain the enemy in New Orleans and protect the state from his ravages." Neither Moore nor Lovell could have realized the ramifications the introduction of irregular forces in eastern Louisiana would have on the region's postwar development.[14]

Partisan warfare evoked mixed emotions among civilians and military men alike. Many citizens regarded partisan rangers, or partisans, as little more than undisciplined outlaws who often provoked brutal retaliation for their actions yet offered little realistic protection to the civilian population. Military men generally condemned partisans as guerrillas whose uncontrolled activities accomplished little other than keeping qualified soldiers out of the regular army.

Lovell, however, presented a strong case in favor of partisan operations in eastern Louisiana, bluntly requesting permission to organize "guerrilla parties with authority to act as this is the only available force in the swamps of Louisiana." His appeal was strengthened by Governor Moore's demand that Louisiana be divided into two departments separated by the river. Moore's insistence that the commands be separated, with an emphasis on the defense of the western part of the state in order to maintain the supplies of beef coming from Texas, reinforced the need for Lovell's partisans east of the river. In May, 1862, responding for the war department, General Robert E. Lee approved the use of irregular forces in eastern Louisiana.[15]

After securing New Orleans the Federals wasted little time in expanding their control of the surrounding region. A portion of the Federal fleet rapidly steamed north to capture Baton Rouge and intimidate the surrounding area. When the fleet dropped anchor off the capital city, a melancholy crowd gathered to observe the might of the invader. While the ships awaited the city's surrender, a group of horsemen fired on a longboat approaching the shore. In response and without warning, the fleet intensively shelled the town. Astonished by the severity of the Federal response, women and children ran shrieking through the streets, seeking safety from the bombardment beyond the bluffs of the river. Horrified by the results, young Sara Morgan mockingly re-

14. OR, Vol. VI, 652–53, 885–90, Vol. LIII, 805.

15. OR, Ser. IV, Vol. I, 395; Jackson, Miss., Mississippian, February 27, 1863; Virgil Jones, Gray Ghosts and Rebel Raiders (New York, 1956), vii–ix; John D. Winters, The Civil War in Louisiana (Baton Rouge, 1963), 153; OR, Vol. VI, 652–53, 885, 889–90, Vol. LIII, 805.

torted, "Hurrah for the illustrious [Admiral David] Farragut, the Woman Killer!!!"[16]

Hoping to exploit the demoralized condition of the local residents and the few Confederate troops in the area, the Federals moved rapidly to apply irresistible pressure on the Florida parishes. These operations targeted particularly the destruction of Camp Moore and the demolition of the New Orleans-Jackson Railroad and aimed generally at the subjugation of the region. To further these goals General Benjamin Butler, commanding the department, ordered General Thomas Williams, in charge at Baton Rouge, to mount a series of demonstrations against Camp Moore. Butler's instructions directed Williams to "punish with the last severity every guerrilla attack and burn all the property of every guerrilla found murdering your soldiers."[17]

During the summer of 1862, Williams launched a series of probing raids into the interior to test Confederate strength and to intimidate the population. On June 7, 1862, the Thirtieth Massachusetts Regiment departed on a mission to capture several suspected "guerrillas," a term universally applied to all Confederate forces operating in the area. The raiders failed in their effort to capture any Confederate forces, but they did lay waste several plantations belonging to prominent Confederate sympathizers. At each plantation all buildings and fences, excepting the slave quarters, were burned, the livestock stolen, and ornamental trees cut down. The commanding officer reported on the success of his endeavor: "I burnt every building on the estate of these once beautiful plantations, except such as were required to cover the negroes left behind. . . . In fact I left nothing but the blackened chimneys as a monument to the folly and villainy of its guerrilla owner."[18]

Applauding this destructive raid, Butler urged Williams to intimidate the local population rapidly so as to ensure the security of the garrison at Baton Rouge. In the last week of June, 1862, Williams dispatched another raiding party in the direction of Camp Moore. At Williams Bridge, across the Amite River near Greensburg, the raiders encountered the camp of Vernon Terrell's Mississippi Cavalry, and a sharp skirmish ensued. The surprised Mississippians initially panicked and fled, but regaining their composure, they returned

16. OR, Vol. XV, 22, 122–23; Joseph Corkern to Jeptha McKinney, August 27, 1862, in McKinney Papers; Sara Morgan Dawson, A Confederate Girl's Diary (New York, 1913), 40–55; Celine F. Garcia, Celine Remembering Louisiana, 1850–1871, ed. Patrick Geary (Athens, Ga., 1987), 69–71; Winters, Civil War in Louisiana, 104.

17. OR, Vol. XV, 24–25.

18. OR, Vol. XV, 19–21.

and fired on the Yankees from the woods. When the main body of Union cavalry came up, a determined charge scattered the rebels, who left several dead and wounded and over a dozen prisoners. After destroying the enemy camp, the Federals proceeded back toward Baton Rouge with their loot and prisoners, but the firing had alerted local residents to the presence of the raiders, and the alarm quickly spread through the piney woods. At a point eighteen miles from Baton Rouge, Confederate cavalrymen ambushed the column at a bend in the road, inflicting six casualties and recovering most of the prisoners. The results of this ambush provided an early example of the importance of citizen involvement to Confederate success in the region.[19]

To force the Confederates to spread thin their meager resources, Union forces probed Confederate defenses at Pass Manchac and along the north shore of Lake Pontchartrain in coordination with the raids from Baton Rouge. The Union plan to put pressure on multiple locations in the Florida parishes and thereby to wear down Confederate resistance and demoralize the civilian population proved quite successful at first. Through the summer of 1862, Union forces kept constant pressure on the north shore of the lake and repeatedly raided the interior of the Florida parishes. From July 25 to August 2, 1862, a Union raiding party backed by gunboats menaced the north shore and environs. The raiders hit all of the villages along the north shore between the Tchefuncte and Pearl Rivers, skirmishing with Confederate partisans and destroying provisions. During the expedition the Federals expressed surprise at the level of destitution existing among the people. Major Frank Peck, commanding the operation, reported that "in many places flour had not been seen for months, the poorer classes subsisting almost entirely upon the meanest quality of corn meal." The raid had exposed a grim reality. Barely one year into the war, suffering and privation already prevailed in large areas of the Florida parishes and southwestern Mississippi.[20]

The frequent raids continued relentlessly into the summer of 1862, deeply distressing civilians and local soldiers away in other theaters of the war who received accounts in letters from home. The increasing ease with which the Federals moved about the territory had a demoralizing effect; many residents felt neglected by the Confederate government. N. R. Jennings loudly denounced the government's failure to defend the Florida parishes: "Our region

19. OR, Vol. XV, 36; Dunbar Rowland, *Military History of Mississippi, 1803–1898* (Spartanburg, S.C., 1978), 409.
20. OR, Vol. XV, 111, 124; Diary of Eli Capell, April 27, November 30, 1862, in Capell Papers.

of the country has literally been cursed and destroyed by the incompetence, ignorance, and arrogance of the military commanders placed over us. [Daniel] Ruggles and Jeff Thompson have only a few guerrilla bands to protect the entire region." Governor Moore reminded the Confederate government of the contributions that Louisianians were making to the war effort. He initially demanded, then later pleaded, for the general government to make a stronger commitment to Louisiana. Citizens also directly petitioned military authorities for protection from the invader. In July, 1862, a committee of prominent citizens from the Felicianas and East Baton Rouge sent a petition to General Daniel Ruggles, commander of Confederate troops in the Florida parishes. The petition noted that the region had been stripped of men as a result of the massive outpouring of support for the Confederate army. Moreover, Florida-parish farmers, the petition alleged, had followed government instructions and reduced their cotton acreage while tripling their output of corn and in general had "manifested a willingness to sacrifice all, even life itself, to advance the common cause." The statement continued: "All is at the mercy of an enemy greedy for destruction, unless they are met by an adequate force. . . . This aid we think is due to so loyal a population if it can be afforded consistently with the general interests of the service."[21]

Seemingly abandoned by their protectors, vulnerable to the depredations of the enemy and facing starvation, the residents of the Florida parishes in the summer of 1862 could have easily given up the game. But the ferocity of the Federal campaign of subjugation ensured that they would not. Although incidents of kindly behavior on the part of the Federals occurred, overwhelmingly the Yankees extended the torch rather than the olive branch to their former brethren. Rather than building on the shattered remnants of unionism in the area and alleviating the exhausted and demoralized condition of the local populace, the Federals' iron-fisted policy encouraged the inhabitants to resist the invader. An exasperated Christian Koch later declared that the Federals seemed completely unwilling to reconcile the people. For the Union it was an opportunity lost, and for those involved, both northern and southern, it meant continuation of the suffering.[22]

21. John Ellis to his Mother [Mrs. T. E. Ellis], June 9, 1862, in Ellis Family Papers; W. Greene Raoul to his Father [Gaston Raoul], June 28, 1862, in W. Greene Raoul Papers, LLMVC; N. R. Jennings to Messrs. Lusher and Davidson, n.d. [1863], in Hennen-Jennings Papers; OR, Vol. XV, 733–36, 740–41, 777–78.
22. Christian Koch to Annette Koch, September 1, 1864, in Christian Koch Papers, LLMVC.

The aggressive policy of Union troops in eastern Louisiana touched both soldier and civilian alike. Scores of citizens were seized by Federal troops as potential Confederate supporters, or as hostages, and were whisked away to Federal prison camps without a word of notice to their families. Mortified by his inability to contain the marauding of the enemy, Lieutenant Colonel J. H. Wingfield wrote his commanding officer, "The depredations committed by the enemy are of the most shameful character on private property and on the persons of our fellow-citizens and helpless women and children." The wanton destruction committed by many of their own troops served to outrage some Federal officers who possessed the foresight to recognize that a people repeatedly subjected to depredations must resist. General Thomas Williams, commanding at Baton Rouge, complained to the Union high command about the constant pillaging committed by the Wisconsin and Michigan regiments under his command. "These regiments, officers and men appear to be wholly destitute of moral sense and I believe that they believe in the face of all remonstrances that they regard pillaging not only as a right in itself but a soldierly accomplishment."[23]

Even though many recognized that war is war, the civilian population nevertheless expressed dismay at the escalating destruction. Anxiously commenting on the frequent Yankee raids near her home, Anna Jennings asserted, "The greatest outrages are committed throughout the country and we tremble as to our fate." Kate Burruss described to her soldier-brother the anxiety prevailing: "We hear of great suffering in many places from the ravages of our dreadful enemies, in this sense we have been blest. One lady near Clinton had on Saturday night all that one could wish, food, carriages, horses, elegant furniture, and on the next Monday she and her family were starving, the yankees have taken everything from her and her children." Jane McCausland Chinn recalled the columns of smoke created by burning houses "as far as we could see," which identified the route taken by Federal soldiers. Horrified by the ruthlessness of some Union troops, Mary A. Stratton, a private tutor from Connecticut, embraced the cause of the South. Stratton wrote one of her former pupils, "I informed my fiancee [a Federal officer] that I would return home, but after seeing the horror Federal soldiers have wreaked upon the South I could not marry him unless he resigned." The growing perception that Union forces would likely destroy everything they encountered stiffened resistance in the Florida parishes and increased de-

23. OR, Vol. XV, 22–23, 80, 122–23, 778, 787, 1119.

mands that the Confederate government initiate offensive operations in the area. Reports concerning the actions of General Butler, Union commander at New Orleans, further mobilized support both for the Confederacy and for retaliatory operations against the Yankees.[24]

Butler's actions in New Orleans and the depredations committed by the troops under his command in the Florida parishes attracted the attention of Confederate authorities eager to stem disaffection in that region and to secure their base of operations for the planned recapture of New Orleans. In late July, 1862, General John C. Breckinridge arrived at Camp Moore at the head of a small army. He had orders to destroy the Union force at Baton Rouge, capture the town, and, if possible, move against New Orleans. Complete success eluded Breckinridge, but he noted some positive results from the effort. In his report Breckinridge bemoaned the striking contrast between the "presence of every comfort, even luxury," found in the encampments of the enemy and his own shoeless and poorly fed troops. Yet, he boasted, his troops had fought enthusiastically, many contesting the order to withdraw despite the severity of the casualties, and the citizens of the surrounding country had exhibited the "warmest patriotism" and provided generous assistance to his army. If neither side could declare outright victory, Breckinridge claimed the strength of his effort had taken pressure off the badly abused surrounding countryside. The Confederates placed a tight picket line around Baton Rouge with orders to harass the enemy relentlessly. Constant probing of the defenses helped convince the Federals that the city was untenable, resulting in their evacuation of the area a few days later. Before departing, the Yankees looted the city, burned large portions of it, and released all the convicts from the state penitentiary. Several warships then steamed up the river and burned the village of Bayou Sara. After restoring order in the city and

24. Ibid.; Anna Jennings to Mr. Odel, June 23, 1862, N. R. Jennings to his Wife, May 24, 1863, both in Hennen-Jennings Papers; Kate Burruss to Edward Burruss, May 8, 1862, M. A. Stratton to Edward Burruss, May 29, 1864, both in Burruss Papers; Emma Lay Lane to her Brother Willie, December 13, 1862, in John Q. Anderson Papers, LLMVC; Sara Dawson, *Confederate Girl's Diary*, 146, 168–85; W. M. Barrow to his Aunt Anna, September 6, 1862, in Barrow Family Papers; Amacker Diary, September 2, 1862, in Amacker Papers; Dixon Diary, August 28, 1862, May 24, 1863, in Dixon Papers; Mary E. Taylor Diary, June 19, 1862, in Hunter-Taylor Family Papers; Zwei Bericht von New Orleans, aus F. N. Freudenthal, Konsul, Hessen-Brunswick, aus New Orleans, in File No. 3818, Book No. 210, pp. 85–86, Hessen-Nassau Hauptstadt Archiven, Wiesbaden, Germany.

containing the fires, Breckinridge placed General Ruggles in charge of fortifying the bluffs at Port Hudson above Baton Rouge.[25]

The operations about Baton Rouge secured for the residents of the Florida parishes a temporary respite from the fighting. This brief interlude in the fall of 1862 provided farmers with an opportunity to harvest their crops and tend to their personal affairs virtually unmolested. Moreover, work could continue on the Confederate stronghold at Port Hudson. But reduced Federal pressure exposed some major problems for Confederate authorities in the area—problems resulting primarily from the effects of the blockade. Although supplies of beef and corn remained adequate to sustain the population through the winter, certain staple commodities and medicines had already reached critical shortage levels. In particular, the shortage of salt had reached crisis proportions, for unlike coffee and other luxury items, salt constituted an absolute necessity, especially for the preservation of meat. By the winter of 1862 local residents had exhausted their supplies, and the popular process of sifting the dirt of smokehouse floors produced but a meager return. This procedure involved digging up the floor of a smokehouse, where meat had been salted for years, and boiling the dirt in water. After a few hours over a heavy fire, the salt-saturated water was drained off and allowed to evaporate, revealing the crystalline deposits. The residents' inability to secure enough salt from such sources of last resort precipitated a crisis in the territory.[26]

The emergency reached such proportions that in December, 1862, Confederate collector F. H. Hatch, based at Tangipahoa, petitioned Confederate secretary of war James A. Seddon to allow local residents to barter with the enemy for salt. Some citizens embarked on perilous journeys to western Louisiana or to the evaporation vats near Mobile to secure the precious com-

25. OR, Vol. XV, 34, 778, 74–83, 1124; T. G. Lea to Lemanda Lea, August 18, 1862, in Lea Papers; Amacker Diary, August 4, 7, 12, 1862, in Amacker Papers; Kendall, "Recollections of a Confederate Officer," 1080–90; OR, Vol. XV, 76–81, 797, 129–31; Amacker Diary, September 2, 1862, in Amacker Papers; Frank to Anne, April 13, 1863, in Anonymous Civil War Letters Collection; Dixon Diary, August 28, 1862, in Dixon Papers; Barrow to Aunt Anna, September 6, 1862, in Barrow Family Papers; Edward Bacon, Among the Cotton Thieves (Detroit, 1867), 31; Sara Dawson, Confederate Girl's Diary, 168–85, 221.

26. F. P. Wall to her Sister, n.d., in McKinney Papers; Amite City News Digest, February 5, 1976; OR, Vol. XV, 242, 602–603, 797; Eugene Hunter to Stella Hunter, October 14, 1863, in Hunter-Taylor Family Papers; John Ball to Joel Stokes, February 13, 1863, in Stokes Papers; Magnolia, Miss., Grand Trunk, October 11, 1862; Ella Lonn, Salt as a Factor in the Confederacy (Birmingham, Ala., 1965), 41.

modity. On one such expedition, Annabelle Pitkins left Washington Parish
headed for Mobile, accompanied by her nine-year-old son and E. J. Allen,
who had lost both an arm and a leg in the Battle of Shiloh. Accosted by
Union cavalry near Madisonville, she pleaded that she was merely returning
home with her husband, who had been wounded in the fighting near Baton
Rouge. When Federal officers suspiciously examined Allen's neatly healed
wounds, Pitkins praised the work of Admiral Farragut's private surgeon, who,
she claimed, had removed the shattered limbs on a ship in the Mississippi. To
protect her precious cargo from the Yankees, who would steal it, and from
Confederate cavalry, who would confiscate a part of it, Pitkins ingeniously
fashioned in her wagon a false bottom large enough to hold one thousand
pounds of salt. After taking on a large supply of salt near Mobile, she returned
by a northerly route via Meridian, Mississippi, and delivered her cargo to
friends and neighbors. Her arduous journey required approximately six weeks.
Although this supply temporarily relieved the suffering of a few individuals,
the salt crisis continued to escalate throughout the war.[27]

The acute shortage of staples afflicting the South as early as the fall of
1862 created severe distress among the population and compounded the
problems facing Confederate authorities. The inability to maintain supplies
of basic necessities revealed the rashness and seeming lack of foresight involved in the secession effort. Providing essential commodities, however,
proved to be only a part of the crisis confronting Confederate authorities on
the home front. The immediate necessity of fielding armies to repel invasion
on numerous fronts severely strained the existing legal system in the Florida
parishes. With the vast majority of men under arms, inadequate resources remained to sustain the prewar legal structure. As a result, Confederate commanders were forced to employ their limited means to maintain a semblance
of civil discipline. In the critical weeks before the late summer fighting
around Baton Rouge and Ponchatoula, Confederate authorities reluctantly
dispatched a cavalry detachment to seek out increasingly aggressive criminal
elements in lower Livingston Parish, where civil authority had ceased to
function.[28]

27. OR, Ser. IV, Vol. II, 242; Mrs. R. J. Causey to R. J. Causey, October 14, 1863, in Causey
Correspondence; Eugene Hunter to Stella Hunter, October 13, 1863, in Hunter-Taylor Family
Papers; Mary Wilkinson to Micajah Wilkinson, August 1, 1862, in Wilkinson Papers; Magnolia
Grand Trunk, October 11, 1862; Amite City News Digest, February 5, 1976.
28. Bayou Sara Ledger, rpr. New Orleans Daily Picayune, October 3, 1861; OR, Vol. XV, 120.

During the spring and summer of 1862, the Amite River swamplands in lower Livingston and Ascension Parishes had attracted criminal elements who exploited the absence of civil authority. Repeated appeals to the military authorities in nearby Ponchatoula finally received a reply following the brutal robbery and murder of two Confederate soldiers near Springfield. The command considered an ardent military response to be warranted by the presence of one Adolph Dies, "a notorious desperado who had proclaimed himself a Lincolnite and with a supposed fifteen men had threatened citizens in the parish." In reality, the purpose of the expedition was to contain lawlessness in the Amite River region and to arrest several fugitives from civil justice.

Accordingly, Lieutenant Alfred Bradley proceeded to Springfield at the head of a detachment of Caruthers' Sharpshooters, C.S.A. Bradley made several arrests, confiscated a few weapons, and, as a bonus, killed Dies and captured a few of his associates. Although this operation may have afforded some relief to the citizens of the territory, the necessity of dispatching troops to police civilians deprived the Confederate military of limited cavalry resources at the height of the campaign season. What was even more significant, growing criminal activity highlighted the emergence of an aggressive contempt for authority that would intensify rather than diminish with the cessation of hostilities between North and South.[29]

The spring of 1863 brought with it renewed Federal thrusts into the Florida parishes. In preparation for operations against Port Hudson, in December, 1862, Union forces reoccupied the ruins of Baton Rouge. By the end of December, General Nathaniel Banks, who had replaced the controversial Butler as commander of the Union Department of the Gulf, had forty thousand troops in Louisiana. In contrast to the massive Federal buildup, Confederate troops had been stripped from the Florida parishes to support other theaters of the war, excepting the six thousand men concentrated about Port Hudson and a few hundred assigned to protect the New Orleans-Jackson Railroad.[30] Concerned that the railroad would allow Confederate troops to be transferred rapidly from Mississippi to Louisiana to reinforce Port Hudson or to threaten an attack on New Orleans, Union planners determined to destroy it. The spring offensive operations would thus begin with an attack on the Confederate base at Ponchatoula.

29. OR, Vol. XV, 120–21.

30. John Durnin to Ann Durnin, September 25, 1862, in Durnin Papers; Sara Dawson, Confederate Girl's Diary, 221; Winters, Civil War in Louisiana, 153, 157, 167.

On March 21, 1863, a two-pronged attack was launched against Poncha-toula. After driving off Confederate skirmishers, the Federals entered the town. The sleepy village had no premonition of the horror that would befall it that day. What resulted constituted an orgy of pillage and destruction. Pan-icked women and children fled the village as the Federals, led by their com-manding officer, Colonel Thomas Clark, looted and destroyed every building they encountered. As he observed the wanton destruction and abuse of citi-zens, Federal colonel Edward Bacon noted that the legendary savagery of the Turks could not have been more thorough. Bacon reflected that the entire command "seemed transfigured by the evil spirits that possess them, and ap-peared more like devils of theft and pillage than like mortal men."[31]

The destruction of Ponchatoula continued unabated through the night. At least one civilian was murdered while attempting to negotiate the protection of his property. Lacking the strength to drive the Federals from the village, the Confederates contented themselves with taking up a defensive position before the Cate Shoe Factory, near present-day Hammond. When reinforcements ar-rived in the afternoon, the Confederates drove the more numerous Federals from the town so quickly that they were forced to torch much of their loot along with most of the town. Behind them remained a deeply embittered pop-ulace whose perception of the war and moral responsibility had received a sharp lesson from the enemy. The lessons learned from the war, though, were only beginning. Hatred for the Yankees would remain for generations, and the lessons in brutality would determine the course of social development through the end of the century. A Federal officer who attempted under flag of truce to return some Masonic jewels looted by his troops described the mood prevail-ing among the citizens and soldiers at Ponchatoula: "They would hardly treat me civilly; they are terribly enraged against us."[32]

In the spring of 1863, Ponchatoula was not the only community to be-come an unfortunate victim of the war. The entire region would find itself squarely in the course of a violent storm. As the increasing might of Federal arms slowly overwhelmed the Confederates, increasing distress overcame the population. During the late spring of 1863, Union troops briefly captured and destroyed much of Clinton, wreaking havoc among the once-stately planta-

31. OR, Vol. XV, 280–91; Bacon, *Among the Cotton Thieves*, 64–86, 114–18; Jackson, Miss., *Daily Southern Crisis*, March 30, 1863.

32. OR, Vol. XV, 284–91; Bacon, *Among the Cotton Thieves*, 64–84; Winters, *Civil War in Louisiana*, 220; Jackson *Daily Southern Crisis*, March 30, 1863.

tions in the area. The efforts of Confederate cavalry and of the citizens who joined them proved able to delay, but not prevent, repeated Federal visits to Clinton and nearby Jackson. What was more significant, in May, 1863, a powerful combined force of cavalry and infantry exploited the Confederates' preoccupation with containing the Federals below Ponchatoula by attacking the railroad above that point. The raiding force destroyed the Cate Shoe Factory and burned the leather tannery near Tickfaw. After driving off a small body of Confederate cavalry and citizens who contested their advance at Independence, the Yankees destroyed the railroad's car manufacturing plant, along with numerous gun carriages. The depots and all structures housing supplies were burned at both Independence and Amite City, and the railroad devastated as far north as Tangipahoa. Although the destruction greatly affected the Confederate war effort in the area, the greatest crisis befell the already-suffering residents: while approaching and departing the area, the raiders burned homes, destroyed fences, slaughtered livestock, and generally "greatly abused the citizens." Other than a few scattered pickets and a handful of partisans deployed in conjunction with elements of Terrell's Mississippi Cavalry, no significant Confederate forces remained in the area to contest the Union marauding. Coordinated pressure from numerous points at the same time allowed the Federals to employ their superior resources and to stretch Confederate defenses beyond the breaking point. By the spring of 1863, the Federals had developed a strategy that worked, and for the luckless residents, the suffering had only begun.[33]

In addition to the raids from Baton Rouge and assaults on the now-inconsequential base at Ponchatoula, the scattered Confederate forces in the region were thrown into confusion by an unexpected raid originating in Tennessee. On April 17, 1863, Colonel B. H. Grierson's Sixth and Seventh Illinois Cavalry and Second Iowa Cavalry departed La Grange, Tennessee, with instructions to destroy the length of the New Orleans-Jackson Railroad and to disrupt enemy supply lines while in route to New Orleans. Grierson proceeded through the state of Mississippi, destroying the railroad and supply depots but generally avoiding the destruction of private property. He noted in his report that at several towns along the way, groups of armed citizens had contested his advance, inflicting a few casualties on his troops. Yet rather than burning their towns or arresting those who resisted, Grierson instead

33. Taylor Diary, April 29–30, May 14, May 24, June 3–9, 1863, in Hunter-Taylor Family Papers; OR, Vol. XV, 406–409, Vol. XXVI, Pt. 1, p. 9.

disarmed the citizens, reassured them of the honorable nature of his troops and mission, and ordered that private property be respected. His action had a dramatic impact on the citizens. Grierson cited numerous incidents in which local residents asserted that they "had been grossly deceived as to our real character." He continued, "I mention this as a sample of the feeling which exists, and the good effect which our presence produced among the people in the country through which we passed." Unlike the troops wantonly destroying people and property in the Florida parishes, Grierson applied the stick to government property and offered the carrot to the citizens. This policy, in his view, did far more to encourage respect for the United States government among the citizens than did burning the roofs above their heads. Unlike regions of central and eastern Mississippi, where support for the secession effort dwindled into disaffection, resistance to the invader continued in eastern Louisiana to the end, proving Grierson's point.[34] The contrast between Union activities in eastern Louisiana and those in parts of southwestern Mississippi constitutes an important element in the focal point of this study. Regions where federal policy had been mild during the war, Grierson's raid being a case in point, experienced much less violence and instability in the postwar period.

Grierson's destruction of the railroad and rebel supply depots caused a crisis for Confederate authorities. Frantic efforts to capture his command failed, largely because of misinformation spread by scouts he dispatched in civilian clothing. Informed that a sizable Confederate force awaited them at Osyka, Mississippi, Grierson abandoned the route to New Orleans and headed for Baton Rouge. Traveling rapidly, his cavalry overwhelmed a small contingent of the Ninth Louisiana Partisan Rangers, who enthusiastically opposed his crossing of the Tickfaw River at Walls Bridge. Following this encounter, the Union raiders proceeded on to the safety of Baton Rouge, virtually unmolested. Grierson's raid successfully disrupted rebel communications, destroyed large stockpiles of supplies, and temporarily disabled considerable sections of the railroad. Bemoaning the success of the raid, Abigail Amacker commented, "It seems we have come to a crisis in our revolution and we certainly cannot remain in the present state much longer." Most important, Grierson had exposed Confederate weakness in the Florida parishes—a weakness that guaranteed increasing Federal visits to the area.[35]

34. OR, Vol. XXIV, Pt. 1, pp. 522–29.
35. OR, Vol. XXIV, Pt. 1, pp. 523–33, 539–40, 547–49; Capell Diary, May 3, 1863, in Capell Papers; Amacker Diary, May 22, 1863, in Amacker Papers; Andrew Booth, *Records of*

As the maneuvers that culminated in the siege of Port Hudson began in the spring of 1863, Union planners determined to employ their expected victory as a catalyst to subjugate all of eastern Louisiana and southwestern Mississippi. Accordingly, Union forces intensified their efforts to interdict the trade in foodstuffs and material between the lakeshore region and the Mississippi Gulf Coast. The Federals made no secret of their intention to disrupt all Confederate intercourse and to starve the rebels into submission, as outlined in General Orders, Number 33. Although the Confederates enjoyed some success in operations about Lake Maurepas, such as the destruction of the ironclad gunboat *Barataria*, the Federals slowly overwhelmed the territory. By the summer of 1863, the situation for many residents had become unbearable. Denied access to their primary market at New Orleans, subjected to destructive Union raids, and flooded with hundreds of refugees ordered out of New Orleans after being enrolled as registered enemies of the United States, the region groaned under the burden of war.[36]

The transformation of the region had been dramatic. On the eve of the conflict in 1860, Edward Stewart, overseer on a lower Livingston Parish plantation, wrote his employer of the seemingly limitless harvest of foodstuffs collected on the plantation. Two years later, facing starvation, Stewart complained that the sixteen refugees he harbored had overtaxed his supply of provisions. With little hope of improving conditions, Stewart notified his employer, John Gurley, that he must now refuse assistance to everyone, including close family friends. Concerning the arrival of yet another boatload of refugees on the north shore, Annette Koch fretted to her husband about their fate: "What will become of all these people that have come to this poor part of the country, there was nothing to eat for them that was already here, and these that come bring nothing with them, they will be sure to starve. Oh the misery of this war when will it cease."[37]

Louisiana Confederate Soldiers and Louisiana Confederate Commands (3 vols.; Spartanburg, S.C., 1984), II, 572.

36. OR, Vol. XLI, Pt. 2, p. 804, Vol. XV, 291; Reminiscences of Jane McCausland Chinn, "The Burning of the Barns," Typescript, LLMVC; Provost Marshall's statement describing registered enemies of the United States, October 4, 1862, in Gurley Papers; John Bettersworth, *Confederate Mississippi: The People and Policies of a Cotton State in Wartime* (Baton Rouge, 1943), 203; *Civil War Naval Chronology, 1861–1865* (Washington, D.C., 1966), Pt. 6, pp. 202–203. James E. Bradley Diary, October 13, 24, 1862, indicates heavy concentrations of refugees from New Orleans in the Amite City and Arcola Station area (James E. Bradley and Family Papers, LLMVC).

37. Edward Stewart to John Gurley, January 18, 1860, May 1, 1862, in Gurley Papers; Annette Koch to Christian Koch, May 13, 1863, in Christian Koch Papers, LLMVC.

Similar circumstances confronted the entire population in the lakeshore region. The Covington *Weekly Wanderer* noted that less than one week's supply of corn remained in the area and that in a two-day period the cost per bushel had increased from $1.75 to $2.25. Sara Sandell grieved for the residents around Ponchatoula, who had exhausted their personal supplies of meat; in April, 1863, Sandell informed her daughter that no meat could be purchased for any price. The deepening crisis forced many residents to make desperate decisions. Annette Koch faced the dilemma of feeding her children or her servants. When she naturally chose to sustain her children, she suffered a near breakdown from the stress associated with her decision to release her servants, who would "surely starve." Lamenting conditions, M. J. Scott sadly noted the necessity of relinquishing the responsibility of raising his two children: "It is enough to say that the war has ruined me, broken me up. Provisions are scarce and dear and clothing is almost entirely out of the question." Scott implored his sister-in-law to take the children away and "act not only the part of a friend to them, but the more holy one—that of the mother." By the summer of 1863, the success of the Federal blockade and interdiction of Confederate trade on the lakes ensured that the local residents would face the constant threat of starvation.[38]

The desperate circumstances prevailing in the lakeshore region and on the Gulf Coast of Mississippi severely strained many residents' commitment to the war effort. Increasingly, they were forced to barter with the enemy to survive, despite Confederate efforts to prevent such practices. By the fall of 1863, the practice of trading cotton or sugar to the enemy for food had become common in the lakeshore region. Lieutenant C. M. Allen, on a reconnaissance mission with elements of the Second Arkansas Cavalry in October, 1863, reported that a general system of contraband trade with the enemy continued in the lakeshore region. Allen indicated that this illegal trade had an obvious demoralizing effect on the people. Many residents no longer trusted the ability of the Confederate authorities to protect and provide for them. Annette Koch complained to her husband that her youngest son had fled during a recent Union raid. Rumors indicated that the Yankees made "conscripts of all such lads as he and all negro men they could catch," so, she

38. Covington *Weekly Wanderer*, April 19, 1862; Christian Koch to Annette Koch, April 6, 1863, Annette Koch to Christian Koch, April 29, May 13, July 1, 1863, April 24, September 18, 20, 1864, all in Koch Papers; M. J. Scott to his Sister-in-law, June 3, 1864, M. J. Scott Letter, LLMVC; Sara Dawson, *Confederate Girl's Diary*, 370–72.

argued, her husband "would have allowed him to take to the woods too." The boy's departure, however, deprived Koch of her last farmhand, forcing her to rely on bartered food obtained from the Federal garrison at Fort Pike. Mrs. R. J. Causey regretfully informed her soldier-husband that desperate circumstances had forced her to barter with the enemy to provide for their children. Although she professed continuing patriotism to the cause of the South, she wrote fearfully of the efforts of Confederate cavalry to interdict this trade.[39]

Recognizing the severity of the situation, Collector F. H. Hatch, suggested that a policy fair to both the people and the government be implemented. He confided to Richmond that since the enemy had made clear his intention to starve the people, "while I would not sanction or encourage trade with the enemy, I would endeavor to regulate these matters in a time of war rather by a policy which would work to the benefit of our cause and to the injury of the enemy than by a rigid application of the law." To dramatize the critical circumstances confronting the citizens of the region, Hatch noted that even as a ranking Confederate official, he, too, faced starvation. He reminded his superiors that the only way to halt the contraband traffic with the enemy would be to deploy the precious few troops in the territory as pickets across the entire region. Hatch's proposal to allow limited trade with the enemy to relieve the extreme suffering of the people obviously met with tacit approval. By the fall of 1863, Mrs. Causey noted that the people had been granted permission to trade two bales of cotton with the enemy. In the end this policy constituted an official acknowledgment of the Confederate government's inability to sustain its citizens and hastened the growing contempt for ineffective authority increasingly evident in the region.[40]

The lingering fear of a slave insurrection also stimulated anxiety as the war continued to drain most males from the region. In November, 1863, Mrs. Causey reinforced her pleas to her husband to return home from the army by noting that a conspiracy to launch a "negro uprising" had been uncovered in their neighborhood. She continued, "I am afraid we will have some troublesome times down here the men are patrolling all of the time but the men are

39. OR, Vol. XXVI, Pt. 1, p. 313, Vol. XLI, Pt. 2, pp. 1084, 1088; Annette Koch to Christian Koch, April 29, May 11, 1863, in Koch Papers; Mrs. R. J. Causey to Causey, October 14, 1863, in Causey Correspondence; P. L. Bonny to Messrs. Cousins, Jones, and J. A. Leblanc, April 23, 1864, in Bonny Papers.

40. OR, Ser. IV, Vol. II, 459–60, Ser. IV, Vol. III, 677–80; Mrs. R. J. Causey to Causey, October 14, 1863, in Causey Correspondence; James A. Seddon Letter, December 19, 1862, J. B. Eustis to P. L. Bonny, November 28, 1863, both in Bonny Papers.

so few in the country that they can not do much good." Similarly, Mary Wilkinson urged her soldier-husband to come home and restore some discipline on the farm; she noted ominously, "I think the negroes has [sic] done without you long enough." These letters are rare examples of the present fear of a slave revolt in eastern Louisiana. Although no slave rebellions materialized, hundreds of slaves deserted their former masters as the presence of the Federal army became more evident. The desertions not only deprived the slaveholders of their source of labor but also highlighted the implications of defeat.[41]

Further adding to the hopeless conditions prevailing in the lakeshore region were growing numbers of deserters, both Union and Confederate, who camped in the woods along the lakes or secreted themselves in the Pearl River swamps. Many of these war-weary men had families in the area and simply returned home to be near them. Others among the deserters constituted desperate characters who preyed on the already-suffering population. Regardless of their motives, the bands of deserters collecting in the lakeshore region added to the unhappy state of affairs.[42]

The demoralization evident in the lakeshore region did not translate into the development of significant unionism. Some historians, influenced by propaganda in the federally censored New Orleans press, have suggested that large sections of eastern Louisiana and southwestern Mississippi experienced a revival of unionist sympathies at the height of the war. That war-weariness and a certain degree of disaffection emerged in the region is indisputable, but little evidence exists to indicate that significant unionism emerged. Infrequent reports submitted by Federal raiders declaring that local residents had professed loyalty to the Union must be qualified by the circumstances under which these statements were made. Only exceptionally committed or foolish persons would fail to say what seemed appropriate to preserve their homesteads and possibly their lives. This is not to say that the region contained no Union sympathizers. A small group of Unionists remained evident from the beginning to the end of the conflict. The evidence merely suggests that the decreasing quality of life associated with the war resulted in no significant up-

41. Mrs. R. J. Causey to Causey, November 19, 1863, in Causey Correspondence; Mary Wilkinson to Micajah Wilkinson, November 9, 1862, in Wilkinson Papers; Capell Diary, March 11, 19, April 8, 1865, in Capell Papers.

42. OR, Vol. XXVI, Pt. 1, pp. 313–14, Vol. XXXII, Pt. 3, p. 755; Mrs. R. J. Causey to Causey, October 14, November 19, 1863, in Causey Correspondence; Steven Ellis to his Mother [Mrs. T. E. Ellis], March 5, 1865, in Ellis Family Papers.

surge of unionism. Indeed, some of the most acclaimed Unionists in the territory appear to have been motivated by self-serving principles.[43] The Christian Koch family remains one of the most frequently cited unionist families. However, a survey of their papers indicates that they, as recent Danish immigrants, felt less loyalty to either side in the American conflict than they did to the Danes in their war with Prussia. The Koches, like many people in the area, simply hoped for peace on whatever terms would bring it speedily.[44]

The Federal ability to employ warships to raid the lakeshore area greatly aggravated the desperate conditions there. By the summer of 1863, Union warships increasingly raided the towns and countryside along the north shore of Lake Pontchartrain, destroying precious food stores, stealing livestock, and devastating farming operations. The frequent intensive raids, which continued into the spring of 1864, so decisively laid waste to the region that Union commanders complained of their inability to find anything else to destroy. Reporting on a Federal expedition he directed in the lakeshore region, Major Martin Pulver asserted that "prospects for doing serious damage to the enemies of our country in that direction looked extremely doubtful, as the inhabitants, what few there were, were very poor." Similarly, Union general Cuvier Grover commented that the livestock his troops had stolen during a raid near Madisonville appeared extremely unhealthy and, in his words, "were hardly worth driving." Through the end of 1863, Federal raiders enjoyed the privilege of devastating the region virtually unbothered. Excepting a handful of partisan rangers, almost no other Confederate forces remained in the area.[45]

While conditions prevailing in the lakeshore region remained particularly critical, as the second year of the war came to an end, increasingly desperate circumstances dominated the entire territory. The massive buildup of forces along the Mississippi occasioned by the fighting at Port Hudson exposed the

43. Testimony of Johnson E. Yerks and William Wilder, "Sub-Committee Investigating Elections in Louisiana," *House Documents, Congressional Hearings Supplement*, House Committee on Elections, 41st Cong., 2nd Sess., No. 1, 1869, hereinafter referred to as *Congressional Hearings Supplement*, 1869; New Orleans *Daily Picayune*, December 10, 1863, October 9, 11, 1864; Ted Tunnell, *Crucible of Reconstruction: War, Radicalism, and Race in Louisiana, 1862–1877* (Baton Rouge, 1984), 8–25; OR, Vol. XV, 406. Limited evidence suggests that some Unionists remained in the Florida parishes for the duration of the war; see unsigned letter (possibly from one Evans) to "Dear friend brother Ellis," January 30, 1864, in Ellis Family Papers.

44. See Koch Papers.

45. Copy of Special Orders No. 27, Col. Edward Dillon to P. L. Bonny and J. C. Robert, May 5, 1864, Eustis to Bonny, November 28, 1863, in Bonny Papers; OR, Vol. XXXIV, 104–106, 869, Vol. XV, 786–87, Vol. XLI, 756–58.

upper Florida parishes to constant maneuvering on the part of both armies. On May 21, 1863, the two-pronged Union drive against the garrison at Port Hudson resulted in a sharp skirmish at Merritt's Plantation near Plains Store. The arrival of massive Federal reinforcements compelled the Confederates to retire within the defenses of Port Hudson, completing the encirclement of the garrison. The longest siege in American history had begun.[46]

Outside the siege lines, fighting raged along Thompson's Creek as both sides attempted to consolidate their lines. Recognizing the precarious position of his small command in the midst of the besieging army, Colonel John Logan, commanding the Eleventh Arkansas Mounted Infantry and partisan units cooperating with him, withdrew to concentrate at Clinton. In a special report to General Joseph E. Johnston, Logan pleaded for additional forces to relieve Port Hudson and to secure a valuable region from the depredations of the enemy that would certainly follow.[47]

Logan's fear that Federal forces would aggressively seek to destroy the war-making potential of the upper Florida parishes proved true. On June 3, 1863, a series of well-executed ambushes enabled Logan to repulse a Union raid on Clinton, but the Confederate advantage proved temporary. Four days later a heavily reinforced Federal column departed Port Hudson for Clinton. In the face of this powerful force, Logan wisely retreated north, leaving only a handful of partisans to harass the Union advance. The Federals entered Clinton, burned all government property, including the railroad depot and a cotton factory, and relieved many citizens of their private property. General Halbert Paine, commander of the expedition, observed that, despite the commanding presence of the Federals, many citizens "exhibited in their demeanor as well as their language great confidence that their army would fall upon us before the capture of Port Hudson."[48]

However, the surrender of Port Hudson in July, 1863, cast a shadow of gloom over the region. Celine Fremaux, a young resident of Jackson, vividly described the universal weeping occasioned by the fall of the Confederate bastion and by the appearance of the starved, tearful defenders trudging slowly by

46. OR, Vol. XXVI, 120–22, 137, 144; Winters, Civil War in Louisiana, 244–45.

47. OR, Vol. XXVI, 128–29, 179–81; Stewart Sifakis, Compendium of the Confederate Armies: Florida and Arkansas (New York, 1992), 90–91.

48. OR, Vol. XXVI, 134–36, 181; Taylor Diary, June 3, 1863, in Hunter-Taylor Family Papers; OR, Vol. XXVI, 72, 111, 126–27, 181–82; Taylor Diary, June 7, 9, 1863, in Hunter-Taylor Family Papers; Garcia, Celine Remembering Louisiana, 119; Winters, Civil War in Louisiana, 277–78.

in defeat. G. T. Harrower, a Federal soldier stationed at Baton Rouge, commented on the depression evident among the local population: "There are very few secessionists to be found here now. They all begin to wish for peace. They are at our mercy. They can never recruit that army—nor can their British and French friends furnish them with arms—the end is near."[49]

Port Hudson did constitute a major setback for the Confederates, but the war continued. On August 3, 1863, Logan fell upon a Union force, including a regiment of the Corps D Afrique, which was impressing blacks to serve in the Federal army near Jackson. The outnumbered Confederates thoroughly routed the Yankees, capturing all their artillery and supply wagons. As the survivors straggled back to the safety of Port Hudson, powerful Union columns departed from that garrison and from Natchez, forcing Logan to retire. In his report concerning the operations about Jackson, General George Andrews, commanding the Federal garrison at Port Hudson, expressed outrage that Logan's force had received considerable assistance from local residents. Andrews noted that among the over one hundred Union soldiers taken prisoner in the battle, "several were captured through the aid of so called citizens." This brief campaign exemplifies the pattern the conflict took in the Florida parishes for the remainder of the war. The character of the war in this final phase would, in turn, serve as a blueprint for the violence that prevailed in the region in the late nineteenth century.[50]

By the late summer of 1863, it was apparent that Confederate forces lacked the strength to repel Union thrusts into the interior of the Florida parishes. The Confederates would continue to confront the Federals, but for the remainder of the war the proximity of powerful Union bases permitted speedy reinforcement of any raiding party in trouble. Realizing their strength and perhaps frustrated by their inability to subjugate the region effectively, the Federals initiated an intensified campaign of terror against the local population.[51] In response, exasperated citizens took an ever-more-active part in operations against the invaders.

A new type of brutality characterized the war in the Florida parishes during its last months. In a letter to a friend serving in Lee's army in Virginia,

49. Garcia, *Celine Remembering Louisiana*, 119–20; Taylor Diary, July 9, 1863, in Hunter-Taylor Family Papers; G. T. Harrower to Helen, August 2, 1863, in G. T. Harrower Letters, LLMVC.

50. OR, Vol. XXVI, 238–40.

51. The Federals also demanded security for their fledgling farming operations in the region (OR, Vol. XLI, 878, Vol. XXVI, 313).

J. M. Doyle summarized the intensification of Federal actions against the citizens with the comment, "The yankees did much more damage this time." Abigail Amacker expressed dismay at the changed appearance of an elderly aunt who had been robbed of everything by Federal soldiers. Amacker confided in her diary, "I believe that grief is killing her." Celine Fremaux described a Union raid on Jackson in early 1864 in which a large body of soldiers drove the children from their schoolhouse. According to Fremaux, the Yankees burned their books and slates and used their desks as troughs to feed the horses. A separate raiding party entered the only drugstore and destroyed all of its contents, leaving the community without any medicine on the eve of yellow fever season. Fremaux commented that the raids occurred with increasing frequency and that "just such sort of narrow, mean, unmanly, sort of acts were perpetuated by every raiding gang." J. Burruss McGehee, Eve Brower, and Carrie McGehee all vividly described the looting and burning of Bowling Green Plantation south of Woodville. Union troops under the command of Colonel J. B. Cook entered and looted the house, smashing everything they did not steal before brutally beating the elderly couple who owned the plantation and then burning the home and all outbuildings.[52]

Attacks even more disturbing to the civilian population occurred. At least two Jackson women were raped by Federal soldiers in early 1864. In one instance, Union troops battered their way into the home of an elderly lady and her granddaughter. The Yankees bound and tied the old woman and gang raped her granddaughter. On the same day, Union soldiers murdered two residents of Jackson. Dr. J. Barkdull, the chief physician at the Louisiana state insane asylum, was murdered by Federal soldiers even as he attempted to produce papers demonstrating that he had taken the Federal oath to secure provisions for his patients. In a callous display of their contempt for the local residents, Union troops staged a congratulatory ceremony for the doctor's murderers in the cemetery during his funeral. Joseph Fluker, sixteen-year-old son of an older lady who had lost her husband and six other sons to the war, was clubbed to death in the center of Jackson by Union soldiers who threw the dying young man face down into a gully filled with water. Celine Fre-

52. J. M. Doyle to Eugene Hunter, October 16, 1864, in Hunter-Taylor Family Papers; Amacker Diary, November 19, 1863, in Amacker Papers; Elers Koch to Christian Koch, September 15, 1864, in Koch Papers; Garcia, *Celine Remembering Louisiana*, 112–27; J. Burruss McGehee to James S. McGehee, February 5, 1904, Eve Brower to James McGehee, February 22, 1904, and Carrie McGehee to James McGehee, n.d., all in James McGehee Papers; *OR*, Vol. XXXIX, Pt. 1, 829–32.

maux remembered Federal soldiers stripping a severely wounded Confederate soldier of his clothing and then taunting her one-armed "school marm," who attempted to assist the dying man. Moreover, she recounted rumors that attributed to the Federals the mysterious appearance of several barrels of poisoned flour in her town. Josephine Pugh credited the pleas of her slaves with saving her life during the looting of her home by a party of Federal soldiers who had murdered her neighbor only moments before. Frightful accounts of the mistreatment and murder of captured Confederate soldiers circulated among the citizens. Bemoaning his miserable existence as a Federal prisoner, Willie Barrow summarized the feeling of many in the Florida parishes with his plea, "Lord deliver me from such hardships."[53]

The outcome of the escalating Federal war on the civilian population was the emergence of an unqualified hatred for the Yankees and for authority in general. The strength of their loyalty to friends and relatives away in the Confederate army, combined with the mutually shared suffering that forced neighbors to rely on one another to an unprecedented degree, created a bond of determination and togetherness. Such a bond helped to overcome the defeatism the Federals expected to result from their aggressive actions. J. N. Waddel summarized the position taken by many families: "I lost all my property, my home and my furniture, had been driven from all I held dear and was in exile, a wanderer among strangers frequently, but I felt I could endure all this with patience, and in the hope that my country some day or other would be free."[54]

As the war entered its final months, hatred helped to sustain the cause of the South in eastern Louisiana. Outraged by the ruined condition of his hometown Clinton and reports of Yankee boasts of the thoroughness of their work, Robert Patrick, on leave from the Confederate army in northern Georgia, vented his contempt over the grave of a Union soldier: "You were not satisfied to remain at home and let us alone; you must come to the South to

53. Garcia, *Celine Remembering Louisiana*, 111–21, 142, 144–48, 155; "Reminiscences of a Union Raid," Typescript, n.d., in Josephine Pugh Papers, LLMVC; Eugene Hunter to Stella Hunter, June 16, 1865, in Hunter-Taylor Family Papers; John Ellis to Martina Ellis, September 16, 1864, in Ellis Family Papers; Barrow Diary, April 10, 1862, in Barrow Family Papers.

54. J. N. Waddel to Eli Capell, January 9, 1866, in Capell Papers; John Ellis to his Mother [Mrs. T. E. Ellis], March 11, 1862, in Ellis Family Papers; John Connell to "Dear Pet," May 1, 1865, Lizzie Hamilton to Albert Batchelor, May 21, 1865, both in Albert Batchelor Papers; Garcia, *Celine Remembering Louisiana*, 137–44; Amite City *Tri-Weekly Wanderer*, April 29, 1865; Amite City *Sunday Wanderer*, February 12, 1865.

murder our citizens, burn our houses, desolate our homes, and lay waste our country; to make war upon women and children, turning them out to die of cold and want, without the slightest compunctions of conscience. You for one have met your just reward, which is a grant of land from the Confederates of three feet by six." Writing from below Woodville, Mississippi, a grieving mother declared her feelings: "You can never imagine my hatred for the Yankees. I despise everything that is connected with them in any way. From henceforth and forever I will school mine to despise more than I now do if it is possible the Yankees, but my hatred for them is so intense I don't think I can increase it." Commenting on its attack on a Federal raiding party in the spring of 1865, Steve Ellis declared that anger alone propelled his unit to victory. Hatred proved to be a powerful motivating force. Instead of embracing the cause of the Union, many local residents, having little left to lose, took desperate steps to strike back against the Yankees.[55]

In the spring of 1864, Colonel John S. Scott replaced Logan as commander of Confederate forces operating in eastern Louisiana. Scott, at the head of the First Louisiana Cavalry, had established a reputation as a cunning and courageous, albeit controversial, commander during operations in Virginia and Tennessee. More important, Scott, like most of the survivors of his cavalry unit, was a native of the Florida parishes. The arrival of the First Louisiana Cavalry occasioned great rejoicing among the men of the command and inspired a new confidence among the long-suffering residents.[56]

Scott moved quickly to consolidate his new command. Aggressive recruiting and conscripting efforts, backed by a stern warning to shirkers and to those who harbored deserters, resulted in the formation of a new battalion for service in eastern Louisiana. The Federals provided further incentive to join the Confederate army by impressing eligible men into their army or arbitrarily arresting them. Dozens of refugees from New Orleans and others eager to fight the Yankees rallied to the call of the charismatic leader. The deprivations of years of war, however, were apparent in the men. Serrano Taylor de-

55. F. Jay Taylor, ed., *Reluctant Rebel*, 132, 201, 223; Nannie C. to Stewart, April, 1864, John Connell to "Dear Pet," May 1, 1865, in Albert Batchelor Papers; Raoul to his Father [Gaston Raoul], June 28, 1862, May 24, 1863, in Raoul Papers; Steven Ellis to his Brother, April 9, 1865, John Ellis to his Sister, March 18, 1862, both in Ellis Family Papers; Serrano Taylor Travel Journal, 1862–63, October 2, 1862, in Hunter-Taylor Family Papers; Garcia, *Celine Remembering Louisiana*, 118.

56. Carter, *Cavalryman's Reminiscences*, 104–107, 117; Steven Ellis to his Brother, April 9, 1865, in Ellis Family Papers.

scribed the appearance of Scott's force to his son-in-law: "We have refugees from New Orleans in Colonel Scott's command—barefoot—a coarse shirt and pants, unwashed for months—for they have no change." Jane McCausland Chinn related that the Confederate force on which the hopes of the residents depended consisted of "old grey bearded men, soldiers in their prime with fiery angry looks, and flustered young lads."[57]

Despite their appearances, Scott expressed great confidence in his men's ability to contain the invader. In order to keep the Yankees off balance, he determined to take the offensive. Partisans operating under his command attacked Federal raiding parties near Madisonville, creating panic among the Union forces there and encouraging them to remain near the protection provided by their gunboats in the lakes. During the late spring and early summer of 1864, in a series of hit-and-run raids, cavalry units commanded by Colonel Frank Powers disrupted Federal communications and supply trains between Baton Rouge and Port Hudson. Elements of Scott's cavalry repeatedly established mobile batteries along the Mississippi and shelled Federal steamers and transports. A Federal raid designed to destroy his base of operations failed when Scott ambushed the Federal column at the Comite River and repulsed it. In a bold maneuver in August, 1864, Scott's cavalry forced the surrender of the Union stockade at Doyal's Plantation below Baton Rouge.[58]

Scott's offensive maneuvers in the Florida parishes created consternation among Union commanders in the lower Mississippi region. Outraged Federal officials at Baton Rouge placed a $10,000 bounty on Scott's head.[59] In a substantive military sense, though, his efforts did little more than provide temporary relief and a bit of hope for the local population. The critical contribution resulting from Scott's command of the department concerns his policy toward citizens under arms.

57. Amite City *Daily Wanderer*, December 8, 1864; Serrano Taylor to Eugene Hunter, June, 1864, in Hunter-Taylor Family Papers; Alex Stuart to his Uncle, December 27, 1863, in William R. Bell Papers, LLMVC; Chinn, "Burning of the Barns," 2; Annette Koch to Christian Koch, April 29, 1863, in Koch Papers; Garcia, *Celine Remembering Louisiana*, 136.

58. Amite City *Daily Wanderer*, December 8, 1864; Taylor to Hunter, June, 1864, in Hunter-Taylor Family Papers; Robert A. Tyson Diary, February 1, 11, 1864, LLMVC; Tom Ellis to Martina Ellis, May 20, 1864, in Ellis Family Papers; W. W. Garig Diary, April 7, 1864, in W. W. Garig Papers, LLMVC; Dixon Diary, April 7, 1864, in Dixon Papers; *OR*, Vol. XXXIV, Pt. 1, pp. 136–38, 877–79, 906, Vol. XLI, Pt. 2, pp. 833, 919, 932; Carter, *Cavalryman's Reminiscences*, 107–109.

59. *OR*, Vol. XLI, Pt. 2, p. 833. F. P. Wall to her Sister, n.d. [1864?], describes a reward of $1,000 for the capture, dead or alive, of Naul and of $10,000 for Scott, in McKinney Papers.

Little evidence exists to indicate that Scott actively encouraged guerrilla warfare, but that he tolerated this method of combat is indisputable. Unlike Confederate commanders in other theaters of the war, Scott issued no directives governing, or statements condemning, guerrilla warfare. By adopting a policy of total war, he, in fact, sanctioned a grisly development of enormous consequence for the future development of the Florida parishes.

Proposals to launch a guerrilla war in eastern Louisiana had been entertained as early as the spring of 1862, but guerrilla warfare constituted something far different from partisan operations. Unlike partisan units, whose usefulness resulted from their adherence to the commands of the regular army, guerrillas operated independently. Autonomous bodies of armed men almost always created problems for both friend and foe. A March, 1862, proposal recommended, "Let 200 determined men in each county take to the woods with their horses and rifles, swear never to bend their necks to the yoke, but war upon our tyrants and all who give them aid and comfort, night and day, as long as the foot of the Yankee presses upon southern soil." In 1862, this ominous suggestion received little support, but by late 1864, the situation proved very different.[60]

Recognizing the odds that faced him, Scott sanctioned the participation of citizens in the war effort by encouraging the formation of citizens' militia. Previous efforts to create and employ militias in eastern Louisiana had proved of little consequence. Scott's plan called for the creation of home-guard units, consisting of men over forty-five, to act as localized reserves in support of regulars when their communities were threatened. These units performed duty as garrison forces and pickets and occasionally supported the army in repelling attacks. Unlike the militia, which recognized the authority of the regular army, by the fall of 1864 increasing numbers of citizens, independent of any civil or military control, engaged in attacks upon the Yankees. W. Greene Raoul expressed the exasperated sentiment of these men: "We had as well raise the black flag at once. They [Federals] are fighting almost upon that principle. We, I think ought to take some measure to retaliate. There is no reason to fear that they will do more, for they are doing all they possibly can now. Submission we can not have, we must fight it out to the last."[61]

60. New Orleans *Daily Picayune*, March 13, 1862.

61. OR, Vol. I, Pt. 2, p. 19; Raoul to his Father [Gaston Raoul], May 24, 1863, in Raoul Papers; Taylor Diary, April 28, 1863, in Hunter-Taylor Family Papers; Amite City *Daily Wanderer*, December 8, 1864.

The Amite City *Daily Wanderer*, one of the few newspapers still publishing by the fall of 1864, encouraged guerrilla activity. The *Daily Wanderer* reminded readers that Spain had survived the burning of its cities and the destruction of its armies to prevail over the French by employing guerrilla tactics. Beginning in the summer of 1864, guerrillas increasingly preyed upon Union forces operating in the area. Occasionally, guerrillas cooperated with regular Confederate units in confronting Union raiders, but in most cases the citizens established prearranged points of ambush and waited in hiding for a Federal patrol. In almost all cases the guerrillas took no prisoners.[62]

These tactics produced fear and outrage among the Federals. The guerrillas proved difficult to catch, and their methods were effective. One group operating in Livingston and lower East Baton Rouge Parishes sought out and killed any Federal stragglers they encountered. The same party frequently ambushed whole patrols, tying up considerable numbers of Federal soldiers in their pursuit. The fighting along both the east and west banks of the Mississippi became increasingly brutal. Both sides were accused of murdering prisoners and looting homesteads. Confederate guerrillas and partisans wreaked bloody vengeance on Federal soldiers they found with looted goods. By the fall of 1864, guerrilla activity made considerable portions of the territory unsafe for Federal soldiers. In response, the Federals burned entire towns, executed many Confederate soldiers as suspected guerrillas, and intensified their efforts to arrest every adult male of combat age. In most cases the guerrillas confined their activities to killing Yankees, but in the lakeshore and Pearl River regions, the war assumed a particularly ugly character. Determined to exterminate one another, guerrilla bands, occasionally operating with Confederate cavalry, and Union forces engaged in wanton acts of murder and destruction. The unfortunate residents became victims of the suspicions and requisitions of both sides. Overcome by scenes of devastation and mangled bodies by the roadside, Annette Koch lamented what had happened to the people: "I have found so much that is bad in the hearts of so many people. They have taken the law in their own hands and do just as they please and I think when things come to that no man is safe."[63]

62. Amite City *Daily Wanderer*, November 10, 1864; Amite City *Sunday Wanderer*, February 12, 1865; OR, Vol. XLI, Pt. 1, pp. 277–78; John Burruss to Edward Burruss, February 18, 1864, in Burruss Papers; Carter, *Cavalryman's Reminiscences*, 113–14.

63. John Burruss to Edward Burruss, February 18, 1864, in Burruss Papers; Annette Koch to Christian Koch, September 18, 20, October 3, 9, 1864, February 6, 11, 1865, Elers Koch to Christian Koch, September 20, October 3, 1864, all in Koch Papers; Priscilla M. Bond Diary,

In early October, 1864, the Federals initiated a major offensive designed to drive Scott's force from the territory and to exterminate the guerrillas by crushing their base of support. This operation effectively laid waste the region. On October 5, 1864, the Yankees moved out of Baton Rouge in two columns backed by cavalry and artillery. As they proceeded through East Feliciana and St. Helena Parishes and the southwestern counties of Mississippi, they burned all government property and huge amounts of private property. They destroyed all food and crops they found and slaughtered or dispersed all livestock. The towns of Liberty, Woodville, Greensburg, Osyka, and Camp Moore were ravaged by the raiders. The Covington *Wanderer* reported that the Federals "committed hellish degradations, robbing and plundering indiscriminately." The Amite City *Daily Wanderer* gave voice to the anxiety of the people. "If the Yankees continue the destruction and heathenish pilfering that they have practiced heretofore upon the residents in the vicinity of Liberty and the adjacent country, if absolute want and starvation do not ensue, something akin will certainly follow." The New Orleans *Daily Picayune* reported that the Federals had destroyed over forty thousand pounds of bacon, twelve hundred shoes, and limitless amounts of clothing and other goods, noting that "the general deemed it a military necessity in taking several citizens." The *Daily Picayune* continued, calling the raid "the most successful expedition emanating from Baton Rouge," for "it cleared the area of Jayhawkers."[64]

The October, 1864, raid did devastate the region, but it did not dissuade citizens from attacking Federal soldiers. On the contrary, the despoiling raid seemed to promote continued resistance, which increasingly relied on citizen involvement. In his report concerning his unit's role in the October raid, Major N. F. Craigue, Fourth Wisconsin Cavalry, described his movement through lower St. Helena Parish. As his command proceeded through the region, they encountered no regular Confederate units, but his column suffered the heaviest casualties of the raid. Craigue reported that as he departed the region, a citizen followed his regiment, killing and wounding several of his

---

March 6, May 3, 1864, June 16, 1865, in LLMVC; Dominique Pochelu to W. R. Bell, March 23, 1864, Alex Stuart to his Uncle, December 27, 1863, both in William R. Bell Papers; Carter, *Cavalryman's Reminiscences*, 113–15; OR, Vol. XLI, Pt. 1, pp. 294, 880–83, Vol. XLI, Pt. 2, p. 933, Vol. XLVIII, Pt. 1, p. 263; Winters, *Civil War in Louisiana*, 392–96.

64. OR, Vol. XLI, Pt. 2, pp. 880–83; Covington *Wanderer*, October 15, 1864; Amite City *Daily Wanderer*, November 29, 1864; New Orleans *Daily Picayune*, October 9, 11, 1864; Carter, *Cavalryman's Reminiscences*, 118; James Durnin to his Sister, September 13, 1864, in Durnin Papers.

men by "firing into them from the bushes." He concluded his report with an ominous note for Federal authorities: "The guerrilla could not be taken." Colonel E. D. Osband, in command of the column that sacked Woodville, also reported that he had suffered casualties as a result of bushwhackers firing on his command "while concealed in the bushes." In the Florida parishes bushwhacking was becoming an art form.[65]

Bushwhacking involved concealing a gunman in the undergrowth along a roadside and cutting a small opening in the bushes that faced the opposite direction from which the foe approached. Unobserved, the assailant then fired into the back of his victim. The confusion created by shotgun blasts from the rear gave a bushwhacker with knowledge of the terrain an excellent opportunity to escape undetected, only to strike again at another prearranged location. The Federals' frustrated and vain efforts to capture bushwhackers in the last months of the war demonstrated their effectiveness. Sadly, this phenomenon would be a lesson too well learned in the Florida parishes.

The October raid and corollary operations in the upper Florida parishes did accomplish a primary objective. As a result of the devastation of the region, Scott, who relied heavily on requisitions from local farmers to feed his troops and horses, withdrew into southwestern Mississippi, leaving only a token force behind.[66] But the bushwhackers had also accomplished an important objective. Their efforts helped to contain the marauding of small groups of Federals, who were more likely to commit atrocities in the absence of a senior officer. As a result the local press continued to urge resistance "to the bloodhounds of Lincoln's despotism."[67]

Although many residents continued to insist through the final weeks of the war that the South would prevail in the end, reality proved contrary to their hopes. Through the dreary winter of 1864 and 1865, new Confederate units emerged in eastern Louisiana, but the surrender of the Confederate armies under Robert E. Lee and Joseph E. Johnston in April, 1865, highlighted the reality of failure. Suddenly, the Federals adopted a policy of appeasement toward the rebels. Yet four years of brutality could not simply disappear. Even after the cessation of hostilities between the regular armies in

65. OR, Vol. XLI, Pt. 1, pp. 881–82, Vol. XXXIX, Pt. 1, pp. 831–32.

66. Capell Diary, March 29, May 28, June 22, July 15, September 6–8, October 18, October 25–29, 1864, January 31, 1865, in Capell Papers. St. Helena Parish Succession Records, Succession Bin W-3, January–July, 1863, May–June, 1864, demonstrate reliance of Confederate units on the local population for sustenance (St. Helena Parish Courthouse, Greensburg, La.).

67. Amite City *Daily Wanderer*, December 8, 1864; OR, Vol. XLVIII, Pt. 1, pp. 128, 157–58.

eastern Louisiana and southwestern Mississippi, guerrilla operations, occasionally on a large scale, persisted. A Federal force traveling through parts of Alabama, Mississippi, and Louisiana to "secure by conciliation and kindness the good will of the people for and toward the representatives of the Federal government" was bushwhacked north of Osyka in late May. The war did not end simply because Washington, D.C., pronounced it over and staged a great celebration in honor of the North's victory. In the Florida parishes the violence had only begun.[68]

As the official war waned, the Florida parishes, like many areas of the South, were ruined. Countless members of the prewar elite and their offspring had succumbed to the ravages of war. With them went the vestiges of stable government. The survivors faced starvation, a society turned upside down, and an uncertain future as a conquered people. In many cases hate and bitterness had replaced hospitality and kindness. Most important, the war challenged in an unprecedented fashion the value system of the people. The presence of the Union Army thrust Federal authority into their lives. Confederate efforts also intruded upon their independent life-style, but the harsh policy of the Federals made clear who was the enemy. In the Florida parishes brutality engendered brutality. Certain agents of the Federal government sanctioned truculence and murder, and the residents responded effectively in like manner. Bloodshed solved problems permanently. The solution was learned; the war had only begun.

68. Amite City *Daily Wanderer*, October 15, 1864; F. P. Wall to Jeptha McKinney, December 17, 1864, in McKinney Papers; Father [Thomas A. G. Batchelor] to Albert Batchelor, September 7, December 26, 1864, in Albert Batchelor Papers; Chinn, "Burning of the Barns," 1; OR, Vol. XLVIII, Pt. 1, pp. 262–64.

· 4 ·

Opportunity Lost:
Incipient Chaos Delayed

In the spring of 1865, the sectional conflict moved into another far more complex phase. Thousands of Union soldiers marched home to a hero's welcome in a land that the war had transformed into one of the most prosperous and productive regions on earth. Except for the loss of many of its sons, the North had remained insulated from the true horror of the war, and after the war, it persisted as a region at the forefront of recasting a national identity. The next phase of the conflict, though similar in many ways to the earlier phase, would be a struggle not of armies but of individuals, ideas, and policies. Hope and opportunity would fall victim to the tempestuous cauldron of chaotic circumstances gathered under the amorphous name *Reconstruction*. Instead of opportunity, many areas of the South would experience a fierce revival of traditional values, which, unburdened by the restraints inherent in antebellum social order, would contribute directly to a continuing cycle of suffering. What could have emerged as a time of healing and fulfilled dreams instead became one of darkness and failed will.

Amid the reality of defeat, residents of eastern Louisiana struggled to revive the sources of stability and prosperity from a world that existed no more. The result of their efforts demonstrated the incompatibility between fealty to the old order and the inevitability of the new. More important, the chaotic conditions associated with Reconstruction reinforced latent suspicions of government and belief in the effectiveness of violence. In the immediate aftermath of the war, the prevailing despair and disillusionment encouraged the plain folk to assert themselves politically and to challenge the planter leadership that had led them to ruin. Real power, however, rested with federal military authorities. In eastern Louisiana, the federal attempt to create a state government suffered from the people's lingering hatred of northerners, which the unprincipled behavior of some governmental participants aggravated. The antebellum elite employed the frustration produced by the presence of an "alien" government to recover their regional dominance and to encourage the violent overthrow of the Republicans. The end result of war and Reconstruction for many in the piney woods of the Florida parishes was an unqualified contempt for authority figures and the knowledge that even the law could be overcome through violence.

The shock of defeat wore off slowly in the Florida parishes. Many solemnly refused to accept that their homeland had been vanquished. The Amite City *Tri-Weekly Wanderer* demonstrated the desperate pretensions of many residents: "I cannot banish the thought that ere the God of battle will manifest himself in our midst, and by the interposition of his strong arm, rescue us from the abyss of ruin which seems yawning to engulf us . . . our nation must unite in one fervent supplication, that Jehovah may deliver us out of the hands of our enemies." Initial dismay and disbelief eventually gave way to anger and despair. The efforts of grieving families to ascertain the value of extreme sacrifice culminating in defeat contributed to the prevailing depression. Mary L. Wall, who lost her three sons and only brother to the war, prayed for a means of understanding their sacrifice. Similarly, J. N. Waddel wrote that his son's death had deprived him of the only thing he truly valued in life. Unlike their northern counterparts, who realized a sense of accomplishment in the death of their loved ones, southerners enjoyed no such consolation. Linus Parker concluded, "Here we are like people blown up in a steamboat, hardly knowing what has happened, how it happened or where we are left."[1]

War-related anger and frustration assumed various forms. Thomas Ellis proclaimed before a congressional investigating committee that his bitterness stemmed from his conviction that he could have fought harder for the Confederacy. In a similar vein, many former Confederates expressed boundless contempt for those who sought to cooperate with the federals. Prominent Baton Rouge attorney James O. Fuqua exemplified this attitude in a letter to his Clinton associate James G. Kilbourne. "Keep these people away from me or I may do them mischief, tell them to keep away that I am armed and dangerous, have got a knife, a big stick, and a little nigger to collect brickbats." Frustrated efforts to understand exactly what had happened produced numerous other scapegoats. In his private letters, for example, Charles E. Kennon condemned the Democratic party as the source of southern troubles.[2]

1. Amite City *Tri-Weekly Wanderer*, April 29, 1865; Mary L. Wall to Kate Burruss, November 7, 1866, in Burruss Papers; J. N. Waddel to Eli Capell, January 9, 1866, in Capell Papers.
2. Testimony of Thomas C. W. Ellis, *Congressional Hearings Supplement, 1869*; James O. Fuqua to James G. Kilbourne, June 8, 1865, in J. G. Kilbourne Family Papers, LLMVC; Lizzie

As white southerners grappled with the problems associated with defeat, blacks experimented with their newfound freedom. The freedmen assumed that Confederate defeat would create unprecedented opportunity for them, and in terms of their liberation from bondage it did. Blacks universally applauded the destruction of the slave system. Some whites expressed ambivalence at the changed state of affairs. Stella Hunter declared, "I am delighted to know that my yard will now be clear of little negroes and our expenses will now be much less though I will be sad to see them say goodbye." But the vast majority of whites expressed outrage with the implications of emancipation. Most planters deeply resented the enormous loss in capital they experienced as a result of the collapse of the slave system. J. N. Waddel declared that "the emancipation of the negro is the greatest injustice ever done to property owners; being nothing more, nothing less than rank robbery." Still others chafed at the notion of extending social and political rights to their former bondsmen. In the months immediately following the surrender, many whites simply refused to treat the freedmen as anything other than slaves. Charging a grand jury in the spring of 1867, Judge E. P. Ellis declared that the "ignorance, prejudice, and superstitions" of the blacks required that an 1855 law concerning the insubordination of slaves "should be still rigidly enforced with regard to the free colored population in our midst."[3]

White contempt for emancipation frequently provoked racial incidents. During the summer of 1865, Lieutenant Edward Ehrlich, commander of the federal garrison at Amite City, and Captain H. H. Rouse, Freedmen's Bureau agent there, reported daily incidents of racial violence in the area. In one instance, Ehrlich reported that the city marshall at Amite City had requested to see the pass of a freedman named Hardy. The pass, which exemplified the rigid restrictions on black mobility in the antebellum period, constituted one of the most hated aspects of the slave system for freedmen. When Hardy proudly announced that he had none and "did not consider it necessary now," the marshall hit him with his pistol and fired several shots at him as he tried to escape. The shooting attracted the attention of several patrons at a nearby coffeehouse who proceeded to empty their pistols at the fleeing Hardy, striking him twice. Ehrlich noted that military authorities had attempted to

Hamilton to Albert Batchelor, May 21, 1865, in Albert Batchelor Papers; Charles E. Kennon to Thomas Ellis, February 24, 1870, in Ellis Family Papers.

3. Capell Diary, December 25, 30, 1866, January 6, 7, 1867, in Capell Papers; Stella Hunter to Eugene Hunter, June 27, 1865, in Hunter-Taylor Family Papers; Waddel to Capell, January 9, 1866, in Capell Papers; Greensburg *Weekly Star and Journal*, April 27, 1867.

arrest the offending parties but failed. Both Rouse and Ehrlich pleaded for additional troops to curb the violence. Along with his report Ehrlich included several letters from prominent white citizens, including Amite City mayor John Wentz, who also requested assistance in curbing the disturbances.[4]

Under the prevailing highly charged circumstances, the freedmen needed and aggressively sought protection. That some whites also requested federal aid indicated the desperate state of affairs. Racial violence in particular aggravated the problem of rebuilding the shattered economy. The war so completely devastated the region that the most pressing problem involved procuring adequate supplies of food.

Starvation loomed in large areas of eastern Louisiana and southwestern Mississippi. Faced with an acute shortage of meat, prominent Livingston Parish planter John Gurley directed his overseer to kill as much wild game as possible while he sought provisions in New Orleans. Through the fall and winter of 1865, his employees killed hundreds of squirrels and ducks, selling some to their equally destitute neighbors. Freedmen's Bureau agents across the region regularly petitioned the bureau headquarters at New Orleans for provisions. Like many local farmers, John Haney virtually ceased planting cotton and concentrated exclusively on food production, though the initial results were less than encouraging. Governor J. Madison Wells desperately sought assistance from a reluctant Washington, D.C. Wells informed President Andrew Johnson that in the last phase of the military campaign, the Federals confiscated a large number of the horses and mules used for agricultural purposes by the population. The governor concluded that this action, more than anything else, contributed to the "great distress and fear of pestilence and starvation plaguing the country." Most unconfiscated cattle and hogs had been slaughtered or dispersed by the Federals, greatly exacerbating the food crisis.[5]

4. Capt. H. H. Rouse to Lt. D. Fenno, September 9, 1865, Lt. Edward Ehrlich to Lt. D. Fenno, October 10, December 19, 20, 1865, "Records Relating to Murders and Outrages," Lt. Edward Ehrlich to Lt. D. Fenno, July 5, 9, 10, August 20, September 18, October 20, 1865, all in Records of the Assistant Commissioner for the State of Louisiana Bureau of Refugees, Freedmen, and Abandoned Lands, Record Group 105, National Archives, Washington, D.C., hereinafter cited as Freedmen's Bureau Reports, NA.

5. Charles Daggs to John Gurley, November 8, 1865, Edward Stewart to John Gurley, November 13, 1865, in Gurley Papers; letters received at Freedmen's Bureau headquarters at New Orleans from A. Finch, November 10, 20, December 1, 10, 1867, January 8, 1868, James Hough, December 31, 1867, W. H. Haugen, January 10, March 6, 31, 1868, all in Freedmen's Bureau Re-

As in many areas of the defeated South, the war promoted drastic economic restructuring in eastern Louisiana. A sample survey of regional farmers demonstrates that fully 76 percent in the Florida parishes suffered acute reductions in the value of their overall wealth. Merchants and professional men fared little better, nearly 73 percent experiencing analogous reductions as a result of the war. Similar patterns prevailed statewide. Much of this decline related directly to the loss of slave property, but other indicators demonstrate that the financial catastrophe was pervasive. The sample survey reveals that during the period 1860 to 1870, 76 percent of Florida-parish farmers experienced a reduction in corn production, whereas 83 percent witnessed a decline in their cotton yields. Most farmers faced similar reductions in their livestock holdings (see Table 8). Although significant decreases occurred among all types of livestock, mules and horses incurred the sharpest losses, declining by 79 and 84 percent, respectively.[6]

Acute reductions in landholdings provide the most conclusive evidence of the economic catastrophe wrought by the war in eastern Louisiana (see Table 9). Between 1860 and 1870, fully 64 percent of Florida-parish property owners experienced a significant decrease in landholdings, a decline sharply contrasting with the trend in the 1850s. Local merchants and professional men who had weathered the war well or had found favor with the federals appropriated much of this property. Land served as the medium to settle many debts in the face of a severe credit contraction. Some planters as well as merchants who suffered comparatively minor losses during the war also seized the opportunity to buy up devalued land or assisted needy neighbors by purchasing a part of their holdings. During the period 1860 to 1870, for instance, Livingston Parish planter Thomas Green Davidson dramatically increased his landholdings. Davidson's total acreage rose from 2,900 to 8,100 acres, though much of the increase involved uncultivated woodlands. Former Federal soldiers who remained in the area, Freedmen's Bureau agents, and others associated with the postwar administration accounted for smaller purchases of land. James DeGrey, Freedmen's Bureau

ports, NA; John P. Haney to E. P. Ellis, April 26, 1868, in Ellis Family Papers; J. Madison Wells to Andrew Johnson, May 27, 1865, in Andrew Johnson Papers, NA; McDonald and McWhiney, "Antebellum Southern Herdsman," 164.

6. *Eighth Census, 1860,* Manuscript, Louisiana, Schedule 1, Free Population, Microfilm; *Ninth Census, 1870,* Manuscript, Louisiana, Schedule 1, Free Population, and Schedule 2, Agricultural Statistics, Microfilm. Figures were derived from a 3 percent sample of the heads of household of each parish.

TABLE 8. ECONOMIC CHANGES IN LIVESTOCK AND CROP YIELDS, 1860–1870

Livestock

Parish	Horses & Mules			Cattle			Hogs		
	% Increased	% Decreased	% Remained Same	% Increased	% Decreased	% Remained Same	% Increased	% Decreased	% Remained Same
East Baton Rouge	28	71	1	75	25	—	33	66	1
East Feliciana	13	77	10	12	77	11	—	88	12
Livingston	29	71	—	20	80	—	20	80	—
St. Helena	—	86	14	—	90	10	33	67	—
St. Tammany	40	40	20	50	50	—	10	50	40
Washington	17	83	—	10	80	10	—	67	33
West Feliciana	50	50	—	20	80	—	20	80	—

Crop yields

Parish	Corn Production			Cotton Production		
	% Increased	% Decreased	% Remained Same	% Increased	% Decreased	% Remained Same
East Baton Rouge	60	20	20	—	100	—
East Feliciana	—	89	11	—	88	12
Livingston	—	80	20	—	80	20
St. Helena	—	75	25	—	100	—
St. Tammany	—	50	50	—	40	60
Washington	33	67	—	—	100	—
West Feliciana	—	86	14	—	60	40

Sources: *Eighth Census, 1860,* Manuscript, and *Ninth Census, 1870,* Manuscript, Agriculture and Heads of Household Schedules

TABLE 9. ECONOMIC CHANGES IN LANDHOLDINGS, 1860–1870

| | Landholdings | | |
Parish	% Increased	% Decreased	% Remained Same
East Baton Rouge	—	68	32
East Feliciana	13	73	14
Livingston	33	60	7
St. Helena	—	67	33
St. Tammany	40	50	10
Washington	25	50	25
West Feliciana	—	33	67

agent at Clinton, secured a homestead, set up a farm, and in 1868 ran for sheriff.[7]

Most disturbing to local residents were the scores of northern speculators who purchased vast areas of farm- and timberland. H. S. McComb purchased huge tracts of timberland at twelve dollars per acre along the line of the New Orleans-Jackson Railroad and eventually seized control of the railroad itself. By the mid-1880s none other than the northern millionaire and railroad entrepreneur Jay Gould emerged as the largest landowner in several upstate parishes. Addressing this trend in a speech before the legislature, J. C. Kathman, chief of the Bureau of Immigration, reported that "some entire portions of the state are rapidly passing into the hands of northwestern farmers." Kathman acknowledged that the transition created "great excitement" among the former slaveowners, who held two-thirds of Louisiana's land prior to the war. Although Kathman included some letters from Florida-parish entrepreneurs

7. *Eighth Census*, 1860, Manuscript, and *Ninth Census*, 1870, Manuscript, Louisiana, Schedule 1, Free Population, and Schedule 2, Agricultural Statistics, Microfilm; (figures derived from a 3 percent sample of the heads of household of each parish); Fuqua to Kilbourne, June 8, December 11, 25, 1865, January 14, 1866, all in Miscellaneous File, James Gilliam Kilbourne Correspondence, LLMVC; transfer of the estate of Thomas A. G. Batchelor to the firm of Levy and Deiter, concluded December 7, 1866, J. G. Kilbourne Record Book, No. 23, 1860–67, pp. 66–74, both in Kilbourne Family Papers; J. Addison to Robert Corbin, July 23, 1874, in Robert A. Corbin Papers, LLMVC; statement of purchase of debtor's note of Mrs. Nancy L. Norwood by Abraham Levi, June 15, 1869, and preparations for seizure of Norwood's property and record of indebtedness to A. Levi, December 5, 1866, to August, 1874, in A. Levi to James Fuqua, November 9, 1874, in James O. Fuqua Papers, LLMVC.

extending northern farmers a welcome, the majority of local whites deeply resented the purchasing power of northern capital and the political implications of northern immigration.[8]

Federal confiscation acts also contributed to the prevailing misery. Many prominent families lost their homes and all their property. The widow and five minor daughters of N. R. Jennings watched as the federals confiscated all their property, leaving them perfectly destitute; desperate efforts to recover their property remained unresolved as late as 1867. Some families fell victim to unscrupulous merchants whose aggressive efforts to collect all debts due forced many to relinquish their homes and other property. Abraham Levi, a prominent Clinton merchant who frequently spied for the Federals during the war, pugnaciously collected from his debtors in the immediate aftermath of the surrender. Levi's assertiveness led his attorney James Fuqua to proclaim, "Look out for his store when the military leave." Martina Ellis also described the acute shortage of cash in the area, which contributed to the moribund economy.[9]

The problems of promoting economic recovery and curbing racial violence were integrally intertwined. Mass unemployment characterized the region in the immediate aftermath of the war. Many among the hundreds of soldiers returning home could find no work. Farming suffered from a lack of draft animals for plowing and a blight of army worms. Almost all industrial concerns had been destroyed during the war, and little capital remained

8. "Report of J. C. Kathman, Chief of the Bureau of Immigration, to the General Assembly of Louisiana," *Louisiana Legislative Documents*, 1868, p. 51; New Orleans *Daily Picayune*, April 22, 1873; E. D. Frost to H. S. McComb, June 27, 28, 29, October 18, 1875, in Francis and Frost Out Letters Collection; *Report of the Joint Committee of the General Assembly of Louisiana on the Conduct of the Late Elections and the Condition of Peace and Order in the State*, 1869, p. 7; Frank Smith to Jeptha McKinney, November 19, 1870, in McKinney Papers; John Hutchins to B. F. Flanders, October 6, 1867, in Benjamin F. Flanders Papers, LLMVC; Evan Harris to Willie McKowen, November 29, 1867, in John C. McKowen Papers, LLMVC; Greensburg *Journal*, February 23, 1866; William Ivy Hair, *Bourbonism and Agrarian Protest: Louisiana Politics, 1877–1900* (Baton Rouge, 1969), 48, 112.

9. S. B. Buckner to Gen. O. O. Howard, October 15, 1865, in Hennen-Jennings Papers; James Fuqua to James G. Kilbourne, June 9, 1865, J. G. Kilbourne Record Book, No. 23, 1860–67, pp. 66–74, both in Kilbourne Family Papers; statement of purchase of debtor's note of Mrs. Nancy L. Norwood by Abraham Levi, June 15, 1869, Levi to Fuqua, November 9, 1874, in Fuqua Papers; William Watson, Sheriff's Fee Book, 1866–70, listing number of property seizures in 1866, LLMVC; OR, Vol. XLI, Pt. 2, p. 229; New Orleans *Daily Picayune*, November 14, 1865; Clinton *East Feliciana Patriot*, November 6, 1869.

available for rebuilding. Perhaps most significant, the railroad had been completely devastated across the length of the Florida parishes.[10]

In June, 1865, the military returned control of the railroad to its governing board. All of the depot buildings, platforms, water stations, and storage houses, excepting the depots at Osyka, Magnolia, and Summit in southwestern Mississippi, had been destroyed. Even though the track was in fair condition from New Orleans to Ponchatoula and in "usable" condition north of Brookhaven, Mississippi, the portion from Ponchatoula to Brookhaven remained completely ravaged. Few serviceable locomotives were available for use anyway. Recognizing that the railroads constituted the key to economic recovery in Louisiana, Governor Wells attacked the corruption of the military authorities, who had blocked restoration of the railroads. According to Wells, the army's hand-picked directors refused to permit repair of the roads unless the stockholders released the government "from reclamations on account of the enormous sums received by its officers since the road had been in their hands."[11]

The dramatic changes associated with defeat, emancipation, and military rule created a profoundly perplexing state of affairs. The transition from slave to free labor seemingly necessitated a period of adjustment, but the prevailing crisis demanded immediate action. Most fundamentally, recovery depended on getting people back to work. Eli Capell summarized the existing state of affairs: "There is a great confusion in the country among whites and blacks as regards hiring for next year." Capell's monthly labor record exemplified the inconsistent working conditions. Of nineteen field hands employed at his Pleasant Hill Plantation in early 1867, only four received daily wages, ranging from thirteen and a half cents to seventy-five cents a day. The others presumably worked for a share of the crop. Most worked erratically, with some laborers frequently absent for weeks at a time. Only five of those employed in March, 1867, continued to work for Capell in March of the following year. Capell's records exhibit growing frustration with his laborers. In December,

10. J. R. Galtrey to Albert Batchelor, September 5, 1867, in Albert Batchelor Papers; Wells to Johnson, May 27, 1865, in Johnson Papers; Amite City *Times*, August 10, 1867; John Ellis to Thomas Ellis, August 10, 1867, in Ellis Family Papers; "Affairs of Southern Railroads," *House Reports*, 39th Cong., 2nd Sess., No. 34, pp. 1–41.

11. "Affairs of Southern Railroads," *House Reports*, 39th Cong., 2nd Sess., No. 34, pp. 1–41; *House Reports*, 40th Cong., 2nd Sess., No. 15, pp. 1–20; "Statement of Governor J. Madison Wells," *Louisiana House Journal*, Extra Sess., 1865, p. 14; Galtrey to Batchelor, September 5, 1867, in Albert Batchelor Papers; Amite City *Times*, July 27, 1867.

1866, he confided in his diary, "I am completely disgusted with free negroes." One week later he explained why: "Negroes very unsettled won't say what they are going to do I never saw such a state of things. Not one on my place except old Tone has as yet said they would stay on with me."[12]

The freedmen understandably proved reluctant to continue serving their former masters in what amounted to a semiservile state. The initial contract between Joseph Embree and his laborers contained many features of the slave system. Embree's employees worked from dawn to dark, with a portion of their salary deducted if the overseer judged their work inferior. Laborers were forbidden to ride Embree's animals or curse in his presence, and leaving the plantation without permission resulted in a stiff fine. Such a situation amounted to an effort to keep the freedmen as close to slavery as possible. But blacks' refusal to labor in the same manner they had in the antebellum period helped expose a crucial flaw of Reconstruction and aggravated prevailing circumstances. Owning no land, blacks lacked means to achieve the self-sufficiency central to the piney-woods freemen's existence. Without funds to purchase food or land on which to grow it, many soon became desperate. The Freedmen's Bureau provided temporary relief to some, but its resources proved woefully inadequate to sustain a significant portion of the state's population indefinitely. As a result, many blacks resorted to stealing privately owned livestock, primarily hogs, in order to survive. Dustin Willard demonstrated the severity of this problem: "The negroes is [sic] doing very bad here there is but a few that will work for a living but steal all the time, on the river it is worse than it is on the hills, there is scarcely any hogs in the country and but few cows. I do believe they will starve us all for there is no law that can reach them." Congressional investigators reported that blacks, accustomed to having everything provided by their former masters, "have taken to filching and stealing fruit, vegetables, and poultry so that the raising of these items literally had to be abandoned to the great distress of the white people."[13] Eli

---

12. Capell Diary, December 30, 31, 1866, January 7, 1867, Eli Capell's Laborer's Record Book, Pleasant Hill Plantation, Book No. 8; 1867–85, all in Capell Papers.

13. Dustin Willard to Micajah Wilkinson, March 18, 1868, in Wilkinson Papers; contract agreement between Joseph Embree and his laborers, February, 1866, in Embree Papers; *House Documents*, "Report of the Special Congressional Investigating Committee of Three," 43rd Cong., 2nd Sess., No. 101 (1657), Pt. 1, 1875, pp. 4–20. The congressional investigating teams examining conditions in the South almost always constituted partisan bodies collecting only that evidence that supporting the position of their party. In 1874, Democrats dominated the House investigating committees.

Capell killed his sixteen remaining hogs rather than see them stolen like most of his others. In the winter of 1867, Freedmen's Bureau agents at Clinton, Amite City, and Madisonville reported extremely high levels of tension between the races owing to the theft of poultry and hogs.[14]

Like many areas of the South in the immediate postwar period, eastern Louisiana emerged as a society adrift, with no clear sense of direction. Central to the prevailing chaotic circumstances was an absence of effective leadership. John Ellis summarized the lack of direction in a letter to his brother Tom: "We have no leader, no one to stand forth with honesty and capacity and will to thwart the tempest. These whom we call leaders are sunk in apathy or afraid to rise." Initially, it appeared that President Johnson's policy toward the defeated Confederates would disenfranchise a large percentage of the prewar elite. Johnson's pardon program excluded higher ranking Confederate civil and military officials, as well as those possessing estates valued at $20,000 or more. By September, 1865, Johnson had abandoned his policy of cautiously granting pardons and instead issued them wholesale, thereby nullifying much of the substance of the pardon program.[15]

The war itself had played havoc with the antebellum elite of the Florida parishes. Federal raiders targeted the property of the "sesech" aristocracy, and some of what survived had been confiscated. As a result, many of the old ruling order, overwhelmed by personal problems, withdrew from public service. Others found it unacceptable to stand for office in the turmoil of the postwar period. B. W. Clark considered the very idea of serving blacks and shirkers repulsive. According to Clark, "electioneering is an uphill battle with me under any circumstances and it would be especially disagreeable for me to go smiling about some rascally deserter and informing him that I would be happy to obtain his vote, when in reality it would afford me great satisfaction to give him a good kicking." The *East Feliciana Patriot* observed that men about Jackson and Clinton directed their energies toward financial recovery

14. Capell Diary, January 4, 1867, in Capell Papers; letters to Freedmen's Bureau headquarters at New Orleans from James DeGrey, November 10, 1867, W. H. Haugen, December 31, 1867, James Hough, December 31, 1867, in Freedmen's Bureau Reports, NA; McDonald and McWhiney, "Antebellum Southern Herdsman," 164.

15. John Ellis to Tom Ellis, January 9, 29, 1870, both in Ellis Family Papers; Joe Gray Taylor, *Louisiana Reconstructed 1863–1877* (Baton Rouge, 1974), 60, 63; Jonathan Dorris, *Pardon and Amnesty Under Lincoln and Johnson: The Restoration of the Confederates to Their Rights and Privileges* (Chapel Hill, 1953), 116–17, 138–41; Eric Foner, *Reconstruction: America's Unfinished Revolution, 1863–1877* (New York, 1988), 190–91.

rather than politics. Still others among the antebellum elite succumbed to the ravages of the war. J. R. Galtrey noted that most of the local power brokers in Amite County, Mississippi, including "Squire Reeves and Mr. Weathersby," died during the course of the war, adding that "everything about here wears the air of dilapidation and decay."[16]

Although death, disenfranchisement, and financial ruin certainly served to remove many from the political spectrum, these issues alone do not account for the wholesale transformation of elected officials in the Florida parishes. Although ex-Confederates dominated the legislative election of November, 1865, few of them had served in the prewar period. Only G. W. Munday of East Feliciana and J. H. Collins of West Feliciana had any prewar experience among those elected from the Florida parishes. Moreover, few of the candidates elected in the piney-woods parishes came from the prewar planter elite. Washington and St. Tammany Parishes returned farmers to the lower house, but only Jacob Magee of Washington Parish possessed the wealth necessary in 1860 to classify as a planter. The balance of legislators elected from the piney woods came from the emerging merchant and professional class. They included among their ranks lawyers, court recorders, and lumbermen. Analogous circumstances prevailed in regional and municipal elections in the piney woods. Only one of the six sitting members of the St. Tammany Parish Police Jury retained his seat in the immediate postwar period. Although F. A. Cousin, police jury president in 1865, also retained his seat on the jury, he was decisively defeated in his bid to secure reelection as president and never attended a session during the following year. In Greensburg, Mayor Henry Williams, a member of one of the largest and most affluent families in the parish, was replaced by local merchant C. H. Hyde. Similarly, in Amite City the mayor and three out of five councilmen failed to retain their seats.[17]

16. J. R. Galtrey to his Uncle Grip, September 5, 1867, in Albert Batchelor Papers; B. W. Clark to Eugene Hunter, July 23, 1865, in Hunter-Taylor Family Papers; Clinton *East Feliciana Patriot*, November 20, 1869; Joe Gray Taylor, *Louisiana Reconstructed*, 54–55, 64–65.

17. List of legislators compiled from *House Journal*, 1860, 1864, 1865, and *Senate Journal*, 1856, 1860, 1864, 1865; *Eighth Census*, 1860, Manuscript, Louisiana, Schedule 1, Free Population, and Schedule 2, Agricultural Statistics, Microfilm; Records of the Louisiana State Government, 1850–88, War Department Collection of Confederate Records, Doc. F-75, Roll 9, NA; St. Tammany Parish Police Jury Minutes, January Sess., March Sess., 1865, August Sess., 1866, all in WPA Louisiana Parish Police Jury Minutes Collection; Amite City *Times*, July 27, 1867; Amite City Council Minute Book, June, 1863–July, 1866, Amite City Hall, Amite, La.; *Seventh Census*, 1850, Manuscript, Louisiana, Schedule 1, Free Population, Microfilm.

A perception of powerlessness contributed to the political transformation in the Florida parishes. The presence of federal garrisons at Baton Rouge, Bayou Sara, Clinton, and Amite City served as a constant reminder that real power rested with an army of occupation. Periodically these garrisons dispatched cavalry contingents to Franklinton, Greensburg, Springfield, and Covington, demonstrating the federal presence throughout the territory. Local governing bodies and the courts functioned under the close scrutiny of resident federal officials. In early 1867 General Philip Sheridan, commanding the Fifth Military District, issued a proclamation that confirmed the impotence of local civil authority. The decree stated, "Existing civil functionaries will be continued but simply provisionally and subject to removal should their conduct not comport with the military commanders' view of their duty." Similarly, the local courts exercised little realistic authority. In the summer of 1865, General E. R. S. Canby pronounced that state courts could resume their duties with the exception of cases involving soldiers or civil officials affiliated with the United States government. William P. Mellen urged the military authorities to submit cases only to those state courts that appeared sympathetic to the interests of Washington, D.C. The Greensburg *Journal* summarized the opinion of many local residents when it declared the federals' usurpation of local authority a violation of the fundamental tenets of republicanism. "Our political position is already sufficiently humiliating, even if our state officials use their utmost energies and talents to conceal the fact that the powers at Washington to which we owe allegiance are adverse to state sovereignty and constitutional liberty."[18]

The absolute control exercised by United States military authorities furthered the changing political climate, particularly among the remnants of the planter elite, who deeply resented the collapse of their commanding power in state government. But the revival of the societal commitment to a peculiarly piney-woods republicanism contributed in a more substantive sense to the changing of attitudes in the eastern parishes. From the late 1830s to the early 1850s, the centrality of the republican tradition to piney-woods perspectives promoted increasing disillusionment with planter-dominated government. Planter power brokers had, however, skillfully manipulated the sectional cri-

---

18. Greensburg *Journal*, February 23, 1866; Greensburg *Weekly Star and Journal*, April 27, 1867; Proclamation of General Philip Sheridan, rpr. Clinton *Feliciana Democrat*, March 21, 1867; Proclamation from headquarters, Department of the Gulf, signed by General E. R. S. Canby, June 27, 1865 William P. Mellen to B. F. Flanders , April 27, 1866, both in Flanders Papers.

sis and the omnipresent fear of slave unrest to create an "us versus them" mentality. This maneuver, in turn, necessitated continuing plain folk acceptance of the rule of their planter protectors.

The catastrophe that secession and the war represented for all white social classes in eastern Louisiana changed all that and encouraged the plain folk to reassess their fealty to the planters. Linus Parker declared that his reflection on the events leading to secession and its results had led him to "wonder at the hollowness of the whole affair." In a chilling reference to the piney-woods tradition of political powerlessness, the Greensburg *Weekly Star and Journal* urged its readers to action by declaring, "You will have a government made for you if you do not make it for yourself." The *St. Helena Echo* reminded the people that the man who works the land has always been oppressed by "class legislation" initiated by the "lordly planters." Calls for the revival of the independent, self-sufficient life-style that characterized the region in less complicated times proved a popular theme of the piney-woods press during the immediate postwar period. The Greensburg *Journal* exhorted a revival of Jeffersonian principles to liberate the people from the manipulation that led to war, ruin, and subsequent exploitation by Yankees, proclaiming, "Home manufacturing is the true road to independence." Likewise, the Amite City *Democrat* reminded its readers of the near utopian existence inherent in the independent and self-sufficient piney-woods way of life. Many newspapers equated the prevailing deprivation with the people's abandonment of self-sufficiency for the unpredictable and dependent circumstances of the market economy. The *East Feliciana Patriot* urged farmers to plant corn, not cotton: "We never did right in so tilling our soil as to enrich others at our expense and we can never reach that level of independence as long as we allow that great mine of wealth, our soil [to] lie dormant. The surest way of relieving ourselves of debt and becoming independent is to raise everything our soil and climate can afford for human consumption."[19]

The resurgent republican ideal demanded that piney-woods farmers free themselves from all agents of exploitation. This included their northern conquerors as well as their planter overlords, who, many plain folk appeared increasingly willing to believe, had manipulated them. Osyka resident J. W.

---

19. Linus Parker to John Burruss, September 27, 1865, in Burruss Papers; Greensburg *Weekly Star and Journal*, April 27, 1867; Greensburg *St. Helena Echo*, September 12, 1891; Greensburg *Journal*, July 20, 1866; Amite City *Democrat*, October 2, 1875; Clinton *East Feliciana Patriot*, April 27, 1867, November 13, 1869, July 2, 1870.

Courtney argued that the poor had fought and suffered through the war merely to support the life-style of the rich. Proclaiming his refusal to submit further to planter selfishness, Courtney declared, "I am determined in my mind not to serve them [planters] any longer they have allways [sic] made laws to oppress the poor." Cotton increasingly came to be seen as the tool for exploiting the less privileged. Deliverance from the shackles of King Cotton became synonymous with independence in the piney-woods press. The St. Helena Echo declared, "Wealth and prosperity will come only through independence and independence will come only through agricultural diversity." Other country newspapers, such as the East Feliciana Patriot and the Magnolia Gazette, urged farmers to plant food crops in order to break the cycle of dependence and limit the wealth of rich manufacturers.[20]

Calls for economic independence, coupled with the results of the immediate postwar elections and the commanding presence of the federal military, created conditions favorable to political realignment in eastern Louisiana. As they had in the 1850s, however, the planters would again delay the arrival of realistic democracy in the piney woods by identifying and promoting fear of another common enemy of southern whites. Planter preeminence, though now subject to an alliance with the increasingly powerful merchant-professional class, who also demanded racial unity and home rule, resurfaced in the face of a determined common enemy. Henry Clay Warmoth, a Republican organizer and successor to Governor Wells, correctly surmised that the old elite intentionally fostered hatred in order to maintain its power. According to Warmoth, Louisiana's problem lay "in the contumacy of the old ruling aristocracy, who believe that they were born to govern, without question, not only their slaves but the masses of the white people." By capitalizing on reinforced racial fears and lingering hatred for the Yankees, the elite again presented itself as the protector of the common man. Carpetbaggers, northerners who supposedly carried all their belongings in a satchel made of carpet material as they came south to exploit the defeated region, and local people who supported the efforts of the Republican party, known derisively as scalawags, provided excellent scapegoats. The old elite aggressively promoted contempt for the Republicans and their supporters. One Democratic party circular de-

20. J. W. Courtney to his Brothers and Sisters, February 7, 1864, in Stokes Papers; Greensburg St. Helena Echo, August 4, 1889, January 23, 30, 1892, January 31, 1896; Clinton East Feliciana Patriot, April 27, 1867, November 13, 1869, July 2, 1870; Magnolia, Miss., Gazette, April 12, 1883; Kentwood Commercial, February 26, 1898.

clared, "Most ill disposed negroes are not half so much deserving our aversion and non-intercourse with them as the debased whites who encourage and aid them, and who become through their votes the office holding oppressors of the people. Whatever of resentment you have should be felt toward the latter and not the colored men." Such statements, typical in the immediate postwar period, implied that the Republicans, not the freedmen, constituted the real enemy. By joining the old elite in vanquishing the power of these intruders, the argument continued, the common people could again enjoy the fruits of their adherence to the Jeffersonian-Jacksonian tradition. Although significant evidence demonstrates that the piney-woods aversion for rule of the elite had resurfaced, racial fears and the new common enemy would again delay the ramifications of this resentment.[21]

Fortunately for the battered ranks of the old elite and their reluctant allies, the Republicans would simplify the task of maintaining and expanding the remnants of their power. J. Madison Wells became governor in early 1865 when Unionist Michael Hahn was elected to fill a seat in the United States Senate. Wells then secured election as chief executive in his own right in November, 1865, defeating an absentee Henry W. Allen, who had fled the country following the collapse of Confederate resistance. Wells, a native of Rapides Parish, had remained a consistent Unionist throughout the war. Although he shared many of the racial views of his Democratic counterparts, Wells emerged as one of a score of political chameleons whose machinations added to the confusion prevailing in postwar Louisiana. Convinced that the ex-Confederates would emerge as the real power brokers, he initially made appointments and supported legislation favorable to that group. However, the growing strength of the Radical Republicans, led by the youthful carpetbagger Warmoth, induced Wells to shift his allegiance frequently. In March, 1867, Congress overcame Johnson's veto and divided the South into five military districts; General Philip Sheridan became the commander of the Fifth Military District, which encompassed Louisiana and Texas. By the spring of 1867, Wells's inconsistency had alienated virtually everyone, prompting an exasperated Sheridan to remove him from office. In his place Sheridan appointed New Hampshire-born Benjamin F. Flanders, whose seven-month tenure signaled the end of presidential Reconstruction and the advent of military Reconstruction in Louisiana.[22]

21. *Report of the Joint Committee of the General Assembly of Louisiana*, 7, 22–23.

22. Greensburg *Journal*, February 23, 1866; Joe Gray Taylor, *Louisiana Reconstructed*, 71, 80–82, 103–104, 140; Baton Rouge *Weekly Advocate*, June 30, 1866; New Orleans *Daily*

The events contributing to the introduction of military, or Radical, Reconstruction are well documented.[23] The primacy of racial fears prompted all but Tennessee among the southern states to reject the Fourteenth Amendment. Rather than see the South returned to the fold with its antebellum power structure intact, Congress initiated a series of acts designed to produce substantive change in the former Confederacy.

The congressional plan required a new registration of voters, a measure intended to disenfranchise secessionist leaders. Moreover, black enfranchisement provided the best means to promote the fortunes of the Republican party in the South and for the freedmen to secure their rights as citizens. The measure approved by Congress on March 2, 1867, was designed to deny the vote to thousands of ex-Confederate civil and military officials. Sheridan directed that the order be interpreted so as to include virtually all ex-Confederates of any standing. His proclamation declared, "Registrars will give the most rigid interpretation to the law and exclude from registration every person about whose right to vote there may be doubt." Republican registrars regularly consulted local Unionists to ascertain the political affiliation of many ex-Confederates before determining their eligibility. In parishes where it proved difficult to locate Unionists to act as registrars, Union soldiers or Freedmen's Bureau agents performed this service.[24]

White conservative efforts to prevail in peace where they had failed in war necessitated the actions of the Radical Republicans in Congress. The popular perception that scores of men imbued with a fierce republican tradition and just emerging from a brutal war were being disenfranchised by their government, however, had enormous implications that Republicans either

Picayune, February 8, 9, 1867; Joseph G. Dawson, III, *Army Generals and Reconstruction: Louisiana, 1862–1877* (Baton Rouge, 1982), 44.

23. See David H. Donald, *The Politics of Reconstruction, 1863–1867* (Baton Rouge, 1965); William M. Evans, *Ballots and Fence Rails: Reconstruction on the Lower Cape Fear* (Chapel Hill, 1967); Foner, *Reconstruction*; Kenneth Stampp, *Era of Reconstruction, 1865–1877* (New York, 1965); Joe Gray Taylor, *Louisiana Reconstructed*; Tunnell, *Crucible of Reconstruction*.

24. *House Documents*, 40th Cong., 2nd Sess., Exec. Doc. No. 291 (1343), 1867–68; *Instructions to Supervisors of Registration with a Transcript of the Constitutional, Naturalization, and Other Laws Pertaining to the Qualification of Electors* (New Orleans, 1868), 6–7; Testimony of John H. Pipes and Martial Amacker, in *Congressional Hearings Supplement*, 1869, 384–97; Charles E. Kennon to John Ellis, September 22, 1870, in Ellis Family Papers; Dorris, *Pardon and Amnesty*, 333–35; Joe Gray Taylor, *Louisiana Reconstructed*, 132, 139, 143; Joseph Dawson, *Army Generals and Reconstruction*, 49; New Orleans *Daily Picayune*, April 21, June 28, 1867. The New Orleans *Tribune*, July 23, 1867, called for loyal persons to help produce evidence to "erase the rebels" from the voters' rolls.

failed to foresee or greatly underestimated. Although only a fraction of the white electorate actually lost the vote, and then only temporarily, the press and public treated the measure as a full-scale repression and a disaster. Local newspapers blasted the Republicans for "perpetuating disunion" and "trampling upon the fundamental virtues of the Constitution." As reports circulated that disqualifications included road overseers, school directors, commissioners of election, sheriffs' deputies, steamboat pilots, and others who held seemingly insignificant positions before the war but had served in the Confederate army or civil service, passions reached a fever pitch. The Amite City *Times* relentlessly condemned efforts to emasculate the white South and the concomitant delivery of local government into the hands of opportunistic carpetbaggers and their minions "from the land of the gorilla and the ape." The *Times* and other state papers also strongly urged those permitted to vote to do so. On the day appointed for the election to approve a constitutional convention, the New Orleans *Daily Picayune* estimated that one-half of the white voters of the state had been denied suffrage.[25]

The results of the constitutional convention election appeared to confirm the massive disenfranchisement of white voters. The convention secured approval by a vote of 75,083 to 4,006. Republicans elected ninety-six of the ninety-eight delegates, with blacks making up one-half of that number. In reality, the election did not provide a truthful indication of the level of disenfranchisement. Hopelessness and disgust served to keep most whites away from the polls. Many recognized that conservatives had no chance for success, while others hoped that a low turnout would nullify the election results. Still others could not yet accept the idea of voting alongside blacks. By the day of the election, even the normally enthusiastic *Daily Picayune* admitted that it, too, had abandoned hope for a conservative victory.[26]

The April, 1868, state and constitutional ratification election provides a much more definitive statement on the level of disenfranchisement. Although far from revolutionary, by Louisiana standards the Constitution of 1868 represented a radical departure from the past. Whites' anger increased

25. Amite City *Times*, July 27, August 10, 31, 1867; New Orleans *Daily Picayune*, April 21, June 28, September 27, 1867; Kennon to Ellis, September 22, 1870, in Ellis Family Papers.

26. New Orleans *Daily Picayune*, September 27, 1867; *Official Journal of the Proceedings of the Convention for Framing a Constitution for the State of Louisiana, 1867–1868* (New Orleans, 1868), 1–6, hereinafter referred to as *Constitutional Convention Proceedings, 1868*; Charles Vincent, "Negro Leadership and Programs in the Constitutional Convention of 1868," *Louisiana History*, X (1969), 339–51; Joe Gray Taylor, *Louisiana Reconstructed*, 146–48.

as this document, which they regarded as written by and reflecting almost exclusively the views of "blacks, Yankees, and scalawags," became public. Thousands who had avoided the earlier election now determined they would participate. The *Daily Picayune* urged readers to vote against the document designed, it argued, to benefit "the camp followers left behind by the Federal army and a lot of white trash of southern origin." The gubernatorial candidacy of the carpetbagger Warmoth, whose public comments to black audiences had gained him notoriety as a Radical, also encouraged white conservative participation. Significantly, though Warmoth's opponent, James G. Taliaferro, represented a reputedly more radical faction of the Republicans, thousands of white Democrats supported his candidacy merely because he was a native of Louisiana.[27]

Republican reports indicated that only 2,169 men had been rejected outright by the registrars, but published lists of voters denied registration indicate that the figure was considerably higher. Moreover, public awareness that General Sheridan demanded a rigid application of the law probably discouraged many from subjecting themselves to the humiliation of rejection. Returns show that approximately 36,029 whites voted in the April, 1868, election. The number of participants amounted to slightly more than 41 percent of adult white males, a dramatic decrease in voter turnout from elections in the late 1850s. Thus, though claims that 50 percent of white males had been denied suffrage are almost certainly exaggerated, following the implementation of the Reconstruction Acts of 1867, nearly one-third fewer whites voted, whether from disillusionment or choice. Both the constitution and Warmoth secured the voters' approval by comfortable majorities. East Baton Rouge, Livingston, St. Helena, and Washington Parishes joined sixteen primarily upstate cotton and Sabine River region parishes in rejecting the constitution.[28]

The prevailing perception that many among the prewar elite had been disenfranchised provided the old aristocracy with a powerful propaganda tool.

27. New Orleans *Daily Picayune*, April 15, 17, 1868; *Constitutional Convention Proceedings*, 1868, 290–309; Thomas G. Davidson to James Taliaferro, April 25, 1868, in James G. Taliaferro Papers, LLMVC; testimony of Charles E. Kennon, in *Congressional Hearings Supplement, 1869*, 217–23; Amite City *Times*, August 31, 1867; Vincent, "Negro Leadership and Programs," 339–51; Joe Gray Taylor, *Louisiana Reconstructed*, 151.

28. *Ninth Census, 1870; Population*, 629; *Historical Statistics*, II, 1072; Donald W. Davis, "Ratification of the Constitution of 1868—Record of Votes," *Louisiana History*, VI (1965), 301–305; Amite City *Times*, September 28, 1867; New Orleans *Daily Picayune*, September 27, 1867; Dorris, *Pardon and Amnesty*, 333–35; Joe Gray Taylor, *Louisiana Reconstructed*, 143–44.

Denying landholding freemen suffrage comprised a fundamental violation of the piney-woods tradition of republicanism. The old elite presented themselves as victims of tyrannical outsiders who sought not to create equality between the races but indeed to make blacks dominant in order to serve their own special ends. The transition in popular perceptions regarding the planter elite would prove decisive in determining the outcome of Radical Reconstruction in Louisiana. Racial solidarity and hostility to outsiders again secured the old elite against the potential for social upheaval. Latent antagonism between white social classes would remain dormant until the common enemy was subdued.

Following the election, the Republicans moved swiftly to consolidate their power. The legislature granted the governor the authority to fill vacant political positions and replace officials considered ineligible. Warmoth accordingly removed many elected officials on the state, parish, and municipal levels and replaced them with party loyalists, thereby alienating many of the business and professional men who filled the immediate postwar void of elected officials. The disaffected consequently flocked to the battered ranks of the old elite. Warmoth further antagonized Florida-parish conservatives by appointing scores of Federal soldiers, Freedmen's Bureau agents, and local Republicans with questionable ethical backgrounds to responsible positions. Other clearly incompetent Republicans gained office either by election or appointment. H. H. Bankston, facing several indictments for fraud and embezzlement of municipal funds, secured appointment as mayor of Amite City. Freedmen's Bureau agent DeGrey was appointed sheriff of East Feliciana despite his limited knowledge of the people and region. In St. Tammany, Warmoth appointed a crippled illiterate black named Populus as parish tax collector to spite an opponent within his own party. Perhaps the greatest regional farce occurred in St. Helena, where John Kemp, an uneducated field hand, albeit a Republican organizer, secured election as parish coroner.[29]

---

29. *Louisiana Senate Journal*, Exec. Sess., 1868, pp. 1–49, 1st Sess., 1869, pp. 16–18; Amite City Council Minute Book, June, 1863–February, 1867, Amite City Hall; Testimony of H. H. Bankston, Thomas C. W. Ellis, James H. George, John H. Pipes, Robert Babington, R. F. Briggs, and Johnson E. Yerks, in *Congressional Hearings Supplement, 1869*, 41, 83–95, 98–110, 236–38, 384–92; James DeGrey to Freedmen's Bureau headquarters at New Orleans, April 18, 30, 1868, both in Freedmen's Bureau Reports, NA; Isaac Evans to James G. Taliaferro, February 28, 1870, in Taliaferro Papers; John Ellis to Tom Ellis, June 13, 1872, in Ellis Family Papers; New Orleans *Republican*, January 7, 11, 1870; Amite City *Tangipahoa Democrat*, July 4, August 2, 1872; Joe Gray Taylor, *Louisiana Reconstructed*, 176.

The Republicans' determination to fill positions exclusively with party loyalists created problems. Many of those appointed to important offices found themselves incapable of performing their duties. An exchange between James H. George, elected district judge from St. Helena, and members of a congressional subcommittee investigating conditions in Louisiana symbolized this problem.

Subcommittee: Do you think opposition to you arose mainly from politics?

George: It mainly arose from politics. The lawyers held a meeting and agreed not to practice under me.

Subcommittee: Why?

George: Two reasons, one that I was ineligible and another that I was elected by negroes.

Subcommittee: How were you ineligible?

George: For lack of a knowledge of the law.

Subcommittee: Then you mean you were incompetent?

George: Yes, that is what I mean.[30]

Under the prevailing circumstances the Republicans naturally faced acute limitations in resources, but their determination to rule absolutely, regardless of the quality of local government, proved both provocative and fateful.

For blacks and white Republicans the advent of Radical Reconstruction represented an unprecedented opportunity. With the future in their own hands, few would willingly relinquish their newfound power, and many would fight to retain it. Most regarded the limitations of some of their number as a product of decades of misrule and brutal oppression. Most local whites, though, viewed the changing circumstances not merely as a loss of control over their own destinies but as an affront to the very idea of order and government. And in eastern Louisiana, as in other areas of the South, the last months of the war had demonstrated an effective means of dealing with a perceived oppressor. With such a vast chasm between the opponents and such bitter lessons learned, the struggle was certain to be painful.

30. Testimony of James H. George, *Congressional Hearings Supplement*, 1869, 41, 85, 95; New Orleans *Republican*, January 12, 18, 1870.

Violence characterized the Florida parishes from the very outset of Reconstruction. Freedmen's Bureau agents, Federal soldiers, and blacks all suffered frequent attacks. The day after the second attempt on his life, Lieutenant Edward Ehrlich reported, "Outrages are committed daily at Amite City." During the summer and fall of 1865, at least sixteen shootings and stabbings occurred in the eastern Florida parishes. Dozens of incidents of assault, battery, and intimidation also were reported. In the few cases local law enforcement sought to prosecute, it failed miserably, often in comical fashion. A jury acquitted George Story of shooting a black woman based on his assertion that he was actually shooting at another man down the street from the victim. The jury apparently not only lacked sympathy for the victim but also considered Story's intentions justifiable.[31]

Federal authorities also proved incapable of dealing with the scope of the violence. Insufficient manpower and a sluggish bureaucracy ensured that before enough evidence could be gathered in one case, several more startling incidents had occurred. Civil authorities refused to share information from ongoing criminal investigations with federal troops and only reluctantly responded to federal demands. The vast majority of local whites refused to cooperate with federal authorities in any way. When summoned to appear before the local Freedmen's Bureau agent, Amite City resident Mark Day responded simply, "To hell with the Yankee."[32]

Although blacks suffered greatly from acts of violence, many proved willing to defend themselves, and others resorted to violence to obtain their own ends. Many blacks who spoke in support of the Democrats became victims of black-on-black terror. Only moments after Stephen Durden, a black resident of Livingston Parish, completed a speech supporting the Democrats, a group of freedmen shot and killed him on a public highway. Such incidents increased in the wake of the September, 1867, election. After touring Washington Parish, Freedmen's Bureau agent W. H. Haugen observed that many

31. Letters received at Freedmen's Bureau headquarters at New Orleans from James Hough, December 12, 20, 1867, Lt. Edward Ehrlich, September 18 (three letters), December 19, 20, 21, 23, 26, 1865, Gen. A. J. Edgerton, September 6, 1866, Capt. H. H. Rouse, September 9, 1865, James DeGrey, April 20, June 20, October 7, 1867, W. H. Haugen, October 10, 1867, and A. F. Hayden to Edward Ehrlich, October, 1865, all in Freedmen's Bureau Reports, NA; Amite City *Times*, August 10, 31, 1867; Col. George Forsyth to District Court Judge at Covington, May 27, 1867, in Ellis Family Papers.

32. James Hough to Freedmen's Bureau headquarters at New Orleans, December 12, 1867, in Freedmen's Bureau Reports, NA.

blacks refused to work, instead resorting to theft, and were "a perfect terror to the country." Armed freedmen also seized several plantations in East Feliciana and St. Helena parishes, threatening to kill anyone who interfered with their operations. Under the heading "An Ugly Sight," the Amite City *Democrat* described the passion of a particular black woman for carrying "a tremendous navy six shooter" with her about the streets of Amite City in search of a "white man who gave her a drubbing." The article concluded, "We hope some of her colored friends will prevail upon her to leave the ugly weapon at home and use the law to protect her." White Republican officials were often accused of instigating these acts of violence. Governor Wells faced accusations that he provided immunity to those who murdered his political enemies.[33]

The level of violence increased dramatically with the emergence of several paramilitary organizations. Prior to this development, despite the presence of numerous thinly disguised "rifle clubs" and other politically inclined groups, most violent incidents had been random acts between individuals. In the wake of the July, 1866, New Orleans race riot, which amounted to no less than a slaughter of blacks by armed whites, however, the necessity of black defensive preparations was manifest. During the spring and summer of 1867, Republican organizers from New Orleans worked aggressively to establish politically inclined self-defense organizations known as Loyal League Clubs among the blacks in eastern Louisiana. Increasing acts of violence against the freedmen, such as the seemingly daily incidents at Amite City, and inequitable labor practices encouraged a newfound militancy and willingness to defend themselves. Throughout the summer of 1867, local Freedmen's Bureau agents and federal officers reported growing political agitation among the freedmen. White residents became increasingly tense with the discovery of each new "incendiary" tract issued by the New Orleans Radical Club, headed by Warmoth and others. Warmoth created near panic in February, 1868, when he proclaimed before a black audience in New Orleans that ex-

33. Amite City *Democrat*, November 20, 1875; Amite City *Times*, August 31, 1867; "Register of Murders and Outrages Committed," description of Stephen Durden murder, August 12, 1868, letters received at Freedmen's Bureau headquarters at New Orleans from W. H. Haugen, January 20, February 29, 1868, James Hough, August 10, 31, September 30, 1867, James DeGrey, October 10, 1867, message received from Lt. Col. G. W. Mitchell, December 20, 1867, all in Freedmen's Bureau Reports, NA; Testimony of William H. Wilder, Henry Clay Warmoth, and Thomas C. W. Ellis, in *Congressional Hearings Supplement*, 1869, 91–94, 98–110, 510; W. H. Sparks to James G. Taliaferro, March 6, 1869, in Taliaferro Papers.

Confederates were "traitors and treason under the Constitution is punishable by death." Union army veteran A. J. Sypher confessed that his formation of a black militia in Rapides Parish "greatly exasperated the majority of the white people in the parish." By August, 1867, Freedmen's Bureau agent James Hough reported that blacks increasingly left work to attend political meetings "where incompetent negroes [created] insubordinate feelings." Hough further noted that armed groups of blacks regularly established picket posts along the public roads and that "travellers passing by [were] halted and subjected to annoyance." Suspicions of impending trouble became a reality in the volatile circumstances surrounding the September, 1867, election.[34]

One of the most militant black paramilitary organizations emerged in western St. Helena Parish. This Loyal League Club embodied the recognition among many blacks that realistic protection from increasing racial attacks rested with themselves. Led by a mulatto farmer named Thomas Turner, the group created consternation by publicly parading with arms and threatening local whites. Hough described Turner as "very troublesome and the terror of all whites in his neighborhood." In the summer of 1867, Turner announced that he had received authority from the commanding officer of the local federal garrison "to hang all the whites." On the roads in lower St. Helena he posted pickets who loudly proclaimed their intentions. On the eve of the September 27, 1867, election, Turner mobilized his forces. Rather than marching on Greensburg as local residents expected, Turner instead headed for Amite City. During the afternoon of September 27, he arrived outside the town at the head of an armed band, which estimates placed at anywhere from 50 to 250. Major James Offley, commanding the federal garrison, informed the militiamen that they would not be permitted to enter the town as an armed body. To the horror of local whites, Offley allowed the blacks to conceal their weapons and march into town en masse. Turner's men voted with-

34. *Report of the Joint Committee of the General Assembly of Louisiana*, 26, 46; letters received at Freedmen's Bureau headquarters at New Orleans from James Hough, August 10, 31, September 30, 1867, A. Finch, September 21, 1867, James DeGrey, August 20, 1867, in Freedmen's Bureau Reports, NA; Amite City *Times*, August 31, 1867; Woodville, Miss., *Sentinel*, August 21, 1871; Testimony of James H. George, John H. Pipes, Thomas C. W. Ellis, Amos Kent, in *Congressional Hearings Supplement, 1869*, 41, 95, 98–110, 223–27, 384–92; John Ellis to Tom Ellis, August 10, 1867, in Ellis Family Papers; New Orleans *Daily Picayune*, May 5, October 8, 1868; Otis A. Singletary, "The Negro Militia Movement During Radical Reconstruction" (Ph.D. dissertation, Louisiana State University, 1949), vi, 6–12; James Stewart McGehee, "Ramble in Autobiography," Typescript, n.d., in James McGehee Papers.

out incident, then camped on the outskirts of town for several days as a demonstration of their resolve.[35]

In permitting Turner's militia to enter Amite City as an organized body and to camp on the outskirts of town, Offley outraged local whites, most of whom proved unwilling or unable to make the connection between black assertiveness and the daily incidents of racial violence perpetuated against the freedmen. Turner had boasted that he was authorized to hang any whites who interfered with his group, and many residents considered the federal commander's actions irrational. Many also remained incensed that Yankee planters had provided arms to some of their black laborers. The Amite City *Times* and other local newspapers angrily contrasted General Sheridan's orders to break up meetings supporting hospitals and monuments for Confederate veterans with his tolerance of secret meetings by armed blacks. The *Times*, though continuing to profess confidence in Major Offley's intentions, declared its own intentions: "The whites can not and will not sit idle and see their families butchered by barbarians. Self defense is God's gift—a deduction from the gift of existence itself."[36]

Limited evidence does indicate that secret white paramilitary organizations functioned in Louisiana prior to the winter of 1867 or the spring of 1868. In a November, 1865, address to the state legislature, Governor Wells announced, "Secret political associations, the members of which are bound to each other by strange oaths, and recognize each other by signs and passwords, are being revived in this city [New Orleans] with affiliations in the parishes throughout the state." Wells failed to speculate on the motives of these secret organizations, nor did he provide any evidence to support his allegations. If the evidence is sparse concerning white paramilitary organizations statewide, even less exists to indicate their presence in the Florida parishes prior to the first months of 1868. It should be noted that white-on-black violence remained so universal and difficult to prosecute that prior to 1868 there was no need for organized white terrorist groups. Substantial evidence indicates that the explosive conditions surrounding the elections in the fall of 1867 and the spring of 1868 promoted the rapid growth of white

35. James Hough to Freedmen's Bureau headquarters at New Orleans, September 30, 1867, in Freedmen's Bureau Reports, NA; Testimony of John H. Pipes, Amos Kent, Thomas C. W. Ellis, in *Congressional Hearings Supplement*, 1869, 98–110, 223–27, 384–92; Amite City *Times*, August 31, 1867.

36. Amite City *Times*, August 31, 1867; Clinton *East Feliciana Patriot*, July 21, 1866; McGehee, "Ramble in Autobiography," in James McGehee Papers.

secret societies across Louisiana. Although many supporters of these groups insisted that they emerged as a response to black assertiveness, they clearly functioned less for self-defense and more as mechanisms for the maintenance of white supremacy. The Knights of the White Camellia and the Ku Klux Klan emerged as the principal groups to fulfill this mission.[37]

Historians have frequently misunderstood the relationship between these two white supremacy organizations. Despite the recurrent misconceptions, both groups functioned separately, with different methods, if not different purposes. In the winter of 1867 and 1868, the first reports of a Ku Klux Klan in Louisiana began to circulate. Organized in Tennessee in 1866, the Klan initially functioned as a social club for Confederate veterans. By early 1867 Klan members had recognized that their secrecy enabled them to function effectively as regulators as well. Ample evidence suggests that by the spring of 1868 several Klan dens existed in the Florida parishes as well as in upstate Louisiana and southwestern Mississippi. The Klan combined an unqualified commitment to white supremacy with a murderous contempt for aspiring blacks and white Republicans. Terror served as the weapon of choice for Klansmen. Murder, arson, and intimidation all played an integral role in the Klan's nightly adventures. Their violent activities demanded absolute secrecy; few ever admitted membership. Klansmen in eastern Louisiana conformed to the stereotype of white-hooded and shrouded specters who traveled late at night and terrorized with impunity.[38]

The Ku Klux Klan's obsessive secrecy has caused some historians to question its existence in Louisiana during Reconstruction or to assume that it functioned as the more popularly recognized Knights of the White Camellia.[39] In contrast to the Klan, though, the White Camellia originated in Louisiana with slightly different intentions. Whereas the former combined fealty to white superiority with a determination to terrorize its enemies into

37. "Address of Governor Wells," *Louisiana House Journal*, Extra Sess., 1865, p. 13.

38. *Report of the Joint Committee of the General Assembly of Louisiana*, xxxi–xxxii, 83–86, 147–56; Dustin Willard to Micajah Wilkinson, March 8, 1868, in Wilkinson Papers; Willie Dixon Diary, February 20, June 16, 1868, in Dixon Papers; Charles Kennon to Tom Ellis, July 5, 1870, in Ellis Family Papers; Mary Alley Scrapbooks, Vol. I, 7–9, LLMVC; Testimony of James B. Wands, Charles Benedict, William H. Wilder, H. H. Bankston, Isham Buckhalter, Thomas C. W. Ellis, in *Congressional Hearings Supplement*, 1869, 83–87, 91–94, 97–102, 218–24, 400–403.

39. See Joe Gray Taylor, *Louisiana Reconstructed*, 145; Tunnell, *Crucible of Reconstruction*, 6; George Rable, *But There Was No Peace: The Role of Violence in the Politics of Reconstruction* (Athens, Ga., 1984), 71.

submission, the latter incorporated a similar commitment to white supremacy into a political and economic agenda. Although equally brutal in their condemnation of assertive blacks and white Republicans, the Knights of the White Camellia who operated in the Florida parishes seldom engaged in terror. Instead, they typically incorporated menacing persuasion with economic intimidation to achieve political ends. The combination of the terror of the Klan and the economic strangulation of the Knights proved a powerfully persuasive arrangement.

Members of the White Camellia openly admitted their affiliation, though the very same men denied any knowledge of the Klan. Local residents apparently felt justified in their determination to preserve the superiority of the white race but proved reticent in discussing an organization that encouraged murder. When congressional investigators in the spring of 1869 repeatedly insisted that the Knights of the White Camellia constituted nothing more than a pseudonym for the Ku Klux Klan, prominent Tangipahoa merchant Charles Kennon exploded: "I know that it is not the Ku Klux. I have never heard it called so." Some residents belonged to both, but the different oaths they took for these groups indicate their contrasting emphases. In swearing loyalty to the White Camellia, one committed himself to "defending the social and political superiority of the white race and in all places to observe a marked distinction between the white and African races." Furthermore, initiates pledged to "vote for none but white men for any position of honor, profit or trust, and to protect and defend persons of the white race against the encroachments and aggressions of an inferior race." Although it contained an extreme commitment to racial superiority and required an apparent willingness to defend that principle, the oath did not include an overt call to violence. A Klansman pledged to "reject and oppose the principles of the radical party in all its forms, and forever maintain that intelligent white men shall govern this country." After swearing to protect "females, widows and their households," the Klansman further pledged his life: "[I will] obey all instructions given me by my chief, and should I ever divulge or cause to be divulged any secrets, signs or passwords of the Invisible Empire, I must meet with the fearful and just penalty of the traitor, which is death, death, death, at the hands of my brethren."[40] Although abundant evidence demonstrates the vio-

---

40. Testimony of Charles Kennon, John R. Wood, Robert Babington, John H. Pipes, Martial Amacker, Thomas C. W. Ellis, E. R. Boissat, in *Congressional Hearings Supplement, 1869*, 98–110, 217–23, 276, 308, 368–71, 384–97; *Report of the Joint Committee of the General Assembly*

lent activities of the Klan, no available evidence indicates that the Knights of the White Camellia participated in violent activities in the Florida parishes.

During the course of Reconstruction, Florida-parish blacks endured constant physical assaults, continual efforts to retain them as virtual slaves, sustained discrimination in all areas, and universal denial of long-overdue civil rights. Without the backing of guns, their desire to enjoy the fruits of liberation from bondage would have ensured their destruction in eastern Louisiana. Yet their organized efforts to protect themselves did result in extreme racial sensitivity on the part of whites long accustomed to black passivity and subordination. By fanning the flames of this racial hysteria, the old elite recovered much of their influence. The near universal support among whites attained by the postwar leadership enabled these men aggressively to pursue their primary purpose, recovery of political control. As in the antebellum period, though, not all whites shared the same priorities. If most whites feared black empowerment and demanded government led by native conservatives, the divergence in priorities exemplified by the nebulous distinctions between the White Camellia and the Klan symbolized a contrast between the white groups that was central to the chaotic conditions of the late nineteenth century. The two organizations shared many of the same ideals and members, but in eastern Louisiana political control proved primary to the White Camellia, whereas Klansmen typically regarded racial dominance as preeminent. The differences in the priorities and methods of these two groups contributed to a growing schism between piney-woods whites in the late nineteenth century from which emerged violently competitive factions.

The distinctions between the two organizations sharpen when their day-to-day operations are examined. The membership of the White Camellia represented the best elements of white society. Most of their leaders in eastern Louisiana, including Tom and John Ellis, John Pipes, and J. B. McClendon, represented the emerging business and professional class, which provided leadership in the immediate postwar period. Others, such as former state senator and Washington Parish patriarch Hardy Richardson, exemplified the old elite's commitment to the movement. The Klan's obsessive secrecy makes

---

of Louisiana, xxxi–xxxii; Walter L. Fleming, The Reconstruction of the Seceded States (Albany, N.Y., 1905), 119, 125; J. C. Lester and D. L. Wilson, Ku Klux Klan: Its Origin, Growth, and Disbandment (New York, 1905), 189–98; John Ellis to Tom Ellis, March 6, December 23, 1869, January 11, 29, 1870, in Ellis Family Papers.

identifying members difficult, but the few in eastern Louisiana whose membership is certain differed from the Knights: they were younger, less affluent, and largely detached from sources of power. Tom Ellis referred to the Klansmen simply as "drinking characters." Other possible Klansmen, such as Robert Babington, a Franklinton businessman and postmaster, represented those associated with both organizations.[41]

In the weeks preceding the November, 1868, election, both white societies initiated offensives that exemplified their respective practices. Having failed in the spring of 1868 to achieve victory through legal means, the Democrats determined to triumph through extralegal activities. The *Daily Picayune* declared in the immediate aftermath of the April election, "The next time an election takes place we will be prepared, and their [Republicans'] intimidation game will not be a very safe one." The most hotly disputed contest in addition to the presidential election and a few local races involved the selection of a congressman from eastern Louisiana. That race pitted an aging Louis St. Martin against a carpetbagger general J. H. Sypher, in a bitter contest characterized by massive fraud and violence.

The white conservative campaign incorporated economic intimidation, psychological terror, and murder. One technique involved a systematic economic lockout of blacks who voted Republican. Acting at the behest of the Knights of the White Camellia, local Democratic executive committees issued protection papers to freedmen who voted Democratic. The papers identified the individual as a Democratic voter who was therefore entitled to retain his employment and to receive valuable services provided by Democrats such as corn grinding and credit extension. Local newspapers and power brokers promoted this effort relentlessly in the weeks preceding the November election. According to congressional testimony, the owners of the Magee Mill and Lumber Company in Washington Parish distributed flyers informing the freedmen that the mill would no longer grind their corn or cut their timber if they failed to vote Democratic. Isham McGee, a black resident of Washington Parish, confirmed that many freedmen voted Democratic simply to avoid losing their jobs or essential services. The Democrats circulated a pe-

41. John Ellis to Tom Ellis, March 6, 1869, in Ellis Family Papers; Testimony of Charles Benedict, John Wood, Robert Babington, John H. Pipes, Martial Amacker, Thomas C. W. Ellis, in *Congressional Hearings Supplement*, 1869, 98–110, 218–24, 308, 368–71, 384–97; *Ninth Census, 1870*, Manuscript, Louisiana, Schedule 1, Free Population, Microfilm; Dixon Diary, June 16, 1868, in Dixon Papers; *Report of the Joint Committee of the General Assembly of Louisiana*, 83–86, 147–48.

tition among whites getting them to pledge that they would not buy from or sell to blacks who failed to vote Democratic. Those who refused to sign came under immediate suspicion. In the Florida parishes as in other regions of the South, voting Republican carried a stiff price.[42]

Another part of the Democratic strategy involved the use of terror. This aspect of the multifaceted campaign of intimidation fell to the Ku Klux Klan. To fulfill their part of the scheme, the Klan employed tactics designed to eliminate black leadership and inspire fear in their Republican opponents. During the interim between the April and November elections, the Klan sought to "turn over" Republican activists. Johnson E. Yerks, a leading St. Helena Parish Republican, informed a congressional investigating team that several prominent blacks presented letters urging them to "turn over" or face death. Yerks himself received a menacing letter signed only "KKK." Headed "Crow Hall Midnight," the letter warned that Yerks was suspected of Radical principles and should beware the hour of midnight. Other prominent Republicans received similar letters. H. H. Bankston testified that the Klan placed cards with mystic warnings on his door and those of other known Republicans. As the election neared, the Klan began making nightly raids in full costume. Black Washington Parish residents Isham Buckhalter and Isham McGee received midnight visits from large groups of Klansmen. Both declared that the Klansmen "dressed in sheets from the top of their heads to their horses' heels" and "wore false faces." The nightriders warned the blacks to vote Democratic or die. Buckhalter testified that blacks knew the Klan members were men and not ghosts but added that most believed they would be killed if they voted Republican.[43]

Republican activists had good reason to fear the Klan. In the two weeks preceding the November election, armed Klansmen in groups fifty to one hundred strong made nightly rides through the streets of Greensburg and Franklinton, creating fear and consternation among friend and foe alike.

---

42. Dixon Diary, June 13, 1868, in Dixon Papers; New Orleans *Daily Picayune*, April 15, 1868; letters received at Freedmen's Bureau headquarters at New Orleans from James DeGrey, April 10, May 10, 1868, W. H. Haugen, May 10, 1868, all in Freedmen's Bureau Reports, NA; Testimony of H. H. Bankston, Isham McGee, James H. George, Johnson E. Yerks, William H. Wilder, John Evans, Charles Benedict, in *Congressional Hearings Supplement, 1869*, 41, 83–97, 218–24; *Report of the Joint Committee of the General Assembly of Louisiana*, 83–86.

43. Testimony of Johnson E. Yerks, Isham McGee, Isham Buckhalter, H. H. Bankston, in *Congressional Hearings Supplement, 1869*, 83–87, 94–95, 397–403; *Report of the Joint Committee of the General Assembly of Louisiana*, 83–86, 147–56.

Other groups of Klansmen made discreet yet menacing midnight rides near the homes of Republican organizers. Even more disturbing, Klansmen unexpectedly dynamited trees late in the evening near Republican homes, greatly heightening the anxiety of the inhabitants. William H. Wilder and H. H. Bankston both declared that the "tree burstings" created extreme fear among local Republicans, black and white. Wilder described panicked families huddled in their homes, waiting to be attacked and afraid to venture out for sustenance, much less to vote. Word circulated later that the tree burstings served as a signal to Klansmen that the election should proceed without violent interruption, indicating that the Klan recognized their campaign of terror had been successful. With little physical harm, the Klan's nocturnal activities effectively neutralized a significant portion of the Republican electorate.[44]

Some black leaders, however, refused to "turn over," so in the days immediately preceding the election, the Klan, seemingly exasperated by their intransigence, systematically eliminated the black and significantly weakened the white Republican leadership. Congressional candidate J. H. Sypher emerged as the principal candidate for elimination. Sypher, widely regarded as ruthless and opportunistic, along with his brother had engineered the appointment to local office of numerous Republicans in eastern Louisiana. His frequent speeches to largely black audiences encouraging self-defense and support for the Republican party enraged many whites in the Florida parishes.

Ten days before the November election, armed groups of whites broke up Republican meetings at Greensburg and Tangipahoa, where Sypher had planned to speak. Rumors circulated that prominent Republicans, including Sypher and John Kemp, president of the local black Republican club, would be killed that night. Learning of the rumors, Sypher wisely cut short his visit to Greensburg and canceled his appearance at Tangipahoa. Kemp received a final warning, which he answered with a telegram to Governor Warmoth requesting troops. Unfortunately for Kemp, his message fell into the hands of Klansmen, who intercepted the youth attempting to send it in a nearby village. Late that evening a body of Klansmen crossed the state line below Osyka, Mississippi, heading south. The Klan routinely employed neighboring dens in extreme cases in order to hamper identification. The nightriders en-

44. Testimony of William H. Wilder, H. H. Bankston, Charles Benedict, Martial Amacker, David Hennessy, in *Congressional Hearings Supplement*, 1869, 83–87, 91–95, 218–24, 392–97; "Register of Murder and Outrages Committed," November, 1868, in Freedmen's Bureau Reports, NA; *Report of the Joint Committee of the General Assembly of Louisiana*, 83–86, 147–56.

tered the village of Tangipahoa and inquired at the hotels for Sypher. Learn-ing of the absence of their prize, they proceeded to Kemp's home outside of town and murdered him. Six days later, Jim Beekham, leader of a black mili-tia forming in western Washington Parish, met a similar fate. Black Republi-can organizers Squire Roberts and Mumford McCoy barely escaped with their lives. The Republican mayor of Amite City placed Roberts under arrest for disturbing the peace on election day and probably saved his life. McCoy, a Greensburg blacksmith and legislative candidate, received a postelection visit from a group of white men who denounced his activism. The visitors warned McCoy that if any whites should be harmed, he would be held per-sonally responsible and that as retribution the Klan would cut off his head. McCoy understandably fled the parish the same day. Many other less promi-nent freedmen suffered similar abuses, including Bill Wheeler, whose eyes were gouged out at Greensburg, and Daniel Lee and Marshall Thompson, both bushwhacked near Amite.[45]

In addition to Sypher, the Klan also targeted other prominent white Re-publicans. James B. Wands, a former Union naval officer from New York, aroused the ire of Democrats by securing from Warmoth appointments as lo-cal tax collector and state representative. If the onerous burden of Recon-struction taxation did not in itself condemn Wands, his aggressive support of the Republican cause did. In the days preceding the November election, Wands distributed Republican ballots in Livingston, St. Helena, and Wash-ington Parishes. Warned of a plot to kill him, Wands fled Franklinton the evening before the election and camped in the woods as Klansmen searched the area. David Hennessy, a member of Warmoth's newly created Metropoli-tan Police Force and a registrar of voters in Washington Parish, was not so lucky. The day before the election, the third attempt to kill Hennessy proved successful. Mass torchlight counterdemonstrations by Republicans and Democrats in Clinton and Jackson avoided bloodshed only because both sides recognized the horrific casualties that could result. Describing a pro-vocative Democratic procession near Olive Branch in East Feliciana Parish that stumbled into a similar Republican procession, Willie Dixon declared,

45. Testimony of James H. George, H. H. Bankston, Thomas C. W. Ellis, William H. Wilder, John Evans, James B. Wands, R. F. Briggs, Robert Babington, J. C. Bach, in *Congressional Hear-ings Supplement, 1869*, 41, 83–87, 90–102, 98–111, 236–38, 368–71; "Register of Murders and Outrages Committed," November, 1868, J. D. Buckley to Freedmen's Bureau headquarters at New Orleans, November 15, 1868, both in Freedmen's Bureau Reports, NA; *Report of the Joint Committee of the General Assembly of Louisiana*, 147–56, 13–14.

"We came very near having a bloody battle with them." A timely absence from the region was all that saved Republican congressman J. P. Newsham of West Feliciana from death at the hands of an outraged mob. Numerous bloody encounters between individuals contributed to an incredibly high level of tension by election day in the Felicianas and East Baton Rouge. In the wake of massive election-day violence and fraud, Freedmen's Bureau agent J. W. Coleman reported from Baton Rouge that "the Bureau appears to be the only protection the freedmen have."[46]

The pressure applied to black voters came from friend and foe alike. To counter Democratic threats and intimidation, white Republicans warned that blacks who failed to vote, and vote Republican at that, would not receive their share of land and mules. Republicans routinely promised the freedmen that once they were in power, their supporters would be appropriately compensated. Moreover, the federal garrisons increasingly demonstrated an unwillingness to intervene on behalf of black Republicans. Prominent Republican William Wilder declared, "The soldiers are worse on the negroes than anybody else." Thus, blacks had the option of risking their lives by voting Republican or of forfeiting their only realistic hope for economic advancement by voting Democratic. Unfortunately for the freedmen, this unenviable predicament would only get worse.[47]

The 1868 Democratic campaign of terror proved remarkably successful. By employing the lessons in brutality learned from the war, the Democrats effectively neutralized much of their opposition. Political violence claimed the lives of at least 204 black and white Republicans statewide. Rowdy, armed Democrats congregated about most precincts, intimidating all who sought to vote Republican. Colorized ballots made a voter's preference easily identifiable, thus expediting coercive efforts. Only precincts guarded by federal troops recorded any Republican votes. White and black Republicans voted

46. Dixon Diary, August 1, 15, 22, 29, September 2, October 19, November 3, 1868, in Dixon Papers; Testimony of James B. Wands, Charles Benedict, in *Congressional Hearings Supplement*, 1869, 97–102, 218–24; letters received at Freedmen's Bureau headquarters at New Orleans from George Dunwell, June 9, 20, 1868, J. W. Coleman, November 20, 1868, H. E. Barton, November 10, 12, 20, 1868, Robert M. Davies, October 14, 20, 1868, all in *Freedmen's Bureau Reports*, NA; *Report of the Joint Committee of the General Assembly of Louisiana*, 17–26, 79–81, 229–30; Baton Rouge *Tri-Weekly Advocate*, September 16, October 5, November 4, 1868.

47. Testimony of William H. Wilder, Thomas C. W. Ellis, Charles Kennon, in *Congressional Hearings Supplement*, 1869, 91–94, 98–110, 217–23; A. Finch to Freedmen's Bureau headquarters at New Orleans, February 20, 1868, in Freedmen's Bureau Reports, NA.

Democratic at most polling stations in St. Helena and Washington Parishes or faced the consequences of failing to vote. Their votes contributed to huge Democratic majorities in both parishes. On the other side, the extent of their defeat alarmed both state and national Republican leadership. Barely 40 percent of the region's Republicans cast ballots for their party's ticket. Except in West Feliciana, where the Republicans scored a substantial victory, every parish in eastern Louisiana returned a Democratic majority. The margin of victory ranged from slightly more than one hundred votes in East Baton Rouge to a 100 percent Democratic vote in Washington.[48]

The Republicans' two-to-one majority among registered voters in the plantation parishes easily offset a similar Democratic majority in the piney woods. Despite the regional preponderance of Republicans, what the Democrats had failed to accomplish through persuasion in April, 1868, they achieved splendidly only seven months later. The key to success remained the unqualified application of violence. Moreover, Democratic efforts contributed to an emerging societal phenomenon. The secret societies, and nightriding in particular, promoted an important camaraderie among country whites. With a dearth of opportunity for fraternizing in rural areas, Republican bashing became an important outlet and social activity. Ominously, violence was at its core. With startling alacrity, violence progressed from a common element in the piney woods of Louisiana and southwestern Mississippi to an integral aspect of every resident's very existence. Long acceptable in affairs of honor, unrestrained brutality emerged as the principal means of societal regulation and governance. Significantly, violence became an aspect of behavior not merely accepted but expected. The events of the 1860s clearly demonstrated that the old adage "violence does not solve anything" was nonsense.

Since Ulysses S. Grant did not require Louisiana's electoral vote to secure the presidency, little formal protest accompanied the presidential election. To ensure that the Republicans retained control of state government, however, Warmoth engineered the creation of two vital agencies. Although federal law prohibited the creation of a state militia, Warmoth established the Metropolitan Police Force to counter Democratic intimidation. Composed of white and black Republicans, the Metropolitans served as the governor's private militia, independent of any other authority. Warmoth secured arms, in-

---

48. Baton Rouge *Tri-Weekly Advocate*, November 4, 9, 1868; *Report of the Joint Committee of the General Assembly of Louisiana*, xxix; Testimony of James H. George, William H. Wilder, Charles Benedict, R. F. Briggs, in *Congressional Hearings Supplement*, 1869, 41, 91–95, 218–24, 236–38.

cluding Gatling guns, in Washington, D.C., which enabled the Metropolitans to become an effective fighting force. More important was Warmoth's Election Act, which provided for the establishment of a Returning Board, to be controlled by reliable Republicans, whose duties included tabulating votes and excluding those from regions influenced by violence or intimidation. Originally intended to prevent fraud, the Returning Board soon proved as adept at stealing elections as did the Democrats. Congressional investigators examining the results of the 1872 Louisiana elections reported that the Returning Board had committed "flagrant and transparent" fraud upon the citizens of Louisiana.[49]

To increase their strength on the local level in the wake of the November, 1868, debacle, the Republican-dominated legislature created several new parishes. Among these, Tangipahoa, carved from portions of each of the four piney-woods parishes in eastern Louisiana, constituted the wealthiest. The new parish spanned the length of the Florida parishes from Lake Maurepas to the Mississippi state line along the course of the New Orleans-Jackson Railroad. Additionally, an act of the legislature granted Warmoth the power to appoint all officials for the new parish. The certainty of Republican domination of Tangipahoa Parish, combined with the exclusion of the railroad from the existing parishes, intensified piney-woods Democrats' hostility toward state government. The unusual procedure creating the new parish government led a suspicious Paris Ellis to assert, "I ascertained while in New Orleans that the Radicals were in ascendancy and offices being let to the highest bidder." Republicans defended the necessity of creating Tangipahoa. H. H. Bankston, defeated for sheriff the preceding year, testified during a congressional hearing, "They robbed me out of my election in St. Helena and I came to New Orleans took an active part in getting the new parish created and asked for the appointment as sheriff." Commenting on the creation of the new parishes and the suspect qualifications of some of the appointed officials, the New Orleans *Republican* maintained that "men must be known to be in full sympathy with the administration before receiving office else its policy can not be carried out successfully, to the victors belong the spoils."[50]

49. *House Documents*, "Report of the Special Congressional Investigating Committee of Three," 1–34; James Longstreet to Henry Clay Warmoth, June 30, 1870, in Henry Clay Warmoth Papers, LLMVC; Joe Gray Taylor, *Louisiana Reconstructed*, 177–82.

50. *Acts Passed by the General Assembly of the State of Louisiana at the Second Session of the First Legislature Begun and Held in New Orleans* (New Orleans, 1869), 83; Paris Ellis to Tom Ellis, March 7, 1869, John Ellis to Tom Ellis, March 6, 13, 1869, in Ellis Family Papers; Testimony of

Republicans believed the creation of new state agencies and parishes would provide the mechanisms to contain Democratic intimidation and to maintain power. Regardless of the strategy they employed in eastern Louisiana, their efforts would probably have failed. As violence became less a method of last resort and more a preferred means for settling disputes, it became increasingly apparent that local Republicans and their northern supporters lacked the resources and resolve to prevail. Moreover, in addition to the odds already against them, the Republicans contributed directly to their own demise.

The corrupt practices of some Republican officials contributed to an unqualified hatred for carpetbagger control among the conservative whites of Louisiana and, more importantly, reinforced their latent disillusionment with government. The dramatic increase in the rates of taxation initiated by the Republican-dominated legislature in itself proved catastrophic for many citizens already heavily burdened by war-related debts, but the hefty increase in salaries the legislature provided for themselves and other elected officials provoked even greater resentment. Likewise, the public became increasingly aware that scores of state jobs were being awarded to northerners who had little interest in Louisiana other than making a personal profit. Vermont native M. H. Twitchell secured the establishment of Red River Parish in upstate Louisiana and filled the payroll with family members and friends. Congressional investigators found that by controlling the legislative, judicial, and tax collecting mechanisms of the parish, the Twitchells amassed great wealth to the detriment of many established families and that the people held the Republican party responsible.[51]

H. H. Bankston, in *Congressional Hearings Supplement, 1869*, 83–87; New Orleans *Republican*, March 10, 1869.

51. "Annual Address of Governor William Pitt Kellogg," *Louisiana House Journal*, 1st Sess., 1876, p. 20; G. Wheat to Maston Newsom, June 17, 1874, receipt for parish taxes, June 22, 1874, both in Maston Newsom Papers, LLMVC; Port Vincent *Livingstonian*, April 25, 1879; New Orleans *Republican*, January 1, 1873; "Report of the Special Congressional Investigating Committee of Three," 104–108; Ted Tunnell, ed., *Carpetbagger from Vermont: The Autobiography of Marshall Harvey Twitchell* (Baton Rouge, 1989); J. Mills Thornton, "Fiscal Policy and the Failure of Radical Reconstruction in the Lower South," in J. M. Kousser and James McPherson, eds., *Region, Race, and Reconstruction: Essays in Honor of C. Vann Woodward* (New York, 1982), 349–91; Oscar Lestage, "The White League in Louisiana," *Louisiana Historical Quarterly*, XVIII (1935), 657–61; Philip H. Sheridan to Orville E. Babcock, January 21, 1875, Gen. Philip H. Sheridan Letter, Newberry Library; Elizabeth Tilton to B. F. Flanders, October 3, 1867, John Hutchins to B. F. Flanders, October 6, 1867, David Barritz to B. F. Flanders, October 9, 1867, all

The public naturally resented higher taxes, particularly when they received little benefit from their sacrifice, and methods of taxation often seemed designed to promote default and seizure more than collection of money. In one instance, Amite City businessman Maston Newsom unexpectedly received notice to pay more than $340 in taxes within ten days or all his property would be confiscated. A congressional investigating committee sent to discover the source of Louisianians' fierce resistance to their government expressed dismay at the policies of the Republican state government. The committee's report exemplified its surprise: "In the parishes taxation has been carried almost to the extent of confiscation. In many of the parishes all the white Republicans and all the office holders belong to a single family. As the people saw taxation increase and prosperity diminish, as they grew poor while officials grew rich, they became naturally sore." The committee further noted that the governor and legislature exercised "extraordinary and exclusive jurisdiction over political questions," commanded a private political militia, created monopolies, abolished courts, and "commanded a degree of power scarcely exercised by any sovereign in the world." The committee concluded that, based on its observations, few could wonder at conditions in Louisiana.[52]

In an 1874 legislative address, Governor Warmoth's successor, William P. Kellogg, acknowledged an emerging trend of enormous consequence for the future development of the region. According to the governor, under the direction of the Republicans, legal fees and court costs had risen to a level that "barred the way to the courts in many instances." He concluded that this tendency would cause many to avoid using the legal system to redress grievances. His fear would soon be proven painfully correct. Despite his insight, though, Kellogg contributed to the problem himself by continually interfering with the courts in favor of friends and allies, creating the impression that the legal system could be manipulated to serve partisan purposes.[53]

---

in Flanders Papers; J. Madison Wells to Andrew Johnson, May 22, 1865, in Johnson Papers. In one of his first actions as governor, Francis T. Nichols, the first "Redeemer" chief executive, promoted legislation "reducing their [legislators'] present extravagant compensations"; see Francis Nichols to E. A. Burke, February 20, 1877, in Francis T. Nichols Papers, LLMVC.

52. "Address of Governor William P. Kellogg," *Louisiana Senate Journal*, 1st Sess., 1874, pp. 12–13; notice of taxes due, signed by James B. Wands, in Newsom Papers; "Report of the Special Congressional Investigating Committee of Three," 3–34; New Orleans *Times*, April 14, 1873.

53. "Address of Governor William P. Kellogg," *Louisiana Senate Journal*, 1st Sess., 1874, pp. 12–13; J. J. Monette to William P. Kellogg, January 22, 1876, J. Regan to William Kellogg, March 17, 1876, in Louisiana State Executive Department, Governor's Correspondence Collection, LLMVC.

In addition to the seeming lack of concern for the state's welfare exhibited by some Republican officials, accusations of theft of public and private funds further damaged their image. Deputy United States Marshall Thomas H. Jenks admitted to a congressional committee that his brother L. B. Jenks embezzled $14,000 in parish funds while serving as deputy tax collector in East Feliciana. Jenks's theft merely continued a trend of missing funds in East Feliciana during Reconstruction. Fraud surfaced there as early as 1869, when only $10,000 of a special $20,000 tax reached the parish treasury. Tangipahoa and Livingston also recorded large discrepancies between the amount of taxes collected and the amount of money deposited in the parishes' treasuries. Municipal funds also mysteriously disappeared under the direction of Republican administrators. The Woodville *Sentinel* repeatedly demanded that the Republican mayor account for missing funds during his two years in office. Comparable accusations appeared in many regional newspapers. The Amite City *Democrat* and the *Tangipahoa Democrat* gleefully published weekly accounts of alleged fraudulent practices. The *Democrat* fanned the flames of outrage by declaring that Republican graft had increased the state debt from $4,000,000 to $75,000,000 during their seven years in power. Allegations involving the theft of personal and educational funds proved even more disturbing to local residents. Prominent Tangipahoa Parish Republican organizer Johnson Yerks faced frequent accusations concerning the theft of funds entrusted to his care by an elderly school teacher. Moreover, in his capacity as Tangipahoa school superintendent, Yerks provoked outrage when an independent investigation revealed that he had embezzled nearly $8,000 in school funds, thereby decimating the parish school system. J. W. Armstead, a black West Feliciana proponent of education, informed congressional investigators that the Republicans' misuse of school funds created scores of Democratic supporters among the freedmen.[54]

54. Testimony of Thomas H. Jenks and J. W. Armstead, in *House Documents*, "Testimony Taken by the Select Committee on Alleged Frauds in the Presidential Election of 1876," 45th Cong., 3rd Sess., Misc. Doc. No. 31, Pt. 1, 1878, pp. 315–18, Pt. 3, 1879, pp. 295–99, hereinafter referred to as "Select Committee on the Presidential Election of 1876"; Citizen to Henry Marston, June 8, 1869, in Marston Family Papers; Lestage, "White League in Louisiana," 633; Woodville *Sentinel*, August 26, 1871; Amite City *Democrat*, August 21, September 18, November 6, 1875; Amite City *Tangipahoa Democrat*, June 7, 1873, September 19, 26, 1874; Mary Lotspich to Maston Newsom, March 20, 1873, in Newsom Papers; "Report of the Joint Committee of Investigation of the Department of Education," *Louisiana Legislative Documents*, 1st Sess., 1878, pp. 1–31.

Most damaging of all to the character of the Republicans were the accusations of massive corruption on the part of the legislature. Through regular newspaper reports, the public remained keenly aware of and increasingly disillusioned with the functions of state government. According to the allegations, in the form of levee and asylum bills Republican legislators routinely pocketed huge sums of state funds. Monies appropriated for the construction and improvement of levees and other state works frequently either disappeared or fell far short of requirements. E. L. Weber, Republican senator from West Feliciana Parish, described the method of fraud he participated in to a congressional commission. On Weber's arrival at the legislature, Senator M. H. Twitchell encouraged him to join a combination of nineteen Republican senators. Twitchell explained that the nineteen senators comprised a one-vote majority that afforded them great opportunity. According to Weber, the combination frequently secured passage of levee bills appropriating millions of dollars for certain parties and companies holding levee bonds and contracts. The members of the combination received from $10,000 to $20,000 of the appropriation for each bill that passed. Weber described scores of levee, asylum, and statehouse bills from which the combination pocketed hundreds of thousands of state dollars. Thomas Durant exposed a similar conspiracy to defraud the state of $6,000,000 of federal levee appropriations. In an 1876 address to the legislature, Governor Kellogg acknowledged that the state had awarded a monopoly contract to the Louisiana Levee Company, but despite the appropriation of millions of dollars, the company had made little effort to meet its obligations.[55] Republican congressman J. H. Sypher acknowledged that the corruption of some Republicans had destroyed the party's chances for success in Louisiana. Similarly, St. Helena Republican J. P. Wall affirmed his commitment to the party but denounced those members "who to obtain their own selfish ends succumbed to a few renegades not worthy to be recognized by any party."[56]

55. Testimony of E. L. Weber, in "Select Committee on the Presidential Election of 1876," Pt. 3, pp. 234–35; "Annual Message of Governor William P. Kellogg," *Louisiana Senate Journal*, 1st Sess., 1876, pp. 8–10; Thomas Durant to Benjamin Flanders, June 7, 1867, in Flanders Papers; C. B. White to William P. Kellogg, May 1, 1875, in Louisiana Executive, Governor's Correspondence Collection; Amite City *Democrat*, November 20, 1875.

56. Testimony of J. Hale Sypher and B. F. Joubert, in "Testimony Taken by the Select Committee to Investigate the Condition of Affairs in Louisiana," *House Documents*, 42nd Cong., 2nd Sess., Misc. Doc. No. 211, pp. 453–62, 541–42; Testimony of James E. Anderson and Thomas H. Jenks, in "Select Committee on the Presidential Election of 1876," Pt. 1, pp. 1–64, 315–18;

Although pervasive corruption existed in Louisiana during Reconstruction, fraud was by no means unprecedented in the Bayou State. Corruption had, in fact, been a standard practice of Louisiana politics since the colonial period. Tax collectors routinely recorded discrepancies between the amount of funds collected and the amount delivered to the state treasury. Officials also frequently awarded state contracts and positions to family members or friends. Reconstruction produced neither the first nor the last corrupt Louisiana official. The significant difference between Reconstruction corruption and that of earlier periods lay in public awareness of the fraud. Newspapers and Democratic politicians relentlessly paraded evidence of corruption before the public, thereby creating the impression that such practices were unprecedented. The propaganda blitz persuaded many that Reconstruction represented an anomaly in Louisiana's tradition of "good" government. Although this fallacy does not absolve corrupt Republican officials from their misdeeds, particularly that of subverting an opportunity for realistic reform, it does help explain the intensity of the conservative reaction. What was more important, in the Florida parishes widely publicized incidents of Reconstruction-era fraud furthered a deep suspicion of government, while the extralegal overthrow of that government advanced a commitment to violent means for the resolution of grievances.[57]

Despite the fact that their leadership had plunged the region into war and catastrophe, during Reconstruction the old elite again emerged dominant. By promoting racial fears and encouraging popular contempt for the Republican government, antebellum power brokers identified another enemy common to the white population, Republicans and assertive blacks, who provided a focus to rally the commoners behind the elite. Again the aspirations of the plain folk would be subsumed by the necessity for unity behind the natural leadership of the planters. But the contest for political dominance between the old elite and the Republicans produced some important lessons that would have an impact on regional development. Planter attacks on Republican leadership

---

Amos Ackerman to B. F. Flanders, May 22, 1872, H. C. Hobart to B. F. Flanders, February 6, 1873, in Flanders Papers; Amite City *Democrat*, September 4, 1875; "Report of the Special Congressional Investigating Committee of Three," 18–30; New Orleans *Republican*, January 7, 11, 1870.

57. List of defaulting tax collectors in *Louisiana Legislative Documents*, 1st Sess., 1853, pp. 1–4; *Board of Trustees of Montpelier Academy v. Dr. Thomas Webb*, May 6, 1841, involving allegations of theft of school funds, in St. Helena Parish Records; Thomas G. Davidson to A. W. Walker, October 23, 1870, involving efforts to purchase black votes, in Ellis Family Papers.

seemed to confirm the intrinsic corruption of government, and their calls for the violent overthrow of the Republicans reinforced an inclination toward extralegal means in eastern Louisiana. Moreover, the legal system appeared subject to partisan maneuvering. Each of these lessons would shape the popular proclivities of Florida parish residents in the late nineteenth century.

· 5 ·

ORGANIZED LAWLESSNESS: CHAOS ASCENDANT

Oh God! Grant us rest from this weariness.
  —Abigail Amacker, Diary

The Democratic campaign to promote contempt for the Republicans and their supporters strengthened the position of the old elite. Conservative leaders effectively manipulated events in support of their own goal to resecure power. By encouraging the belief that Republican officials systematically looted the state of its wealth, the Democrats produced a near hysterical demand for their ouster. The planters naturally assumed that with the Republicans eliminated, they would dominate regional politics in the post-Reconstruction period. But the means the elite promoted to destroy the Republicans, violence and contempt for governance, created conditions beyond their ability to control. Following the collapse of the Republican government, the planters would find themselves victims of their own success. The unprecedented publicity surrounding cases of Republican fraud and impropriety demonstrated just how corrupt government could be, thus augmenting the plain folk's suspicion of authority. Many piney-woods residents recalled the failure of government to address their needs in the antebellum period, and an enlightened few recognized that their own desires had always been subsumed by the grand strategy of the planter elite. Each time assertiveness or discontent had surfaced among the plain folk, the elite had circumvented their intentions with appeals for unity in the face of a common threat. The Spanish colonial government, abolitionists, Federal troops, and carpetbagger government had all served as the common enemy against which to rally the forces, and throughout, racial unity served as the foundation for their appeals.

In the post-Reconstruction period no apparent common enemy would emerge. Blacks, no longer enslaved or politically independent, would pose far less of a threat. With these threats removed, contempt for the old elite quickly manifested itself in the piney woods. In the first major post-Reconstruction election, voters in Tangipahoa Parish, the scene of the fiercest late-nineteenth-century disorders, decisively voted down the old elite in favor of independent candidates. The results from Tangipahoa during the state election of 1879 startled members of the old elite as well as the Democratic party. In particular, the defeat of judicial candidates O. P. Amacker and J. M. Thompson, both members of the prewar elite and conservative leaders during Reconstruction, indicated the changing political climate. Although the Democrats ran strong in all the towns excepting the village of Tangipahoa, they generally did poorly at all rural precincts.[1]

In the late nineteenth century the Florida parishes served as a microcosm for examining the South as a whole. In the Felicianas and East Baton Rouge, stability returned as the old elite, augmented by some new faces, effectively returned to power. In the piney woods, however, a continuing cycle of social and political instability predominated. The rejection of planter leadership in the piney woods produced a corresponding vacuum in governance. The planter elite had so thoroughly dominated social, political, and economic development in the region that the plain folk, unaccustomed to power, proved incapable of governing themselves. The piney-woods republican tradition, as manifested in eastern Louisiana, virtually demanded defiance of governance. At least thirty years of suspect government had amply reinforced latent suspicions of authority. Leadership failed primarily both because of its inability to overcome the powerful factions that rapidly emerged and because of its failure to cope with the incredible levels of violence.

Suspicions that the Republicans practiced electoral fraud seemed confirmed in 1872 when the Republican-dominated Returning Board seated the regular Republican William Pitt Kellogg as governor over John McEnery, who ran as a Fusion candidate endorsed by both the Democrats and the minority Warmoth faction of the Republican party. Thereafter, conservative Louisianians ceased to regard the state government as legitimate. By 1873 most of the country parishes were in open revolt against the government. Local political contests dramatically aggravated the prevailing hostility. In the Florida parishes, where local judges exercised enormous influence, judicial races provoked the greatest controversy. For the remainder of the century, the dominant regional party or faction could often be identified by those seated at the parish and district judicial benches.

1. Amite City *Independent*, December 6, 1879.

In a hotly contested 1873 race in the Sixth Judicial District, comprising the piney-woods region of the Florida parishes, Democratic incumbent E. P. Ellis faced challenges from Regular Republican Ashford Addison and Independent Republican William B. Kemp. Despite some irregularities, far less violence characterized this election than those of 1868. The results indicated an Ellis victory by more than 1,000 votes. Democrat Bolivar Edwards defeated his Republican challenger F. M. Bankston by a similar margin for district attorney. However, determined not to lose their grip on power, particularly in a parish created and designed to be a Republican stronghold, the Returning Board threw out the results and declared Kemp and Bankston the winners. Although many black voters avoided the polls as a result of earlier events, little evidence of direct voter intimidation existed to sustain the Returning Board's findings. In addition, the Democrats commanded a 2,500-vote majority over the Republicans in the piney-woods parishes. Nevertheless, other Florida-parish contests, particularly the parish judgeship and legislative seats, were determined in a similar manner. The most provocative debate centered on the seating of Kemp, whom many regarded as a consummate opportunist and scalawag. When federal authorities at New Orleans sustained the Returning Board's findings, open rebellion flared in eastern Louisiana. The *Tangipahoa Democrat* called for active resistance: "To resist by lawful means Kellogg's taxes, when Kellogg's tools and lickspittles are his judges is worse than nonsense. There is no justice for the people in these bogus courts. They are filled with usurpers, who were put in office because right or wrong, they would meekly do their master's bidding." Such appeals underlined the necessity of extralegal resolution of grievances.[2]

The seating of the defeated Republican candidates provided the proverbial flint to the tinderbox of Democratic outrage. As Democrats in Tangipahoa, Livingston, and St. Tammany organized to prevent the seating of the "usurpers," mass meetings in East Feliciana, St. Helena, and Washington

2. Amite City *Tangipahoa Democrat*, September 27, 1872, February 1, 7, 1873; "Annual Address of Governor William P. Kellogg," *Louisiana Senate Journal*, 1st Sess., 1874, pp. 4–7; "Report of the Special Congressional Investigating Committee of Three," 338–40; John Ellis to Tom Ellis, January 29, May 30, June 4, 1873, Alexandra to Maggie, July 28, 1873, copy of court order summoning witnesses to appear in the case of *E. P. Ellis v. W. B. Kemp*, April 21, 1873, in Ellis Family Papers; *W. B. Kemp v. E. P. Ellis*, in *Reports of Cases Argued and Determined in the Supreme Court of Louisiana* (New Orleans, 1873), Vol. XXV, No. 4655, pp. 253–63; *Report of the Joint Committee of the General Assembly of Louisiana*, xxix; New Orleans *Daily Picayune*, April 25, May 9, 1873; Amite City *Independent*, November 7, 1874; Port Vincent *Triune*, July 22, 1873.

urged support for their neighbors. James G. Kilbourne and G. W. Munday, prominent members of the old elite in East Feliciana and St. Helena, respectively, directed the Democratic response. The widespread reaction exemplified regional white unity and the resurgent authority exercised by the planters.[3]

Armed bodies of men seized the courthouses in Tangipahoa, Livingston, and St. Tammany Parishes in support of the Democratic officials functioning under the authority of the McEnery pretender government. Sporadic violence erupted in St. Helena and Washington as residents vented their frustration. In Livingston Parish armed citizens removed the seat of justice from Springfield to the Democratic stronghold at Port Vincent on the Amite River. Initially, state officials seemed overawed by the determination of the resistance and did nothing, but as frightened Republicans rushed to the safety of New Orleans with accounts of open rebellion, Kellogg determined to act.[4]

To suppress the insurgency he secured an additional $30,000 in armaments from the federal government and dispatched an elite brigade of the Metropolitan Police Force to contain the severest outbreaks. Three of the seven deployments of Metropolitans in 1873 served to quell disturbances in the Florida parishes. The *Daily Picayune* reported the mood prevailing in eastern Louisiana: "The people feel deeply this new outrage. The Kellogg usurpation, infamous before, brought now into closer contact with the citizens, grows irksome beyond endurance. If these outrages are repeated, the citizens will meet force with force. The hireling bands of a pretended authority, denounced in the United States Congress as a vile usurpation, resting only on fraud and force will be resisted."[5]

The Metropolitans arrived in Amite City on April 19, 1873, at a late hour in the evening. After surrounding the public buildings and disarming the surprised guards, they forced the Democratic officials to step down and installed their Republican opponents. With their mission accomplished, the Metropolitans perilously held their position for three days before departing shortly before dawn on the fourth day. This force then combined with another

---

3. New Orleans *Daily Picayune*, April 25, May 9, 1873; "Address of Governor William P. Kellogg," *Louisiana Senate Journal*, 1st Sess., 1874, pp. 4–7; John Ellis to Tom Ellis, May 20, 1873, June 4, 1874, in Ellis Family Papers.

4. New Orleans *Daily Picayune*, April 25, 29, 1873; "Address of Governor William P. Kellogg," *Louisiana Senate Journal*, 1st Sess., 1874, pp. 4–7; John Ellis to Tom Ellis, May 20, 1873, June 4, 1874, in Ellis Family Papers.

5. New Orleans *Daily Picayune*, April 25, 29, 1873; "Address of Governor William P. Kellogg," *Louisiana Senate Journal*, 1st Sess., 1874, pp. 4–7.

brigade dispatched from New Orleans to conduct the dangerous journey across Livingston Parish. After fighting off some bushwhackers, the Metropolitans returned the seat of government to Springfield and installed the Republican officials. A similarly successful operation forced the opening of the parish court at Covington in St. Tammany Parish a few months later. Although these expeditions successfully disrupted the functioning of the local Democratic government, their inability to deploy garrison forces ensured the weakness of the Republican officials. As a result, by 1873 virtual chaos reigned in the piney woods.[6]

Kellogg hoped that an effective Metropolitan Police Force, backed by federal troops, would allow him to regain lost ground in the country parishes, but the steadily decreasing numbers of the federal occupation army soon rendered it virtually ineffective beyond New Orleans. Moreover, outrageous incidents such as the Colfax Massacre, in which armed whites slaughtered at least a hundred blacks, demonstrated that Kellogg exercised little realistic authority outside the Crescent City. The September, 1874, defeat of the Metropolitans at the hands of the White League, a paramilitary force committed to white supremacy and supporting the McEnery claim to the governorship, radically curtailed the effectiveness of the governor's private militia. Even with the unflinching support of the Grant administration and a rump federal force quartered primarily in New Orleans, by late 1874 the Kellogg government tottered on the brink.

When word reached the piney woods of the Metropolitans' defeat in New Orleans, most of the Republican officials fled the region. President Grant's assurance that federal troops would support their claims to office prompted some to return and resume, as much as possible, their duties. The Republican Amite City *Independent* warned the Democrats: "The new Rebellion will be crushed. The president has ordered troops stationed at White League strongholds all over the state." Similarly, the New Orleans *Republican* declared that if the Democrats persisted in their efforts to "clean out" the Yankees, southerners could expect the same treatment in the North: "A brutal mob in any northern city might at any time revenge this intolerance in a manner painful to all sentiments of humanity. As there are more southern people who go

6. "Address of Governor William P. Kellogg," *Senate Journal*, 1st Sess., 1874, pp. 4–7; New Orleans *Daily Picayune*, April 23, 25, 28, 29, 1873; New Orleans *Times*, April 19, 24, 28, 1873; Amite City *Independent*, September 5, November 7, 1874; Amite City *Tangipahoa Democrat*, October 31, 1874; John Ellis to Tom Ellis, May 30, June 4, 1873, in Ellis Family Papers.

North than northern people who go South, this balance of insult and possible injury must go against our section." Unmoved by these threats, the Amite City *Democrat* declared in response: "Let us organize, unite, and arm for the task, they can call us White League, Ku Klux or what not. The mercenaries that prowl around the country forcing themselves into offices against the express will of the people will be attended to in due time." The same paper urged the use of violence as the best means to destroy their enemies. By the close of 1874, state authority in Washington Parish had completely collapsed; the remainder of Louisiana would soon follow.[7]

The power of the federal army alone sustained the government of William Pitt Kellogg. In the Florida parishes Kellogg's authority rarely extended beyond the garrison towns of Baton Rouge and Bayou Sara. By 1874, he commanded only a fraction of the electoral strength necessary to maintain his administration. As a result, the Republicans increasingly relied on the actions of the Returning Board to retain control of state government. Revulsion for the increasingly impotent administration encouraged the growth of a movement to join the Florida parishes with Mississippi. "We have lately heard from numerous persons in the Florida parishes on the subject of the annexation of this part of Louisiana to Mississippi," the Amite City *Democrat* reported, giving voice to this idea. "There is decidedly strong feeling in favor of it and that feeling is growing everyday." Although the movement soon faded, it demonstrated that many Florida-parish residents despised the government more than they loved Louisiana.[8]

As the prestige of state government declined in the eyes of the majority in eastern Louisiana, local government assumed an increasing importance. Daniel Wedge informed congressional investigators that the people of eastern Louisiana respected local officials but had no confidence in state authority. Conservatives intensified their efforts to secure control of the local court-

---

7. New Orleans *Republican*, April 5, 1873; Amite City *Independent*, September 5, 1874; Amite City *Democrat*, September 4, December 11, 1875; Amite City *Tangipahoa Democrat*, September 26, 1874; New Orleans *Daily Picayune*, May 9, 1873; Resolutions adopted at White League meeting in Bayou Barbary, Livingston Parish, September 5, 1874, in Alley Scrapbooks.

8. Amite City *Democrat*, April 1, 1876; D. A. Weber to William P. Kellogg, March 6, 1876, in William P. Kellogg Papers, LLMVC; E. R. Platt to William P. Kellogg, September 14, 1874, describing additional troops en route to Baton Rouge, in Ellis Family Papers; "Report of the Special Congressional Investigating Committee of Three," 1–34; S. E. Claille, *Intimidation and the Number of White and Colored Voters in Louisiana in 1876 as Shown by Statistical Data Derived from Republican Official Reports* (New Orleans, 1877), 31; New Orleans *Daily Picayune*, May 4, 1873.

houses in response to the growing irrelevance of state government. Increasingly, their efforts proved successful. Joseph Thompson, a member of the McEnery pretender legislature made this announcement from Covington in the fall of 1874: "We in St. Tammany have taken possession of the court-house and public offices—have turned over the keys to the officers elect and intend to hold possession. I hope that the other Florida parishes have done the same."[9]

With startling speed, conservatives in each of the remaining Florida parishes bludgeoned their way back into power. Convinced that politics offered no hope for an honest trial, they instead relied on a proven means for success, violence. Since 1871, several counties in southwestern Mississippi, particularly Amite and Wilkinson, had experienced frequent racial troubles, often on a massive scale. Wilkinson County blacks, many of them Union army veterans, boasted a well-armed and disciplined militia that frequently picketed roads and marched en masse through towns. Their forthright actions created alarm among local whites and neighboring Louisiana conservatives, who typically cooperated closely. Madison Batchelor reported that a plot had been uncovered among blacks in Amite County to rise and slaughter as many whites as possible "about a certain day." By the summer of 1875, with Kellogg's authority rapidly deteriorating, East Feliciana whites determined to act. Armed mobs drove all black elected officials from the parish, threatening them with death should they return. Kellogg provided encouragement but little else. By summer's end the threat of federal intervention had produced an uneasy peace.[10]

Nevertheless, sensing victory and Republican weakness, the Democrats continued to push their advantage. On October 7, 1875, an armed mob marched on the courthouse at Clinton, shot and wounded black sheriff Henry Smith, and forced him to resign on pain of death. The mob then entered the courthouse, halted the proceedings, and also forced the Republican judge to resign. A few days later, a leader of the mob, Dr. J. W. Saunders, nearly succumbed to a massive dose of poison administered by his maid. A hysterical crowd promptly hanged the maid, Babe Mathews, in the court-

9. Testimony of Daniel Wedge, in "Select Committee on the Presidential Election of 1876," Pt. 3, p. 138; Joseph M. Thompson to Tom Ellis, September 17, 1874, in Ellis Family Papers.

10. Madison Batchelor to Albert Batchelor, September 6, 1874, in Albert Batchelor Papers; Woodville Sentinel, August 26, 1871; Louisiana House Journal, 1st Sess., 1876, pp. 94–99; Henry Marston to J. F. Temple and Sons, August 5, 1875, Henry Marston to J. W. Burbridge and Co., August 5, 1875, both in Henry Marston Letter Books, No. 4, p. 228, Marston Family Papers.

house square and marched on Baton Rouge to arrest her brother-in-law, former representative John Gair, whom Mathews had implicated as the instigator of the plot. Apprehended by the mob in Baton Rouge, Gair, a leading East Feliciana Republican since the advent of Radical Reconstruction, never reached Clinton. Mobs similarly forced the resignation of Republican officials in West Feliciana and St. Helena. A mass meeting in East Baton Rouge produced a petition demanding that the Republican officials resign or face the consequences. Commenting on the events in the Felicianas, the Amite City *Democrat* remarked caustically, "The insolent, ignorant, negro Sheriff Smith of East Feliciana has at last resigned."[11]

With state officials apparently unable or unwilling to contain the violence, whites in the plantation parishes continued to "bulldoze" the territory effectively. The term *bulldozing* describes the attainment of goals through armed might by crushing the opposition into submission. Under the pretext of preventing the theft and resale of seed cotton by blacks, armed bands of regulators terrorized the freedmen and Republican sympathizers in the Felicianas and East Baton Rouge. Nightriders brutally abused and murdered many blacks in an effort to return them to a state of economic and political dependence. Blacks responded in kind by forming the Sage Hill Club, which retaliated by murdering at least two whites. By the eve of the election of 1876, chaos prevailed throughout the Florida parishes. The *Daily Picayune* declared Louisiana to be in a complete state of anarchy.[12]

11. *Louisiana House Journal*, 1st Sess., 1876, pp. 94–99; Amite City *Democrat*, November 20, 1875; Marston to Temple and Sons, August 5, 1875, Henry Marston to Jacob Wall, October 14, 1875, in Marston Letter Books, No. 4, pp. 228, 250, Marston Family Papers.

12. Testimony of John DeLee, E. L. Weber, Henry Reid, J. W. Armstead, J. S. Dula, T. M. Clark, George Swayze, Julius Green, in "Select Committee on the Presidential Election of 1876," Pt. 3, pp. 140–42, 198–234, 266, 295–99, 351–63, 383–88, 506–509; Testimony of Isaac Guy, M. F. Jamar, Benjamin Rogers, G. W. Munday, J. G. Kilbourne, George Norwood, all in *House Documents*, 44th Cong., 2nd Sess., Misc. Doc. No. 34, Vol. V, Pt. 3, pp. 165, 238, 241–43, 332, 457, 480, hereinafter referred to as "Congressional Investigating Committee at Clinton, 1877"; E. L. Weber to William P. Kellogg, April 10, 1876, Richard Walther to William Kellogg, April 24, 1876, Joseph W. Armstead to William Kellogg, May 1, 1876, copy of Proceeding from the Inquest on the Death of Max Aronson on the Plantation of H. S. Perkins, May 13, 1876, all in Kellogg Papers; J. A. Glasper to Stephen Packard, January, 1877, in Louisiana Executive, Governor's Correspondence Collection; Henry Marston to A. Foster Elliot, October 17, 19, 1875, in Marston Letter Books, No. 4, p. 251, Marston Family Papers; Amite City *Democrat*, November 27, 1875; New Orleans *Daily Picayune*, May 4, 1873; Philip H. Jones, "Reminiscences of Days Before and After the Civil War," Pamphlet, n.d., in Annabel Smith Diary, LLMVC.

With the Kellogg administration near collapse by the spring of 1876, many black and white Republicans abandoned the party in an effort to salvage their political careers or save their lives. Kellogg attempted to shore up the party in rural areas by replacing some wavering parish officials with loyal Republicans. Yet almost as soon as the new officials received their commissions, mobs forced their resignation or flight. The Bayou Sara *Ledger* reported that "four members of the West Feliciana police jury were forced to resign, in open session, last Monday, to save trouble, in the face of blue jackets, who are stationed at a stone's throw from the seat of justice in our parish."[13]

During the course of 1876, increasingly chaotic conditions prevailed in eastern Louisiana. Murder and bushwhackings occurred with painful frequency as lawless elements exploited the lack of legal authority. Arson, attributed to disgruntled blacks, destroyed significant portions of the towns of Clinton, Jackson, and Amite City. Most important, by early summer large sections of eastern Louisiana and southwestern Mississippi appeared on the verge of a race war. Following the murder of white regulator Max Aronson in West Feliciana Parish, conservatives intensified their campaign of terror against local blacks. Multiple lynchings of freedmen suspected of Aronson's murder climaxed when armed blacks massed near Pinckneyville, Mississippi. Whites from across eastern Louisiana and southwestern Mississippi converged on the region. Before darkness brought a halt to the slaughter, according to reports, fifty freedmen had been killed outright and half a dozen others lynched along the roadside as an example of the futility of their rebellion. With black resistance effectively crushed, the last hope for the Republican party in eastern Louisiana flickered out.[14]

In the wake of the Pinckneyville massacre, scores of blacks who had previously testified about the scope of Democratic intimidation recanted their statements before a congressional commission at New Orleans. Other blacks abandoned the Republicans during the election of 1876 based on the

---

13. Amite City *Democrat*, April 1, 1876, Bayou Sara *Ledger*, rpr. Amite City *Democrat*, May 20, 1876; Joseph Armstead and George Swayze to William P. Kellogg, May 1, 1876, Agnes Jenks to William Kellogg, September 23, 1876, both in Kellogg Papers.

14. Cornelia Stewart to Albert Batchelor, May 23, 1876, Albert Batchelor to Cornelia Stewart, May 25, 1876, in Albert Batchelor Papers; copy of Proceeding from the Inquest on the Death of Max Aronson, May 13, 1876, in Kellogg Papers; Testimony of M. F. Jamar, in "Congressional Investigating Committee at Clinton, 1877," 238; Amite City *Democrat*, April 22, May 13, 20, 1876; New Orleans *Daily Picayune*, March 24, 1876; James S. McGehee, "Ramble in Autobiography," Typescript, n.d., in James McGehee Papers.

strength of Democratic promises of schools and higher wages. Samuel Houston, a Republican party official in St. Tammany Parish, noted "the times were getting poorer and they [blacks] were getting poorer with them, the Democrats gave kind and conciliatory speeches to the blacks and generally outgeneraled the Republicans." Nevertheless, the Republicans managed to "steal" the election, in part by rejecting the returns from East Feliciana and portions of West Feliciana, East Baton Rouge, Livingston, and Tangipahoa. With the freedmen firmly cowed, however, and Republican state authority generally smashed, Louisiana had effectively returned to the rule of native whites. As a final demonstration of their contempt for Republican government, a committee visited and shot and wounded the newly elected governor Stephen Packard, who quickly abandoned his claim.[15]

Jubilant celebrations heralded the collapse of Republican government in Louisiana. It mattered little that "John Sherman's theft" had secured Louisiana's electoral vote for the Republican presidential candidate, Rutherford B. Hayes. In their eyes, from the depths of defeat and despair Louisiana whites had secured a brilliant victory over the Yankees. For the moment native Louisiana whites felt unified and confident. In reality, the victory over Reconstruction would prove more catastrophic to many regions of the South than had defeat in war. For blacks, the greatest of triumphs, liberation from bondage, concluded with the advent of decades of political exploitation and grinding poverty. For whites, a generation of bitterness and brutality had distorted their perceptions of the traditions they held dear and of the methods appropriate to sustain them.[16]

---

15. Testimony of Samuel H. Houston, in *House Documents*, "Testimony Taken by the Select Committee on the Recent Election in Louisiana," 44th Cong., 2nd Sess., Misc. Doc. No. 34, Pt. 2, 1877, p. 263, hereinafter cited as "Select Committee on the Recent Election in Louisiana"; New Orleans *Daily Picayune*, October 31, 1876; Testimony of Thomas McWilliams, Henry Reid, J. W. Armstead, Andrew Duncan, T. M. J. Clark, T. W. Dalton, Julius Green, in "Select Committee on the Presidential Election of 1876," Pt. 3, pp. 139, 266, 295, 300–14, 381–83, 503–507; *Report of the Board of Returning Officers, Session 1876, to the General Assembly of the State of Louisiana Relating to the Election Held November 7, 1876*" (New Orleans, 1877), 1–12. Concerning blacks' defection from the Republican party, see Henry Marston to J. W. Burbridge and Co., September 29, 1876, in Marston Letter Books, No. 4, p. 320, Marston Family Papers.

16. Regarding Sherman's role in manipulating the vote in Louisiana in 1876, see Testimony of Republicans James E. Anderson, Thomas H. Jenks, Agnes Jenks, and J. Hale Sypher, in "Select Committee on the Presidential Election of 1876," Pt. 3, pp. 1–325. Also see unsigned statement presented to B. F. Flanders concerning John Sherman's role in the 1876 Louisiana election and subsequent patronage, January 28, 1889, in Flanders Papers.

With the collapse of the Republicans, many areas of the post-Reconstruction South witnessed a restoration of stability under the direction of the old elite. Despite the continuity of racial and class oppression, their resumption of power signaled the return of societal equilibrium. In Louisiana, the sudden federal refusal to sustain the Republican government, combined with the prevailing disorder in rural parishes, created a momentary power vacuum. In most of the delta and sugar parishes, the planters easily reasserted their dominance, but in some areas of the state, particularly the piney-woods region of eastern Louisiana, local residents resisted the return of the prewar status quo.

In a determined but haphazard manner many voices urged the people to concentrate on personal concerns rather than on the political agenda of the elite. The expanding influence of the emerging merchant-professional class exacerbated the challenge to planter power. Calls for new leadership surfaced in all areas of the Florida parishes. In a direct attack on the legacy of planter dominance, the Baton Rouge *Capitolian-Advocate* declared, "The old war horses of antebellum days have become so mixed in their political theology, so crochet and rank by reason of a thousand political entanglements and creeds, that the only salvation for the country is in placing its politics in the hands of the young men." Recognizing the necessity of explaining their rejection of the old elite, the same paper continued: "There can be no doubt that these [old elite] and these alone have caused a large proportion of our discord, strife and bitterness within the party in past years, and with all seriousness we assert that the only means of escape in the future is to trust our political fates to new men."[17]

Although in the delta parishes their vast patronage enabled planter interests to maintain the lion's share of authority, in the piney woods, where the planter elite had always maintained only a precarious grip on power, a serious challenge emerged. At the forefront of this dispute, the piney-woods press gave voice to the dissenters. Among the most aggressive of the newspapers in eastern Louisiana, the Franklinton *New Era* condemned the efforts of Feliciana planters to dominate politics in the piney-woods parishes. The political intrigues of delta planters in the piney woods represented a particularly sore topic for many in the eastern parishes. Similarly, the Amite City *Florida Parishes* published letters attacking the "political bosses and bloats" who had long dominated the region and who now sought to entrench their power further. The same paper attacked government mismanagement and the failure

17. Baton Rouge *Capitolian-Advocate*, August 15, 1888.

of local politicians to address the will of the majority. As an alternative to maligning the prevailing conditions, the Amite City *Democrat* reminded its readers of the independence and security inherent in the piney-woods life-style, attributes the residents had virtually abandoned to conform to the agenda of the planter elite.[18]

The sharpest break with the politics of the past occurred in Tangipahoa Parish. The new parish initiated the move to resist the resurrection of the prewar status quo when its voters repudiated the old elite in the initial state elections in 1879. Indeed, Tangipahoa was aptly suited for this leadership. The rapid economic and demographic transformation of Tangipahoa, occasioned by its proximity to the New Orleans-Jackson Railroad, exacerbated the post-Reconstruction instability. The possibilities created by the railroad encouraged scores of opportunists to settle in the parish. By the early 1870s, Tangipahoa was second only to East Baton Rouge among the Florida parishes in the number of white residents, and the parish seat, Amite City, joined Clinton in a tie as the second largest town in eastern Louisiana. The influx of new settlers, combined with the weakened status of the antebellum elite, permitted the rise of numerous factions that competed fiercely for political control. This situation, in turn, provoked resentment on the part of the traditional piney-woods dwellers and the old elite, many of whom had opposed the railroad and now fiercely resisted its associated consequences.[19]

As events would demonstrate, Tangipahoa experienced some of the most ferocious societal divisions in the nation during the late nineteenth century. The popular proclivity for violence and the consistent legal tolerance of it in Tangipahoa gave rise to such expressions of dismay as Pulitzer Prize–winning editor Hodding Carter's factual account "Not Much of a Man if He Hadn't." Despite the savagery of its conditions, Tangipahoa was not alone. Factional politics and economic competition destabilized the piney woods of much of Louisiana and especially of the Florida parishes for the next three decades.[20]

Bitter factional disputes emerged in Louisiana immediately following the overthrow of the Republican state government. With the Republicans re-

18. Franklinton *New Era*, August 15, 1888; Amite City *Florida Parishes*, July 15, August 5, 12, 1891; Amite City *Democrat*, October 2, 1875.

19. Amite City *Independent*, December 6, 1879; New Orleans *Daily Picayune*, December 8, 1897; *Ninth Census, 1870: Population*, 154–57, 629; *Tenth Census, 1880: Manufactures*, 123–24, 249.

20. Hodding Carter, "Not Much of a Man if He Hadn't," *Southern Legacy* (Baton Rouge, 1966), 48–63.

moved as an effective force, the Democrats rapidly fragmented into three primary groups: the moderate patricians, the lottery-dominated ring faction, and the reactionary Bourbons. Bitter divisions among these three statewide factions contributed significantly to turbulent political conditions in the Florida parishes. Few local political contests operated beyond the intrigues of these Democratic groups. In the winter of 1892, the *Daily Picayune* observed that bitter hostility prevailed among the Democrats in eastern Louisiana. Weary of the infighting and disappointed by the lack of unity, congressional candidate C. J. Boatner expressed the feelings of many Democrats in an 1894 speech: "I am heartily tired of factional fights and want to see the party united as in the days of 1868 to 1879." Others placed party above personal ambition in a vain effort to reduce the infighting. B. T. Young declined the nomination for representative from St. Helena in an effort to alleviate factional antagonisms.[21]

The dramatically weakened Republicans also suffered from infighting and factional divisions. They, too, endured bitter internal disputes resulting from the popular aversion for the rule of the old elite. The struggle of younger Republicans to cast off the domination of sugar-planting interests ripped asunder party organization in the Florida parishes, adding to the political chaos. In a heated denunciation of the efforts of old-line Republicans to maintain their dominance, the Kentwood *Commercial* declared, "There was a time perhaps when two or three men could manipulate the politics of the parish behind locked doors but it won't do now." The *Commercial* joined the *Weekly Picayune* in prophesying "an end to the Republican organization here" if its members did not negotiate a speedy conclusion to their internal troubles.[22]

21. C. J. Boatner to Steve Ellis, March 12, 1894, Tom Ellis to Steve Ellis, December 4, 1879, Steve Ellis to Tom Ellis, September 23, 1883, M. S. Newson to Tom Ellis, December 14, 1883, multiple letters regarding Democratic factional fighting, July, 1885–August, 1887, S. M. Robertson to Steve Ellis, August 25, 1893, T. E. Warner to Steve Ellis, September 10, 1894, all in Ellis Family Papers; Charles Lea to Hardy Richardson, March 20, 1879, in Hardy Richardson Papers; Lemuel Conner to his Mother [Fanny Conner], April 27, 1884, in Lemuel Conner Family Papers, LLMVC; New Orleans *Daily Picayune*, January 23, 30, 1892; Greensburg *St. Helena Echo*, September 26, October 3, 10, 1891, January 23, February 13, 1892; Amite City *Independent*, December 22, 1883; Kentwood *Commercial*, January 1, March 13, 1897; Franklinton *New Era*, August 31, 1887, August 15, 1888; Amite City *Florida Parishes*, October 1, 8, 1890, August 12, September 16, 1891.

22. Kentwood *Commercial*, April 4, August 1, 1896, June 5, 1897; New Orleans *Weekly Picayune*, September 10, 1896, New Orleans *Daily Picayune*, December 5, 1897; Steve Ellis to Tom Ellis, April 5, 1892, in Ellis Family Papers.

Factional fighting debilitated party loyalty and correspondingly the entire regional political structure, but factionalization was not limited to politics. During the course of the late nineteenth century, bitter divisions also emerged along social, cultural, and economic lines. Temperance advocates provoked almost constant controversy by aggressively encouraging prohibition. Local tavern keepers and patrons of the illicit "blind tiger" moonshine distilleries often forcefully opposed the efforts of the "drys." Hostility surrounding the temperance movement climaxed in June, 1890, when two days of rioting disrupted communities in northern Tangipahoa and St. Helena Parishes, as well as portions of neighboring Pike County, Mississippi. Heated controversy also frequently plagued the efforts of railroad promoters and educational reformers. The prevailing antipathy often provoked extreme controversy over seemingly insignificant issues: efforts to purchase a building to serve as the parish courthouse repeatedly engendered hostile factions in Tangipahoa as did the controversy created by a ban on slingshots in Amite City.[23]

Perhaps the most significant division in white society centered on racial attitudes. In particular, this controversy pitted racial moderates against those who demanded unqualified white supremacy. During the last phase of Reconstruction, many whites advocated racial cooperation as a tool to overcome the Republican government. As early as the fall of 1874, the impassioned debate surrounding this issue had created a rift in the once-solid ranks of Florida-parish Democrats. Addressing those who supported racial cooperation, Democratic organizer Charles Kennon declared his opposing position: "We can never control the negro vote for the simple reason that it involves social equality which we can never accept. Let our banner be *white* and keep it unsullied." Other whites disagreed, preferring instead to grant blacks suffrage, which they, in turn, would control. The *Weekly Picayune* observed that blacks were learning "who would give them employment and treat them kindly." In return for political support, blacks would be granted limited op-

23. Kentwood *Commercial*, July 9, 1895, August 22, 1896; Amite City *Florida Parishes*, October 8, 1890, March 11, 1891; New Orleans *Daily Picayune*, February 10, 1889, October 16, 1897; Amite City *Democrat*, November 6, 1875; E. D. Frost to H. S. McComb, July 15, 1875, in Francis and Frost Out Letters Collection; E. W. Preston to Robert R. Reid, April 27, 1897, in Robert R. Reid Papers, LLMVC; R. L. Duvall to Robert Corbin, March 17, 1892, in Corbin Papers; broadside "To the Citizens of the Parish of Tangipahoa," in Louisiana Broadside Collection, LLMVC; Amite City Council Minute Books, No. 1, January 30, 1886. "Blind tiger" referred to both illegally manufactured moonshine and liquor distributed without paying the federal tax, *i.e.*, blind to the federal tax (interview of Junie Ricks, Franklinton, La., February 3, 1996).

portunities for advancement. What was more important, some secured employment in white-owned businesses. For the cooperationists black employment provided a cheap and easily exploited source of labor. Black votes and
labor contributed to the empowerment of one white faction at the cost of the
unqualified hatred of the other.[24]

It should be noted that despite the factionalization of white society, blacks
were victimized by all white groups. The *Weekly Picayune* summarized the
prevailing racial climate in eastern Louisiana: "The question of white supremacy is not an issue here as it is well understood that the citizens will not
tolerate anything else." Completely cowed by the massive violence characterizing the final months of Reconstruction, blacks retained only the unenviable options of suffering either exploitation or intimidation. Although the
advantages of controlling black votes and labor proved readily apparent to all
whites, one primary group determined to exclude blacks, whereas the other
sought to use them. This strategical fissure contributed significantly to the
eruption of bitter factional feuding.[25]

A second issue contributing to the emergence of societal factions involved
the economic transformation of the region. During the 1870s and 1880s, economic conditions improved substantially in eastern Louisiana. Considerable
new industry, primarily lumber mills, brickyards, and cotton mills, located
predominantly along the course of the railroad. Included were some large
firms, such as the Isabella (later Banner) Lumber Company at Kentwood in
northeastern Tangipahoa Parish and the Gullet Cotton Gin manufacturing
plant at Amite City. Other industrial concerns included shoe and box factories, vegetable canneries, and railroad repair facilities. The steady pace of industrialization proved most significant in Tangipahoa Parish. By 1880, Tangipahoa ranked fifth in overall manufacturing production statewide (see Table
10). In addition, scores of truck farms dotted the landscape alongside cotton
fields and herds of grazing livestock. The rapid rate of development initially

24. Charles Kennon to Tom Ellis, November 11, 1870, October 6, 1874, Tom Ellis to Steve
Ellis, April 1, 1884, in Ellis Family Papers; resolutions adopted by White League meeting at
Bayou Barbary, Livingston Parish, September 5, 1874, in Alley Scrapbooks; Amite City *Florida
Parishes*, August 26, September 16, 1891; New Orleans *Weekly Picayune*, February 24, March 2,
April 9, 1896; New Orleans *Daily Picayune*, February 22, July 4, 1897, January 10, 1898; Lea to
Richardson, March 20, 1879, in Hardy Richardson Papers; Testimony of Samuel H. Houston, in
"Select Committee on the Recent Election in Louisiana," Pt. 2, p. 263; Testimony of J. W. Arm-
stead, Robert C. Wickliffe, John Kennard, in "Select Committee on the Presidential Election of
1876," Pt. 3, pp. 297–99, 548–49, 592.
25. New Orleans *Weekly Picayune*, April 9, 1896.

TABLE 10. MANUFACTURING ESTABLISHMENTS, 1880

Parish	No. of Establishments	Capital	Average No. of Employees	Value of Production
East Baton Rouge	13	$45,850	97	$91,800
East Feliciana	11	$24,000	22	$36,300
Livingston	5	$22,500	25	$41,700
St. Helena	15	$16,400	29	$51,332
St. Tammany	12	$12,450	56	$55,100
Tangipahoa	9	$174,109	207	$334,800
Washington	—	—	—	—
West Feliciana	—	—	—	—

Source: *Tenth Census, 1880: Manufactures*

created a labor shortage. Moreover, it heightened the tension between planters and commercial interests, who were competing directly for laborers. E. D. Frost, regional director for the Illinois Central Railroad, successor to the New Orleans-Jackson line, complained to H. S. McComb that fierce competition for laborers raged between planters and railroad interests in the Florida parishes. Likewise, the Amite City *Gazette* published letters from St. Helena planters who desperately sought cotton hoers.[26]

Despite the increasing diversity characterizing the economy of eastern Louisiana, staple-crop agricultural production remained central. Cotton continued to dominate, though small-scale rice and sugar cane production also increased in the piney woods. Yet in 1880, the implications of the war and Reconstruction persisted. Overall, cotton production in the Florida parishes remained far below prewar levels despite the increasing use of fertilizers. Although production rivaled antebellum amounts in the piney woods, it continued well below the prewar norm in the plantation parishes. The decrease

26. E. D. Frost to H. S. McComb, November 3, 1875, in Francis and Frost Out Letters Collection; Amite City *Gazette*, May 23, 1890; Amite City *Democrat*, November 20, 1875; Amite City *Tangipahoa Democrat*, August 9, 1872; Kentwood *Commercial*, March 16, July 1, 9, 16, 1895, March 14, 1896; U.S. Department of Agriculture, *Report of the Chief of the Bureau of Soils for 1905* (Washington, D.C., 1905), 252; Amite City *Florida Parishes*, November 26, 1890, March 4, 1891; Newsom Brick Yard and Sawmill receipts, in John Thomas George Papers, LLMVC; Charles Gayarre to L. E. Simonds, July 4, 1875, November 12, 1877, both in Gayarre Collection; Liberty, Miss., *Southern Herald*, August 25, 1883; New Orleans *Weekly Picayune*, November 1, 7, 1894; Illinois Central Railroad Company, *Where to Locate New Factories in the States of Kentucky, Tennessee, Mississippi, Louisiana, on the Line of the Southern Division of the Illinois Central Railroad* (Cedar Rapids, Iowa, 1892), 118–48; *Tenth Census, 1880: Manufactures*, 123–24, 249.

was likely related to the average decline in land under production and provided further evidence of the diversification of the economy. Moreover, the reduced yield of cotton per acre may have resulted from difficulties encountered in securing sufficient labor to harvest crops. Table 11 demonstrates the level of agricultural productivity in each of the Florida parishes based on a sample survey of farmers in the immediate post-Reconstruction period.[27]

Brisk economic growth attracted additional sources of capital and labor to the region. Hundreds of northern settlers and investors migrated south in search of cheap land and labor. Business advocate Charles Gayarre informed inquiring northern industrialists that southern labor could be worked sixty hours a week, adding that management "will not be interfered for many years to come by the impatient demands of overtaxed workmen."[28]

Several new communities dominated by northern immigrants, in particular Kentwood and Roseland, developed along the railroad. Other previously established towns such as Hammond also encouraged northern immigration. Newspapers there proclaimed its benefits and actively encouraged new settlement. One broadside distributed by industrial promoters in Kentwood proclaimed the village "free from malarial influences, poisonous snakes and other reptiles, and annoying insects of all kinds" and, addressing the greatest concern of northern immigrants, declared, "At Kentwood the people are polite and kindly disposed towards northern people and always treat them well."[29]

The population of some of these settlements quickly surpassed that of many previously established towns along the railroad. Moreover, the rapid rate of economic development encouraged commercial interests in older communities such as Clinton, Franklinton, and Greensburg to petition for the construction of spur railroads through their towns. The Franklinton New Era urged its readers to encourage the construction of a railroad to stimulate economic development in Washington Parish.[30]

27. Tenth Census, 1880, Manuscript, Louisiana, Schedule 2, Agricultural Statistics, Microfilm (figures based on a 3 percent sample of farmers in each parish); Tenth Census, 1880: Manufactures, 123–24, 249; Capell Diary, December 30, 31, 1866, January 7, 1867, Eli Capell's Laborer's Record Book, Pleasant Hill Plantation, Book No. 8, 1867–85, all in Capell Papers; Amite City Gazette, May 23, 1890.

28. Charles Gayarre letter published in New Orleans Bulletin, n.d. [1885], in Gayarre Collection.

29. Broadside, n.d., in Kent Papers.

30. Franklinton New Era, May 21, 1896; Greensburg St. Helena Echo, September 17, 1892, June 10, 1893, March 15, 1895.

TABLE 11. AGRICULTURAL PRODUCTION, 1880

Parish	% Farmers Growing Rice	% Farmers Growing Cane	% Farmers Growing Cotton	Cotton Produced in Bales	Avg. Amt. Cotton Grown in Bales	Avg. No. Acres to Produce 1 Bale	Avg. No. Acres Owned	% Farmers Owning Land	% Farmers Share-Cropping	% Farmers Renting for Cash	% Farmers Owning Livestock	Avg. Value Livestock Holdings
East Baton Rouge	0.0	14.2	80.9	5,756	17.0	1.70	277.0	52.0	14.0	33.0	90	$452.00
East Feliciana	4.0	17.0	95.0	11,098	9.26	2.62	176.0	39.0	43.9	17.0	88	$212.00
Livingston	23.5	17.6	58.8	1,344	4.6	2.90	296.4	82.0	11.7	5.8	94	$311.56
St. Helena	8.5	12.0	96.0	5,328	5.4	2.52	151.5	62.5	33.0	4.0	100	$177.83
St. Tammany	25.0	25.0	31.0	102	2.4	2.26	121.8	87.0	12.5	—	100	$267.00
Tangipahoa	28.5	14.0	82.0	2,934	6.0	2.74	240.0	82.0	14.0	3.5	96	$368.48
Washington	28.5	23.8	72.7	2,338	3.1	3.50	260.8	89.0	11.0	—	100	$199.66
West Feliciana	0.0	3.0	92.8	11,810	8.6	1.70	94.5	35.7	32.0	32.0	93	$133.65

Sources: Tenth Census, 1880, Manuscript, Heads of Household and Agriculture Schedules

However, the influx of northern settlers and ideals threatened the traditional social structure of the Florida parishes as never before, leading to a dangerous polarization of society. Many of the region's traditional residents accordingly resisted the changes brought by northerners and frequently felt animosity for the settlers themselves. Although it aggressively courted northern immigrants, the Kentwood *Commercial* admitted that outside the towns "back in the woods," many residents resented Yankee intrusion. The *Commercial* also reluctantly noted that a mass meeting designed to promote support for northern immigration among established residents "was very poorly attended." Less inclined to play down the issue, the Amite City *Independent* observed that many older residents exhibited overt hostility to northerners settling in the area. The New Orleans *Daily Picayune* reported that in contrast to depending on Yankee immigration, promoters in Amite City were employing local capital to develop the existing resources of their town.[31]

Northern settlers and capital challenged the existing order in the Florida parishes in two important ways. Their money fueled the economic growth occurring primarily along the railroad, which in itself threatened the traditional piney-woods life-style of eastern Louisiana. The intrusion of numerous industrial concerns and the purchase of huge tracts of timberland jeopardized the conventional existence prevailing in the Florida parishes. Moreover, the northern work ethic and conception of property rights differed from the established relaxed attitude regarding work and landholding. The societal transition initiated by these changes produced concomitant blocs of supporters and opponents, increasing regional divisiveness. In essence, progress had reached a region where most were unprepared for it, many resented it, and some would violently resist it.

The problems plaguing the Florida parishes derived directly from the events of the preceding decades. The weakened status of the old elite, the multiple societal factions emerging, and the challenge posed to the traditional culture contributed to a continuing cycle of instability in the piney woods. In the most significant development, the events of the war and Reconstruction had created a culture of violence in the eastern parishes.

By the closing months of Reconstruction, few piney-woods residents conducted their daily affairs unarmed. Sixteen years of fighting Federal troops and Republican government had demonstrated the effectiveness and finality

31. Kentwood *Commercial*, March 30, April 6, 13, December 14, 1895; Amite City *Independent*, November 14, 1874; New Orleans *Daily Picayune*, March 27, 1897.

of brutality. From the year immediately preceding the outbreak of war to the year of the close of Reconstruction, the murder rate increased 900 percent. Similarly, the level of assault increased by approximately 377 percent. Such extraordinary rates of violence did not simply end with the conclusion of Reconstruction. In his last annual address to the legislature, William Kellogg summarized the enduring condition of the Bayou State: "The great need of Louisiana is peace—peace and the enforcement of the laws, with the active concurrence of the people for whose protection the laws are devised." Kellogg could not have realized that twenty years later his words would prove even more relevant than when he first spoke them.[32]

Incredibly high rates of violent crime characterized the piney woods of the Florida parishes throughout the late nineteenth century. Complete regional official criminal statistics for the period are available only for the years 1877 and 1907. But existing records indicate that in the thirty-year period following the close of Reconstruction, the piney-woods parishes experienced not a return of stability but a dramatic increase in the number of murders while the population less than doubled. The smallest change occurred in St. Tammany, where four reported murders in 1877 increased to six in 1907. Tangipahoa reported the most significant change; the number of murders there increased from three to forty-six in the same period. The numbers for attempted murder and assault demonstrated similar increases over the recorded level in 1877.[33] Significantly, the plantation parishes of East Baton Rouge, East Feli-

32. "Report of the Attorney General," *Louisiana Legislative Documents*, 1860, pp. 3–42, 1877, pp. 1–48; "Annual Address of Governor William P. Kellogg," *Louisiana House Journal*, 1st Sess., 1876, p. 22.

33. "Report of the Attorney General," *Louisiana Legislative Documents*, 1878, pp. 1–40; "Report of the Attorney General to the General Assembly," *Louisiana Legislative Documents*, 1906–1908, Vol. I, 3–51; *Twelfth Census, 1900: Population*, 22–23; Sixteenth Judicial District Court Minute Books, Nos. 4–6, Tangipahoa Parish Clerk of Court Archives, Amite City, La.; New Orleans *Daily Picayune*, October 26, 1896, June 15, July 12, 1897. The increase in the number of murders in the remaining parishes from 1877 to 1907 was: Livingston, 0 to 8; Washington, 1 to 5; East Feliciana, 4 to 6; East Baton Rouge, 3 to 16. Complete figures for West Feliciana and St. Helena are unavailable. Unfortunately, Justice Department reports for the most chaotic period in the region, 1890–1900, are incomplete. In some cases the district attorney failed to file a report; most significantly during the most crucial years, 1896–1898, he reported that all indictments and records in criminal cases were missing (see *Report of the Attorney General to the General Assembly of Louisiana*, 1896–1898 [New Orleans, 1898], 51). Although the rates of murder in East Baton Rouge Parish did increase this corresponded with the substantial population growth in that relatively urbanized parish.

ciana, and West Feliciana did not experience similar increases. Two of the plantation parishes either witnessed a decrease in the number of violent crimes or remained about the same even though they experienced similar population growth. Despite severely chaotic conditions during Reconstruction, the return of the antebellum elite to most positions of authority in the plantation parishes allowed for the restoration of stability.[34]

The breakdown of legal authority amid the highly charged racial and political circumstances during the last years of Reconstruction virtually required that all residents be armed. With an armed camp established, few were willing to be the first to conduct their affairs unarmed. The Kentwood *Commercial* observed, "A good many peaceable citizens carry guns simply because dangerous men carry them." The editor declared his research indicated that proportionately more people carried concealed weapons in the Florida parishes than in any other region of the nation. Despite these allegations, similar situations prevailed in other areas of the country. Most regions, however, enjoyed the discipline provided by a popularly supported legal system, which the Florida parishes lacked.[35]

As early as the spring of 1879, local newspapers urged legislation to contain the proliferation of concealed weapons. Many recognized that though weapons may have proved essential in defeating the Reconstruction government, they now constituted a menace. In the spring of 1890, the Amite City *Gazette* reported, "Saturday night last one would have supposed Amite City had been turned into a frontier town and wild Indians had made an attack so numerous were the pistol shots." Violent crimes frequently went unnoticed for hours because of a general acclimation to gunshots. The Kentwood *Commercial* complained that the reports of weapons at the scene of one violent crime had "caused no alarm or excitement as the people of the town are not unaccustomed to hearing the discharge of firearms during the night." Kentwood attempted to control the random discharge of weapons in town by building a shooting gallery "for the rowdy boys." James S. McGehee reflected sadly on the upbringing of Florida-parish boys: "[They] had grown up in a country where youths were permitted by public opinion to carry revolvers at an age when they scarcely had sufficient discretion for pen knives. Human

---

34. For a differing example of the interrelationship between planters and plain folk under stressful circumstances in the late nineteenth century, see Christopher Waldrep, *Nightriders: Defending Community in the Black Patch, 1890–1915* (Durham, N.C., 1993).

35. Kentwood *Commercial*, September 12, May 2, 1896.

life there has always been held far too cheaply." Not surprising, women also frequently carried guns for self-protection.[36]

In a series of articles beginning in the winter of 1890, the Amite City *Florida Parishes* provided perhaps the best explanation of the regional obsession with violence. "Four years of war added to ten years of alien carpetbag rule, fourteen years of demoralization and destruction could not have been expected to leave the people of this state in a very settled condition, nor with a very high regard for the majesty of the law." The editor emphasized that by the close of Reconstruction few local residents had retained any respect for established legal authority. Ominously, the same paper observed that the absence of effective law enforcement since the close of Reconstruction had permitted "a few lawless and irresponsible men in the community who have nothing to lose to terrorize a whole community." Local newspapers fanned the flames of chaos by dramatically publicizing events and essentially making heroes out of notorious criminals. Many newspapers encouraged a culture of violence by the nature and emphasis of some of their articles. One such article, entitled "How to Whip a Bigger Man than Yourself," described a series of tricks to overcome a more powerful opponent.[37]

With the order and stability provided by a dominant planter class removed, as well as the absence of federal troops, the piney woods of the Florida parishes declined into anarchy. The popular desire to return to a less-regulated existence foundered on the reality of the prevailing circumstances. The rapid economic transformation occurring primarily along the railroad impeded efforts to return to a simpler way of life. Many openly opposed the implications of modernization. Local newspapers vigorously attacked what they perceived to be the exploitation inherent in capitalism. The Kentwood *Commercial* predicted that the abuses of capitalism would produce "a revolution the magnitude of which few have ever dreamed of." Similarly, the *East*

36. Amite City *Independent*, April 26, 1879; Amite City *Gazette*, May 23, 1890; Kentwood *Commercial*, March 30, 1895, August 29, 1896; New Orleans *Weekly Picayune*, August 2, 1894, March 26, 1895; New Orleans *Daily Picayune*, November 21, 1896; New Orleans *Times Democrat*, December 9, 1888; James Stewart McGehee, "Ramble in Autobiography," in James McGehee Papers; newspaper article, *Daily Picayune*, n.d. [1900?], describing armed women in Tangipahoa, in John W. Lambert Papers, LLMVC.

37. Amite City *Florida Parishes*, November 5, 1890, February 11, 1891; newspaper article, [Amite City *Advocate?*], n.d., in Duncan Francis Young Scrapbooks, Vol. 4, pp. 12–13, Department of Manuscripts and Rare Books, Howard-Tilton Memorial Library, Tulane University, New Orleans.

Feliciana Patriot condemned the "merciless creditors" who exploited honest working people. The *Patriot* joined the *St. Helena Echo* and other papers in urging readers to strive for self-sufficiency and economic independence.[38]

The negative impact of modernization proved readily apparent. Many lumber mills provoked widespread resentment by compensating workers in script redeemable exclusively at their own company stores, which often sold merchandise at exorbitant prices. Such restrictive practices kept many laborers in poverty. Likewise, the railroad incurred the wrath of many residents. Some farmers condemned the high freight charges that cut substantially into their meager profits. Others deplored the railroad's decimation of their livestock. Most important, many deeply resented the railroad's exploitation of its own laborers. Regional director E. D. Frost observed that the railroad had aroused the hostility of local residents primarily because of its failure to pay its workers. Frost summarized the prevailing animosity simply by noting, "We have broken so many promises." The *St. Helena Echo*, always at the forefront in condemning unfair labor practices, declared: "It is fast becoming the old, old question of capital vs. labor, freemen vs. capitalist slavery. Let the farmers stop, think, and take measures to protect themselves."[39]

As abundantly demonstrated in the newspapers, a fierce determination to maintain one's independence and honor remained central to the piney-woods existence in the Florida parishes. In a society now heavily armed and extensively schooled in the effectiveness and finality of brutality, conditions proved conducive to chaos. In an effort to rationalize the chaos that gripped the eastern Florida parishes, the New Orleans *Daily States* explained, "The people of the Florida parishes are generally rough and of an independent, too often fierce spirit unrestrained by the efficient enforcement of criminal justice."[40]

Like the social structure and economy of the region, the system of justice in the Florida parishes was completely transformed as a result of events associated with the war and Reconstruction. The remnants of the prewar legal system that survived the war collapsed before the purges initiated during Re-

38. Kentwood *Commercial*, July 30, 1895; Clinton *East Feliciana Patriot*, April 27, 1867; Greensburg *St. Helena Echo*, August 24, 1889, September 12, 1891, January 14, 1898; Amite City *Independent*, January 7, 1882.

39. E. D. Frost to H. S. McComb, October 18, June 27, 1875, in Francis and Frost Out Letters Collection; Greensburg *St. Helena Echo*, January 16, 1892; Amite City *Democrat*, December 4, 1875; New Orleans *Weekly Picayune*, November 27, 1895.

40. New Orleans *Daily States*, rpr. Kentwood *Commercial*, January 1, 1897; New Orleans *Daily Picayune*, April 12, 1899; New Orleans *Weekly Picayune*, August 2, 1894.

construction. With real power concentrated in the hands of federal authorities, the majesty of civil justice declined. The system installed by the Republican government proved incapable of coping with the ever-increasing cycle of violence. Moreover, popular perceptions of the fraudulent rise to power of and corruption in the Republican system negated respect for the courts among residents.

Tangipahoa and East Feliciana Parishes experienced the widest chasms between legal authority and popular approval. In Tangipahoa the Republicans appointed as sheriff a widely despised man accused of prewar criminal activity, and a large portion of the population believed that the local judges held office fraudulently. In East Feliciana popular outrage resulted in the violent ouster of the local sheriff and judges. The similarities between these two parishes, however, end with redemption. The return of the planter class to power in East Feliciana allowed for the establishment of a respected assertive legal system in a social framework that retained many elements of the antebellum system. The rapid economic transformation of Tangipahoa and the concomitant factionalization of society and politics hindered efforts to reestablish a respected system of justice there.

Throughout the late nineteenth century, the local courthouse served as the premier political prize in many regions of the rural South. In the Florida parishes, judges commanded the greatest power and respect, though the district attorney and sheriff also retained considerable influence. Central to an understanding of the chaos that emerged at its worst in Tangipahoa Parish is a comprehension of the incoherent system of justice that prevailed there. Unfortunately for the residents, the district judgeship fell directly under the control of one faction, the district attorney often appeared partisan to another, and a progression of sheriffs proved cowardly and incompetent. Although all of the piney-woods parishes experienced inordinant rates of violence, as a result of the legal chaos prevailing in Tangipahoa, it not only sustained comparatively exceptional levels of violence but continued a regional tradition attracting scores of lawless elements.

The turbulence within the legal system rendered it largely ineffective, promoting increasing disaffection with the mechanisms of justice. Violent criminals in the charge of the sheriff frequently escaped, as did inmates of the parish prisons. Henry Crittenden, who escaped from Tangipahoa sheriff P. P. McMichael while en route to the state penitentiary, announced that he would kill all who had testified against him, causing several families to flee the region. Most escapees, such as Hardy Strickland, who fled the courthouse during an exchange of gunfire between his friends and sheriff's deputies, were not pursued after their escape. Criminal dockets were often stolen or destroyed, and at one point the Washington Parish courthouse mysteriously burned down amid a series of heated cases. In the absence of an effective system of justice, feuding emerged as the primary mechanism for redress of personal grievances.[41]

The incompetence of several sheriffs, in particular P. P. McMichael and F. P. Mix of Tangipahoa, encouraged the violence. Neither made any realistic effort to control the ever-widening cycle of brutality. When asked how a mass-murderer could so blatantly snub the legal system, a female member of one of the notorious feuding families responded curtly, "They were afraid to arrest him." In vain, concerned citizens frequently filed charges against local sheriffs for failure to perform their duties. Similarly, the district attorney frequently appeared reluctant to prosecute either those aligned with his own faction or particularly dangerous elements. The New Orleans *Daily Picayune* observed that in the late-nineteenth-century piney woods, the old, honor-bound means of settling disputes, in face-to-face confrontations, had given way to "skulking, cowardly assassins," thus paralyzing the legal system with fear. The failure of the mechanisms of justice to arrest the increasing violence led a group in Washington Parish to urge, "Deal out the justice of Judge Lynch with an unsparing hand."[42]

Sheriff McMichael's failure to fulfill his duties proved particularly shameful. Throughout the 1890s, the bloodiest decade in the region's history, McMichael remained completely unwilling to confront the most violent elements. Moreover, he seemed to resent those who possessed the aggressive nature he lacked. For months prior to the fall of 1896, merchants in Hammond had been bullied by a notorious thug who was "trying to run the town with a small gang at his back." When Hammond city marshall Tom Rhodes courageously confronted the gang, a shoot-out resulted, leaving one of their number dead and Rhodes seriously wounded. To the dismay of the residents who applauded Rhodes's bravery, McMichael promptly arrested him for creating a

41. Kentwood *Commercial*, March 30, 1895, June 6, 1896, January 1, March 20, 27, June 12, July 3, 1897; Amite City *Florida Parishes*, June 10, 1891; Greensburg St. *Helena Echo*, August 15, 1891, January 22, 1897; New Orleans *Daily Picayune*, January 20, 29, 1891, June 14, 15, July 1, 1897; New Orleans *Weekly Picayune*, June 2, 1896; "Report of the Attorney General to the General Assembly of Louisiana, 1896–1898," *Louisiana Legislative Documents*, 1898, p. 51.

42. New Orleans *Daily Picayune*, December 14–15, 1897, January 31, February 10, 1898, June 12, 1898; Kentwood *Commercial*, June 12, July 3, 1897; Sixteenth Judicial District Court Minute Books, Nos. 5 and 6, 1893–99, Tangipahoa Parish Clerk of Court Archives, Amite City.

disturbance. The remaining gang members continued to roam free, "making threats." Sheriff Mix likewise incurred the wrath of East Feliciana residents. After accompanying a "dangerous negro maniac" to the asylum at Jackson, the sheriff was angered to find the facility full. Rather than returning the man to jail in Tangipahoa, Mix simply released him in Jackson.[43]

The shortcomings of the legal system mirrored a more substantive problem. Conditioned by brutality and a fierce tradition of independence, many residents rejected the idea of government intervention in what they considered private affairs. Feuding families frequently expressed contempt for the interest shown by nonparticipants, though some of the feudists themselves, particularly younger unattached men, seemed to revel in the publicity surrounding the later phases of the feuds. Feudists and families often regarded the system of justice as merely another hostile faction. Many considered government to be inherently corrupt and partisan, whereas others regarded murder as the definitive means of defending independence and honor. In court, defendants repeatedly appealed to a warped Jeffersonian tradition that permitted a man to confront a perceived threat aggressively, and juries accordingly sustained their pleas. With juries unwilling to convict, the efforts of peace officers were neutralized and the entire system demoralized. Commenting on the prevailing attitude toward the legal system in the piney woods, the *Weekly Picayune* observed that the people seemed to fear the courts "more than smallpox."[44]

In the winter of 1890, the *Florida Parishes* summarized conditions in the piney woods. The editor observed, "From a period of anarchy we have progressed to one in which the law breaker is at least brought to trial." Despite this positive step, he noted, few criminals filled the local jails. He concluded with an impassioned appeal for jurors to convict the guilty, noting, "We can have no prosperity until we have peace; we can enjoy no peace as long as the criminal laws of the land are violated openly and with impunity." At the conclusion of a session of the district court seven years later, the same paper lamented that despite the large number of locally and illegally distilled and distributed blind tiger whiskey cases heard, not a single conviction had resulted. In a complaint similar to that voiced years before, the editor noted that "the court officers do what they can but the juries favor whiskey and

43. New Orleans *Daily Picayune*, February 7, 1889, October 31, 1896; Kentwood *Commercial*, October 24, 1896, January 23, 1897.
44. New Orleans *Weekly Picayune*, August 2, 1894.

won't convict." Following the April, 1891, bushwhacking of Jack Hall in Livingston Parish, the *Florida Parishes* argued that his murder was a logical step. Hall had been tried for the murder of Bud White a few months earlier, but a jury had failed to convict him.[45]

In an 1894 article entitled "What Is the Reason?," the Roseland *Herald* observed that of the thirteen true bills returned by the sitting grand jury, none had resulted in convictions. The indictments, ranging from trespass to murder, were all dismissed by a jury composed of men "who will never convict, no matter what the evidence may be." The *Herald* continued, "If this is true then justice has fled, and the courts are a mere farce, a travesty on justice." As late as 1908 Governor Newton C. Blanchard complained that juries "are too often influenced in their actions by the local surroundings, by the sentiment or feeling in the community favorable to the accused and thus fail to convict." Instead of improving the system, these appeals from the press and from authority figures had little, if any, positive effect. The *Daily Picayune* noted that every celebrated case appearing before the Sixteenth Judicial Court at Amite City in June, 1897, had been dismissed. In some cases the jury deliberated only five minutes before returning a verdict of not guilty. The only exception epitomized the popular response to the system: a party of armed feudists, upon learning that their case would actually go to trial, marched out of court derisively mocking the proceedings. The court responded by disbanding the jury and canceling the session.[46]

Outraged by what it called the "Reign of Blood" in the piney-woods parishes, the *Daily Picayune* printed an assessment of the legal system there. The report commended Sixteenth Judicial District judge Robert R. Reid for his efforts but condemned the incompetence of Tangipahoa sheriff McMichael. A similar report presented by an 1897 grand jury also praised the efforts of Judge Reid but gingerly criticized McMichael and District Attorney Duncan Kemp. Both reports reserved their strongest criticism for the mass of the population. The *Picayune* denounced the residents for their pervasive disrespect of the law. According to the *Picayune* this condition resulted from a persistent effort of some to bring justice into disrepute, thereby creating a condition in which juries refused to convict out of sympathy for the accused or

45. Amite City *Florida Parishes*, November 5, 1890, April 29, 1891, April 30, 1897.
46. Roseland *Herald*, June 15, 1894; *Message of Governor Newton C. Blanchard to the General Assembly, 1908* (Baton Rouge, 1908), 58–59; New Orleans *Daily Picayune*, June 8, 10, 12, 13, 14, 15, 17, 19, 1897.

out of fear of being killed by friends of the criminals. The *Picayune* concluded, "The burden is placed where it belongs upon the people." In separate articles the same paper and others noted that in the past fifty years Washington Parish had convicted only one accused murderer amid the relentless violence.[47]

The *St. Helena Echo* called for radical changes to counter the ineffectiveness of the judicial system. The *Echo* urged that court officials be made appointive lest the region continue "onward and downward to financial ruin." Like most other observers as well, the paper admitted that without a change in the character and accountability of the population, any effort to restructure the system of justice would be doomed to failure. Judge Reid provided perhaps the best summary of the prevailing conditions in a January, 1897, charge to a sitting jury: "The failure to perform the duties entrusted to you is the fruitful source of mobs and riots, the people become incensed against the machinery of justice by reason of such failure; evil doers become emboldened by immunity from punishment for crime and the result is a hatred and contempt for them and anarchy and lawlessness spread their reign of terror over the community."[48]

In a culture dominated by an extremely sensitive concern for honor and independence, an ineffective legal system spelled disaster. Seemingly insignificant issues frequently resulted in serious "difficulties," a term popularly employed among the press and people to describe honorable violent confrontations. Difficulties differed from "cowardly murders" and bushwhackings, both of which connoted craven assassinations or murders conducted under criminal auspices. Bushwhacking almost always indicated a planned-in-advance, feud-related homicide. In examining events in the piney woods of eastern Louisiana in the late nineteenth century, it is important to remember that the majority of residents tolerated murder as a means of settling differences. Thus, most difficulties, and the murders that resulted, were considered justifiable.

Difficulties caused 79 of the 133 homicides whose specific events and circumstances have been identified in the Florida parishes during the period 1882 to 1898.[49] Of the total, 20 murders occurred under criminal circum-

47. New Orleans *Daily Picayune*, June 15, July 12, 1897, October 26, 1896; Kentwood *Commercial*, March 27, 1897.

48. Greensburg *St. Helena Echo*, September 30, October 7, 1893, also rpr. New Orleans *Daily Picayune*, August 2, 1897; New Orleans *Daily Picayune*, January 14, 1897.

49. These figures include four murders in southwestern Mississippi related to or directly influencing events in the Florida parishes.

stances. These incidents ranged from the bungled train robberies of the notorious Eugene Bunch to the random murders of inoffensive tramps camping along the railroad. In one particularly grisly incident, a pair of highway bandits robbed and murdered a traveling salesman, horribly mutilating his corpse to inhibit identification. In the same period, 19 bushwhackings occurred, as did 6 racially motivated murders. Most of the remaining 9 murders were feud-related instances in which the victim received wounds in the back. Such occurrences differed from difficulties in that they manifested no sense of honor. Significantly, a considerable proportion of the difficulties and almost all of the bushwhackings were feud related.[50]

In addition to the almost daily incidents of personal violence, collective terror and nightriding continued to plague the region. In the late nineteenth century many areas of the South witnessed the rise of terroristic organizations known as "Whitecaps," who employed such terror tactics as nightriding. Usually inspired by economic competition, Whitecaps often engaged in violent acts against oppressive employers or industries. In most cases in the region, however, blacks served as the target of Whitecap violence. Whitecaps fre-

50. Amite City *Florida Parishes*, January 7, 28, April 29, 1891, March 23, August 10, 1892, April 12, 26, 1893, January 23, 1904; Greensburg *St. Helena Echo*, January 31, July 11, 25, August 29, 1891, May 21, June 18, July 9, August 20, September 17, 24, 1892, May 27, June 10, 1893, September 20, 1895; Kentwood *Commercial*, March 30, June 11, 25, July 9, 16, December 28, 1895, January 11, April 24, September 12, October 24, 1896, April 10, July 10, August 7, November 13, 1897, February 5, March 19, 1898; Liberty *Southern Herald*, April 5, 1884; Magnolia *Gazette*, August 25, September 8, 1882, May 31, July 26, 1883; Osyka, Miss., *Two States*, November 23, 30, 1888; Amite City *Gazette*, August 19, 1887; Amite City *Independent*, July 15, 1882, May 26, 1883; Baton Rouge *Daily Advocate*, August 6, 1888; New Orleans *Daily Picayune*, January 26, February 2, 5, April 20, 1883, May 9, 1887, December 17, 1888, January 22, 25, 26, 1889, January 11, 20, 1891, July 12, 1894, October 10, November 21, December 23, 25, 1896, March 15, 27, April 6, May 25, June 12, July 4, 20, 29, August 24, 26, November 9, 22, December 11, 13, 1897, January 31, May 31, June 8, July 13, 1898; New Orleans *Weekly Picayune*, November 2, December 9, 1894, March 24, 26, November 21, 1895, January 10, April 22, 27, June 4, July 14, September 7, 1896; A. C. Bankston to his Uncle Simon, August 18, 1876, in William Bond Papers, LLMVC; W. D. J. Warner to Tom Ellis, September 15, 1874, in Ellis Family Papers; W. W. Draughon to Judge Robert Reid, June 15, 1900, newspaper clippings, New Orleans *Times Democrat* and Greensburg *St. Helena Echo*, n.d., all in Reid Papers; Sixteenth Judicial District Court Minute Books, Nos. 4–6, Tangipahoa Parish Clerk of Court Archives; Minutes of the Pike County, Mississippi, Circuit Court, Books A–B, Pike County Courthouse, Magnolia, Miss.; unidentified newsclipping, March 3, 1894, and two newsclippings, n.d., [1888?], in Young Scrapbooks, Vols. 5 and 6.

quently drove blacks from employment and sought to force their code of morality on the resident population. Jews also suffered at the hands of White-caps, though such persecution had less to do with religion than with per-ceived price gouging by Jewish merchants. One observer described the situa-tion in early 1893: "There is a good deal of excitement here about what is called whitecaps. They are running all the darkeys off from people's mills and farms at a dreadful rate. It is rumored that all the Jews in Summit are going to Jerusalem." Whitecaps met in secret, concealed their identities from the gen-eral population, and often included mystic rituals in their initiation process. Will Purvis, the celebrated Mississippi Whitecap who escaped fate when his head slipped through the hangman's noose, maintained that Whitecaps func-tioned as a direct outgrowth of the Ku Klux Klan.[51]

The success of nightriding during Reconstruction had not escaped the notice of residents in the Florida parishes and southwestern Mississippi. Moreover, nightriding continued to provide a source of camaraderie in a re-gion otherwise virtually devoid of entertainment. But Whitecapping re-mained a deadly serious business. Whitecaps terrorized the community and paralyzed economic development. In the Florida parishes Whitecaps were seldom motivated by high ideals. Instead, they typically functioned as racial regulators, keeping the blacks down and assaulting the interests of economic competitors.

Whitecaps frequently posted armed pickets near sawmills and brickyards to prevent blacks from working. In one instance in the summer of 1895, sev-eral Whitecaps called together a group of black laborers working for a sawmill in central Tangipahoa Parish. The nightriders informed the blacks that they could no longer work at the mill, and to demonstrate their resolve, they singled out a man whom they had already warned. The unfortunate fellow pleaded that he had not understood them initially but would cease working

51. Sister [Lillie Stokes] to J. J. Stokes, February 6, 1893, in Stokes Papers; untitled newspa-per article datelined Laurel Hill, La., January 22, 1893, in John Burruss McGehee Papers, LLMVC; Francis Williams Griffith, *True Life Story of Will Purvis* (Purvis, Miss., 1935), 1–12; Napier, *Lower Pearl River's Piney Woods*, 84; William F. Holmes, "Whitecapping: Agrarian Vio-lence in Mississippi, 1902–1906," *Journal of Southern History*, XXXV (1969), 165; New Orleans *Daily Picayune*, July 10, 1887, March 30, 1894, October 15, 1896; New Orleans *Weekly Peli-can*, July 16, 1887; Greensburg *St. Helena Echo*, November 15, 1895; Baton Rouge *Capitolian-Advocate*, July 1, 1888; Kentwood *Commercial*, November 16, 1895, February 1, April 4, 1896; Amite City *Florida Parishes*, January 14, February 4, 11, 1891.

immediately. The Whitecaps coldly responded that the time for amends had passed and cruelly murdered him in front of all the gathered workers. Similar incidents occurred with painful frequency.[52]

Unlike in neighboring Mississippi, where local authorities aggressively combated Whitecapping violence with the enthusiastic support of the governor, in the Florida parishes, where the Whitecaps commanded broad support, little official sanction hampered them. One group, the Phantom Riders, which operated extensively in Tangipahoa, St. Helena, and Washington Parishes, functioned as a pseudolegal unit. The Phantom Riders whipped and terrorized accused thieves, wife beaters, and the like, always reserving their most severe treatment for blacks. They boasted among their number some prominent local figures, which strengthened their immunity from criminal prosecution and furthered acceptance of extralegal violence among the population. In an article highly critical of the Phantom Riders, the Republican New Orleans *Weekly Pelican* observed the silence surrounding their activities: "No notice of them [Phantom Riders] whatsoever has appeared in our daily papers. The murderous doings were suppressed for fear, it is said that some good (?) citizens might be implicated in such questionable acts."[53]

Some of these groups considered their actions both morally justified and essential to securing regional stability. The constitution of the Knights of the Mystic Ring, based at Amite City, declared, "It shall be the duty of every member to protect the weak, the innocent, and the defenseless, from the indignities, wrongs, and outrages of the lawless, the violent, and the brutal." These were clearly high-minded ideals for an organization focused on secret, paramilitary operations.[54]

Their expressed intentions to address the ineffective legal system notwithstanding, the Whitecaps themselves posed an extreme threat to regional stability. The danger resulted not simply from their extralegal activities but from the possibilities inherent in a situation in which multiple clandestine militias terrorized a community at will. Individual efforts to im-

52. Kentwood *Commercial*, June 11, 1895; Magnolia *Gazette*, November 9, 1882; Sister to Stokes, February 6, 1893, in Stokes Papers; Amite City *Florida Parishes*, January 14, February 4, 11, 1891; New Orleans *Daily Picayune*, October 15, 1896, April 5, 1899; New Orleans *Weekly Picayune*, August 2, 1894.

53. New Orleans *Weekly Pelican*, July 16, 1887; New Orleans *Daily Picayune*, July 10, 1887, February 22, 1897.

54. Handwritten constitution of the Knights of the Mystic Ring, in Thomas E. Warner Family Papers, LLMVC.

press upon the residents the necessity of controlling Whitecap lawlessness typically failed miserably.

Throughout the late 1890s, Kentwood served as a center for Whitecap activities. Located barely five miles from the Mississippi state line, it offered a safe haven for Magnolia state fugitives as well as for many indigenous desperadoes. When C. T. Curtis, the northern-born editor of the local newspaper, criticized the prevailing lawlessness, he quickly received two death threats. Curtis responded with an admission of his own cowardice and a lengthy apology to those he had offended. His weekly apologies apparently failed to appease his antagonists; one month later the same paper reported that Curtis had "mysteriously disappeared."[55]

Wilfred Colvert, a former editor of the Chicago *Vindicator* and a former secret service agent as well, replaced Curtis. Initially Colvert appeared uniquely suited for the stressful role of a "fighting editor." But he, too, soon earned the wrath of the Whitecaps. In December, 1895, Colvert announced, "We have heard of one person who does not like the *Commercial* or its editor and we are considering the advisability of shutting up the shop." Colvert continued to direct the paper, seeking, as far as possible, to distance himself from the prevailing factional violence. Despite his efforts, the *Commercial* reported in March, 1897, that its editor had received two notes ordering him to "git" out of town on pain of death and signed "Captain Whitecaps." Instead of fleeing like his predecessor, Colvert retreated from his critical position on lawless elements and instead allowed his paper to degenerate into the mechanism for publicizing the views of the most violent local faction.[56]

The greatest threat to regional stability posed by Whitecapping involved the possibility that the nightriders could fall under the control of one ill-intentioned individual or group. In a January, 1891, address to a sitting grand jury, Judge Walter Thompson lamented that this possibility had become a reality: "I predicted then that no matter how good the motives of the parties who started this organization [whitecaps] it would fall under the control of parties who would use it as a means of private vengeance and oppression. Subsequent events have confirmed my predictions." If the brutality practiced by terroristic nightriders was not in itself enough, a private, clandestine militia in the hands of a rancorous competitor could wreak havoc on the local economy and provoke the emergence of counter paramilitary organizations.

55. Kentwood *Commercial*, August 13, 20, October 1, 1895.
56. Kentwood *Commercial*, December, 1895, and March, 1897.

Such a situation would result in little less than complete societal chaos. In the Florida parishes perfect conditions for such chaos were already in place.[57]

With the last of the enemies common to southern whites removed, the regional dominance of the planter elite correspondingly collapsed. In the absence of effective and respected leadership, powerful social and economic divisions that split white society emerged. The lack of a competent legal system allowed for rampant criminal activity, including nightriding, which threatened the social and economic stability of the territory. Moreover, the closing months of Reconstruction witnessed the emergence of an armed camp in the piney woods and the triumphant success of violence. An even more appalling period of misery and terror would follow. With their common enemies removed, the white factions turned on themselves in a frenzied carnage of factional warfare that terrorized the population and decimated the economy. The combination of an obsession with violence and an absence of commanding leadership created conditions conducive to disaster in the piney woods.

57. Amite City *Florida Parishes*, January 14, 1891.

Sawmill and Laborers at Hyde Station, *ca.* 1893. The use of black labor (center and upper far right) proved a central element in promoting Whitecapping activities and feud-related violence.

Courtesy Samuel C. Hyde, Sr.

Albert Sidney Johnston Hyde, *ca.* 1893. Hyde later became a prominent physician in the area. The rifle in his left hand is indicative of the prevailing culture of violence. *Courtesy Samuel C. Hyde, Sr.*

Millowner and Democratic Party Chairman Sam Hyde and Family at Hyde Station, Louisiana, *ca.* 1893
Courtesy Samuel C. Hyde, Sr.

Sawmill Workers and Family at Arcola Station, *ca.* 1893
Courtesy Samuel C. Hyde, Sr.

Young Sawmill Manager in Tangipahoa, *ca.* 1893
Courtesy Samuel C. Hyde, Sr.

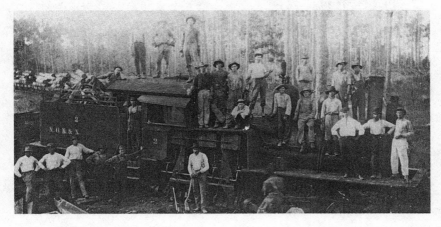

Timber and Railroad Workers Repairing a Dummy-Line Railroad, *ca.* 1898
Courtesy Center for Regional Studies, Southeastern Louisiana University

Students from a Rural One-Room Schoolhouse, *ca.* 1894. The school, located between Hyde Station and Tangipahoa, was typical of piney-woods school facilities.
Courtesy Samuel C. Hyde, Sr.

Black Timber Cutters, with Gear, *ca.* 1898
Courtesy Center for Regional Studies, Southeastern Louisiana University

White Timber Cutters amid a Virgin Stand of Long-Leaf Pine, *ca.* 1898
Courtesy Center for Regional Studies, Southeastern Louisiana University

City Councilmen of Tangipahoa, *ca.* 1897. Avery Draughon (third from left) served as mayor of Tangipahoa and as a deputy sheriff during the height of the feud-related violence. His effort to control the Whitecaps created enemies for him among the Branch men, which led to his murder in 1899.

Courtesy John Walter Lambert Papers, Louisiana and Lower Mississippi Valley Collections, LSU Libraries, Louisiana State University

Black Field Laborer near Amite City, *ca.* 1900. Cotton production remained central in the regional economy in the late nineteenth century.
Courtesy Buddy Bell

Group of Timber Cutters, *ca.* 1898. The bottle of whiskey held by the man second from the right and the pistol flashed by the man at the extreme right both reflect the prevailing culture of violence.

Courtesy Center for Regional Studies, Southeastern Louisiana University

Downtown Tangipahoa, *ca.* 1898. The site of the most intense postwar instability, Tangipahoa was the center of the feud-related violence of the 1890s.

Company H, First Louisiana Infantry Regiment, on Dress Parade at Hammond Station, 1898. This unit assisted members of the Courthouse faction in defending the Tangipahoa Parish courthouse when it was threatened by the mob seeking to lynch the Cotton murderers in September, 1896.

Downtown Tangipahoa, *ca.* 1898. The women are standing on the New Orleans-Jackson Railroad Line (later the Illinois Central Railroad). Bill Davidson was murdered in front of the building on the right.

Courtesy John Walter Lambert Papers, Louisiana and Lower Mississippi Valley Collections, LSU Libraries, Louisiana State University

Company K, First Louisiana Infantry Regiment, 1898. The troops are departing from Hammond Station at the outset of the Spanish-American War.

Courtesy Center for Regional Studies, Southeastern Louisiana University

Parade Revelers During the Tangipahoa Parish Fair in Amite City, *ca.* 1898
Courtesy Buddy Bell

New Orleans Newspapers, 1897–1899. The headlines exemplify the sensationalism of the New Orleans press in covering the admittedly shocking events occurring in
the piney-woods parishes.

Courtesy Center for Regional Studies, Southeastern Louisiana University

·6·

WAR WITHOUT HONOR:
CHAOS ENSCONCED

In a swampy area along a roadside in northeastern Tangipahoa Parish, three men waited nervously. One, a teenage boy with little experience in such matters, crouched anxiously in a clump of bushes about one hundred yards up the road from the others. If all went as planned, he would announce the approach of the unfortunate victim with a series of bird calls. The two assassins, both armed with double-barreled shotguns and Winchester rifles, remained concealed in the thickest undergrowth near a stream bed. A can of turpentine and a pile of cigarette butts lay at their feet. As morning turned to midday, the bushwhackers settled in for another day of patient waiting. Their rival had survived another morning. Perhaps he would come tomorrow, and if not, they just might shoot somebody else then anyway.[1]

Similar situations occurred regularly in the Florida parishes as well as in many other regions of the late-nineteenth-century rural South. With the close of Reconstruction, large areas of the South returned to a semblance of the stability they knew in the antebellum period, but in other regions, unrestrained violence remained a fundamental component of everyday life. In some relatively isolated areas of the piney-woods and mountain South, scores of fierce feuds erupted. Many of these found their origins in the struggle for economic and political primacy that characterized much of the post-Reconstruction South. The frequency and endurance of white-on-white violence indicated the presence of a retarded system of justice and the continuity of a frontier mentality. Moreover, it demonstrated a breakdown in the social homogeneity that prevailed among native whites during Reconstruction. More important, the widespread acceptance of violence unregulated by traditional

1. Similar descriptions of bushwhackings were found in New Orleans *Daily Picayune*, July 4–5, November 9, December 11, 1897; New Orleans *Times Democrat*, July 4–5, 11, December 11, 1897.

interpretations of honor indicated a perverted understanding of the Jeffersonian-Jacksonian concepts of independence and honor—a perversion that contributed to the emergence of a distorted perception of individual rights. In the Florida parishes, violence resulted from perceived threats to individual liberty, but it also functioned as a matter of economic or political policy, frequently motivated by but transcending concerns for independence and honor.[2]

Among the piney-woods dwellers of eastern Louisiana, the Jeffersonian tradition served not as a blueprint for creating good citizens but instead as the instigator of an obsessive concern with liberty and independence. Rather than promoting agrarian virtue, the republican tradition as manifested in the Florida parishes produced a suspicion of government and of authority figures in general. This perverted tradition demanded resistance to restraints on liberty even to the point of employing dishonorable means, such as shooting perceived agents of oppression in the back. The planter elite's shrewd manipulation of a series of enemies common to southern whites from the antebellum period to the close of Reconstruction prevented this philosophy from coming to fruition. However, planter leadership did contribute to the precarious circumstances prevailing in the late nineteenth century by focusing on perceived threats to white liberty and encouraging extralegal means to resolve grievances. Planter dominance of the region had been so pervasive that in the power vacuum created by the rejection of their authority in the piney woods, the plain folk proved incapable of effectively governing themselves. With common threats eliminated and planter leadership correspondingly weakened, the debauched Jeffersonianism ascended, producing a society overwhelmed by violence and ultimately ungovernable.

The feudists themselves were not the only ones who demonstrated the presence of a perverted republican ideal. Although the unwillingness of certain individuals to address the chaotic conditions can certainly be attributed

2. For examples of late-nineteenth-century southern violence, see Michael Hyman, *The Anti-Redeemers: Hill-Country Political Dissenters in the Lower South from Redemption to Populism* (Baton Rouge, 1990); O. V. Burton, *In My Father's House There Are Many Mansions: Family and Community in Edgefield, South Carolina* (Chapel Hill, N.C., 1985); Stephen Cresswell, *Mormons, Cowboys, Moonshiners, and Klansmen: Federal Law Enforcement in the South and West* (Tuscaloosa, Ala., 1992); Robert P. Ingalls, *Urban Vigilantes in the New South: Tampa, 1882–1936* (Knoxville, 1988); Charles Mutzenberg, *Kentucky's Famous Feuds and Tragedies* (New York, 1917); Altina Waller, *Feud: Hatfields, McCoys, and Social Change in Appalachia, 1860–1900* (Chapel Hill, N.C., 1988).

to cowardice, this faintheartedness in itself does not account for the reaction of the majority. The tacit tolerance of lawlessness by the mass of the population signified instead the centrality of a misguided impression of individual rights. By employing only those aspects of the Jeffersonian tradition conducive to their social and political agenda, local power brokers promoted in the people an intense but distorted republican legacy, which violently rejected government and other sources of restraint on their individual liberty. The refusal of the mass of the population to address the lawlessness reinforced the impression that individual liberty was most effectively manifested through the barrel of a gun. In an effort to explain the source of the chaotic conditions prevailing in the Florida parishes, the New Orleans *Daily Picayune* described the residents as peculiar people "exceedingly jealous of what they deem their rights, and it was mainly through their misconception of what those rights really were that the troubles originated."[3]

Evidence of this dangerous tradition is readily apparent. One recent immigrant to the area received a chilling response to an article he published castigating the prevailing violence and distorted sense of personal rights common to the region. A derisive response from a long-term resident warned that the newcomer had lived in the territory too briefly to understand "society here," adding contemptuously, "his stay here will be short unless before he leaves some domestic misfortune should happen to him or his, which heaven forbid will help him understand the social qualities of this community."[4]

Such ominous circumstances were furthered by a legacy of instability connected to the criminal and rebellion-minded elements of the initial settlers. The plain folk's strong proclivity for rebellion against the existing order simmered as the political agenda of the ruling elite repeatedly subsumed their aspirations. Lingering suspicions of authority, combined with the increasing demands of the market economy and years of unprecedented brutality, contributed to the emergence of a peculiar set of social mores. By the late nineteenth century, suspicion of governmental corruption and the absence of a unifying common enemy permitted the dangerous end product of this tradition to emerge and unleash a vicious cycle of violence and anarchy.

The political power vacuum existing in the post-Reconstruction piney woods created the opportunity for new leadership, but the men who filled that void lacked both the stature of the old elite and the unifying issues the

3. New Orleans *Daily Picayune*, April 12, 1899.
4. Amite City *Independent*, August 20, 1887.

planters had manipulated so effectively in support of their dominance. The factionalization of politics and the rapid economic transformation occurring in certain areas rendered stability increasingly elusive; societal equilibrium proved exceedingly difficult to secure in a region where, in the absence of a common threat, many refused to be governed. Furthermore, the region's fledgling political leaders faced the resentment of many of the old elite, who not only offered little assistance but withdrew their active support from a legal system in crisis.

Among the more important families who sought to fill the political void in this turbulent period were the Reids, led by brothers Joseph and Robert. The Reid brothers, both practicing attorneys, migrated from Madison County, Mississippi, in 1866 and settled near Amite City. By the late 1870s the Reids had established themselves as an alternative to the old elite and had secured a strong political base. Robert, a graduate of the Virginia Military Institute and one of scores of Louisiana politicians who continued to rise in the ranks of the Confederate army throughout the late nineteenth century whether or not they actually possessed a service record, emerged as the family's consummate politician. The Reids' growing influence in regional politics climaxed when Robert secured election to the highly influential district judgeship.[5]

Like that of many other political newcomers, the Reids' success provoked resentment from many members of the old elite. Congressman S. M. Robertson repeatedly expressed deep reservations about the character of the Reids to his friend Steve Ellis. Similarly, Charles Lea informed Washington Parish patriarch Hardy Richardson that a "bloodless revolution" would be necessary to terminate the rule of the Reids. The efforts of the Reids and other emerging political families to promote education and stability consistently suffered from a lack of support among the old elite.[6]

Resistance to the Reids and allied families also centered on their methods and their factionalization of the Democratic party. The Reid faction, like

5. Twenty-Fifth Judicial District Court Minutes, Succession No. 852 A, Register of Doctors, Tangipahoa Parish Conveyance Records, December 2, 1882, Succession of Dr. Columbus Reid, No. 443, April 13, 1886, all in Tangipahoa Parish Clerk of Court Archives, Amite City, La.

6. Tom Ellis to Steve Ellis, December 4, 1879, Steve Ellis to Tom Ellis, November 15, 1887, S. M. Robertson to Steve Ellis, August 11, 25, 1893, July 24, 1896, T. M. Akers to Steve Ellis, August 8, 1894, Steve Ellis to Tom Ellis, September 4, 1894, T. M. Babington to Steve Ellis, September 19, 1894, S. W. Settoon to Steve Ellis, September 9, 1895, Milton Strickland to Tom Ellis, February 15, 1896, all in Ellis Family Papers; Charles Lea to Hardy Richardson, March 20, 1879, in Hardy Richardson Papers; New Orleans Daily Picayune, April 4, 1897.

many of the newly powerful families, aggressively exploited the divisions created by the Louisiana lottery and the increasing power of the Farmers' Alliance. The lottery's perceived manipulation of state government served as an exceptionally divisive issue among Louisiana voters. By 1892 the Reid faction of Florida-parish Democrats openly defied the regular party, provoking considerable resentment. The prolottery and anti-Reid *St. Helena Echo* observed, "This faction with its audacious leaders in bitter hostility to the Democratic party is drawing lines deep." In a blatant effort to employ an old strategy to sustain the power of the regular Democrats, the *Echo* equated the assertiveness of the Reid faction with an assault on white superiority. "It must be noted that white supremacy, the peace and happiness of the people of our state is seriously threatened."[7]

Part of the Reid faction's political success resulted from both its determination to contain the prevailing lawlessness and its willingness to use force. The Reids' aggressive methods brought them into frequent conflict but also gained them powerful allies, most notably Tangipahoa Parish millowner, postmaster, and Democratic party chairman Sam Hyde. As with all the piney-woods political factions, though, the Reid organization's primary purpose remained local political control. In this endeavor they proved extremely successful through most of the late nineteenth century. By the early 1890s the Reid faction frequently directed regional Democratic strategy and parish policy through secret sessions of the Tangipahoa Parish Executive Committee that met at the courthouse in Amite City. Many of those excluded from this process deeply resented the secret sessions. The New Orleans *Times Democrat* condemned their iron-fisted political control as "undemocratic." As a result, many Florida-parish residents viewed them as merely another political faction embroiled in the internecine warfare that overwhelmed the region. Despite this perception, the legitimacy of their often marginally legal efforts to control criminal elements led the newspapers to dub them the "Courthouse faction."[8]

A rival group, which many regarded as partial to one feuding faction, coalesced around elements associated with the district attorney's office. Al-

7. Greensburg *St. Helena Echo*, January 23, February 13, 1892; Amite City *Florida Parishes*, July 22, 29, August 19, 1891.

8. Amite City *Florida Parishes*, January 14, August 12, 1891; New Orleans *Daily Picayune*, July 4, 5, 1897; New Orleans *Weekly Picayune*, September 6, 1896; New Orleans *Times Democrat*, September 14, 1890, July 11, 1897; Kentwood *Commercial*, June 11, 1895; Greensburg, *St. Helena Echo*, January 23, 30, 1892; Settoon to Steve Ellis, September 9, 1895, Strickland to Tom Ellis, February 15, 1896, both in Ellis Family Papers.

though a Confederate veteran, William B. Kemp allied himself with the Republicans in the wake of the war, attaining notoriety when he secured appointment as district judge from Governor Kellogg after being defeated at the polls. With the close of Reconstruction, Kemp recast himself again into a race-baiting spokesman for the rights of local whites, especially Confederate veterans. In 1896 his son, Duncan, secured election as district attorney, gaining the support of some and the boundless contempt of others by his perceived ability to manipulate the legal system in support of friends. In reference to his maneuvering, the Kentwood *Commercial* observed that "he is generally like a flea, very hard to catch." Far from the aggressive legal officer circumstances required, Kemp consistently appeared reluctant to prosecute or delayed the trials of feudists opposed to the Courthouse faction. The delays in many cases allowed the accused time to murder or intimidate witnesses and secure alibis. Addressing the absence of reports filed with his office from the Sixteenth Judicial District, exasperated attorney general M. J. Cunningham included a note indicating that all indictments and records of criminal cases in Tangipahoa Parish had been stolen.[9]

By the early 1880s the old elite had clearly lost the advantage in the piney-woods parishes to the emerging factions. Both the Courthouse faction and the diverse elements aligned against them commanded broad support in each of the five parishes. Politicians and office seekers typically identified themselves as Reid or anti-Reid men. A "Reid Democrat" came to symbolize one who adhered to the Florida-parish faction of Democrats committed to securing local control independent of the regular party. The Courthouse faction frequently antagonized the state Democratic party by obsessively concentrating on local contests and exhibiting little interest in statewide races. Although influenced by pro- and antilottery agitation and the growth of the Farmers' Alliance, each faction operated independent of statewide trends, lending support to the group that seemed best situated to promote its interests.[10]

9. Booth, *Records of Louisiana Confederate Soldiers* III, 531; Kentwood *Commercial*, January 30, 1897; Amite City *Florida Parishes*, October 8, 1890; Amite City *Tangipahoa Democrat*, February 1, 1873; Greensburg *St. Helena Echo*, July 26, 1895; New Orleans *Daily Picayune*, December 21, 1897; Sixteenth Judicial District Court Minute Books, Nos. 5 and 6, Tangipahoa Parish Clerk of Court Archives; *Report of the Attorney General to the General Assembly of Louisiana, 1896–1898*, 51; *Report of the Attorney General to the General Assembly of Louisiana, 1898–1900* (New Orleans, 1900); *Report of the Attorney General to the General Assembly of Louisiana, 1900* (New Orleans, 1902), 7.

10. H. R. Williams to Robert Reid, April 8, 1900, in Reid Papers; Tom Ellis to Steve Ellis, December 4, 1879, Akers to Steve Ellis, August 8, 1894, Steve Ellis to Tom Ellis, September 6,

As the dominant faction, the Reids endured intense hostility. St. Helena attorney Milton Strickland declared to friends in Tangipahoa his enmity toward the Reids: "Your friends and mine can never have any chance in this district in business or politics unless the rule of those Reids is overthrown and their reign closed. Everywhere they are attempting to defeat and crush out every man who will not wear the Reid collar, let us fight them to the death." Without an effective legal system, the Courthouse faction embodied the only realistic hope for stability. Accordingly, many of the old elite reluctantly supported that faction in an effort to contain the prevailing lawlessness. Livingston Parish senatorial candidate F. M. Hinson declared himself outraged to learn that the Ellis family had placed their dwindling support behind the Courthouse faction.[11]

However, the Reid contingent never commanded the absolute control that would have been necessary to bring stability to the region. The local district attorney and most sheriffs typically remained outside their realm of influence or were controlled by competing factions. Moreover, the Courthouse faction, like the other political cliques that filled the power vacuum created by the decline of the old elite, lacked the deferential support the planters had always enjoyed. Part of this problem resulted from the character of some of the faction's most important supporters. Throughout the early 1890s, Sam Hyde remained embroiled in seemingly constant tort-action lawsuits, primarily resulting from disputed timber transactions and labor controversies. He also possessed a notoriously quick temper, engaging in his first shootout at sixteen. Similarly, Joe Reid endured the contempt of many piney-woods residents, as demonstrated by Congressman S. M. Robertson's comments to a supporter in Amite City: "I note what you say about Joe Reid. It is astonishing to me that such a man, known as he is, to the community in which he is now located, so well, can have any political influence." Reid's reputation suffered significantly from his alleged participation in an 1891 killing in Amite City.[12]

1894, Settoon to Steve Ellis, September 9, 1895, Strickland to Tom Ellis, February 15, 1896, F. M. Hinson to Steve Ellis, March 15, 1896, all in Ellis Family Papers.

11. Strickland to Tom Ellis, February 15, 1896, Hinson to Steve Ellis, March 15, 1896, both in Ellis Family Papers.

12. Robertson to Steve Ellis, August 25, 1893, in Ellis Family Papers; Sixteenth Judicial District Court Minute Books, No. 5, Tangipahoa Parish Clerk of Court Archives; Amite City Democrat, May 6, 1876; Kentwood Commercial, June 11, 1895; Amite City Florida Parishes, December 3, 1890, January 7, 14, 1891; New Orleans Daily Picayune, September 6, 1896, February 9, 11, 1897.

234 PISTOLS AND POLITICS

The continual instability was dramatically complicated by the arrival of a new family. Led by brothers A. H. (Lance) and Joel J., the Goss family migrated to the Louisiana-Mississippi border region under suspicious circumstances. At least some members of the family had been heavily involved in Whitecap atrocities in and about Marion County, Mississippi. In sharp contrast to practices in Louisiana in the 1880s and 1890s, successive Mississippi governors, particularly John M. Stone and Anselm McLaurin, sought to crush the Whitecap menace. Their efforts resulted in many arrests and the dispersal of the remaining fugitives. During this same period, portions of the Goss family resettled in Osyka, Mississippi, and in the village of Slaughter in East Feliciana Parish.[13]

Soon after their arrival in the region, the Goss brothers introduced practices that would eventually cost both their lives. Like scores of other pharmaceutical drummers, druggists, and practitioners of "country medicine," both of the Gosses claimed the title "doctor."[14] The brothers combined a passion for politics with a determination to eliminate economic competition in the communities in which they located. To secure these goals they directed Whitecap groups that systematically terrorized and sometimes murdered competing pharmacists and merchants. Their ambition to exercise political control over specific regions led them to employ Whitecaps to terrorize the labor of competing merchants and of politically opposed millowners. The Gosses' criminal activities brought them into almost constant conflict with the courts and local residents.[15]

The Goss family troubles began almost immediately upon their arrival in the region. Lance Goss participated in a movement to dominate the region

13. New Orleans *Daily Picayune*, December 1, 8, 9, 29, 1888, January 12, 1889, March 30, April 1, 12, 1894, November 12, 1895, December 27, 1896; Francis Williams Griffith, *True Life Story of Will Purvis*, 5–8, 30.

14. J. J. Goss allegedly possessed a degree from the Georgia Eclectic Medical College, specializing in female and chronic diseases (Magnolia *Gazette*, March 22, 1883, Greensburg *Gazette*, June 17, 1882).

15. Greensburg *St. Helena Echo*, July 25, 1891, June 18, 1892; Amite City *Florida Parishes*, July 29, 1891, June 29, 1892; New Orleans *Times Democrat*, n.d., describing Goss's involvement in the murder of Varnado, in Reid Papers; New Orleans *Daily Picayune*, December 1, 8, 9, 12, 29, 1888, January 12, 1889, December 23, 1896, February 22, July 11, December 29, 1897, June 8, 15, 17, 29, 1898; Minutes of the Pike County, Miss., Circuit Court, Book A, 553–55, 563, 565, 569, 576, Book B, 11–12, 16, 18, Pike County Courthouse; Sixteenth Judicial District Court Minute Book, No. 5, 1892–96, Tangipahoa Parish Clerk of Court Archives; Baton Rouge *Capitolian-Advocate*, August 8, 1888.

about Slaughter in lower East Feliciana Parish. This effort, in a stable delta parish, met with an aggressive response from the local planter hierarchy. Led by planters from East Baton Rouge and West Feliciana Parishes as well as the local sheriff, an armed group of more than one hundred men forcibly drove the Goss group from East Feliciana. Similarly, Joel Goss fled Osyka, Mississippi, after apparently directing the murder of competing druggist Felix Varnado. A jury failed to convict Goss even though both of the assassins stated that Goss had paid them to kill Varnado. In this case, Goss initiated a pattern his family would employ in the future: the killers were to be compensated with a business established at the Gosses' expense. Moreover, each would receive an additional one hundred dollars. Joel Goss's boasts that all who testified against him would be put to "a long sweet sleep" and his seemingly obvious involvement in the murder of the popular Varnado created a strong public reaction that forced the Goss brothers to flee. Prophetically, they migrated to the increasingly lawless environs of Tangipahoa Parish.[16]

The Varnado murder embarrassed the residents of Pike County. In the wake of the trial, a citizens' commission met at Osyka and released a statement condemning the murderers, adding that none of the accused, including "doctors" Joel J. Goss, Lance Goss, W. M. Tetts, and Bill Rials, were "old citizens of Pike County." The commission noted that the relentless threats issued by Lance Goss, who joined his brother in Osyka after fleeing Slaughter, that they "would kill anyone who testified against them" had outraged local residents. Many regretted that the law had not reacted to the Gosses' frequent public boasts that they intended to murder Varnado. Despite the intensity of the public reaction (sixteen additional deputies were hired to keep order during the trial), the court's attitude toward the Gosses appeared to be simply that they should get out of Mississippi. Responding to a warning that some of the accused might flee before the resumption of the next term of court, the presiding judge said, "At least the country will be rid of them." In essence,

16. Baton Rouge *Capitolian-Advocate*, August 8, 1888; New Orleans *Times Democrat*, July 11, 1897; New Orleans *Times Democrat*, n.d., describing Goss's involvement in the murder of Varnado, in Reid Papers; Osyka *Two States*, November 23, 30, 1888; New Orleans *Daily Picayune*, November 24, 30, December 1, 8, 9, 12, 19, 20, 29, 1888, January 12, 1889, December 23, 1896, February 22, 1897; New Orleans *Times Democrat*, December 9, 11–13, 1888; Minutes of the Pike County, Miss., Circuit Court, Book A, 553–55, 563, 565, 569, 575, 576, Book B, 11–12, 14–15, 16–18, Pike County Courthouse. See also New Orleans *Daily Picayune*, June 15, 1898, for another example of Joel Goss hiring contract murderers.

the courts served only to drive the felons away with the knowledge that they could get away with murder.[17]

In coming to Tangipahoa Parish, the Gosses had entered the heart of a region ripped asunder by factional politics and without effective law enforcement, perfect conditions for the implementation of their method to acquire economic and political power. Their operations would soon bring them into conflict with the dominant Courthouse faction, which, in turn, would create for them a natural ally among the opponents of the Reids.

By 1890 the Gosses were directing a group of Whitecaps that operated freely in the region. Despite some popular concerns, the Goss group initially attracted broad support, including that of some prominent residents, with their moralistic appeal and aggressive "negro bashing." Whitecaps frequently attacked prostitutes, wife beaters, and the like but also whipped, murdered, and generally terrorized blacks, driving scores from the region. Their nightly adventures also terrorized many whites. In one highly publicized operation, Whitecaps raided the village of Tangipahoa, entered the homes of several women of supposed "ill repute," and warned them to leave town or die.[18]

In these endeavors the Whitecaps continued to command some public support, but their relationship with many prominent residents soon soured when Lance Goss exposed his ambitious plans. Goss announced that he intended to organize companies of Whitecaps throughout the region led by himself and his brother Joel. His first priority was to eliminate the prominent Draughon brothers of Tangipahoa, particularly Avery Draughon, who served as one of the few effective deputy sheriffs. Earlier as mayor of Tangipahoa, Avery Draughon had sought to curtail Whitecap depredations in his village by arresting Joel Goss, thus incurring the Gosses' wrath. Moreover, Goss proposed to drive away black labor from the mills at Kentwood, Tangipahoa, and Hyde Station in the belief that blacks belonged in the fields rather than in relatively high-paying mill jobs. The plan called for the Whitecaps to burn the mills, kilns, and other property belonging to those who resisted, but his real motive appeared to center on his effort to secure the support of the emerging Populist movement to further his own political ambitions. Regard-

17. New Orleans *Daily Picayune*, December 8, 29, 1888, January 12, 1889; New Orleans *Times Democrat*, December 9, 12, 1888; Minutes of the Pike County, Miss., Circuit Court, Book A, 553–55, 563, 565, 569, 575–76, Book B, 11–12, 16, Pike County Courthouse.

18. New Orleans *Times Democrat*, July 11, 1897; Amite City *Florida Parishes*, January 14, February 4, 11, 1891; New Orleans *Daily Picayune*, February 22, December 11, 1897.

less, either plan brought him into direct conflict with members of the Court-house faction, in particular with Sam Hyde, a friend of the Draughons and a millowner who employed black labor.[19]

Members of the Courthouse faction accordingly joined the Whitecaps with the stated intention of seizing control and redirecting their energies. In partic-ular, they wanted to protect the Draughons and halt the flow of cheap black labor from the region. Within weeks, they had secured control of the White-caps and elected Hyde captain. Outraged by the nightriders' change of direc-tion, the Goss brothers, more determined than ever to break their opponents, departed with their supporters and created a new Whitecap organization.[20]

The schism in the Whitecaps weakened but did not wreck the Goss group's plans. The Whitecaps continued to terrorize black mill workers. Dur-ing one late night effort to drive off laborers employed by the Draughons, however, one of the blacks met their attack with a shotgun allegedly provided by the Courthouse faction and "brought down several of the boys," including Lance Goss. This shootout exposed the identities of many of the participants and the underlying motives of the Goss faction, temporarily breaking up their operation. With their support evaporating, the Goss brothers wisely fled the region, but before departing, Lance Goss made public threats against promi-nent members of the Courthouse faction, whom he blamed for the White-caps' demise.[21]

The brothers relocated in Purvis, Mississippi. After allowing time for ten-sions to relax in the Florida parishes, Lance returned to Tangipahoa and reen-tered politics. Joel cooperated with a highly publicized band of Whitecaps that terrorized the region about Marion County, Mississippi, among whose participants was the notorious Will Purvis. Mississippi state authorities, un-like those in Louisiana, aggressively pursued Goss, who Purvis claimed was part of the group that framed him for murder, forcing him to flee again and to return to Tangipahoa Parish.[22]

19. Amite City *Florida Parishes*, January 14, February 4, 11, 1891; New Orleans *Daily Picayune*, February 22, December 11, 1897; New Orleans *Times Democrat*, July 11, 1897.

20. New Orleans *Times Democrat*, July 4, 11, 1897; New Orleans *Daily Picayune*, February 22, 1897.

21. Amite City *Florida Parishes*, January 14, February 4, 11, 1891; New Orleans *Daily Picayune*, February 22, December 11, 1897; Kentwood *Commercial*, June 11, 1895.

22. New Orleans *Daily Picayune*, March 30, 1894, November 12, 1895, February 22, 1897; New Orleans *Times Democrat*, July 11, 1897; Griffith, *True Life Story of Will Purvis*, 4–12; Kent-wood *Commercial*, November 16, 1895.

Upon his return to the Florida parishes, Goss reorganized the Whitecaps. This time, the Goss faction concentrated on controlling businesses in Amite City and aggressively courted the local Populists with their message condemning the political elite and advocating mill work for whites only. Specific Amite City merchants received notices ordering them to leave town or face the consequences. This time, however, the Gosses had challenged the Courthouse faction at their strongest point, and they moved quickly to "down the Goss Faction." Moreover, Lance Goss's apparent effort to destabilize the economy by damaging railroad property brought him into conflict with a well-financed major corporation, the Illinois Central Railroad. Nonetheless, the Gosses' promotion of white labor and calls for the disenfranchisement of blacks, whose votes were increasingly manipulated by the Courthouse faction, continued to attract supporters in northeastern Tangipahoa. Their direct association with the emerging Populist-Republican Fusion party in a loudly proclaimed effort to seize power from the dominant Courthouse faction set conditions perfect for the onset of a bitter feud.[23]

In the absence of effective law enforcement, feuding filled the vacuum for addressing perceived injustices. In the late nineteenth century numerous family feuds erupted in diverse regions of the rural South. Most of them involved personal quarrels between families that abated when the primary feudists were killed or driven from the area. Few regions endured multiple unrelated feuds occurring in the same period. Moreover, in most cases, as in the celebrated Hatfield-McCoy feud, the local system of justice endeavored to curtail the violence, and at least some of the feudists suffered the consequences of their crimes.[24]

The brutality engulfing the Florida parishes differed from that of other regions in that the legal system there was subject to, rather than separate from, the feuding. Not only were the representatives of the legal system completely cowed by the violence, but feudists so permeated the system itself that it proved ineffective, functioning as merely another partisan tool of the feudists. In addition, unlike other states, where concerned governors monitored and interceded in affairs, in Louisiana only a sustained statewide cry for inter-

23. Kentwood *Commercial*, February 15, 1896; New Orleans *Daily Picayune*, December 23, 1896, February 22, December 11, 1897; Amite City *Florida Parishes*, January 14, February 4, 11, 1891, June 29, 1892; Greensburg *St. Helena Echo*, June 18, 1892; New Orleans *Times Democrat*, July 11, 1897; Sixteenth Judicial District Court Minute Books, No. 5, Tangipahoa Parish Clerk of Court Archives.

24. For an insightful examination of the Hatfield-McCoy feud, see Waller, *Feud*.

vention moved a reluctant governor Murphy J. Foster to make even a cursory effort at controlling the violence in the Florida parishes. As a result, none of the criminal elements ever faced the implications of their actions before a determined court of law. The concentration of feud-related murders along the railroad demonstrates the centrality of economic development to the violence (see Map 2), but the scattering of homicides throughout the sparsely populated piney woods indicates that the regional breakdown of legal authority transcended the implications of economic competition associated with the railroad.

One of the first and most significant conflicts that emerged in postwar eastern Louisiana was the bloody Tanner-Kirby feud. Waged primarily in Livingston and St. Helena Parishes, this feud had its origins in a personal quarrel from the late Reconstruction period. As with many of the celebrated feuds, the name assigned it by the press constituted something of a misnomer. The conflict pitted the Kirby and Jackson families and their supporters against the large Lanier family and their allies.

The feud began amid the chaos of Reconstruction. The absence of legal intervention in the increasingly brutal internecine warfare required that the families involved take measures to defend themselves. Significantly, no evidence indicates that either side ever sought legal intervention on its behalf. Instead, all parties chose to resolve their differences personally and without government intervention. The bushwhacking of Captain Pierce Lanier, Sr., in February, 1883, and the retaliatory murder of one of the Kirbys near the same spot dramatically intensified the brutality. Public interest was piqued when the news circulated that Captain Lanier's body had been soaked in coal oil and burned, possibly before he died.[25]

By the spring of 1883, when the feud reached its height, both factions engaged in brutal offensive operations. Following a series of individual murders inflicted on both sides, the Kirbys determined to deliver a fatal strike against their enemies. Four members of the Kirby faction, led by Bill Kirby, bushwhacked and killed two Laniers on the Greensburg-Springfield highway; a third survived by fleeing into the town of Greensburg. In the wake of these murders, the Amite City *Independent* reported, "Three Laniers, one Kirby, and two Jacksons are still alive, it is hoped this will end the feud in which six or seven men have died." On May 20, 1883, the Kirbys engineered a second bushwhacking: amid the thick undergrowth along Hog Branch in Livingston

25. Baton Rouge *Capitolian-Advocate*, May 22, 24, 1883.

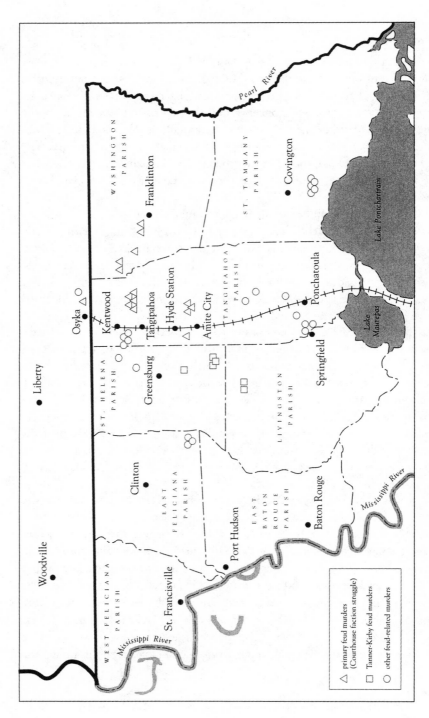

Locations of Principal Feud-Related Murders in the Florida Parishes, 1883–1899

Parish, they waited for a group of Laniers. The ambush resulted in the death of two more Laniers as well as Bill Kirby. After some sporadic sniping at one another, the feud finally subsided in early 1884 when the remnants of the Lanier family departed St. Helena Parish.[26]

The Tanner-Kirby feud captured the attention of local residents and provided a poignant lesson in the importance of individual action and the irrelevance of the legal system. In its wake, scores of feuds developed across the Florida parishes. Many utilized the opportunity to settle old scores. Others felt compelled to slay their antagonists lest they themselves be slain. All recognized that little, if any, effort would be made to arrest them, and few juries would convict anyway.

Each individual feud resulted from circumstances peculiar to the combatants. Some ensued because of seemingly petty personal quarrels, whereas others had their origins in intensive economic or political competition. The Ricks-Bond feud, which flared intermittently throughout the course of the early 1890s and claimed at least five lives, had its origin in a broken marital engagement. A joint picnic in northern St. Helena Parish designed to restore amicable relations between the two families in the summer of 1892 left two dead and two wounded. By contrast, the Settoon-Johnson feud in Livingston Parish arose from the introduction of economic competition into the area. The shooting began when the Johnson faction established a general merchandise store in Springfield. The new store competed directly with the existing one owned by former state senator J. S. Settoon. The Settoon faction's desire to secure their commercial position in and around Springfield continued to provoke sporadic violence throughout the mid-1890s.[27]

Other feuds, such as the McClendon-Overton conflict, resulted directly from the failure of the legal system. An East Feliciana Parish jury's failure to convict B. W. McClendon of the highly suspicious murder of Bill Overton prompted Overton's brother Tom to kill McClendon with a specially loaded shotgun. This murder, in turn, provoked additional reprisal killings. Similarly,

26. Special edition of the Amite City *Independent*, presenting highlights from the period July 15, 1882–May 26, 1883; Magnolia *Gazette*, May 31, 1883; New Orleans *Daily Picayune*, December 14, 1897; Baton Rouge *Capitolian-Advocate*, May 22, 24, 1883; W. D. J. Warner to Tom Ellis, September 15, 1874, in Ellis Family Papers; "Biennial Report of the Attorney General to the General Assembly of Louisiana, 1888–1889," *Louisiana Legislative Documents*, 1890, p. 80.

27. Greensburg *St. Helena Echo*, July 9, 1892; New Orleans *Daily Picayune*, October 22, 1894; New Orleans *Weekly Picayune*, August 2, 1894, June 27, 1895; A. C. Bankston to his Uncle Simon, August 18, 1876, in Bond Papers.

the long-enduring Jolly-Cousin feud in St. Tammany Parish originated in a legal dispute over a piece of land that an ineffective legal system never properly adjudicated. This feud, which lasted more than thirteen years, climaxed in 1897 with a pitched battle involving pistols, shotguns, and clubs that left four dead and two wounded.[28]

By far the most dramatic feud, and the one that best illustrated the relationship of the eastern Louisiana piney-woods mentality and its peculiar pattern of development to the continuing cycle of violence, was the Hyde-Goss feud. This conflict resulted from the struggle for political and economic control between the Courthouse faction and a diverse collection of political aspirants and criminal elements.

Significant differences separated the two feuding factions. Most of the supporters of the Courthouse faction who participated in the armed struggle were family men, with an average age of thirty-six. Over 90 percent maintained regular positions of employment, whereas 60 percent owned property. Four of the eleven principal feudists supporting the Courthouse faction possessed estates valued at more than $1,000. No evidence indicates that any of them had ever been indicted on criminal charges. By contrast, single younger men made up the majority of the feudists aligned with the Goss group. Most of these men, who averaged twenty-five years of age, worked only erratically, which allowed them greater time to concentrate on the business of feuding. While 15 percent of this group owned property, only one of the thirteen primary supporters maintained an estate valued at more than $1,000. Fully 85 percent faced criminal indictments during the course of the 1890s.[29]

The bitter divisions separating the two factions did contain an economic basis. By employing cheaper black labor, businessmen aligned with the Courthouse faction endured the open contempt of their opponents. Ultimately, though, the competition centered on the dilemma of racial cooperation and the corresponding political ambitions of a few men determined to secure the kind of government that suited their interests best. The opportu-

28. New Orleans *Daily Picayune*, January 26, 1883, January 20, 29, 1891, March 27, November 22, 27, 1897, August 10, 1898; Amite City *Democrat*, November 13, 1875; Kentwood *Commercial*, December 4, 1897.

29. *Tenth Census, 1880*, Manuscript, and *Twelfth Census, 1900*, Manuscript, Louisiana, Tangipahoa Parish, Schedule 1, Population, and Schedule 2, Agricultural Statistics, Microfilm; Sixteenth Judicial District Court Minute Books, Nos. 4–6, Tangipahoa Parish Clerk of Court Archives; Minutes of the Pike County, Miss., Circuit Court, Books A–B, Pike County Courthouse.

nity created by the demise of the antebellum elite proved obsessively attractive to some. And in their efforts to secure political power, these emerging political aspirants employed methods that proved disastrous in a region where everyone was schooled in the effectiveness of violence and where less government remained a cherished ideal. The advantages in time and mobility the single, younger, largely unemployed supporters of the Goss faction commanded would be augmented by yet another benefit, the self-imposed restraints under which their opponents operated. Courthouse faction supporters consistently functioned within the limits of a legal system that commanded little popular respect and a code of honor that their enemies had already abandoned. In the Florida parishes the time for honor-bound resolution of conflict had passed. Planter rhetoric insisting that southern rights or native white rights were under attack from abolitionists, Yankees, and carpetbaggers contributed to the growth of a distorted impression of what those rights actually were. The lines between defense of human bondage, white supremacy, and a desire to maintain a life-style independent of the demands of more modern society and government had for many become blurred, as had, concomitantly, perceptions of justice. During the period 1861 to 1877, society had demonstrated a tolerance of extralegal means to defend these individual perceptions of liberty. The Courthouse faction's inability to accept this transition in the absence of an effective system of justice would, for them, spell disaster.

The Goss group's failure to attain commercial supremacy through intimidation stimulated an intensification of their political appeals as they challenged the Courthouse faction, who now consistently disrupted their operations. Lance Goss in particular remained deeply embittered over the breakup of the Whitecaps. Moreover, Joel Goss's effort to reestablish the Whitecaps at Amite City had brought the full weight of the Courthouse faction down on the family. Joe Reid especially resented the Goss faction's methods as well as the threat it presented to the power of the Courthouse faction. Accordingly, he persuaded the sheriff to have Joel Goss, who remained a fugitive from justice in Marion County, Mississippi, arrested and returned to stand trial there. Again Goss secured acquittal, reappearing in Amite City and boasting of his intention to have arresting deputy Bob McMichael, Joe Reid, and Avery Draughon killed.[30]

30. New Orleans *Times Democrat*, July 11, 1897; New Orleans *Daily Picayune*, February 22, December 11, 1897, June 15, 17, 1898.

To confront their enemies in the Courthouse faction, the Goss brothers allied themselves closely with the emerging Populist-Republican Fusion party, which challenged the rule of the Democrats statewide in the 1896 election. Recognizing that the best chance to challenge the control of the Democrats in Louisiana lay in unity, the remnants of the Republican party combined with the increasingly forceful Populists. The Populist emphasis on labor and agriculture and its commitment to improving the quality of life of the common man attracted a large following in Louisiana. The combined ticket commanded the support of black and white workers alike, cutting into traditional sources of Democratic support.

The Fusion party emerged as a serious threat to the race-baiting, do-nothing rule of the Louisiana Bourbon Democrats. In the piney woods of the Florida parishes particularly, the highly charged election represented a serious factional confrontation. Although the gubernatorial challenge the Fusion candidate John Pharr posed to Democrat Murphy Foster stimulated some interest, the area was gripped by the intensity of the regional contests. Local attention concentrated primarily on the challenges to Judge Reid and Sheriff McMichael. In addition, the challenge posed by Lance Goss to the Courthouse faction's candidate for coroner, Dr. J. M. Craig, provided additional interest.

After a grueling campaign, the Fusion party appeared poised for victory, based on their organization of local blacks into Fusion party clubs. In the last hours before the election, however, Hyde and other members of the Courthouse faction persuaded blacks to support the candidacy of Judge Reid, regardless of whom they voted for in the governor's race. Accordingly, the majority of blacks supported Pharr for governor but provided the decisive margin to reelect Judge Reid and defeat Lance Goss.[31]

On election day, April 21, 1896, a large crowd gathered to observe the voting at the precinct in Tangipahoa. When it became apparent that blacks were voting in support of the Courthouse faction despite the threats issued, members of the Goss family became enraged. Deason Goss, twenty-year-old son of Lance Goss, accordingly approached Sam Hyde, who had been crippled in his youth by polio, and gave him a sound drubbing, which seemed to reduce the prevailing tension. A few moments later, Lance Goss approached Hyde, demanding an explanation. When Hyde turned to walk

31. New Orleans *Daily Picayune*, April 22, 23, 1896; Amite City *Florida Parishes*, April 24, 1896.

away, Goss promptly drew his pistol and shot him in the back. While falling, Hyde drew his own revolver and emptied it into Goss. The shooting provoked a general exchange between supporters of each man. In the aftermath, Lance Goss lay dead, struck eight times. Sam Hyde, shot once in the back and once in the stomach, appeared mortally wounded.[32]

Hyde survived his wounds, but the feud was now on in earnest. The Goss family, particularly the deceased man's wife and his sister Ida Goss Fenn, swore vengeance against all those who participated in his death. To many residents, the Gosses had good reason to be angry. Although only five empty chambers were found in Hyde's gun, Lance Goss had been struck eight times, indicating that others had fired on him. Moreover, Goss's nephew, Willie Knapp, who had also fired on Hyde, barely survived the wrath of his uncle's killers. Goss family members repeatedly claimed that the entire incident resulted from a prearranged conspiracy to kill both Goss and Knapp, who had been condemned by some for his participation in a killing in East Feliciana a few years earlier.[33]

Despite its prevailing again at the voting booths, the Courthouse faction emerged from the election of 1896 badly bruised. Several of its strongest supporters had been involved in a violent personal confrontation that left one of them severely wounded. More important, its candidates had faced a surprisingly strong districtwide challenge. Even though the faction carried the parishes of Tangipahoa and St. Tammany, its majorities in each had noticeably dropped. The decline in support for the Courthouse faction candidates proved more drastic in St. Helena and Livingston, where the Courthouse ticket prevailed by only twenty-eight and fifty-nine votes, respectively. The greatest shock came in Washington Parish, where Judge Reid himself was defeated by nearly a three-hundred-vote margin.[34]

32. New Orleans *Daily Picayune*, April 22, 1896, February 22, December 11, 1897; Amite City *Florida Parishes*, April 24, 1896; New Orleans *Times Democrat*, April 22, 1896, July 11, 1897; Kentwood *Commercial*, April 24, 1896. The violence in Tangipahoa conforms to the statewide pattern of violence in this election; see telegrams to Governor Murphy J. Foster, April, 1896, in Murphy J. Foster Papers, Center for Political and Governmental History, Baton Rouge.

33. Amite City *Florida Parishes*, April 24, 1896; Kentwood *Commercial*, April 24, 1896; New Orleans *Daily Picayune*, April 22, 1896, February 22, July 4, December 11, 1897; New Orleans *Times Democrat*, April 22, 1896, July 11, 1897; Greensburg *St. Helena Echo*, July 25, 1891.

34. Amite City *Florida Parishes*, April 24, 1896; New Orleans *Daily Picayune*, April 23, 1896; Settoon to Steve Ellis, September 9, 1895, Strickland to Tom Ellis, February 15, 1896, Hinson to Steve Ellis, March 15, 1896, W. H. McClendon to Steve Ellis, April 12, 1896, and Robertson to Steve Ellis, July 24, 1896, all in Ellis Family Papers.

The power of the Courthouse faction was inversely proportional to the appeal of the Fusion ticket. Beginning in the late 1870s the strength of the Farmers' Alliance increased steadily in the Florida parishes. The combination of farmers committed to improving their standard of living and of those delivering themselves from capitalist exploitation embodied in the Alliance rapidly gained strength in the post-Reconstruction period. Its rhetoric espousing the virtues of an independent agrarian life-style played well in the piney woods. With the emergence of the Populist crusade in the early 1890s, the agrarian movement became far more radicalized. Florida-parish farmers collectively transported their goods overland and by lake steamer to New Orleans to force the railroad to lower its freight rates for hauling produce. Locally the Populists increasingly vented their disappointment on the Courthouse faction, which demonstrated little, if any, interest in their program. In a frustrated outburst one Tangipahoa Parish farmer wrote: "We are tired of being ridden by the political bosses of Amite City and we demand that something be done toward giving the white Democrats of the parish an opportunity to say who shall fill the offices for the next four years." Such statements also exemplified the consistent theme of white supremacy that permeated the rhetoric of piney-woods Populists. The racist appeal reinforced their resentment of the Courthouse faction, which allied itself closely with millowners who employed cheaper black laborers. As a result, blacks in the Florida parishes demonstrated far less interest in the local ticket than they did in the statewide Fusion effort.[35]

The declining strength of the Courthouse faction also resulted from the inability of its members to govern effectively. Although the faction had been dominant for years, criminal elements and lawlessness continued to prevail in the piney woods. In an effort to encourage greater citizen support for law enforcement, Judge Reid and other faction members organized the Law and Order League. The constitution of the league acknowledged, "A spirit of lawlessness prevails in certain portions of this parish which the regularly constituted authorities have thus far failed to suppress and the welfare and se-

35. Amite City Democrat, September 25, November 20, 1875; Amite City Gazette, June 28, 1889; Greensburg St. Helena Echo, August 22, 1891, September 23, 1893; St. Francisville Feliciana Sentinel, June 22, 1889; Amite City Florida Parishes, October 1, December 17, 1890, July 8, August 12, 19, 1891; New Orleans Daily Picayune, June 19, April 25, 1896; D. Caffery to Steve Ellis, September 20, 1893, in Ellis Family Papers; newspaper clipping from the Wesson, Miss., Southern Industry, May 16, 1885, in Young Scrapbooks; James S. McGehee, "Ramble in Autobiography," Typescript, n.d., in James McGehee Papers.

curity of a large majority of the population, white and colored, are jeopardized by these parties, who under cover of darkness seek to regulate the affairs of both employees and employers in defiance of civilization." The statement concluded with a call for citizens to take action against those who "singly or in bands seek to disturb the industrial and social harmony of any portion of the parish."[36]

Although the league constituted a noble effort to encourage citizen involvement in containing growing lawlessness, it failed for a variety of reasons. Fear discouraged many residents from associating themselves with an organization committed to bringing to justice the most violent elements. Others maintained a steadfast rejection of the right of government to interfere in personal matters. Scores of piney-woods dwellers remained dedicated to the idea of individual action, spurning the intervention of government. The prevailing attitude that some folks "needed a killing" and that government served as an unwanted interloper in the natural course of human affairs served consistently to stifle efforts to restore stability in eastern Louisiana. Finally, the Courthouse group failed to extricate itself from the morass of factional fighting occurring in the piney woods. Opponents relentlessly accused faction members of prejudice in directing the courts and thus rejected their authority. Lacking the strength and public support to enforce stability, the Courthouse group saw its prestige steadily decline.

The expanding cycle of violence prompted local residents increasingly to appeal directly to state officials for relief. A petition sent to Governor Foster by "Indignant Citizens" of Livingston and St. Helena Parishes revealed the near anarchy reigning in the piney woods. The petition requested the governor's intervention to halt the constant unprovoked "shooting of people on the Greensburg-Springfield road" by unknown parties. Foster's reluctance to intervene in the increasingly turbulent Florida parishes prompted some residents to adopt desperate measures, some of which threatened the political structure. The single greatest challenge to legally constituted authority occurred in September, 1896, in Tangipahoa Parish.[37]

The threat arose in conjunction with the brutal murder of the Cotton family at Tickfaw. The axe murder of the entire family of five by two blacks, John Johnson and Arch Joiner, provoked unprecedented rage in the southern

36. Amite City *Florida Parishes*, February 4, 11, 1891.
37. Greensburg *St. Helena Echo*, January 13, 1896, January 22, 1897; New Orleans *Daily Picayune*, September 27, 29, 30, 1896.

portion of the parish. After securing a confession, Judge Reid ordered the prisoners sent to New Orleans for their own protection. An outraged mob halted the train on its return to Amite City and threatened the deputies who had transported the accused men to New Orleans. Determined to force the return of Johnson and Joiner, a mob of more than 500 marched on Amite City, threatening to kill Judge Reid and other officials. In the midst of the crisis, Joe Reid, Sam Hyde, and Charles Bradley arrived at the head of about 75 supporters of the Courthouse faction. Hastily sworn in as deputies, the men barricaded themselves and prepared to be stormed while Judge Reid and Sheriff McMichael sent frantic telegrams appealing for assistance to Governor Foster. Responding rapidly under the circumstances, Foster ordered a company of state militia to Amite City and placed three more on alert. Led by Adjutant General Allen Jumel, Company H of the First Louisiana Infantry Regiment arrived only hours before the mob reached the town. Fortunately, bloodshed was avoided when the mob halted before the barricades established on the outskirts of Amite City. A conference held between a committee from the mob and parish officials defused the situation when the officials consented to return the accused to Amite City to stand trial. Within days after their arrival in Amite City, Johnson and Joiner were taken from the courthouse by a mob 250 strong and lynched at the site of the murders; this time parish officials did not intervene.[38]

The Courthouse faction emerged from the Cotton tragedy severely weakened. The affair dramatically exposed the limitations of its authority. Moreover, the confrontation with the mob had strengthened its enemies, who loudly condemned the protection of "negro murderers." Many refused to recognize that these men had acted in support of parish officials, not on behalf of the accused murderers. For the faction's enemies the time seemed right to settle some scores.[39]

Following the death of Lance Goss, his family engaged in elaborate preparations to fulfill their threat to kill all those involved in his demise. In support of this effort, they recruited the assistance of a large family living near Tangipahoa, the Gill family, who embodied the piney-woods life-style and

38. New Orleans Daily Picayune, September 24, 27, 29, 30, October 4, 15, 1896, January 21, July 4, 1897; Kentwood Commercial, October 3, 1896, January 23, 1897; Greensburg St. Helena Echo, January 22, 1897; Annual Report of the Adjutant General of the State of Louisiana for the Year Ending December 31, 1896 (Baton Rouge, 1897), 7–8.

39. New Orleans Daily Picayune, September 29, 30, 1896, January 21, 1897; Greensburg St. Helena Echo, January 22, 1897.

mentality. They congregated in a remote area near the Tangipahoa River appropriately named "Gilltown." Their tendency to intermarry, especially with the closely related Ricks family, made them a tightly knit, somewhat xenophobic clan with distant blood connections to the Gosses. Several sons of the family patriarch Frank Gill, in particular Alonzo, Alex, Gage, and Obe, had served as stalwart members of the Goss Whitecap band. The Gills raised much of their own food, cutting a little timber and occasionally distributing blind tiger whiskey for cash. During the early 1890s the Gill boys compiled an impressive record of arrests, ranging from attempted murder to forcible disruption of peaceable assemblies. Their frequent brushes with the law had steadily increased their contempt for the Courthouse faction but created for them important friends in the Kemp family, who typically served as their counsel.[40]

In recruiting the assistance of the Gills, Ida Goss Fenn and Joel Goss continued the pattern they had established earlier in Mississippi. The Gills would be set up in a business financed by the Gosses and would be paid a set amount of cash for each murder. By November, 1896, the group had secured a small general merchandise store in Tangipahoa, which Alonzo Gill and his brothers operated. The Tangipahoa location would provide an excellent setting for the murder of the first intended victim, Bill Davidson. On Christmas Eve, 1896, while Alonzo Gill served as lookout, Obe Gill and his friends Monroe and Otto Bamber cornered Davidson and shot him four times in the back. Although Davidson returned fire before he died and wounded one of the assassins, they all escaped into the nearby river swamp, leaving the first in a line of Courthouse faction members dead in the streets of Tangipahoa.[41]

Despite the success of their plan, the Goss family had little to celebrate. Only hours before the Davidson murder, Joel Goss lost his life in a difficulty in Amite City. Deputy Sheriff Bob McMichael's attempt to arrest Goss's son Walter for the attempted murder of an Amite City businessman provoked a

40. New Orleans *Daily Picayune*, February 22, July 4, 1897, April 9, 12, 1899; New Orleans *Times Democrat*, July 4, 11, 1897; Kentwood *Commercial*, March 6, 1897; Sixteenth Judicial District Court Minute Books, Nos. 5–6, Tangipahoa Parish Clerk of Court Archives; interview of Ricks, June 21, 1988.

41. New Orleans *Daily Picayune*, December 25, 26, 1896, February 22, July 4, December 11, 1897, June 15, 1898; Kentwood *Commercial*, February 27, 1897; New Orleans *Times Democrat*, January 11, July 11, 1897; Sixteenth Judicial District Court Minute Books, Nos. 5–7, multiple entries temporarily assigned docket no. 219, Tangipahoa Parish Clerk of Court Archives; interview of Ricks; interview of Orin Davidson, Arcola, La., June 18, 1988.

challenge from Goss. When Goss threatened to have McMichael murdered if the deputy arrested his son, McMichael shot him point-blank in the head, killing him instantly. With the sheriff's brother responsible for this questionable killing, the sheriff's department was rendered even more ineffective at an extremely critical moment.[42]

No one resented the killing of Bill Davidson more than his cousin Sam Hyde. The Davidson murder left nine fatherless children and deprived the Courthouse faction of a staunch supporter. Many residents were particularly incensed that Davidson had been shot multiple times in the back. On the evening of the murder, supporters of the Courthouse faction gathered in Tangipahoa. They learned that the Gills and Bambers had purchased a large quantity of ammunition before fleeing into the river swamp. As they conferred in front of the telegraph office, several shots were fired into the gathering, wounding one of their number. The assailant escaped undetected.[43]

Under intense pressure from friends of Davidson, some of whom initiated legal action for nonfeasance, Sheriff McMichael reluctantly agreed to attempt the arrest of the Gills and Bambers. Local residents reported that the fugitives camped in the swamp at night, then returned to their homes in the morning. In the predawn hours of February 20, 1897, McMichael dispatched two deputies by train to direct the arrests while he remained safely in Amite. When the train arrived in Tangipahoa, Sam Hyde, Charles Bradley, and fourteen others were waiting. After being deputized, the posse proceeded to Gilltown and surrounded Frank Gill's fortresslike home shortly before dawn.[44]

As they awaited first light, members of the posse observed Obe Gill emerge from an isolated spot in the river swamp known as the "hideout" and approach the house. With neither of the deputies nearby and naïvely believing that Gill, charged with a treacherous murder, would actually surrender to officers backed by a posse of the victim's friends, the posse allowed him to proceed unwittingly through their lines. For supporters of the Courthouse faction, it would prove a fatal mistake. Deputy Ellzy Dees, thinking he could

42. New Orleans Daily Picayune, December 23, 24, 1896, June 17, 1898; New Orleans Times Democrat, January 11, 1897; Kentwood Commercial, January 23, 1897.

43. New Orleans Daily Picayune, December 25, 26, 1896, February 22, July 4, December 11, 1897; New Orleans Times Democrat, July 11, 1897; interview of Davidson.

44. New Orleans Daily Picayune, February 21, 22, July 4, 5, 1897; New Orleans Times Democrat, February 21, 22, 1897; Kentwood Commercial, February 27, 1897; Sixteenth Judicial District Court Minute Book, No. 5, pp. 100, 284, Tangipahoa Parish Clerk of Court Archives; interview of Ricks.

persuade Gill to surrender peacefully, approached the house and became a hostage of the parties inside. Once inside, Dees realized that they had anticipated just such a move, as nearly a dozen heavily armed men manned the barricaded doors and windows. A fierce shootout lasting several hours ensued. During the course of the firing, two members of the posse were wounded. Sam Hyde, who had moved close to the house, demanded the release of Deputy Dees as the condition for the posse's withdrawal. Dees was released, but Hyde, situated behind a stump in the yard, found himself pinned down by the firing from the house. After Hyde remained unable to retreat or return fire for several hours, Frank Gill appealed to him to withdraw in peace. Understandably reluctant to expose himself to their fire, Hyde called for someone in the house to serve as a shield while he departed. Felder Ricks accordingly walked between Hyde and the house to the edge of the property. Upon reaching the fence line, Ricks heeded the calls from the house and dropped to the ground, and the Gills opened fire, striking Hyde once in the back as he scrambled for cover. The effort to arrest Obe Gill had failed miserably.[45]

Local officials made no further attempts to arrest the Bambers and Gill in connection with Davidson's murder, but Governor Foster's offer of a reward for their arrest and Judge Reid's threat to request state militia units to secure their capture if they did not appear for the June, 1897, session of the district court proved effective. At the head of twenty heavily armed men, the fugitives appeared at the courthouse, learned that they would actually stand trial the next day, and fled, warning everyone not to pursue them. The Gills maintained that they could not receive a fair trial before Judge Reid, and they understandably feared incarceration in the stronghold of their enemies. Their escape, however, produced grave consequences: six days later Gurley Mixon and Alex Martin, prosecution witnesses in the Davidson killing, were mysteriously murdered at Tangipahoa in separate incidents. Moreover, their open defiance of legally constituted authority with the backing of armed supporters effectively neutralized the system of justice. In his summary for the years 1897 and 1898, Attorney General M. J. Cunningham reported that no criminal indictments had been returned in Tangipahoa Parish since June, 1897.[46]

45. New Orleans *Daily Picayune*, February 21, 22, July 4, 5, 1897; *Kentwood Commercial*, February 27, 1897; New Orleans *Times Democrat*, February 21, 22, 1897; interview of Ricks.

46. New Orleans *Daily Picayune*, June 8, 13, 15, 17, 21, July 4, 5, December 11, 1897; New Orleans *Times Democrat*, July 4, 5, 11, 1897; *Kentwood Commercial*, June 19, 26, August 7, 1897; interview of Ricks; *Report of the Attorney General to the General Assembly of Louisiana, 1896–1898*, 51.

With the Gills and Bambers now acting as the primary feudists of the Goss faction, the newspapers assigned this group the name "Branch men," because of the proximity of numerous branches or streams to Gilltown. With clearly little to fear from the legal system, the Branch men determined to continue the process of eliminating their enemies before the same could be done to them. They recruited the assistance of a notorious desperado, Julius Parker, to assist in the murder of Sam Hyde.

Parker possessed many qualities that could be deemed psychopathic. He had fled Westville, Mississippi, "under a cloud" a few years earlier, charged with, among other things, abuse of a young boy and cruelty to animals. His time in the Florida parishes had been equally troublesome. Parker lived in poverty after abandoning his wife and children for a teenage girl. To secure funds, he sold some blind tiger whiskey and frequently offered to kill for money. The promise of large sums of cash and a business opportunity easily persuaded him to join the conspiracy to murder Hyde.[47]

The Branch men knew that in his capacity as postmaster Hyde would file a monthly report in Amite City within the first three days of the month. The three assassins secreted themselves in the thick underbrush along Dry Branch near Arcola Station and waited four days for their victim. On the evening of July 2, 1897, Hyde responded to a warning that the assassins were after him with a knowledgeable comment: "If there will be shooting going on I suppose I will be doing some of it." Undeterred, Hyde proceeded the next morning toward Amite alone. At the spot assigned for the bushwhacking, the Branch men emptied their shotguns into Hyde's back and fled, scattering turpentine to confuse the bloodhounds certain to pursue them.[48]

This murder established a pattern the bushwhackers continued to follow. Prearranged points of ambush would almost always be located along creek beds, where horses often slowed for a drink, or at sharp bends in the road. Heavy brush on the side of the victim's approach concealed the killers, while

47. New Orleans *Daily Picayune*, July 4–6, 8–12, August 3–7, 24, September 2–4, 10, November 9, 1897; New Orleans *Times Democrat*, July 11, August 3, December 11, 1897; interview of Ricks.

48. New Orleans *Daily Picayune*, July 4–6, 8–12, 14–16, August 3–7, 24, September 2–10, October 8, November 9, 1897; Baton Rouge *Daily Advocate*, July 4, 1897; Kentwood *Commercial*, July 10, 17, August 7, 1897; Chicago, Ill., *Chronicle*, July 4, 1897; Lizzie Bradley to Mary Hyde, July 20, 1897, G. W. Walker to Mary Hyde, April 16, 1899, both in Samuel C. Hyde Papers, in possession of Margaret Hyde Quin, Amite City, La.; interviews of Ricks, R. A. Kent, Jr., Fluker, La., August 1, 1991; and Eugene B. Watson, Fluker, La., December 27, 1980.

on the opposite side the foliage was clipped—hence the name *bush-whacking*—to facilitate a clear shot. Shotguns ensured the victim would be hit even by a nervous assassin. A final shot from a pistol or rifle guaranteed the victim's death. To discourage pursuit, turpentine and coal oil were typically scattered to erase scents. Hyde received thirty-six buckshot in his back, knocking him from his horse, and a single rifle slug in the back of his head while he was on the ground. The thoroughness of their work ensured that the third time his enemies shot him would be the last.[49]

Immediately following Hyde's armed funeral, Joe Reid, Charles Bradley, and other supporters of the Courthouse faction gathered to formulate a strategy for dealing with the Branch men. Outraged residents forced Sheriff McMichael to step down temporarily and appealed to the governor to declare martial law. The Tangipahoa Parish Police Jury reinforced their efforts by offering an unprecedented reward for Hyde's murderers. Several unrelated murders in Tangipahoa Parish in the following weeks increased the tension. Governor Foster promised state militia to secure the fugitives' arrest. Fearing retaliation if they remained overnight in the Amite City jail, Obe Gill and the Bamber brothers agreed to turn themselves in to stand trial for the Davidson murder only if they would be incarcerated in New Orleans. The trio had good reason to be fearful. As they quietly boarded the train at Tangipahoa for transport to New Orleans, their plan became public. An effort to intercept the fugitives and avenge Sam Hyde's death failed when the horse of a rider dispatched to alert the men gathered at Hyde Station collapsed en route.[50]

Under intense public pressure sheriff's deputies soon made several arrests in connection with the Hyde murder. The evidence accumulated against Alex Gill, Julius Parker, and Joe Goins proved particularly convincing, though additional evidence seemed to implicate some of Alex Gill's brothers, Walter Goss, and Otto Bamber. District Attorney Duncan Kemp, observing the systematic destruction of his rivals in the Courthouse faction with great interest, failed to pursue the matter aggressively. To the contrary, Kemp and

49. New Orleans *Daily Picayune*, July 4, 5, November 9, December 21, 1897; New Orleans *Times Democrat*, July 4, 5, 1897; Bradley to Hyde, July 20, 1897, Walker to Hyde, April 16, 1899, in Hyde Papers, in possession of Margaret Hyde Quin.

50. New Orleans *Daily Picayune*, July 5, 6, 8, 9, 11, 12, 14–16, 20, 29, August 2, 3, 5–7, 1897; New Orleans *Times Democrat*, July 4–6, 9, 11, 14, 15, 1897; Kentwood *Commercial*, July 10, 17, August 7, 1897; Sixteenth Judicial District Court Minute Book, No. 5, Tangipahoa Parish Clerk of Court Archives; interviews of Ricks and Herbert Hart, Kentwood, La., February 2, 1991.

his father, along with Judge Reid's bitter political foe Milton Strickland, served as legal counsel to the accused. Joe Reid accordingly directed the prosecution personally. In an eloquent and emotional appeal, Reid urged the jury to pass judgment based on the evidence and to deliver the "country from anarchy and ruin, and prove the potency of the arm of justice." Despite his efforts a series of relatives asserting the innocence of the accused and a liberal dose of threats against the jurors secured not-guilty verdicts for all.[51]

The decision provided a definitive illustration of the impotence of the legal system. In its wake a reign of terror engulfed the piney woods as the Branch men sought out those who opposed them. Persons coming to northern Tangipahoa now did so at the risk of their own lives. An elderly minister, one of the few members of the local religious establishment courageous enough to condemn the violence, received a near fatal beating at the hands of several Branch men. The same group attacked staunch supporters of the Courthouse faction Ben and Seaborn Hart, who saved themselves by grabbing their own weapons and barricading themselves in a store in Tangipahoa. Others were not so fortunate. Branch men forced the city marshall of Tangipahoa and others to kneel before them publicly and blow into the barrels of their pistols. Described as a "drunken militia," Parker, some of the Gill boys, and other Branch men rode through the streets of Tangipahoa firing into stores, making threats, and terrorizing merchants. Sites suitable for bushwhackings were established along the roads to Gilltown in anticipation of retaliation. The Branch men notified friends who might be traveling at night to place a lantern on the left side of the horse and to whistle a specific tune or they might be killed. As a climax to the fall activities, some of the Branch men bushwhacked young Willie Mixon, who possessed information concerning the Davidson murder, under circumstances similar to the Hyde killing.[52]

Joe Reid and other survivors of the Courthouse faction continued to press the criminal cases outstanding against the Branch men, particularly the unresolved Davidson murder. Members of the Gill and Goss families repeatedly

51. New Orleans *Times Democrat*, July 11, 14, 15, 19, August 3, 1897; New Orleans *Daily Picayune*, July 14–16, August 3, 5–7, 24, September 2–4, 7, 10, October 8, November 9, December 11, 1897; Kentwood *Commercial*, August 7, 28, September 4, 11, 18, 1897; W. W. Draughon to Robert Reid, June 15, 1900, in Reid Papers.

52. New Orleans *Daily Picayune*, September 4, 7, 10, 16, October 8, November 9, 16, 24, 1897; Greensburg *St. Helena Echo*, December 17, 1897; New Orleans *Times Democrat*, December 3, 11, 12, 1897; Kentwood *Commercial*, October 30, November 13, 27, December 18, 1897; Reminiscences of Dr. J. W. Lambert, Typescript, n.d., in John Lambert Papers.

announced their intention to kill the Reids. The Reid brothers foiled several prepared bushwhackings by alternating their route when they traveled to court in neighboring St. Helena and Washington Parishes. In early December, 1897, the Gills received a tip that Joe Reid would be handling cases at the Washington Parish Courthouse in Franklinton. An effort to bushwhack him on the road to Franklinton failed when Reid took an unexpected shortcut. Unbeknownst to Reid, the assassins pursued him into Franklinton. On the evening of December 9, 1897, four of the Branch men waited nervously outside the courthouse for Reid to depart. As he descended the steps, one of them approached from behind and fired five shots. One hit Reid in the back and killed him. Although a large crowd gathered to condemn the murder, only two volunteered to join a sheriff's posse departing in pursuit of the killers.[53]

Three days later a Baptist minister became the next victim of the Branch men. S. B. Mullen, an itinerant preacher from Simpson County, Mississippi, arrived in Amite City on personal business. Unfortunately for Mullen, the Branch men mistook him for a detective. Following their typical pattern, several men approached Mullen from behind and shot him point-blank in the back on the steps of the Amite City Hotel. The *St. Helena Echo* led the condemnation of the minister's murderers: "Oh heaven pity! And if there be any power to save, hear the cries of the poor widows and orphans and save this country from the further shedding of blood."[54]

The series of successive murders committed by known parties provoked a statewide demand for order in the eastern Florida parishes. Many locals were also outraged that members of the Branch faction boldly entered Amite City during Joe Reid's funeral and made threats around the town. Newspapers across the state called for action to reestablish law and order in the piney

53. New Orleans *Times Democrat*, December 11–13, 1897; New Orleans *Daily Picayune*, December 11–21, 29, 1897, January 3–4, 6–7, 10, 1898; Kentwood *Commercial*, December 18, 1897; Amite City *Florida Parishes*, rpr. New Orleans *Daily Picayune*, January 10, 1898; interview of Ricks.

54. Greensburg *St. Helena Echo*, December 17, 1897; New Orleans *Times Democrat*, December 13–14, 25, 1897; New Orleans *Daily Picayune*, December 13–16, 20–21, 1897; Kentwood *Commercial*, December 18, 1897. Although the mistaken-for-a-detective theory remained the most widely accepted version of Mullen's murder, others interpreted the situation differently. Some noted that Mullen resembled Judge Reid, while others, pointing out that Mullen came from the same region as Julius Parker, assumed the Branch men feared the information he possessed.

woods. The Crowley *Signal* complained that murder in Washington and Tangipahoa Parishes constituted little more than a misdemeanor. The New Orleans *Daily Picayune* declared: "Law has ceased to be supreme and society in the parish of Tangipahoa has degenerated to that primitive state where each individual must look out for himself as best he can. The entire state demands that the reign of law shall be restored in Tangipahoa, no matter what the cost." The Shreveport *Times* came to a similar conclusion: "Nowhere in the state does a feeling of such dread and terror exist as in Tangipahoa. Only a determined and unflinching effort to discover and punish the assassins will redeem Tangipahoa from its Baptism of Blood." The *Times* maintained that lawlessness in the Florida parishes damaged the reputation of the entire state. Similarly, the Plaquemine *Journal* condemned those responsible for the murders: "The soil of Tangipahoa has literally been drenched with blood of late, most of those who have lost their lives being the victims of cowardly and heartless assassins. There is no coward so vile and despicable as he who strikes a fellow being from behind under the favoring shadows of night or the protecting trees of a forest. These black hearted miscreants have made the name of that fair section of the state a byword and a reproach."[55]

Increasing calls from the press and the public demanded intervention by the governor. The Baton Rouge *Daily Advocate* insisted the governor must intervene "with firmness and decision." In an eloquent appeal the *Daily Advocate* declared, "Every instinct of humanity cries out against such monstrous criminals." The same paper urged that the sitting legal officials be forced to resign and the state place justice "in the hands of men who will enforce the law and see that these enemies of civilization are brought to the gallows." The New Orleans *Times Democrat* insisted that Governor Foster force the resignation of Sheriff McMichael, District Attorney Kemp, and Judge Reid for failure to maintain order. In the wake of the murders of his most trustworthy supporters, Reid, too, was accused of being timid in his response to the violence, and his enemies continued to regard him as part of the problem. In an interview with the *Daily Picayune,* Deputy Sheriff Millard Edwards explained the situation in Tangipahoa and neighboring parishes: "It is well

55. Crowley *Signal* and Baton Rouge *Capital Item*, rpr. Franklinton *New Era*, December 17, 1898; New Orleans *Daily Picayune*, December 11–14, 21, 1897; New Orleans *Times Democrat*, December 11–13, 1897; Baton Rouge *Daily Advocate*, Plaquemine *Journal*, Shreveport *Times*, and Amite City *Florida Parishes*, all rpr. New Orleans *Daily Picayune*, January 4, December 21, 1897.

known to everyone that a terrible feud exists in the region, every other man is a friend of one side or the other and thus it would be impossible to organize a posse of 50 men to serve warrants." Edwards noted further that those not involved in the feud were terrified of the participants and therefore would not support the peace officers. John King, superintendent of the Gullet Cotton Gin Company at Amite City, reaffirmed Edwards' observations: "The feud is so severe that everyone goes about armed, everyone knows who killed Joe Reid. There are two parties arrayed against each other and each has many influential friends there so that it is practically impossible to suppress the lawlessness. If the people rose in mass to suppress the violence it would be one faction against the other and a bloodbath."[56]

Under mounting statewide pressure, Governor Foster convoked a conference to discuss the violence increasingly referred to as the "Bloody Tangipahoa Troubles." Foster expressed dismay that he had received an urgent telegram from Deputy Edwards rather than from the sheriff. The telegram stated, "Certain murderous parties having relatives scattered about the parish are safe from molestation by the law." It further indicated that Joe Reid's murderers arrived in Franklinton at 6:30 P.M. and were trailed directly to a specific house in Gilltown by reliable bloodhounds after the killing. But, the deputy alleged, it would take a small army to arrest the suspects. The conference convened in New Orleans on December 20, 1897, with Governor Foster and Attorney General Cunningham in attendance. Judge Reid, as representative of the Courthouse faction, and District Attorney Kemp, whose family increasingly served as counsel for the Branch faction, were present. The newspapers noted that the representatives of each group slept at different hotels, adding, "The relations between the two factions are not amicable." Sheriff McMichael and several deputies also attended.[57]

The meeting lasted two days but, other than condemning the incompetence of McMichael, achieved little of substance. The governor, too, seemed baffled by the incredibly chaotic circumstances and chose to remain aloof. Other than promising troops if the violence persisted, he took no action. Commenting on the ambiguity surrounding the meeting, the *Daily Picayune*

56. Baton Rouge *Daily Advocate*, December 28, 1896, and rpr. New Orleans *Daily Picayune*, December 21, 1897; New Orleans *Times Democrat*, December 23, 25, 1897; New Orleans *Daily Picayune*, December 15–16, 1897.

57. New Orleans *Daily Picayune*, December 20–21, 1897; New Orleans *Times Democrat*, December 23, 25, 1897.

bemoaned the prevailing conditions in the piney woods. "When a community reaches that stage where they believe that whenever a few citizens get together they constitute the people, and on that ground argue that the people are superior to the law, it is pretty hard to convince them to the contrary and those who have to do the convincing will have to travel over a rocky road."[58]

The governor's conference proved to be an unqualified victory for the Branch men. Governor Foster had failed to dispatch troops, and the remnants of the once-powerful Courthouse faction had been humiliated and left seemingly without support. Some speculated that Foster's inaction resulted from his reluctance to intervene in the factional feuding lest it cost him the political support of one of the groups. Others saw his inaction as consistent with his hands-off approach to the personal quarrels of white Louisianians. Rather than attempt to conduct the scheduled trial of the Branch men accused in the murders of Davidson, Mixon, and Joe Reid without state support, parish officials canceled the January term of the district court, thereby highlighting the absolute intimidation of justice. They attempted to justify the cancellation of the district court on a technicality, alleging that the jury had been improperly drawn. The *Daily Picayune* lamented, "A feeling of unrest prevails here and trouble is looked for." Exasperated, the Franklinton *New Era* complained, "In Washington and Tangipahoa the law is held in contempt because it is not enforced."[59]

In the wake of the governor's conference, William Kemp helped secure the release of Obe Gill and the Bamber brothers from prison in New Orleans. When officials in Meridian, Mississippi, arrested Julius Parker and forcibly returned him to stand trial in Tangipahoa, charged with burglary and abandoning his family, the officials at Amite City reluctantly admitted him to jail and endured the criticism of the more courageous Mississippi deputies. Nine new murders in the five months following the governor's conference confirmed the continuing absence of law enforcement in Bloody Tangipahoa. When those accused of the Davidson murder finally came to trial in June, 1898, the *Daily Picayune* reported their acquittal with the contemptuous comment "the state having made no case against them."[60]

58. *Ibid.*

59. New Orleans *Daily Picayune*, January 7, 10, 13, 1898; Sixteenth Judicial District Court Minute Books, Nos. 5–6, Tangipahoa Parish Clerk of Court Archives; Franklinton *New Era*, December 17, 1898; "Report of the Attorney General to the General Assembly of Louisiana, 1896–1898," *Louisiana Legislative Documents*, 1898, p. 51.

60. New Orleans *Daily Picayune*, January 7, 16, 18, 20, 31, February 10, 12, 17, March 9, 13, April 3, 4, 23, May 31, June 4, 6–8, 12, 18, 1898; Franklinton *New Era*, December 17, 1898;

With their victory over the system of justice and their enemies complete, the Branch men returned to Whitecapping. Merchants and millowners were visited and ordered to dismiss their black laborers on pain of death. Their effort to force the dismissal of blacks from the huge Banner Lumber Company in Kentwood, however, provoked a serious challenge. When the directors of the Banner Company refused their demands, Branch men killed one company foreman near Franklinton and bushwhacked another near Spring Creek. In response, an armed posse of more than a hundred Banner employees, exasperated citizens, and sheriff's deputies from three different parishes pursued the Branch men for weeks in a wild series of encounters that included several shootouts and deaths. Convinced by experience that terror tactics would sustain their seeming immunity from the law, some of the Branch men fired into the train bringing the posse into the piney woods, thus reinforcing the determination of their pursuers to arrest them. Such aggressive efforts to capture them created a sustained howl from the families and supporters of the fugitives, who, dismayed by the forceful attempt to enforce the law, denounced the "unjust" persecution of the "boys." As he scanned a meeting in support of the Branch men's right to eliminate those who threatened their liberty, state adjutant general Allen Jumel, speaking for the other side, noted that feud-related violence had spiraled out of control because the victims "could not secure juries with the moral courage to bring in verdicts against the parties charged with crimes." He concluded, "This was the fault of the people not the courts."[61]

Hard pressed by deputies under the direction of Jumel and Deputy Sheriff Avery Draughon, the Gills and Bambers agreed to submit to a court hearing. As before, however, they came backed by an armed mob, posted bond, and departed, contemptuously mocking the "army" that had pursued them. Nonetheless, the *Daily Picayune* declared that the Branch men were "now convinced that any overt act on their part [would] mean prompt pursuit, arrest, and punishment and no longer [would] they be able to carry matters out at their own sweet will." The editor marveled that the people had not considered concerted action earlier, proclaiming "a new era of security and confidence in Tangipahoa." As if to highlight the naïvité of this statement,

Kentwood *Commercial*, November 13, 27, 1897, February 5, 12, 26, March 5, 19, 1898; Sixteenth Judicial District Court Minute Books, Nos. 5–6, Tangipahoa Parish Clerk of Court Archives.

61. Franklinton *New Era*, April 8, 1899; New Orleans *Daily Picayune*, April 4–8, 10, 12–14, 1899; newspaper article, n.d., from Greensburg St. *Helena Echo*, in Reid Papers; Sixteenth Judicial District Court Minute Books, Nos. 5–6, Tangipahoa Parish Clerk of Court Archives.

when tensions cooled a few months later in Tangipahoa, Avery Draughon was murdered under painful, brutal circumstances by Gage and Alonzo Gill.[62]

Among those who participated in the futile effort to capture Draughon's killers were the seventeen-year-old sons of two previously assassinated members of the Courthouse faction. Accompanying the "Tangipahoa contingent," which sought to arrest the Gills and Bambers for the Draughon and other murders, were the eldest son and nephew of Sam Hyde and the eldest son of Bill Davidson.[63]

•

The violence that consumed the Florida parishes in the late nineteenth century demonstrated that when left to their own devices, the piney-woods dwellers proved incapable of effectively governing themselves. A peculiar pattern of regional development and a distorted perception of individual rights that accepted violence as the means to an end subverted the honorable and progressive intentions of the Jeffersonian-Jacksonian idea of independence, rendering the system of justice impotent. This perverted tradition created in many residents an obsession with independence that compelled them to reject in a violent manner governance and legally constituted authority. When the bonds of planter dominance and concomitant exploitation were finally broken, the result was anarchy and the degeneration of a central element of piney-woods society, honor. In the end those without honor prevailed, contributing to a legacy of violence that ensured the Florida parishes would maintain inordinately high rates of brutality into the middle of the twentieth century.

Significantly, the pattern of development in the Florida parishes during the nineteenth century demonstrated that planter dominance had been good for the region, promoting stability and prosperity and reinforcing the sense of honor essential to agreeable interpersonal relations in many areas of the South. However, conditions created by the planters had repeatedly subverted the ambitions and customs of the plain folk, corrupting the purity of their traditions and contributing correspondingly to decades of bloodshed. Moreover, the planters' political agenda reinforced an obsessive concern with per-

62. New Orleans *Daily Picayune*, April 10, 12–14, 1899; Draughon to Reid, June 15, 1900, newspaper article, n.d., from Greensburg *St. Helena Echo*, both in Reid Papers; newspaper article, n.d., from New Orleans *Daily Picayune*, in John Lambert Papers.

63. New Orleans *Daily Picayune*, April, 1899.

sonal liberty, raised the specter of unseen enemies threatening that liberty, and produced a learning ground for the effectiveness of violence in the form of war and Reconstruction. By creating a popular obsession centered on the menace posed by common enemies and encouraging violent resistance to them, the ruling elite provoked the emergence of a dangerous tradition in eastern Louisiana. With the common enemies eliminated and a disillusioned public resentful of decades of corrupt governance and economic exploitation, planter leadership itself became the enemy and was accordingly rejected by the commoners. The ominous tradition nonetheless remained, and in the absence of the determined leadership the planters had previously provided, it ascended and overwhelmed the region.

A more appropriate summarization may be that planter dominance provided an effective means of governance whereas their self-serving agenda proved incompatible with the value system of the piney-woods residents of eastern Louisiana. The planter elite did provide strong leadership in a deferential society—leadership that allowed for stability in otherwise potentially chaotic regions of the South, such as the Florida parishes with their strong legacy of rebellious and criminal elements. But their heavy-handed tactics ensured that the ultimate lessons internalized by many would be contempt for authority and the effectiveness of violence. Sadly, the intricacies of the planter-plain folk relationship contributed to a chaotic pattern of development and the establishment of a culture of violence for the residents of the Florida parishes. Whether such conditions could be overcome amid the changes of the new millennium remained to be seen.

· 7 ·

ADJUSTING TO A NEW MILLENNIUM: CONTINUITY AMID CHANGE

Few observers could have fathomed the dramatic changes that would accompany the advent of the new millennium. Traditional customs and means of accomplishing tasks would be challenged in previously unimagined ways. Profound communication and transportation advances would help facilitate startling breakthroughs in science and technology, all of which dramatically improved the lives of millions of Americans. In many regions of the nation, the improving conditions were complemented by advances in the mechanisms for dispensing justice and a heightened level of political stability. Changes suggesting the advent of modernity included not just innovation, but also accountability.

The residents of southeastern Louisiana celebrated the arrival of the new century with due anticipation. The past nonetheless maintained a powerful shroud over the region. In this long-troubled portion of the Bayou State, visions of hope and expectations for change remained muted by the realities of life that surrounded the residents. In the Florida parishes, abundant portents suggested the new era might eerily resemble the old.

The startling levels of brutality in the late nineteenth century, and the statewide calls for order in the Florida parishes, did produce some initial results. By 1900, two of the most identifiable faces of the dysfunctional legal system in the piney-woods parishes would be removed from office. In Tangipahoa Parish, Sheriff Pleasant P. McMichael would step aside prior to the end of his term. McMichael's failure to perform the duties incumbent upon his office had contributed mightily to the spiraling violence, provoking condemnation in the press and a personal rebuke from the governor. In an unusual move, a Tangipahoa Parish grand jury gently criticized McMichael, declaring him "able and efficient though at times a little too lenient with prisoners." The report continued that "through his regard for his fellow human beings," he had allowed three prisoners, all Branch men and each charged with murder, to escape. His successor, F. P. Mix, had previously served effectively as sheriff from 1876 to 1892, and it was hoped his return would contribute to a restoration of stability. Similarly, District Attorney Duncan Kemp was defeated in his bid for reelection by Robert Ellis. At Kentwood, site of many acts of violence and intimidation precipitated by the Branch men, Kemp received only 9 of 125 votes cast, suggesting a strong desire for change in that troubled community. The Kentwood *Commercial* declared Ellis "a sober man who will make a great district attorney." Kemp was later killed in a "desperate street duel" by C. F. Hyde. Nine shots were exchanged between the two men in the streets of Amite City.[1]

The magnitude of the broken system of justice characterizing the piney-woods parishes in the late nineteenth century was highlighted in the Louisiana attorney general's report for 1900. M. J. Cunningham complained that "if the police and sheriffs would do their duty by arresting and incarcerating all persons violating the law it would be obeyed." He noted further that with the exception of East Baton Rouge Parish, no annual reports had been filed from the Florida parish district attorneys. In a follow-up special report submitted the same year, Cunningham asserted that he had been advised by the district attorney in the Sixteenth Judicial District that all indictments and records of criminal cases in Tangipahoa Parish had been stolen.[2]

St. Helena and Livingston Parishes, also in the Sixteenth Judicial District, likewise secured new sheriffs in the first years of the twentieth century, and it was hoped that new leadership would foster stability. Other aspects of development were emerging at the same time that seemed poised to assist in restoring order and the rule of law. As part of his annual address to the Louisiana Legislature in May, 1900, Governor Murphy J. Foster argued that the Constitutional Convention of 1898 had been held to address problems with the organic law of the state. The elections that preceded the new constitution had, according to Foster, "aroused and excited political and partisan sentiment to the highest pitch, even to bitter and acrimonious exasperation, perhaps more so than ever in our political history." In his closing remarks the governor advised his audience, "with political peace assured and the menace

1. New Orleans *Times Democrat*, December 23, 25, 1897; New Orleans *Picayune*, December 20–21, 1897, March 11, 1908; Sixteenth Judicial District Court Minute Books, Nos. 5, 6, and 11, Tangipahoa Parish Clerk of Court Archives; Kentwood *Commercial*, February 17, 24, March 3, 10, 1900; Duncan Kemp to Judge Reid, August 27, 1898, in Reid Papers, LLMVC.

2. "Report of the Attorney General of the State of Louisiana, 1898–1900" (New Orleans, 1900), 5–6; "Report of the Attorney General to the General Assembly of Louisiana, 1900" (New Orleans, 1902).

of former conditions removed, the people are in a condition to lend all of their energies to a still further development of the state and its resources." The "menace of former conditions" the governor referenced was of course the Populist Revolt, which had shaken the Louisiana political establishment to its core and whose challenge to Democratic dominance had resulted in perhaps the bloodiest election in Louisiana history in 1896.[3]

At the 1898 constitutional convention, President E. B. Kruttschnitt announced that the convention existed for one sole purpose, "to eliminate from the electorate the mass of corrupt and illiterate voters who have during the last quarter of a century degraded our politics." According to Kruttschnitt, "with unanimity unparalleled in the history of American politics," the voters had entrusted to the Democratic party "the solution of the question of the purification of the electorate." In short, the constitution was designed precisely to take the vote from blacks and poorer whites to safeguard against their joining together in a revolutionary effort at self-improvement as they had in the Populist Revolt. Governor Foster boasted that the new constitutional restrictions on suffrage had perfectly eliminated complaints regarding the fairness of elections in the state. His immediate successor as governor, W. W. Heard, declared Louisiana elections "absolutely fair and peaceful," in consequence of the laws regulating the exercise of suffrage. The contraction of democracy in the Bayou State included new laws prohibiting anyone from running for office unless they were a registered voter who had maintained receipts demonstrating payment of poll taxes two years in a row, and who resided in the state for two years and in the parish for one prior to voting. The state Democratic party assumed the rooster as a symbol of its newly ensconced dominance. Heralding the massive Democratic majorities that characterized the elections following the constitutional convention, the *St. Tammany Farmer* proclaimed "Crow Rooster Crow—Another Grand Democratic Victory."[4]

The unquestioned dominance of the Democratic party carried a distinct

3. "Message of Governor Murphy J. Foster," *Official Journal of the Proceedings of the Senate of the State of Louisiana at the First Regular Session of the First General Assembly, 1900* (Baton Rouge, 1900), 18–30.

4. "Message of E. B. Kruttschnitt, President of the Convention," *Constitution of the State of Louisiana Adopted in Convention at the City of New Orleans, May 12, 1898* (New Orleans, 1898), 9–10; "Message of Governor Murphy J. Foster," *Senate Journal,* 1900, 18; "Message of Governor W. W. Heard," *Official Journal of the Proceedings of the Senate of the State of Louisiana at the Second Regular Session, 1902* (Baton Rouge, 1902), 4; Amite City *Tangipahoa Parish News,* June 10, 1926; *St. Tammany Farmer,* April 2, 23, 1904.

set of implications in the Florida parishes. Not only did the virtually mono-lithic state elections reduce political strife, but many believed the elimina-tion of competition would advance stability in the region similar to the way opposition to the Union Army and the Reconstruction government had energized white unity in the preceding decades. Populism had played a con-tributing role in the struggle between the Courthouse faction and the Branch men, and some observers believed that marginalization of the Populists would defuse tensions. The Republican party, deeply mistrusted by most of the re-gional white population, had similarly been crushed. Looking back on his eight years in office, Governor Foster noted that his administrations had been "stormy ones," adding that "future historians will undoubtedly record the past eight years as an epoch making period." Foster concluded that the absolute triumph of the Democratic party revealed that "the ordeal has been safely passed and that we have entered upon a new and brighter era." Political monotheism eliminated one source of rivalry and contention, offering a bit of hope to those who sought stability.[5]

Similar cautiously optimistic visions of the future appeared in the regional press. The Baton Rouge *States* noted that "with good juries and non-preju-diced testimony convictions can be had, and with convictions, crime will cease and the Florida Parishes will become the garden spot that nature de-sired them to be." The Amite City *Florida Parishes* spoke of a "crusade to eradicate the evil that has stifled progress" in the region. Whether such sen-timents amounted to reasoned observations or merely expressions of hope would be revealed in the functioning of a legal system that had failed to offer justice to so many in the recent past. As the new century dawned, a holdover from the previous year would provide a perfect test case to identify progress or more of the same from the legal system. The 1899 murder of Avery Draughon, and the subsequent criminal proceedings, would serve as a litmus test for identifying change or continuity in the regional system of justice.[6]

One of the oldest communities in the eastern Florida parishes, the village of Tangipahoa had also long been home to some of the most savage feud-re-lated violence. Since the feud-related murders began, Avery Draughon, whose

5. *St. Tammany Farmer*, April 2, 23, 1904; Kentwood *Commercial*, February 15, 1896; *St. Helena Echo*, August 22, 1891, June 18, 1892; newspaper clipping from the Wesson, Miss., *Southern Industry*, May 16, 1885, in Duncan Francis Young Scrapbooks, Howard-Tilton Library, Tulane; New Orleans *Picayune*, April 22, 23, December 23, 1896, February 22, December 11, 1897; New Orleans *Times Democrat*, July 11, 1897; "Message of Governor Foster," *House Jour-nal*, May, 1900, 31.

6. Baton Rouge *States*, February 21, 1901; Amite City *Florida Parishes*, November 22, 1913.

266 • PISTOLS AND POLITICS

family was deeply invested in Tangipahoa, had remained at the forefront of efforts to restore order. His service to the community included tenures as city councilman, mayor of Tangipahoa, and parish deputy sheriff. He also served as constable of the surrounding ward. His standing in the region was reinforced by the general belief that he was the leading candidate for sheriff in the upcoming race to replace the ineffective P. P. McMichael. As far back as 1891, Draughon had assumed a leading position in attempting to curtail Whitecap depredations in the area, incurring the hostility of the Branch men as a result.[7]

In the first months of 1899, along with deputies Dick Amacker and W. L. Mullins, Draughon had played a key role in leading the posse that sought to arrest the Branch men following their December, 1898, effort to intimidate the directors of the Banner Lumber Company at Kentwood. The murder of one Banner Company foreman, attempted murder of another, and direct intimidation of the company director, E. V. Preston, stimulated a renewed vigor in efforts to contain the lawlessness. Though several of the Branch men, including Julius Parker, had either been arrested or had surrendered for their role in intimidating Preston, Alonzo Gill had avoided arrest even though he continued to appear from time to time in Tangipahoa. In March, 1899, Gill was arrested in Tangipahoa by Draughon and Amacker and transported to prison in New Orleans at Gill's request, "on account the jail at Amite City was filled with negroes."[8]

At the time of his arrest Gill claimed it was a political stunt on the part of Draughon to advance his candidacy for sheriff. He said that he had been advised of the indictment by Deputy Sheriff Millard Edwards but that neither Edwards nor anyone else had made any effort to arrest him until he encountered Draughon. In June, 1899, Alex, Alonzo, and Gage Gill, along with Julius Parker and Otto Bamber, pled guilty to intimidation, the state having made no case on the murder charge, and were sentenced to thirty days in jail with no fine.[9]

7. Amite City *Progress*, October 1, 1936; Amite City *Florida Parishes*, January 14, February 4, 11, 1891; New Orleans *Daily Picayune*, February 22, December 11, 1897, April 10, 12–14, 1899; *St. Tammany Farmer*, October 14, 1899. In Louisiana, the subpolitical divisions within each parish are known as wards.

8. E. V. Preston to Judge Reid, April 27, 1897, in Robert Reid Papers, Center for Southeast Louisiana Studies, Southeastern Louisiana University, hereinafter referred to as CSLS; Sixteenth Judicial District Court Minute Books, No. 6, docket no. 148, State of Louisiana vs. Julius Parker et al., Tangipahoa Parish Clerk of Court Archives; New Orleans *Picayune*, March, 20, April 5, 14, June 10, 1899.

9. New Orleans *Picayune*, March 20, 1899; Baton Rouge *Daily Advocate*, June 10, 1899.

Having again failed to prosecute a murder and attempted murder, and having only lightly prosecuted organized lawlessness, the regional legal system was again revealed as ineffective. The Baton Rouge *Daily Advocate* derisively noted that for having sought to bring down one of the most important economic engines in the area, specifically the Banner Lumber Company, the convicted Whitecaps would likely serve no more than ten days. The New Orleans *Picayune* complained that "the authorities in Tangipahoa seem incapable of making arrests for the numerous assassinations that occur among them, but when, by some chance, an arrest is made no jury is found that will convict. The result is that the outlaws have everything their own way, while the peaceable people have no assurance that at any moment they will not be murdered by cowardly assassins." While many observers bemoaned the result, at least some of the Branch men proved emboldened by the limits of justice.[10]

The continuing power of honor and the need to publicly prove one's manhood now came into play. On October 7, 1899, as he waited at the Tangipahoa station to board a train to serve some papers in Kentwood, Avery Draughon was accosted by brothers Alonzo, Gage, and Jim Gill. Willie Ricks and Joe Knopf, both Gill cousins, served as witnesses to what unfolded. Two of the brothers held guns on Draughon as they searched him for weapons. Satisfied that he was unarmed, they forced him to keep his arms raised as they beat and verbally abused him through the streets of Tangipahoa. Observers reported that the Gills shouted that they intended to curse and abuse him in front of the entire town as he "had had his brags." When they reached H. J. Sanders's store, Gage Gill kept a pistol trained on Draughon as Alonzo continued to beat him. Convinced he was about to be killed, Draughon made a desperate grab for a small pistol concealed in his vest that the Gills had overlooked. As he drew the weapon, Alonzo knocked his arm up, discharging the only shot Draughon would fire as Gage Gill shot him from behind. The Gills then fired wildly, emptying their pistols and hitting Draughon at least twice as he staggered from the store toward his house. Hearing of the shooting, his young wife met the dying man in the street and helped him toward his home. Alonzo Gill raced to a carriage and retrieved a Winchester rifle, which he aimed at Draughon only to be stopped by Jim Gill, who told him, "You have done enough." Three days later, Draughon succumbed to his wounds at Hotel Dieu hospital in New Orleans. Yet another advocate for stability had been eliminated.[11]

10. Baton Rouge *Daily Advocate*, June 10, 1899; New Orleans *Picayune*, April 4, 1899.
11. Sixteenth Judicial District Court Minute Books, No. 6, docket no. 304, State of Louisi-

The Draughon killing could be seen as just another Tangipahoa tragedy perpetrated by a group whom press reports were now labeling "the notorious Gill brothers." But this incident was clearly different. The prominent victim was attacked in broad daylight in the middle of town in front of many witnesses, not on a lonely road by a killer hiding in the bushes. The dead man had been mayor of Tangipahoa for six years, was a police officer, and was on the threshold of being elected sheriff. He was, in many senses, the very face of the legal system—both a peace officer and a political official. Reports circulated that the killers had selected a day when all of Draughon's closest friends were out of town, many at a picnic in a neighboring community, adding credence to the belief that it was premeditated. Popular outrage increased as witnesses came forward claiming the Gills had announced their intention to kill all of the "clique" opposed to them and had left town laughing and waving their hats, free of any fear from the system of justice.[12]

In his brother's defense, Alex Gill made a statement claiming that Draughon was the aggressor and had long had it in for his family. He disputed the widely held belief that Draughon's leadership of the posse that pursued the Branch men following the murder of the Banner Lumber Company foreman was the source of the trouble. Instead, Gill argued that his family was being persecuted only because they did not belong to Draughon's political faction. He urged the public to await the results of a trial before passing judgment on the perpetrators. His statement closed with an assault on the character of Avery Draughon. Gill asserted that though he was alleged to be a man of high standing, Draughon had been defeated several times when a candidate for office and only served as a deputy sheriff when court was in session.[13]

Draughon's murder marked a clear escalation in the violence and created dismay among outside observers, many of whom increasingly pointed a finger at residents of the region. A series of articles appearing in the New Orleans *Picayune* highlighted the exasperation of observers growing weary with the endless brutality occurring in the piney-woods parishes. Appearing under titles that underscored the interminable nature of the violence,

ana vs. Alonzo and Gage Gill, Tangipahoa Parish Clerk of Court Archives; W. W. Draughon to Robert Reid, June 15, 1900, in Reid Papers, LLMVC; New Orleans *Picayune*, October 8–10, 1899, January 23, 1901; *St. Tammany Farmer*, October 14, 1899; Baton Rouge *Daily Advocate*, October 12, 1899, January 17, 1901.

12. New Orleans *Picayune*, October 8, 10, 1899, January 24, 1901; *St. Tammany Farmer*, October 14, 1899.

13. New Orleans *Picayune*, October 10, 1899.

such as "Tangipahoa War Again" and "Tangipahoa in Turmoil Again," the *Picayune* articles cast doubt on the courage and moral character of the local population. "Now even cool citizens are demanding harsh measures be taken at once to stop forever this trail of blood in Tangipahoa Parish. They point with horror to widows and orphans and the new graves made with assassin's bullets in the last few years and say that it is time that the staunch and staid citizenship of the Parish assert their manhood and put down lawlessness." The same paper noted further, "not a single individual has been punished for the assassinations in this parish," but added a knowledgeable lament, "and so the bloody work goes on, and each time an attempted murder is made or an assassin gets in his work, good citizens with pale faces say that it must stop. That it has gone far enough, but thus far few, very few, have shown the least disposition to put their shoulder to the wheel and help stop it. While this shows up bad for the parish it is all too true and cannot be disputed."[14]

The initial outcry had an impact on the Gills, who quickly went into hiding. News reports cast the Draughon killing as a new level of horror in a long-troubled region and wondered aloud if this would be the final straw to initiate change. "Some characterize the brutal deception practiced on Avery Draughon as worse than shooting a man from ambush and want to see if the people will stand it." Readers were advised that the Draughons had many friends and that his murder had aroused "fighting blood." One paper declared, "It is safe to say this matter will not rest, as other shooting affairs in this parish have." The Baton Rouge *States* reported evidence of palpable rage—"the death of Draughon whose uncle was a delegate to the Constitutional Convention of 1898 has left smoldering embers of hate"—directed at the Branch men. On October 10, 1899, affidavits were sworn out against the Gills and a posse summoned. The next morning, Deputy Sheriff W. J. Mullins arrived with a posse of eighteen men and immediately began scouring the country east of the Tangipahoa River between Kentwood and Tangipahoa. The posse departed at 2:00 A.M. and returned at 7:00 P.M. weary and with no luck in locating the fugitives.[15]

In response to a call for assistance from Mullins, that same evening Sheriff P. P. McMichael, somehow reinstated to office after being removed for nonfeasance, arrived with about thirty additional men to assist in the search.

14. New Orleans *Picayune*, October 8, 9, 1899; Baton Rouge *Daily Advocate*, October 12, 1899; Baton Rouge *States*, February 21, 1901.

15. W. W. Draughon to Robert Reid, June 15, 1900, in Reid Papers, LLMVC; New Orleans *Picayune*, October 9–13, 1899; Baton Rouge *States*, February 21, 1901.

The hunt was scheduled to begin at 6:30 A.M., yet when the 7:05 A.M. train for Amite City arrived, the entire posse boarded the train and left. The withdrawal of the posse provoked outrage. "Many were thoroughly disgusted at the childish actions of assembling the men and then dilly dallying for so long." Others believed that success could be better attained through different methods, specifically by negotiating with the perpetrators for their surrender. Friends of the Gills claimed they would turn themselves in after tensions had cooled, though many openly scoffed at the notion.[16]

Again, Sheriff McMichael proved unwilling or unable to do his job as the body count under his tenure continued to mount. An exasperated Governor Murphy J. Foster, who less than a year earlier had been forced to send his adjutant general and state militia to deal with the same group, now offered a $400 reward for the arrest of Alonzo and Gage Gill. Some regional residents believed the time for an arrest had passed, suggesting instead the need for a more permanent resolution. Amid mounting outrage, the governor's involvement, and with a price on their heads, the accused retreated further from public view. A ludicrous story emerged that the Gills had traveled to South Africa to join the British in fighting the Boers. According to this account, the Gills had fled to New Orleans via Covington where they secured positions on the freighter *Montezuma* as hostlers en route to South Africa. Tangipahoa sheriff's deputies, along with some hired detectives and the Covington chief of police, searched the area but found nothing.[17]

While the killers remained in hiding, skipping a separate trial scheduled for later that month on charges they intimidated Tangipahoa businessman H. J. Sanders, a stark contrast to popular perceptions of justice emerged in East Feliciana Parish. Only days after the Draughon killing, a telegram arrived in the small community of Wilson advising that former resident J. L. Smith and a small group of men were heading there "to take the town." Prominent citizens were awakened, and when they arrived, Smith and three others were arrested. As the town marshal and two deputies transported them to the parish prison in Clinton, they were overtaken by a posse that seized Smith and hanged him from a tree. Leaders of the lynch mob explained that for the past year the region had suffered from cattle rustling and other law-

16. New Orleans *Picayune*, October 12, 13, 1899.

17. Sixteenth Judicial District Court Minute Books, No. 5, Report of the Grand Jury, Tangipahoa Parish Clerk of Court Archives; Baton Rouge *States*, November 16, 17, 25, 1899, June 27, 1900, February 21, 1901; New Orleans *Picayune*, October 9, 1899; Draughon to Reid, June 15, 1900, in Reid Papers, LLMVC; interviews of Eugene B. Watson, 1980, and R. A. Kent, Jr., 1991, Fluker, La.; *St. Tammany Farmer*, October 28, 1899.

lessness, and that Smith was a prime suspect. Warned not to return to the
area, Smith's companions were permitted to depart for their homes in neighboring Wilkinson County, Mississippi, where they lived alongside Smith's
newly made widow and five fatherless children. Members of the mob made
clear that the lawlessness prevailing in the piney-woods parishes would not
be tolerated in the Felicianas. Order, as interpreted by the governing elite,
would be maintained by any means necessary. The extralegal actions of the
mob, and the seemingly tacit approval of local legal officials, sent a powerful
message to would-be criminal elements to keep out. Though it was indeed
a lynching, the swift and definitive action in East Feliciana highlighted the
dichotomy between the forced order of the plantation region and the prevailing chaos in the piney-woods parishes. No arrests were made, nor did any
public outcry arise, suggesting popular approval of even criminal acts to keep
order.[18]

Ultimately a trial date in the Draughon case was set, and an agreement
was reached to have the Gills surrender and face a jury of their peers. All
eyes were focused on Amite City for what was heralded as the most important
case in the history of the parish. Officials authorized the construction of a
special enclosure around the courthouse to keep back the crowd, and everyone who entered the courthouse was searched for weapons. The New Orleans
Picayune announced the start of the trial with the comment, "this case was
the last killing of a number of homicides that have startled the country and
caused the appellation of 'Bloody Tangipahoa' to be applied to the parish."
Judge Robert Reid presided over the proceedings and former district attorney
Duncan Kemp along with Judge Reid's longtime political foe Milton Strickland and Sentell Davidson represented the defendants. Newly elected district
attorney Robert S. Ellis led the prosecution team that included attorney Clay
Elliott and District Attorney Gordon Goodbee of St. Tammany Parish, who
had been hired by friends and relatives of the deceased to assist in the prosecution.[19]

After a struggle to seat a jury acceptable to both sides, the prosecution
began by offering ten witnesses including a physician, postmaster, train con-
ductor, ticket agent, and multiple merchants and timber workers, all of whom
confirmed the story that the Gills as a group attacked, abused, and ultimately
murdered Draughon. The following morning, the regional press reported that

18. New Orleans *Picayune*, October 16, 18, 1899.
19. Sixteenth Judicial District Court Minute Books, No. 6, docket no. 304, Tangipahoa
Parish Clerk of Court Archives; New Orleans *Picayune*, April 29, 30, 1899, January 22, 25,
1901.

the businesses of two prosecution witnesses, including the post office at Tangipahoa, had been burned to the ground the evening after their testimony. The defense followed, offering seven witnesses including Alonzo Gill and two relatives who claimed the Gills acted in self-defense. District Attorney Ellis closed the testimony with a prophetic statement to the jury: "If the state has not made out a clear case of murder against the accused it could never make out one in any case." After deliberating barely forty-five minutes, the jury returned with a verdict of not guilty.[20]

As residuals to the case, B. J. Scarborough, a friend of the Gills and briefly a member of the jury, was arrested for perjury, and five eyewitnesses to the shooting were called who testified that defense witness Bud Wall was not even in Tangipahoa the day of the killing. Despite the defense attorney's efforts to suppress the statements, several prosecution witnesses testified that they had been visited by Branch men and warned not to testify against the Gills. The acquittals placed these people at risk, and the fear of retribution they felt augmented observers' dismay at the verdict. Some regional newspapers, now convinced that legal justice could not be obtained in Tangipahoa, openly called on the people to take matters into their own hands. The Baton Rouge *States* insisted, "the great need of this section is for the law abiding, who number 95 percent of the population, to organize and punish the lawless. There is no organization now and public opinion cannot make itself felt." Suggestions that the region revert to a more primitive state, where vigilante justice and lynch mobs enforce order rather than the rule of law, were a tangible sign that many Tangipahoa residents remained ensconced in a frontier mentality seemingly immune to the progress occurring around them.[21]

Less than a week after the trial closed, an even more appalling crime occurred just a few miles from the site of the Draughon killing. On February 2, 1901, a group of white men, who had been drinking at a party, inexplicably attacked the home of black farmer Arthur Nickerson near Arcola, Louisiana. The group murdered Nickerson and his five-year-old daughter before sexually assaulting a thirteen-year-old daughter and Nickerson's wife even as she hid their youngest child under the bedcovers. A third daughter was shot and

20. *St. Tammany Farmer*, February 2, 1901; New Orleans *Picayune*, January 22–27, 1901; Sixteenth Judicial District Court Minute Books, No. 6, docket no. 304, Tangipahoa Parish Clerk of Court Archives.
21. Sixteenth Judicial District Court Minute Books, No. 6, docket no. 304, Tangipahoa Parish Clerk of Court Archives; New Orleans *Picayune*, January 24–26, 29, 1901; Baton Rouge *States*, February 21, 1901; *St. Tammany Farmer*, February 2, 1901.

wounded by the gang, which reportedly boasted that they intended to kill the entire family but had run out of ammunition.[22]

Even in a region long accustomed to atrocity, this crime proved shocking. Press reports referred to the men as "debased and lost to all shame," noting further, "because the parties killed were negroes does not palliate the crime." Tangipahoa Parish sheriff F. P. Mix, who had replaced McMichael at the last election, and newly elected St. Helena Parish sheriff E. B. Watson each led a posse in pursuit of the six perpetrators who, with one possible exception, were generally considered men of ill repute and known troublemakers. The six men were quickly rounded up with Watson, "a state university man" and Louisiana's youngest sheriff at twenty-seven, receiving considerable praise for his aggressiveness in capturing five of the six.[23]

Yet the legacy of the region's past, so recently illuminated by the Draughon case, continued to cast a long shadow. In an article titled "Will Tangipahoa Prosecute the Nickerson Outrage?" the New Orleans *Picayune* vented its disdain for the parish's system of justice. A visit by prominent Amite City attorney and secretary of the state senate W. H. McClendon to New Orleans provided insight into the despair of regional residents and the contempt of the region's largest press organ.

Picayune: "What is the sentiment in Tangipahoa over the Nickerson killings?"
McClendon: "There is outrage."
Picayune: "Will the perpetrators be prosecuted?"
McClendon: "Like all other cases have been prosecuted in Tangipahoa the past eight years."
Picayune: "You mean indifferently?"
McClendon: "The record speaks for itself."
Picayune: "Where will they be tried?"
McClendon: "Right in Amite City."
Picayune: "And you think indifferently?"
McClendon: "I think like all other cases have been prosecuted."[24]

Amid such chaotic circumstances few, if any, residents could feel safe. The savagery of the Nickerson tragedy nonetheless highlighted the vulnerability

22. New Orleans *Picayune*, February 3–7, 1901.
23. Baton Rouge *States*, February 21, 1901; New Orleans *Picayune*, February 5–7, 1901.
24. New Orleans *Picayune*, February 7, 1901.

of those occupying the lowest rung of society. No one understood resistance to change regardless of the progress occurring better than black southerners. Forthright assertiveness on the part of African Americans could bring dire consequences in almost any part of the South at the turn of the twentieth century. And in a region "where the influence of the law was scarcely felt," assertiveness could bring a death sentence. The very pillar of racial segregation, the infamous *Plessy vs. Ferguson* decision, was a product of southeast Louisiana.

Even in the face of such obstacles, some Florida parish blacks did seek to improve their condition. More than half of school-age black children attended school at least part-time in all of the Florida parishes except East Feliciana and St. Tammany. Tangipahoa Parish blacks formed a business league to promote their economic fortunes, and some risked their lives by obtaining employment in the lumber industry. Remaining Whitecap groups continued to ruthlessly enforce efforts to keep blacks out of the relatively high paying timber industry jobs. In the spring of 1899, nightriders attacked the quarters of black laborers at the Brackenridge Lumber Mill in Livingston Parish, firing shotguns into their homes to intimidate the laborers, killing one young man in the process. In the summer of the same year, Whitecaps boldly entered the Kent Mill at Kentwood, forcing all black men to cease working at once on pain of death and leaving signs warning them to never return. In a dramatic 1911 incident, a gang of about twenty Whitecaps attacked two logging trains of the J. J. White Lumber Company in St. Helena Parish near the Mississippi border, leaving twenty-one men injured. General manager W. M. White begged for peace, insisting that 50 percent of his laborers were Caucasian and that company policy required that white men be employed for every position whenever possible.[25]

Suppression of black Louisianians went far beyond a few nightriders—it was ensconced in the very highest levels of state law. The Louisiana state constitution of 1898 effectively eliminated African Americans from the electorate. Addressing those to be disenfranchised, one speaker patronized, "What we seek to do is undertaken not in a spirit of hostility, but in the belief

25. "Report of the Superintendent of Public Education," *Louisiana Documents*, II (Baton Rouge, 1906), 190–94; Dunbar Rowland, ed., *Official Letter Books*, VI, 161–62; Hair, *Bourbonism and Agrarian Protest*, 124–27; Amite City *Florida Parishes*, July 16, 1910; New Orleans *Picayune*, April 29, August 9, September 10, 1899; Sixteenth Judicial District Court Minute Books, No. 2, State of Louisiana vs. Ben Kinchen, docket no. 19, Livingston Parish Courthouse; "Train Is Attacked," *Southern Lumberman*, January 14, 1911, p. 28; "Train Fired Upon," *Lumber Trade Journal*, January 15, 1911, p. 26.

the state should see to the protection of the weaker classes. We owe it to the ignorant, we owe it to the weak, to protect them just as we would a little child and prevent it from injuring itself with sharp edged tools placed in its hands." In a wild racial rant at the same convention, Dr. J. L. M. Curry, representing the Peabody Educational Fund, condemned northerners who advocated mixed-race schools. Curry warned opponents of the dominant Democrats that no allies were coming as they had earlier, "like a horde of carpetbaggers, hungry as dogs and merciless as wolves to prey on the conquered section." The message was clear: Blacks should stay in their place, poorer whites should be grateful for their whiteness and remain silent, and the two groups should stay powerless and separate. In the lawless environs of the eastern Florida parishes immiseration, and the powerful social convulsions it can produce, loomed close.[26]

In his influential study *The Mind of the South*, W. J. Cash argued that southern society was governed by an uneasy set of relations he called the "proto-Dorian convention." According to Cash, in order to sustain white supremacy, lower-class whites deferred to the leadership of their wealthy, powerful neighbors, who in return outwardly treated them as equals. Poorer whites were essentially given the crumbs from a meager table to keep the elite in power. Yet despite outward appearances, the elite frequently held lower-order whites in contempt. Similarly, poorer whites often deeply resented the privilege and prestige enjoyed by the powerful. As a result, there also existed what Cash called the "savage ideal," wherein poor whites, and some wealthy whites, vented their anger at prevailing conditions through hostility to the least empowered—specifically, black people. A horrific series of events occurring in Washington Parish in the fall of 1901 gave credence to Cash's logic and underscored the volatility of conditions prevailing in the piney woods of southeastern Louisiana.[27]

The site of the drama was the small, isolated community of Balltown in northeast Washington Parish near the Mississippi border. In October 1901, while her husband was in nearby Columbia, Mississippi, Mrs. John Ball manned the family store alone. A black man named Bill Morris entered the store and requested some items. When Mrs. Ball turned to retrieve the requested items, reports indicated that Morris grabbed her and dragged her to a nearby thick growth of bushes, where he sexually assaulted her before beating her in the head with a pine knot and leaving her for dead. He then

26. *Constitution of the State of Louisiana Adopted in Convention at the City of New Orleans, May 12, 1898* (New Orleans, 1898), 9–10, 31–34.

27. W. J. Cash, *The Mind of the South* (New York, 1941).

returned and robbed the store before saturating his feet with oil, to throw off bloodhounds that might be used in pursuit, and proceeded to his cabin four miles distant. Mrs. Ball, however, survived the attack and crawled to her father-in-law's home and reported what had happened. Learning of the assault on his wife, her husband, along with several men from Columbia, rushed back to Balltown to create a posse and track the assailant. The New Orleans *Picayune* reported, "When he is captured there will be no trial and he will be either hanged or burned."[28]

Morris was quickly located and returned to the site of the assault, where he was chained to a tree. After securing a "confession," members of the posse piled pine knots and straw around him "almost to his shoulders," and he was burned alive. Local law enforcement made no effort to prevent the lynching or seek justice against any members of the mob. But there was clearly concern that the initial assault and subsequent lynching had created a charged atmosphere. In the wake of reports indicating that black residents had been meeting every night since the lynching, concerned whites encouraged law officers to keep an eye on the meetings. In particular, a black camp meeting at Duncan's Chapel, alternately known as Oak Grove Church, near Balltown, was said to be led by a preacher who exhorted followers that the only way to get even for the Morris lynching was to play "tit for tat." Several days later, the local constable visited the camp meeting and discovered a makeshift restaurant being run by a black man named Crea Lott. When the constable asked him for his license, Lott became aggressive and cursed the officer, who retreated to secure aid. When the constable returned with a small posse, the blacks were prepared and waiting. What followed would forever be known as the Balltown Riot.[29]

As the posse approached, Lott and others at the camp fired on them, killing one white man, mortally wounding another, and injuring several others. The posse cornered the shooters, along with women and children, in Lott's restaurant and the church. Lott and the unnamed preacher both attempted to fight their way out only to be shot and killed by the posse. Unable to entice the others barricaded in the buildings to come out, the posse set fire to the buildings and shot at those who tried to flee. Some of the blacks escaped into the surrounding woods, while the least fortunate died in the fire. In the end, three whites and eleven blacks, including three women and one child, died

28. New Orleans *Picayune*, October 24–25, 1901; *St. Tammany Farmer*, November 2, 1901.
29. New Orleans *Picayune*, October 24, 25, 29, 1901; *St. Tammany Farmer*, November 2, 1901.

in the riot. Riders were dispatched to Franklinton and Columbia with news of the fight, and scores of white men poured into the area the following day. Louisiana governor W. W. Heard placed the First Troop of Louisiana Cavalry on standby before determining they were not needed. In the following days, terrified blacks were seen streaming about the countryside fearful of the unbridled wrath of the white posse, who sent a message to black leaders asking if they had had enough. Receiving an unmitigated "yes" in reply, white leaders urged the posse to return to their homes. Questioned about legal action in the aftermath of the riot, District Attorney Gordon Goodbee explained that the grand jury would determine what action should be taken in the Morris lynching, but he doubted they would consider the Balltown Riot.[30]

The Balltown Riot provided yet another example of a dysfunctional legal system in the Florida parishes, though in the case of racial violence it proved more consistent with conditions prevailing across the South. An unfortunate certainty of the late-nineteenth- and early-twentieth-century South remained the unshakable preeminence of white supremacy. It provoked regular incidents of white-on-black violence, and the courts seldom intervened in such extralegal brutality. What made the piney woods of the Florida parishes atypical was the sustained inordinate rates of white-on-white violence amid a hapless legal system. Other regions of the South, such as Izard and Union Counties in Arkansas, Cherokee and Cleburne Counties in Alabama, Sevier County, Tennessee, Edgefield County, South Carolina, and even regions of north-central and western Louisiana, experienced high rates of white-on-white violence. Yet few of these and other regions of the South endured a cowed legal system amid the type of rapid, multifaceted progress occurring in the Florida parishes.[31]

30. Amite City *Florida Parishes*, November 2, 1901; New Orleans *Picayune*, October 29, 30, 1901; *St. Tammany Farmer*, November 2, 1901. Reports on the number of casualties in the Balltown Riot vary, with some placing the number of dead at nine blacks and two whites.

31. Governor James B. Berry to A. J. Witt, January 15, 1883, in Governor J. B. Berry Correspondence, and Governor Daniel Jones to Samuel Carradine, March 1, 1897, in Governor Daniel W. Jones Correspondence, both in Arkansas History Commission–State Archives, Little Rock; Pocahontas, Ark., *Randolph Herald*, April 6, 1893; *Biennial Report of Attorney General William C. Fitts* (Montgomery, Ala., 1894), 17; *Biennial Report of Attorney General Henry C. Thompkins* (Montgomery, Ala., 1884), 9–10; *Biennial Report of Attorney General T. N. McClellan* (Montgomery, Ala., 1887), 9; *Biennial Report of Attorney General William L. Martin* (Montgomery, Ala., 1894), 12–20, all in Alabama State Archives, Montgomery; Birmingham *Age Herald*, March 7, 15, June 21, 22, 24, 1893; List of persons murdered and severely injured by whitecaps in Sevier County, manuscript in J. C. Houck Papers, Calvin McClung Historical Collection, Knox County Public Library System, Knoxville, Tenn.; D. A. Wayland to John C.

Though frequently overshadowed in historical accounts by neighboring Acadiana and New Orleans, the Florida parishes seldom went unnoticed. From the colonial period through the Civil War, the region had always been strategically important. Yet it remained an economic and political backwater, utterly reliant on cotton and timber for jobs and politically subservient to the wealthier and more powerful interests of the state. Such circumstances began to change in the aftermath of Reconstruction, and by 1900, unbridled progress provided a new, and unexpected, crucible for the prevailing social instability. As the nation progressed into the new century, the Florida parishes were poised to enjoy a more healthful, happy existence of enhanced opportunity on the cusp of modernity. In short, a new era of vision and opportunity awaited the residents; yet the killing continued. And holding fast to antiquated perceptions of honor and justice amid profound change offered a perfect formula for tragedy.

Houck, March 20, 1897, M. F. Maples to Houck, March 22, 1897, D. W. Payne to Houck, March 23, 1897, G. E. Sharp to William Parton, April 1, 1897, all in J. C. Houck Papers, McClung Collection; Thomas H. Davis, *The Whitecaps: A History of the Organization in Sevier County* (Knoxville, 1899); Burton, *In My Father's House Are Many Mansions*; Matthew Hernando, *Faces like Devils: The Bald Knobber Vigilantes in the Ozarks* (Columbia, Mo., 2014); Kenneth C. Barnes, *Who Killed John Clayton? Political Violence and the Emergence of the New South, 1861–1893* (Durham, N.C., 1998); Gilles Vandal, *Rethinking Southern Violence: Homicides in Post–Civil War Louisiana, 1866–1884* (Columbus, Ohio, 2000); Kenneth Bridges, "The Tucker Parnell Feud," *Encyclopedia of Arkansas History and Culture* (2009).

The Great Southern Lumber Company at Bogalusa. At the height of its capacity in the early twentieth century, the mill produced more board feet of lumber than any other company worldwide.

Courtesy Judge Leon Ford Collection, Center for Southeast Louisiana Studies, Southeastern Louisiana University

E. V. Preston, Director of the Banner Lumber Company at Kentwood. The White-cap efforts to force the dismissal of black laborers and otherwise disrupt company operations included assaults on company trains, the murder of one foreman, and the direct intimidation of Preston, who responded by turning company employees and supporters into a posse that forthrightly pursued the Whitecaps.

Courtesy Judge Leon Ford Collection, Center for Southeast Louisiana Studies, Southeastern Louisiana University

Street Scene in Amite City, *ca.* 1920. Note the convergence of tradition and modernity as automobiles and horse-drawn wagons maneuver on dirt streets below electric power lines.

Courtesy Fajoni-Lanier Collection, Center for Southeast Louisiana Studies, Southeastern Louisiana University

Armed Escort to the Tangipahoa Parish Courthouse. Louisiana National Guardsmen escort six condemned Italians from the railroad depot to the parish courthouse in Amite City, where the men would be hanged for the 1921 murder of Independence merchant Dallas Calmes. The intense publicity and passion surrounding the case nearly provoked an international incident between the United States and Italy.

Courtesy Jesse Earl Mixon Collection, Center for Southeast Louisiana Studies, Southeastern Louisiana University

The "Rickety" Tangipahoa Parish Jail at Amite City. Scene of numerous escapes and intrigues, the jail was used to house the six Italians convicted in the Calmes murder on the eve of their execution. Fears of mob violence by locals, or a breakout attempt by the Mafia, led to a military-enforced cordon about the jail that included a moat to keep the crowds at a distance.

Courtesy Jesse Earl Mixon Collection, Center for Southeast Louisiana Studies, Southeastern Louisiana University

The St. Helena Parish Jail at Greensburg. One of the oldest in the Florida parishes, it typified the poor condition of places of incarceration available to law enforcement challenged with maintaining peace in a region acclimated to violent criminal behavior.

Courtesy Public Health in Louisiana Collection, Center for Southeast Louisiana Studies, Southeastern Louisiana University

Lynching, 1900. These four African American men were taken from the city jail in Ponchatoula and lynched by local residents exasperated by a series of thefts and home burglaries, including one where a white woman was beaten. Regional press reports indicated that though law enforcement had done all it could to contain the burglaries, local vigilantes believed the time had come to take more aggressive action in the south end of Tangipahoa Parish.

Courtesy Judge Leon Ford Collection, Center for Southeast Louisiana Studies, Southeastern Louisiana University

Baseball Team Sponsored by Natalbany Lumber Company, *ca.* 1910. Although baseball and other sources of entertainment were greeted with optimism and the hope that they could help deliver the region from the cycle of violence, sporting endeavors too found themselves drawn into the pattern of chaos, frequently due to the presence of alcohol and the intense passions of the fans.

Courtesy Judge Leon Ford Collection, Center for Southeast Louisiana Studies, Southeastern Louisiana University

Slidell Liquor Company, St. Tammany Parish, 1908. Partaking of nickel soft drinks and ten-cent beer and chewing tobacco as well as groceries and dry goods, the small gathering of young and old, black and white, at this establishment reflected the importance of such country stores in the rural Florida parishes both to secure supplies and as sites for fraternization. St. Tammany, East Baton Rouge, and West Feliciana Parishes remained the only "wet," alcohol-legal parishes in this region in the first decade of the twentieth century.

St. Tammany Historical Association Collection, Center for Southeast Louisiana Studies, Southeastern Louisiana University

Typical Strawberry Tenant Farm in the Florida Parishes, *ca.* 1900. The family of pickers arrayed before their small, dilapidated house are about to enter their weed-infested field as more affluent landowners look on.

Courtesy Strawberry Photo Collection, Center for Southeast Louisiana Studies, Southeastern Louisiana University

· 8 ·

A Pathway to Peace

In *The Adventures of Tom Sawyer*, Mark Twain wisely noted, "the less there is to justify a traditional custom, the harder it is to get rid of it." The words seem tailored to fit the continuing proclivity toward violence evident in the Florida parishes. Yet as the region entered the twentieth century, traditional customs, especially those categorically opposed to the rules of civilization, would be challenged in previously unimagined ways. The needs and expectations of a global industrializing order arrived in force, offering an opportunity to break with the dark days of the past and embrace the vision of the future. Blessed with a pristine environment and abundant natural resources, southeast Louisiana became a target for comprehensive development that offered a pathway to a radically altered way of life—provided that the residents could overcome the customs of the past.

In the first decades of the new century, significant population shifts, with one notable exception, furthered the existing dichotomy in the region. The exception emerged in the plantation parishes. As the new century dawned, East Baton Rouge Parish came to enjoy the fruits of location and opportunity. Already home to a thriving river port that serviced the needs of the surrounding parishes through a tenuous network of connecting roads, the parish's primary town, Baton Rouge, was awarded a further impetus for development when in 1882 the state legislature designated it as the permanent state capital. The following year, rail connection southward to New Orleans and northward ultimately to Memphis via the New Orleans and Mississippi Valley Railroad further augmented growth in the river port. Under the leadership of Mayor Robert A. Hart, residents approved a series of bond issues that led to the construction of a new city hall, the paving of many streets, and the opening of several new schools. In 1896 a Coca-Cola bottling company arrived, and by the first decade of the new century, wholesale supply houses, like the Holmes and Barnes Ltd. Wholesale Grocery firm, were established and servicing much of southeast Louisiana into southern Mississippi.[1]

The arrival of Louisiana State University at Baton Rouge should have offered still another engine for growth, but for limitations created in the state legislature. In 1898 the legislature appropriated only ten thousand dollars for LSU, a figure that by 1904 had increased to only fifteen thousand dollars—a paltry sum for an institution designed to advance the quality of life in the state. The city caught a huge break when in 1909 Standard Oil directors made the decision to locate a large refinery at Baton Rouge. It became operational several years later, and by 1915 the city savored the benefits big oil could bring to a community that would be inextricably linked to the industry.[2]

Unlike East Baton Rouge, the remaining plantation parishes, East and West Feliciana, entered a sort of socioeconomic malaise—one that typified large regions of the South in the late nineteenth and early twentieth centuries. The grandeur and power of the plantation masters had been badly battered by the years of war and Reconstruction. Although, with some exceptions, stability had largely characterized the region in sharp contrast to the chaos prevailing in the piney-woods parishes, it was built across the vast chasm separating the owners of property and their labor. Manuscript census returns and other sources reveal a recovering planter class, at least partially restored to prewar levels of dominance, ruling over vast numbers of desperately impoverished sharecroppers and landless laborers along with a smattering of craftsmen, merchants, and small farmers.[3]

As they ever had, black residents occupied the lowest rung of society. Largely confined to the same clusters of shacks that had housed them during their years of enslavement, African Americans, denied the redistribution of land they needed to be economically viable, endured grinding poverty amid little reason for hope. The specter of African American assertiveness in

1. New Orleans *Daily Picayune*, November 30, 1899; Hair, *Bourbonism and Agrarian Protest*, 101; Mark T. Carlton, *River Capital: An Illustrated History of Baton Rouge* (New York, 1981), 128–36.

2. Baton Rouge *States*, June 24, 1910; Carlton, *River Capital*, 142,153.

3. *Twelfth Census of the United States*, 1900, Manuscript Population Statistics by Heads of Household, Doc. F2, Roll 118 (National Archives Microcopy No. T623, Roll 564); James S. MGehee, "Ramble in Autobiography," Typescript, n.d., in James McGehee Papers; Henry Marston to J. W. Burbridge and Co., September 29, 1876, in Marston Letter Books, No. 4, p. 320, Marston Family Papers; Baton Rouge *Capitolian-Advocate*, August 15, 1888; Franklinton *New Era*, August 15, 1888; Amite City *Florida Parishes*, July 15, August 5, 12, 1891.

black-majority regions across the South created near hysteria among many of their white neighbors. Efforts at self-improvement in the Felicianas during Reconstruction had been violently smashed so effectively that with rare exception, blacks had embraced the message to "know their place." Common whites, many of whom fared little better economically, were ever reminded that their whiteness made them part of a privileged class and they should therefore help "regulate" the prevailing social circumstances. The needs of white supremacy in a black-majority region inhibited plain folk assertiveness just as it kept the former bondsmen in check. In contrast to the piney-woods parishes or neighboring East Baton Rouge, limited opportunities beyond the farm remained available as the northern plantation parishes entered the twentieth century.[4]

Census statistics reveal the prevailing stasis in development that characterized life in the Felicianas at the turn of the new century. In contrast to the pronounced population increases occurring in most of the piney-woods parishes, as well as in East Baton Rouge, in the first decades of the twentieth century, East Feliciana experienced limited growth, and West Feliciana decreasing population numbers. At the same time, the percentage of blacks increased, suggesting that those among the less fortunate segment of the population who could migrate, namely lower-income whites, did in many instances seek advanced opportunities elsewhere. Limited chances for personal improvement, along with the oppressive political climate of the Bourbon era in plantation regions of Louisiana, undoubtedly contributed to the moribund population figures (see Table 12).

Bourbon politics carried profound implications in the late-nineteenth-century South, and its legacy continued into the early twentieth. So named because they were alleged to have never "learned anything or forgotten anything," Bourbon Democrats fused hostility to virtually every public expenditure, such as education or infrastructure improvements, with crass racism. Unlike many mainstream Democrats who sought to improve the living conditions of the poor where they could, Bourbon politicians employed racial rhetoric to distract voters from their poor record of service to Louisiana. In his seminal study *Bourbonism and Agrarian Protest*, William I. Hair noted

4. J. N. Waddel to Eli Capell, January 9, 1866, in Capell Papers; Greensburg *Weekly Star and Journal*, April 27, 1867; contract agreement between Joseph Embree and his laborers, February, 1866, in Embree Papers; Amite City *Democrat*, September 4, November 20, December 11, 1875; *Louisiana House Journal*, 1st Sess., 1876, pp. 94–99; James S. McGehee, "Ramble in Autobiography," James McGehee Papers; Shugg, *Origins of Class Struggle in Louisiana*, 251–54; Cash, *Mind of the South*.

TABLE 12. POPULATION CHANGES, 1890–1910

Parish	Total Population (1890)	Black Population (1890)	Total Population (1910)	Black Population (1910)
East Baton Rouge	25,922	16,428	34,580	21,342
East Feliciana	17,903	12,707	20,055	14,536
Livingston	5,769	871	10,627	1,377
St. Helena	8,062	4,589	9,172	4,573
St. Tammany	10,160	3,762	18,917	6,731
Tangipahoa	12,655	4,712	29,160	9,135
Washington	6,700	2,065	18,886	5,458
West Feliciana	15,062	12,786	13,449	11,012

Sources: Eleventh Census of the United States, 1890, Vol. I, Population, 22–23, 501; Thirteenth Census of the United States, 1910, Vol. I, Population, 158.

that Bourbonism was strongest where cotton remained the major crop and where blacks outnumbered or enjoyed parity with whites—a definition that precisely identified the Felicianas.[5]

Although Bourbon politics, and the calls for white unity behind the Democrats, extended to all regions of the Florida parishes, the result in the piney-woods parishes proved quite different from the social stasis emerging in the Felicianas. As demonstrated by the rapidly expanding population in the eastern parishes, increasing opportunity proved evident in the piney woods, and it necessarily stimulated calls to overcome the challenges of the past. The primary challenge, of course, remained the need to curb the violence and establish a measure of political stability. Just how far the region could go in recasting cultural identity served as the crucible for charting the future. The consternation at the limits of justice, recently underscored in the Draughon case, proved well founded. In virtually every other sense, Tangipahoa served as a model of progress in a time of significant change that was altering the very character of the nation. Impressive innovations in science and technology linked urban areas to the rural countryside in unprecedented ways. In what scholars refer to as the "organizational synthesis," expedited, efficient links to urban areas rapidly began to change the character of rural society. The piney-woods parishes' close proximity to the South's greatest

5. Hair, Bourbonism and Agrarian Protest, 24; Shugg, Origins of Class Struggle in Louisiana, 312–13.

metropolis, New Orleans, ensured the region would be on the vanguard of change.[6]

The process began in the region shortly before the onset of the Civil War. The construction of the New Orleans-Jackson Railroad in the mid-1850s profoundly affected development in the piney-woods parishes, and especially in Tangipahoa. The troubled parish had literally been created to accommodate the railroad, and the transformation of the area had been comprehensive and continuous. After incorporation into the larger Illinois Central Railroad (ICRR), the trunk line began to spawn numerous spur and "dummy line" railroads, used in logging operations, that further advanced the regional transportation networks and economic development.[7]

The Amite City *Florida Parishes* summarized the dramatic change in mobility the railroad occasioned: "Times were when a trip to New Orleans was akin to a trip around the world and neighbors would gather to see them off and there would be weeping over the perilous journey." The paper boasted that now a visit to the Crescent City required only a matter of hours. The Baton Rouge, Hammond, and Eastern line soon made east-west travel equally expeditious and brought newfound accessibility to previously isolated regions of Livingston, St. Tammany, and Tangipahoa Parishes, among other areas. A proposed line connecting Bayou Sara in West Feliciana Parish to Bogalusa in Washington Parish via Amite City stimulated widespread support, as did a plan to run a line north and south from the East Louisiana Railroad line at Covington to connect Mandeville in St. Tammany Parish with the Washington Parish seat at Franklinton. Each of these ventures attracted the support of leading families in the respective parishes.[8]

While beneficial in their own right, technological innovations also brought new concerns that contributed to community stress. Simply put, the railroads could be dangerous to both livestock and pedestrians, and cat-

6. Robert H. Wiebe, *The Search for Order, 1877–1920* (New York, 1967); Louis Galambos, "The Emerging Organizational Synthesis in Modern American History," *Business History Review*, XLIV (1970), 279–90; Galambos, "Technology, Political Economy, and Professionalization: Central Themes of the Organizational Synthesis," *Business History Review*, LVII (1983), 471–93.

7. E. D. Frost to H. S. McComb, September 4, 1875, in W. M. Francis and E. D. Frost Out Letters Collection; J. B. Kemp to E. P. Skene, September 15, 16, 17, 1897, King to Skene, September 15, 1897, and Map of the Line of the New Orleans-Jackson Railroad from Canton, Mississippi, to New Orleans, circa 1861, all in Illinois Central Railroad Collection, Overflow Reports; Thomas Ellis to John Ellis, January 26, 1858, in Ellis Family Papers.

8. Amite City *Florida Parishes*, August 3, 1907, July 5, 1913; Franklinton *New Era*, July 7, 1900, January 16, 1904.

astrophic wrecks were not uncommon. In November 1903, a high-speed mail train on the Illinois Central line plowed into an accommodation train loading passengers at Kentwood. The crash completely destroyed the two rear coaches of the latter before fire consumed the remaining portion, adding to the horror. Thirty persons were killed and dozens more injured. Potentially as dangerous were intentionally provoked incidents that seemed certain to happen in the wild-west environs of the Florida parishes. Placing a crosstie across the track in an effort to derail a train and tampering with the couplings on the cars proved a favorite tactic of would-be vandals.[9]

The railroads also contributed to regional stress in subtler ways. Locals expressed frustration at their inability to control or even influence the policies of the railroads. An Amite City effort to mitigate potential danger by requiring trains to slow significantly within city limits provoked an immediate injunction on the town from the federal court in New Orleans. Efforts to get the railroads to scale back on "exorbitant" freight and hauling charges likewise fell on deaf ears. The railroads were accused of favoring certain communities over others. Hammond, a town founded by northerners in southern Tangipahoa Parish, was regularly accused of being a favored site of the ICRR. One newspaper editor vented that the railroad "nurses Hammond like a sick child," arguing that through the construction of terminals, hotels, parks, and the like, all with railroad money, Hammond had transformed from "a water stop to a thriving town."[10]

The railroads, particularly the ICRR, countered negative images of the industry with publicity stunts such as a "Get Acquainted Train" that stopped along the route and offered presentations and literature extolling the virtues of the railroad. They also purchased full-page ads in regional newspapers arguing that criticism of the railroad was misplaced. The power the railroads enjoyed in both Congress and the Louisiana Legislature rendered dissatisfaction with the industry little more than a nuisance. The railroads nonetheless

9. *St. Tammany Farmer*, November 21, 1903; Hammond *Daily Herald*, June 8, 1909; Sixteenth Judicial District Court Minute Books, No. 5, Tangipahoa Parish Clerk of Court Archives.

10. "List of Authorities on Behalf of Defendants in the Suit of I.C.R.R. Co. vs. Town of Amite City, No. 37971, U.S. Circuit Court, New Orleans, 1912," and "Restraining Order Against Mayor C. M. Mixon of Amite City and His Agents," forbids arrest or prosecution of any servant or employee of the ICRR, U.S. Circuit Court, New Orleans, December 15, 1911, both in Reid Papers, CSLS; Amite City *Florida Parishes*, December 23, 1911, June 21, August 2, 16, 1913, October 29, November 19, 1921, January 14, 1922; Franklinton *New Era*, September 5, 1907.

added another source of divisiveness and uncertainty in an already politically unstable and socially chaotic region.[11]

Despite concerns, the railroads served as a powerful engine of comprehensive change. Communities throughout the piney-woods region of the Florida parishes embraced the necessity of reliable access to the railroads. In an unprecedented move, scores of residents signed petitions calling for road taxes to improve the notoriously poor quality of regional roads. The modernizing effort, largely initiated in Tangipahoa Parish, centered on the need for roads to become publicly supported. Previously, most roads had either been private endeavors or subject to an antiquated system wherein parish police juries appointed road overseers who supervised maintenance work required of residents in each ward. In one example of this virtual corvée labor, Tangipahoa resident Marvin Harris received a summons to appear in Arcola on a specific date at 7:00 A.M. "to work on the Greensburg road division of public road number one" and to bring with him one spade. Failure to work on the roads could result in an indictment. In November 1900, Livingston Parish resident Robert Palmer received a sentence to pay a five-dollar fine or serve ten days in jail for failure to work on a parish road.[12]

The forced labor of untrained citizens typically produced poor-quality roads. Progress demanded new ways of thinking. Many residents nonetheless remained skeptical about the changes being thrust upon them. As proponents of progress were busily electing delegates to a "good roads convention" to be held in Baton Rouge, police jury members across the region came under fire for endorsing public support of road improvements and education. Some complained that even when voters approved taxes to support road improvements, they produced little result. One Tangipahoa Parish editor noted that even though a road tax had been approved, the only efficient roadways were those located in wards serviced by convict labor. Speaking in Tangipahoa, former governor J. Y. Sanders agreed that convict labor had initially constructed quality roads in the parish, but added that they soon became im-

11. Amite City *Florida Parishes*, August 2, 1913; Franklinton *New Era*, September 5, 1907; Amite City *Florida Parish Times*, June 7, 1924.

12. Springfield *Livingston Times*, October 5, 1906; Amite City *Florida Parishes*, March 8, 15, 1902; F. P. Martin to Joe Reid, August 18, 1895, in Reid Papers, CSLS; "Summons, State of Louisiana, Parish of Tangipahoa, to Marvin Harris," June 14, 1896, in Reid Papers, LLMVC; State of Louisiana vs. Robert Palmer, docket no. 32, November 20, 1900, and State of Louisiana vs. Delanie Adler, docket no. 61, November 14, 1901, both in Twenty-First Judicial District Court, Division A and B, Minute Book No. 2, Livingston Parish Courthouse; *St. Tammany Farmer*, May 16, 1908.

passable because of poor design. Sanders argued that Tangipahoa alone had spent $70,000 on roads but still had not a single efficient road in the parish. He advocated applying engineer-approved designs, including leveling and proper drainage, to road construction.[13]

The increasingly heated debate over changing transportation networks reflected the arrival of mechanization. Regional newspapers became filled with competing ads between horse-and-buggy rigs and automobiles. Demonstrations were held to show that a tractor could outperform a mule. Signaling the end of an era, in November 1924 the Amite City *Florida Parish Times* reported that Tangipahoa Parish now had more automobiles than horses—2,823 to 2,658 respectively. Perhaps not surprising in a region replete with trigger-happy folk, when heavy, fast-moving conveyances encountered one another on narrow, poor-quality roadways, regular shootings were reported between motorists contesting the roads.[14]

Even as residents embraced railroads and automobiles, a reliable and less controversial mode of transportation, waterways, also furthered connection to the outside world. Permeated by slow-moving streams that fed a series of lakes offering a direct connection to New Orleans and ultimately the Gulf of Mexico, the region had long relied on steamer service. By the first decades of the twentieth century, "elegant passenger service" from a variety of locations provided efficient and comfortable travel from ports primarily concentrated in Livingston and St. Tammany Parishes. In addition to passenger service, the steamers—departing from ports such as Port Vincent, French Settlement, and Springfield in Livingston Parish, along with Madisonville, Mandeville, and Covington in St. Tammany Parish—offered reliable, inexpensive freight service. In the first week of November 1899, the steamers *Josie Weaver*, *Rosa A.*, *J. R. O'Rourg*, and *John F. Popp* carried 145 bales of cotton, 332 barrels of rosin, 40 barrels of turpentine, 900 barrels of sand, and 6 bales of moss among other commodities from the port at Covington to New Orleans.[15]

Improving communication networks complemented the evolving trans-

13. Amite City *Florida Parishes*, October 24, 1903, April 15, 1905, August 10, 1907, June 21, 28, 1913; Hammond *Louisiana Sun*, January 3, 1913.

14. Amite City *Florida Parish Times*, January 7, 1922, November 29, 1924; Amite City *Florida Parishes*, March 25, 1922; Kentwood *Commercial*, May 14, 1919.

15. Copy of excursion ticket for "Elegant Passenger Steamers Louise and Daisy," copy of ticket for steamer "Alice," and account ledger with steamer "Jesse" for Hugh Jenks, December, 1919, all in Livingston Parish Papers Collection; Amite City *Tangipahoa Parish News*, September 15, 1927; Springfield *Livingston Times*, September 27, 1907; *St. Tammany Farmer*, November 4, 1899.

portation links and likewise hastened progress in the piney-woods parishes. Declaring that "the protection of women and children is only one of the chief values of the telephone on the farm," by 1913 the Cumberland Telephone and Telegraph Company of Atlanta had arrived in the region to compete with emerging local enterprises like the Amite River Telephone Company of French Settlement and the Washington Parish Telephone Company based at Franklinton. Radio soon followed, dramatically furthering connection to the outside world and revealing ways of life based on order.[16]

Exposure to outside influences hastened transformation of some key aspects of life. Communities across the region began to clamor for electric lights and natural gas. Municipal sewerage systems emerged to replace outhouses and chamber pots. At the same time that the Florida parishes embraced technological innovations, some called for prohibition of traditional practices such as the free ranging of livestock. The *St. Helena Echo* heralded the decisive victory of a measure to prohibit free-ranging hogs in the parish, after a similar measure had been defeated only a few years earlier, as a sign that residents of St. Helena "have caught the spirit of progress." The Hammond *Vindicator* nonetheless acknowledged that such changes were not universally embraced. A fence law approved in one of the southern wards of Tangipahoa Parish was voided by the police jury. The *Vindicator* noted that the intensity of the controversy centered on cattle tick eradication.[17]

The Texas fever tick was known to carry debilitating consequences for cattle. Free-ranging cattle easily disseminated the tick, reducing livestock values and inhibiting the emergence of a dairy industry that attracted increasing interest as the boll weevil continued its devastating march across the South. A Louisiana State Board of Agriculture and Immigration report insisted that livestock would grow in importance in the area only if local, state, and federal agencies cooperated in tick-eradication efforts. Eradication methods, however, required unprecedented government intrusion into the operations of fiercely independent piney-woods farmers. Government mandates required that cattle be rounded up every two weeks and driven to dipping vats. In the spring of 1915, the Amite City *Times* reported that the police jury, with the strong support of dairymen, endorsed the effort to con-

16. Amite City *Florida Parishes*, June 28, 1913, April 7, May 20, 1922; receipt of capital stock purchase of five shares in the Amite River Telephone Co. for H. and S. Jenks, October 7, 1910, in Livingston Parish Papers Collection; Franklinton *New Era*, July 7, 1900.

17. Amite City *Florida Parishes*, April 22, 1922; Amite City *Florida Parish Times*, February 16, September 20, 1924; *St. Helena Echo*, reprinted in Franklinton *Era Leader*, January 15, 1925; Hammond *Vindicator*, June 14, 28, 1929.

struct dipping vats across the region. The Franklinton *Era Leader,* acknowledging World War I–era calls to produce more food, explained that not only did the tick inhibit growth, but infested animals could not be sold on the open market. The paper urged farmers to make tick eradication a paramount concern. Such aggressive demands on the operations of private individuals nonetheless attracted determined opposition. At least two government entomologists were murdered just across the border in neighboring Mississippi at the height of the controversy.[18]

King cotton, long the source of wealth for some and oppression for others, remained abundant in the region in the first decades of the twentieth century. The days when cotton meant wealth for the elite, independence for the plain folk, and enslavement for African Americans had given way to an era of sharecropping and hardscrabble poverty for most in the cotton trap. Yet old ways die hard, and many continued to see cotton as the way to prosperity. Farmers were encouraged to plant fewer, cleaner acres in cotton, and some reports suggested improved fortunes for cotton farmers. Annual reports from the New Orleans Cotton Exchange in the fall of 1901 revealed the commercial value of the crop at $47.63 per bale, compared to $38.55 in 1900 and $25.08 in 1899. Yet by 1906 the market had leveled off, and farmers were being encouraged to cooperate to secure fifteen cents per pound for their cotton. The Amite City *Advocate* referred to cotton as a "treacherous commodity," urging that it be grown only as a surplus crop. By the early 1920s, regional farmers were struggling to sell their cotton to local merchandising firms acting as brokers. In 1923 the large B. Stern Company and the Amite Hardware Company, both located in Amite City, purchased barely half the number of bales compared to the preceding year.[19]

Overproduction and oversupply had buffeted markets for years. Despite a lift in prices during World War I that continued erratically into the early 1920s, the bane of cotton farmers arrived in the form of the boll weevil. On May 27, 1909, the Franklinton *New Era* reported ominously that "the boll

18. "Report of the Louisiana State Board of Agriculture and Immigration," *Louisiana Documents,* II (Baton Rouge, 1906), 25–26; Amite City *Times,* April 30, May 7, 1915; Amite City *Florida Parish Times,* January 27, 1923; Hammond *Vindicator,* March 29, June 28, September 13, 1929, Ponchatoula *Enterprise,* August 19, 1921; Amite City *Tangipahoa Parish News,* April 29, 1926, June 30, July 21, 1927; Franklinton *Era Leader,* July 5, July 19, September 6, November 22, 1917; New Orleans *Picayune,* September 11, 1928.

19. *St. Tammany Farmer,* April 21, 1900, October 5, 1901; Franklinton *New Era,* January 27, 1906; Amite City *Advocate,* February 1, 1906; Amite City *Florida Parish Times,* January 7, 1922, October 13, 1923.

weevil is showing up in the state." It was believed that cotton farming in the southern counties of Texas had created a bridge for the destructive beetle to cross the Rio Grande from Mexico. The St. Tammany Farmer reported that it had been identified in Bee County, Texas, in 1894 and was progressing seventy-five miles north and twenty-five miles eastward each year. Insecticides, beating the bushes, and a natural insect enemy of the weevil had all failed to stop the advance. By 1903, a $50,000 reward was being offered for any idea that might control a problem that seemed to defy solution.[20]

Unlike cotton, whose days were numbered in the Florida parishes, the timber industry was thriving, while also undergoing a rapid transformation. The virgin stands of longleaf pine proved irresistible to northern speculators and local timber barons alike. Aggressive deforestation began in the 1880s, and by 1900 the areas neighboring the expanding networks of railroads were being reduced to cutover wastelands with little reforestation underway. In April 1924, the Florida Parish Times reported that thirteen million acres of prime Louisiana timberland had been reduced to virtually valueless wasteland. The same paper noted that some timber men now acknowledged the value of leaving seed trees, but most still did not. Smaller, locally owned mills were likewise selling out to large northern firms that frequently operated with a "cut and get out" mindset that saw little value in reforestation.[21]

The vast stands of virgin cypress found in lower Livingston, Tangipahoa, and St. Tammany Parishes also attracted interest. The Williams Lumber Company and the Rathborne Lumber Company, located just south of Ponchatoula, employed eight hundred men who lived in modern communities constructed by the companies. The Rathborne community assumed the name "Cypremoor" to indicate that cypress would be cut and that it was located on the edge of a vast moor or swamp. Mill officials lived in fabulous homes in parklike settings removed from the laborers.[22]

The gem of the regional mills located farther north. In the first decade of the twentieth century, members of the famed Goodyear family of timber barons arrived to scout the vast spans of untouched pine forest in Washington Parish. Brothers Frank and Charles Goodyear described Washington Parish as home to the heaviest stands of timber they had ever seen. Within

20. Amite City Florida Parish Times, November 15, 29, 1924; Franklinton New Era, May 27, 1909; St. Tammany Farmer, December 5, 1903; Franklinton Era Leader, June 4, October 1, 1925.

21. Amite City Florida Parish Times, January 21, 1922, April 19, 1924; Kentwood Commercial, March 9, 1906;

22. Ponchatoula Enterprise, April 1, August 19, 1921

a matter of years, the Goodyears had created a self-contained community known as Bogalusa, which would be home to the Great Southern Lumber Company, the largest lumber mill in the nation. By 1926, twenty-four lumber companies operated in the Florida parishes. The four largest alone—the Great Southern, the Natalbany Lumber Company near Hammond, and the Rathborne and Williams mills below Ponchatoula—employed 3,325 men and 17 women.[23]

In addition to the infusion of wealth generated by the vastly expanded timber industry, new opportunities connected to the rapid progress occurring also arrived. The ever-growing use of automobiles demanded improved roads, which necessarily tapped another ubiquitous natural resource in the region. Gravel pits sprang up from the Felicianas to Washington Parish as the product revolutionized travel along Louisiana roadways. Large concerns such as the Holloway Gravel Company at Amite City and the Gano Gravel Pit at Franklinton employed both skilled and basic labor at the pits as well as dump-truck drivers, sales representatives, and the like. An even more lucrative industry arrived when oil was discovered in the region. In the summer of 1901, the St. Tammany Farmer reported that oil had been discovered in the area about Hammond. Within months, wells were being drilled in both Tangipahoa and St. Tammany Parishes. Oil executives, who rushed to the area, were careful to avoid offending existing attitudes about land ownership and usage. In September 1901, the Farmer reported that oilmen had hosted "one of the most successful barbeques in the state" at Lees Landing in lower Tangipahoa Parish. The event was designed to bring together local landowners and oil company people to discuss the changes the new industry would bring.[24]

After an initial rapid push, the oil industry developed slowly in the area. But new economic engines were popping up across the region. Upon demonstrating all-weather viability during a massive 1912 flood that nearly destroyed the West Feliciana community at Bayou Sara, Baton Rouge, safe atop the Istrouma Bluffs, grew rapidly along with its primary benefactor, the Standard Oil Company. In the immediate aftermath of the Civil War, the

23. St. Tammany Farmer, May 7, 1904; Owen Hyman, "The Great Southern Lumber Company in Bogalusa, Louisiana, 1902–1935," Southeast Louisiana Review, IV (2012), 6–36; C. W. Goodyear, Bogalusa Story (New York, 1950); Quick, "The History of Bogalusa"; Frank E. Wood, Industrial Directory of Louisiana, 1925–1926 (New Orleans, 1926), 77–85.

24. Wood, Industrial Directory of Louisiana, 72; Amite City Florida Parish Times, November 3, 1923; Amite City Progress, January 11, 1940; Amite City Tangipahoa Parish News, September 15, 1927; St. Tammany Farmer, July 20, August 17, September 7, 28, 1901.

Gullett Cotton Gin Company relocated from New Orleans to Amite City. In addition to bringing scores of skilled and unskilled positions to the region during a turbulent era, the Gullett Company enjoyed the distinction of being the oldest manufacturing establishment, from point of continued operation, in the state. As the largest industry of its kind in the nation, the factory produced cotton gins that were shipped to locations across the South from its vast production warehouse located adjacent to the Illinois Central Railroad. At its height of production, the Gullett Company employed more than 150 men, most of whom were skilled mechanics. A variety of smaller corporations also located in the area. The Roseland Veneer and Package Company filled orders on the international market, as did the Standard Box and Veneer Company of Hammond. Other emerging companies catered to local needs, such as the Hammond Bottling and Ice Company and the Abita Springs Water Company, chartered in St. Tammany Parish in the fall of 1899. Arguing that factories build towns, in the fall of 1901 the *St. Tammany Farmer* noted that Covington alone boasted a broom factory, sawmill, planning mill, rice and grist mill, and an electric light and ice plant. The same article advised that the Southern Industrial Institute, currently under construction, would produce boots, shoes, personal apparel, and household furnishing goods.[25]

Despite the advancing industrialization, the region remained primarily agricultural largely due to the arrival of new types of farming. In the last decade of the nineteenth century commercial dairy farming arrived, and by 1900 it was spreading rapidly, filling the void left by the decline of cotton farming. The *St. Helena Echo* pointed out that not only did dairy farming return a good profit, but the cows also fertilized the land. In the summer of 1910 the first meeting of the Dixie Dairymen's Association was held on the LSU campus in Baton Rouge, signifying the growing importance of dairy farming in the Florida parishes. Industrious farmers along the uplands of the Chappapeela Ridge in eastern Tangipahoa and Washington Parishes also planted tung oil orchards. The product of the trees was considered essential to the production of paints and varnishes, but the industry enjoyed at best mixed results.[26]

25. Baton Rouge *States*, May 3, 4, 1912; "Report of the Commissioner of Labor and Industrial Statistics to the General Assembly of the State of Louisiana" (New Orleans, 1916), 149–51; Amite City *Tangipahoa Parish News*, October 17, November 7, 1925, September 15, 1927; Amite City *Florida Parishes*, June 21, 1913; New Orleans *Picayune*, September 25, 1902; *St. Tammany Farmer*, September 23, 1899, October 12, 1901.

26. Amite City *Florida Parishes*, September 12, 1900; Hammond *Vindicator*, March 29,

A huge new agricultural enterprise, one that would revolutionize farming in the central Florida parishes, arrived at the turn of the century in the form of strawberries. The composition of the soil, proximity of the railroads, and abundance of available labor created a perfect combination for strawberry farming. The new crop provided a profound stimulus for the regional economy. In the first week of May, 1915, 105 railroad carloads of berries were shipped from Tangipahoa Parish alone. Six years later, heralding the most productive season on record, the Ponchatoula *Enterprise* noted that over 1,400 carloads with an average of 700 crates to the car had been shipped from Tangipahoa at the handsome price of $3.50 per crate. Berry farming stimulated the growth of an expanding network of industrial concerns such as canning factories, cold storage plants, and box companies that constructed crates for shipping the berries. By the 1930s, strawberry farming had been completely intertwined with the regional identity. Festivals, stadiums, and scores of other enterprises would be named for the fruit that would become synonymous with the region.[27]

Capitalizing on the changing identity of the area, in the spring of 1922 Amite City sponsored a "Get Acquainted Day," replete with brass bands, sporting events, circus acts, games, and theater. The mass event—which also included a minstrel show, trade fair, and cash prizes for contests, including prettiest girl and laziest man—was designed to show the world that Tangipahoa was open for business and breaking free from its reputation for bloodshed. Yet ads celebrating and encouraging participation in the event included announcements that "full police protection including in addition to local officials a strong presence of picked men to work in plain clothes," as well as a security contingent from the "enforcement division of the prohibition forces" would be present. The announcements warned, "anyone arrested that day for disorderly conduct need not expect a pardon." On the day of the event, local papers announced that an additional contingent of men wearing badges that read "Law and Order" would also be enforcing the peace. Though they were present to ensure a good time, they undoubtedly served as grim

1929; *St. Helena Echo*, December 23, 1910; Baton Rouge *States*, June 15, 1910; Amite City *Lanier's Digest*, October 25, 1929; Records of the Tangipahoa Tung Oil Company, Tangipahoa Tung Oil Collection, CSLS.

27. Amite City *Florida Parishes*, February 29, 1908, June 28, 1913; Amite City *Florida Parish Times*, March 5, 1922; Hammond *Vindicator*, March 29, 1929; Amite City *Times*, May 7, 1915, March 19, 1920; Ponchatoula *Enterprise*, April 8, August 19, 1921; Independence, La., *News*, April 16, 1926; Amite City *Tangipahoa Parish News*, September 15, 1927.

reminders of the historical reality of the troubled region. For that one day at least, Amite City was revealed as both a frontier town and one seeking to embrace the opportunities of the modern order.[28]

To be successful, progressive initiatives require support from more activist government. Unfortunately for proponents of modernity, government mandates and regulations had been anathema for much of the regional population since the hard days of the Civil War and Reconstruction. Memories of high rates of taxation, impressment of personal property, and political impotence burned bright for many, as did societal awareness that such onerous burdens had been overcome through unbridled violence. The requirements of progress seemed destined to collide with the prevailing social conditions in the Florida parishes. Yet change did come. Despite the determined resistance such painful memories provoked for some efforts, in other areas progressive reform proved more acceptable.

Health initiatives in particular served as a widely embraced aspect of reform. Tales of the "hookworm South" remained popular among critics of the states of the old Confederacy. But the reality was less the lazy, inbred ignorance so widely disseminated by those with only contempt for the South, and more a quality of life occasioned by the ubiquitous presence of certain parasites and challenging maladies such as pellagra. Significant advances in confronting the great scourge of the nineteenth century, yellow fever, had been made through quarantine stations that remained evident in the Florida parishes during fever season. Scientific advances also improved survival rates for tetanus, or lockjaw as it was commonly known, though it continued to be a problem particularly in isolated regions of Washington and St. Helena Parishes.[29]

The residents of southeast Louisiana had good reason to support improvements in health care. Morbidity statistics released by the Louisiana State Board of Health for 1918 ranked St. Tammany fourth and Tangipahoa twelfth among the 64 parishes for rates of infectious disease. The following year, although conditions had improved in Tangipahoa, St. Tammany remained the fourth-unhealthiest parish in the state, with East Baton Rouge

28. Amite City Florida Parishes, March 18, 25, April 1, 7, 1922.

29. H. L. Mencken, "The Sahara of the Bozart," in Prejudices, Second Series (New York, 1920); Erskine Caldwell, Tobacco Road (New York, 1932); Todd Savitt and James Young, Disease and Distinctiveness in the American South (Knoxville, 1988); bill of George Sables for thirty days' service as quarantine guard in Springfield, Livingston Parish Times, October 5, 1906; Amite City Florida Parishes, August 2, 1913; Amite City Tangipahoa Parish News, July 7, 1927.

reporting the second-highest rates of infectious disease among the Florida parishes. The report complained that only 23 of the 64 parishes filed regular monthly reports. Included in that number were East Baton Rouge, East Feliciana, Tangipahoa, St. Helena, and Livingston, suggesting more progressive health organization in those parishes. Malaria, gonorrhea, and syphilis were reported as the most chronic maladies in all of the Florida parishes.[30]

Health concerns were dramatically amplified by the international influenza pandemic that raged in the immediate aftermath of World War I. Dr. Oscar Dowling, president of the state board of health, reported that influenza first arrived in Louisiana in September, 1918, and that 9 percent of the state population had been affected, or 244,410 people, with a death rate of 2.2 percent, before the contagion had abated. Though the influenza epidemic did not carry the devastating consequences in southeast Louisiana that it did in some other regions of the world, the heavy press coverage and fear it produced amplified consciousness of health concerns as demonstrated in board of health reports.[31]

A 1927 report saw the highest rates of infectious disease in East Baton Rouge and Washington among the Florida parishes, though overall rates had declined somewhat from the preceding decade. Malaria, hookworm, diphtheria, measles, and typhoid fever proved the most common maladies respectively, though pellagra killed nearly twice as many people in East Feliciana as in second-ranked East Baton Rouge among the Florida parishes.[32]

That health concerns were assuming a more prominent place in the minds of early-twentieth-century policy planners was reflected in efforts to combat mental illness. The Louisiana State Insane Asylum at Jackson, in East Feliciana Parish, served as a model for progressive thinking in a region that often consigned the mentally ill to prison or life as an outcast. The hospital employed considerable numbers of southeast Louisiana residents on its campus designed to isolate the sick while exposing them to the potential curative benefits of country life. In his May, 1900, address to the state legislature, Governor Murphy J. Foster referred to the hospital as the most important state institution and urged increased funding. Foster expressed pride that the hospital serviced individuals from multiple states, noting that patients had increased in number from 804 in 1892 to the current 1900 total of 1,653. In

30. "Biennial Report of the Louisiana State Board of Health to the General Assembly of the State of Louisiana, 1918–1919" (New Orleans, 1919), 23.

31. *Ibid.*, 12–13.

32. "Biennial Report of the Louisiana State Board of Health to the Legislature of the State of Louisiana, 1926–1927" (New Orleans, 1927), 70, 157–60, 241–43.

all, 78 employees worked at the facility with many keeping families on the hospital grounds.[33]

Health initiatives and other progressive reforms require the support of educated individuals. Unfortunately, the Louisiana legislature in the early twentieth century, much like the one today, did not seem to place high value on educating its citizens. In 1910, legislation directed 21.2 percent of state and local expenditures to education, relegating Louisiana to number 43 of 46 in terms of resources devoted to education by the individual states. By 1920, Louisiana had risen to number 42 of 48, though appropriations had decreased to 20.9 percent of state and local totals. The centrality of education for overcoming the challenges of the past and embracing the opportunities of the future nonetheless remained abundantly apparent. Some parish police juries sought to shore up an underfunded system of education by appropriating funds, at times over the objections of some constituents. School attendance reflected the shortcomings in funding. In 1904, white children in Louisiana attended school for seven months on average compared to a little over four months for black children. Washington Parish led the region for white attendance with 84 percent, followed by St. Helena with 80 percent, and East Feliciana with 78 percent student attendance. The lowest white attendance figures were in St. Tammany, where 74 percent of eligible students attended. East Baton Rouge led the region in black student attendance with 75 percent, followed by Livingston with 73 percent and West Feliciana with 69 percent attendance. The lowest black attendance figures were again found in St. Tammany, where 32 percent of black children went to school. In an effort to address attendance, in the winter of 1906 the St. Tammany Teachers Association broke with the past by adopting a resolution pledging to work to make education compulsory in Louisiana.[34]

A powerful vehicle for advancing educational opportunities in the region arrived on September 14, 1925, when Hammond Junior College opened in Tangipahoa Parish. The rapidly growing institution was renamed Southeast-

33. "Message of Governor Murphy J. Foster," in *Official Journal of the Proceedings of the Senate of the State of Louisiana at the First Regular Session of the First General Assembly, 1900* (Baton Rouge, 1900), 15; *Twelfth Census of the United States*, Manuscript, Heads of Households, 1900, Doc. F.2, Roll 118.

34. Amite City *Florida Parishes*, March 8, 1902, October 24, 1903, January 16, 1904; Kentwood *Commercial*, February 23, 1906; Franklinton *New Era*, August 6, 1904; Amite City *Tangipahoa Parish News*, May 27, 1926; "Report of the Superintendent of Education," *Louisiana Documents*, II (Baton Rouge, 1906), vi–vii; "Louisiana State Department of Education Circulars," Circular No. 1787, in Livingston Parish Papers Collection; *St. Tammany Farmer*, September 5, 1903; C. S. Stewart to My Dear Judge, April 29, 1899, in Reid Papers, LLMVC.

ern Louisiana College and later Southeastern Louisiana University. Southeastern would serve not only as the source of higher education for thousands
of regional residents, but also as a crucial economic engine for the area and
the source of scores of local teachers.[35]

Teaching had long been a profession dominated by women, and the Florida parishes proved no different. Whether in one of the single-room K–11
schoolhouses that dotted the countryside or in a more refined private school
such as the Silliman Female Institute in East Feliciana Parish or the Dixon
Academy at Covington, women filled the lion's share of teaching positions.
The same held true in regional Sunday schools. In their capacity as educa-
tors, women shaped thinking among whole generations of young men and
women on subjects that extended beyond the classroom, such as manners,
morals, and ethics. Yet seeking to instill values in residents of a volatile region could often be dangerous. In an article titled "A Cowardly Threatening
Letter," the *St. Tammany Farmer* expressed outrage that Miss Iona Purser
had received a letter asserting, "you are hereby notified that if you don't stop
wearin the britches and runnin that farse you call a Sunday school you will
catch a good cow hidin on the road someday goin home take warnin yours in
ded ernest [sic]." Moving beyond anonymous threats, in 1909 "a lawless band"
tore up the Red Bluffs School near Covington and terrorized the teacher.
The same group was suspected of later leaving a note of warning to the
teacher, an older woman who enjoyed the support of parish officials but was
known to have struggled with some of her patrons.[36]

Teaching offered a point of relevance and empowerment to women who
otherwise remained largely marginalized. Women of the area had occasionally figured significantly in the carnage that plagued the piney-woods parishes, but more often had endured their second-class status in safe obscurity.
The progress occurring regionally, together with the changing national social climate, stimulated increasing assertiveness among women, which in
turn provoked a reaction among some men. Governor Ruffin G. Pleasant's
opposition, along with a majority in the state legislature, to a federal man-

35. Ronald Harris, *We Hail Thee Now Southeastern: Remembering the First Seventy-Five
Years of Southeastern Louisiana University* (Hammond, La., 2000); Hammond *Vindicator*, June
7, 1929; Amite *Progress*, October 1, 1936.

36. Sarah L. Hyde, *Schooling in the Antebellum South: The Rise of Public and Private Education in Louisiana, Mississippi, and Alabama* (Baton Rouge, 2016); Sally G. McMillen, "Southern
Women and the Sunday School Movement, 1865–1915," in Samuel C. Hyde, Jr., ed., *Plain Folk
of the South Revisited* (Baton Rouge, 1997); *St. Tammany Farmer*, August 11, 1900; New Orleans
Picayune, January 24, 1909.

date endorsing suffrage for women provoked a memorable response from one outraged Florida parish matriarch. In reply to the Louisiana legislature's vote against women's suffrage, "Mrs. Morrill" vented, "they don't have brains they have a fungus growth of antiquated ideas from a prehistoric age."[37]

Some men in the Florida parishes seemed determined to keep women in their place, while others went further and sought to roll back their status. In a region characterized by a dysfunctional legal system, an article published in the Amite City *Florida Parish Times* seems almost incomprehensible. In opposition to women serving on juries, the author asserted that women's "deliberative powers do not yield as readily to logic and reason as do those of men." In 1924 the Livingston Parish police jury passed two notable ordinances directed specifically at women. The first mandated that women were not allowed "to wear one-piece swim suits, knickers, or any other dress that exposes their lower extremities." The *Florida Parish Times* complained, "if it stands, this law will cost Livingston businesses a lot." The second law forbade roadside "spooning," along with "petting parties" and lovers "fussing in public." The social attitudes of some seemed decidedly at odds with the cultural changes occurring around them.[38]

In a pointedly demeaning example of the second-rate status often attributed to women, a *Tangipahoa Parish News* editorial called for stronger protections for teenage boys from lascivious women—"divorcees and prostitutes who prey on our young men." The writer argued that young men should enjoy the same protections afforded women and called for "a return to modesty in women"—a code phrase that seemed to say know your place and remain there.[39]

Another factor that seemed poised to advance civilized order in the region was the arrival of a multitude of new forms of entertainment. The days when a corn shucking or barn raising offered a rare opportunity for socializing and entertainment were passing. So too, it was hoped, were the days when getting drunk and shooting someone served as one of the few ways to be noticed. More developed forms of entertainment had been evident in urbanizing Baton Rouge and in the more highly cultured Felicianas since

37. "Message of Governor Ruffin G. Pleasant to the General Assembly," *Official Journal of the Senate of the State of Louisiana, First Regular Session of the Second General Assembly, 1920* (Baton Rouge, 1920), 30–31; Kentwood *Commercial*, April 24, 1896, August 6, 1920; Amite City *Florida Parishes*, April 24, 1896; New Orleans *Picayune*, April 22, 1896, February 22, July 4, December 11, 1897.

38. Amite City *Florida Parish Times*, January 6, 1923, August 16, 1924.

39. Amite City *Tangipahoa Parish News*, November 7, 1925.

the mid-nineteenth century. In 1855, the town of Clinton alone boasted two theatrical troupes, a Shakespearean society, several poetry reading circles, and a thespian orchestra. Yet few sources of organized entertainment beyond church revivals and political barbecues extended to the piney-woods parishes. The stark cultural contrast between the western plantation parishes and the eastern piney-woods parishes contributed to an aura of superiority in the Felicianas. Clinton resident Robert Patrick described the piney-woods folk as virtually without culture, declaring his family had "blessed little to do with them."[40]

As transportation and communication networks spread across the region, it became easier to learn about sources of entertainment and to get to them. The result was a veritable explosion of the fruits of the emerging entertainment industry in the Florida parishes. By the mid-1920s, movie houses, known as "picture shows," and theaters had sprung up across the piney-woods parishes. In Amite City, entrepreneur Sam Currier opened a movie and road-show theater that included high-speed centrifugal cooling fans along with oscillating fans on the walls. The Choctaw Theater, as it was known, opened to great fanfare, hosting a "high class photo play" the first evening followed by the moving picture *Classified*, starring Corinne Griffith, on the second evening. The famed Columbia Theater, which remains a primary engine of the cultural life of Hammond to this day, opened in the same period. Also in Tangipahoa Parish, the Liberty Theater in Independence welcomed guests to its Sunday showings, noting that unlike surrounding communities, Independence had no Sunday blue law to prohibit theater and sporting events on the Sabbath. The Woodman Opera House opened in Amite City, and the same town also revealed its growing Catholic population by hosting a first-ever Mardi Gras celebration. Traveling circus acts began to visit the region, and a variety of towns constructed stages for homegrown theatrical productions. In the summer of 1903, the Covington Pavilion hosted an "extravagant three part play" put on by the St. Tammany Tribe Improved Order of Red Men.[41]

Festivals emerged to celebrate the product of the regional economy. Sev-

40. Clinton *American Patriot*, November 3, December 15, 29, 1855; Clinton *Feliciana Democrat*, April 14, 21, June 2, 9, 30, October 20, 1855; Augustus Carpenter to his Sister, July 9, 1856, in George H. Carpenter Family Papers; Taylor, ed., *Reluctant Rebel*, 9.

41. Amite City *Tangipahoa Parish News*, November 28, 1925, June 3, 10, 24, 1926; Hammond *Vindicator*, August 30, 1929; Amite City *Florida Parishes*, October 24, 1903; Amite City *Tangipahoa Parish News*, September 30, November 25, 1926, July 7, 1927; Independence *News*, March 5, 1926; *St. Tammany Farmer*, August 22, 1903.

eral communities hosted strawberry festivals, with Hammond home to the largest of the era. Scouting also arrived to offer young men an alternative to the traditional leisure activities of the countryside, many of which involved the use of guns. But far and away the biggest entertainment came in the form of organized sports. In December 1899, the United States Senate acknowledged the growth of athletics at American colleges. New Hampshire senator William E. Chandler remarked that team sports, such as football and baseball, offered a wholesome venue for physical and emotional development. Chandler urged that cultivation of such sports at government academies be given the sanction of law. Such high-profile attention stimulated the rapid expansion of team sporting endeavors. By 1901, community clubs were emerging across the state of Louisiana. Over the course of one week in the summer of 1901, the Covington Baseball Club defeated the Columbia Club and the Stauffer Eshleman Club, both out of New Orleans. The *St. Tammany Farmer* noted that both games were played in front of large crowds that "included lots of ladies." At least four baseball clubs were chartered by 1905 in sparsely populated Washington Parish alone, with the teams frequently crossing the state border to play teams from Tylertown, Columbia, and other communities in southwest Mississippi. A spirited 1905 contest between teams from Franklinton and Mt. Herman revealed the rudimentary status of the sport. The Franklinton *New Era* reported that a heated dispute was raging over who won the game since it had been called in the fifth inning due to rain. One writer argued that Mt. Herman won since they were leading when the game was called. The other insisted that such a game should be considered a draw. The newspaper made clear that the rule was not yet clear.[42]

Though baseball proved the premier attraction, football was not far behind. As team sports spread to high schools, communities across southeast Louisiana invested in large football stadiums and elaborate homecoming events. Standout players became local heroes, and towns came to identify with the team mascots and school colors. Concerns about player safety in a contact sport carried little weight in a region accustomed to violence. In the winter of 1903, the *St. Tammany Farmer* reported dryly that football had

42. Amite City *Florida Parishes*, February 3, 1923; Hammond *Vindicator*, May 3, 1929; Amite City *Tangipahoa Parish News*, November 6, 1925, April 15, 22, 29, May 6, 27, 1926, June 23, 1927; New Orleans *Daily Picayune*, December 8, 1899; *St. Tammany Farmer*, June 29, July 6, 1901; Franklinton *New Era*, August 5, 26, 1905; New Orleans *Picayune*, September 18, 1899; Jack T. Kirby, *Rural Worlds Lost: The American South, 1920–1960* (Baton Rouge, 1987), 300–303.

claimed nineteen fatalities nationwide as of Thanksgiving Day. The report noted that scores of other players had been hospitalized.[43]

Other sports, such as basketball, became increasingly popular in the aftermath of World War I, and each offered an outlet for friendly competition between communities and clubs. Proclivities toward violence nonetheless never remained far from the surface in southeast Louisiana, despite appeals for sportsmanship. Kentwood officials filed a lawsuit after a report was published declaring games at the city ball park had become home to constant profanity "where white lightening is the popular and abundant drink." The report criticized the town marshal for "taking his gun and winning the game when the local team cannot win itself." In an article titled "An Ugly Spirit," the Independence News reported that when the local team visited Ponchatoula, the players were treated to mass verbal and physical abuse. The report closed, "it is a known fact that Ponchatoula has never shown a brotherly feeling toward Independence but they could, at least, disguise this condition when we are there as their guests."[44]

With abundant new economic opportunities, technological advances that made life easier, and varieties of new methods to entertain and ventilate aggressive or competitive behavior, early-twentieth-century residents of the piney-woods parishes should have been able to move beyond the burdens of the past. Income, wages, and prospects were all up, yet the high rates of homicide did not correspondingly come down, nor did the legal system, despite some initial optimism, reflect manifest improvement. Perhaps most curious of all, with the exception of the statewide press's sustained howls for the public to take action to restore order, no popular upheaval, calls for outside intervention, or electoral revolution against sitting officials occurred. In virtually every other sense, the piney-woods parishes were entering the modern order. In terms of justice, accountability, and faith in the rule of law, the region remained on the frontier.

43. Amite City Lanier's Digest, November 8, 1929; Ponchatoula Enterprise, August 19, 1921; Amite City Tangipahoa Parish News, October 31, 1925, September 15, 22, October 13, November 10, 1927; St. Tammany Farmer, December 5, 1903.

44. Amite City Florida Parish Times, July 16, 1921; Independence News, February 5, March 5, 1926.

· 9 ·

A PECULIAR SOCIETY DEFINES ITSELF: EQUILIBRIUM

Our bloody days are over, our only red is the red of strawberries.
— W. H. McClendon, speaking at a picnic in Tangipahoa Parish

Consider a society where abundant opportunity beckoned amid bountiful natural resources and rapid progress that offered a vastly improved quality of life. Consider also that in less than a generation, the same region would endure continuing levels of violence that arguably made it the most dangerous rural region in early-twentieth-century Louisiana. Feuds, affairs of honor, and spontaneous acts of violence would continue with startling regularity—yet they would be augmented by new, disturbing acts of brutality. The violence included a small precursor for what today is known as "ethnic cleansing"—a mass hanging that provoked an international incident, large-scale rural race riots, and a dangerous labor dispute that included events defying the most cherished norms of southern culture and identity. Far from retreating amid the progress characterizing the new century, the challenges confronting civilized society adapted to, and overcame, the mandates of the new era.

What can explain why residents of a region experiencing unprecedented growth and opportunity would accept a legal system that offered little protection or justice and almost required people to cling to an antiquated perception of individual rights and accountability? Why did the saner, soberer members of society fail to cooperate to bring about reform and stability? It is simply not enough to report on historical events, particularly profound departures from the norm, and explain them away as *the way things were*. Moreover, detailed analysis of troubled conditions in the past can help us understand, and confront, criminal behavior in the present. Descriptive statistical analysis offers a potential method for explaining why the killing continued during a time of sustained growth amid a populace that accepted things for what they were. Students of sociology are familiar with the term *collective behav-*

ior and use it, at times, to explain seemingly irrational mass behavior. Such interpretive methods are useful but less definite than statistical analysis. A more effective way of interpreting conditions prevailing in the Florida parishes may be found through the use of methods that can demonstrate the presence of equilibrium. In essence, the evidence suggests that for at least a sixty-year period following the close of Reconstruction, society achieved a dynamic working balance wherein individuals frequently resolved perceived personal grievances violently and the residents, accustomed to such behavior, accepted it as the norm of society. In such a condition, the legal system was compromised, and those not involved in the violence chose safe obscurity rather than forthright action for reform. High rates of homicide accordingly continued and were accepted as a part of life by regional residents who lacked incentive to demand change and/or feared the consequences of challenging the status quo. The prevailing status quo therefore resembled a condition revealed in a method of analysis known as *game theory*, or more precisely *Nash equilibrium*.[1]

Game theory may be defined as the study of mathematical models of conflict and cooperation between intelligent, rational decision makers. Simply put, a game is being played by a group of individuals whenever the fate of an individual in the group depends not only on his own actions, but also on the actions of the rest of the individuals in the group. The dangerous conditions confronting society in the piney-woods parishes conform to this scenario. The game must contain a precise set of elements, including players, information and actions available to each at the point of decision, and payoffs for each outcome. Game theorists, typically economists, mathematicians, and the like, use these elements along with a solution concept to identify a set of equilibrium strategies. Equilibrium refers to a stable state in which either a single outcome or a set of outcomes occurs with known probability. Nash equilibrium, named for Princeton University professor John Nash, who advanced understanding of the concept, suggests that each player chooses a strategy that also takes into account the strategy of the other players, but no players change their strategy even though they realize the other players are aware of their intentions. In Nash equilibrium, players lack incentive to change; instead, the incentive is to keep things as they are. If the outcome of

1. For explanations of game theory and Nash equilibrium, see Peter Morris, *Introduction to Game Theory* (New York, 1994); Guillermo Owen, *Game Theory*, 2nd ed. (New York, 1982); Ken Binmore, *Essays on the Foundations of Game Theory* (Cambridge, Mass., 1990); Avinash K. Dixit and Barry J. Nalebuff, *Thinking Strategically: The Competitive Edge in Business, Politics, and Everyday Life* (New York, 1991).

the game suggests equilibrium, that does not necessarily mean that it is best for all players in the game or society as a whole, only that there is balance.[2]

In this scenario, the players in the Florida parishes would include those engaged in violence, and the people at large, a category that would include the victims of homicide. Information and action would be the knowledge that the legal system is ineffective and thus juries are cowed by awareness that an accused killer is likely to walk free and could exact revenge on prosecution witnesses or jurors who vote to convict. The payoff for the killers is the freedom to eliminate rivals or those who offend them absent concern that there will be determined consequences for their actions. The payoff to the people at large is the ability to remain in safe obscurity by refraining from being proactive in opposition to the prevailing absence of justice.

If a matrix is established that offers options to those prone to violence to keep killing or reduce the violence, and the options to the people at large are to become proactive against the violence or remain safely silent, the presence of equilibrium may be identified. Significant evidence exists to suggest that some among those prone to violence may have been psychotic. Remorseless, premeditated murder alone suggests the possible presence of abnormality. Yet most identified killers maintained a rather normal life outside incidents of violence, suggesting that they were less psychotic and more a product of the prevailing culture. Accordingly, the biggest payoff to killers, acting rationally amid the prevailing cultural circumstances, would be to continue being known for a resolution to violence to keep others cowed, less likely to retaliate through word or action, and maintain the status quo that allowed them freedom to act with violence. The biggest payoff to the people at large, similarly acting rationally amid prevailing conditions, is to remain silent, accepting that what is past is in the past; why provoke known killers? In short, let bygones be gone. The evidence demonstrates that the most visible killers, along with the people at large at the advent of the twentieth century, embraced precisely those options.

The problem for society in the Florida parishes is that both those inclined to kill and the people at large have become culturally conditioned to the status quo. Potential killers realize that they can solve a personal difficulty or protect their honor by eliminating a rival effectively, and with finality, through violence. Ever-new groups of killers continue homicidal behavior because there is no incentive to change. Correspondingly, the people at large

---

2. Binmore, *Foundations of Game Theory*, 1–5; Dixit and Nalebuff, *Thinking Strategically*, 76–77.

become accustomed to the safety of silent obscurity and, with a few minor exceptions, continue to embrace the prevailing status quo as well. With no indication of changed behavior among those prone to violence, and no forth-right or visible improvement in the system of justice, the people too have no incentive to change. For both those inclined to kill, and the people who live among them, even as the years go by, the incentive remains to continue the status quo (see Payoff Matrix).

As a result, the piney-woods parishes of southeast Louisiana may be in a condition that resembles Nash equilibrium because both those prone to violence and the people at large have a chosen strategy and neither side can benefit by changing strategies while the other side keeps theirs unchanged. Or, more succinctly stated, neither side has an incentive to change. As such, society enters a sort of stasis where it is in no one's best interest to tip the balance. The existing troubled conditions continue to prevail: many among those prominent in killings from the previous decade or so remain at large while the people, including families of victims, eventually become resigned to their loss—their hostility to, or fear of, the killers never enough incentive to demand change. And the cycle continues, with new killers and victims in a society becoming generationally accommodated to the aberrant state of affairs.

The matrix is designed to provide a reasonable explanation for why society in southeast Louisiana continued on a destructive course despite the progress occurring in so many other areas. The results are consistent with the existing evidence and therefore offer a far more rational interpretive model than the alternative of concluding the region was rife with sociopaths and cowards. If, then, by the first decades of the twentieth century the Florida parishes were in equilibrium, albeit *undesirable equilibrium,* how is that relevant to a study of this nature? The research supporting this project is designed both to inform about conditions from the past and to suggest why they continue in some forms into the present. The nature of equilibrium necessarily indicates a functioning balance that becomes the norm of society. It is important to note that equilibrium does not translate to stability, or an ordered society governed by and subject to the rule of law. Instead, equilibrium refers to the prevailing status quo, whether favorable or unfavorable to society at large. In this case, violence becomes an accepted part of their lives, or more ac-curately stated, it becomes not merely an accepted but an *expected* response to certain situations. The notion that "some folks need a killing," that the consequences of one's actions become secondary to the fear of public and pri-vate humiliation, and the "he had it coming" defense in criminal jury trials, all become a part of the reality of life, just as their presence compromises the system of justice and sustains the cycle of undesirable equilibrium. The process continues until some individual or group makes a *credible commitment* to break the mold of equilibrium. In other words, things stay as they are until

Payoff Matrix

Victims and People at Large

		Proactive against Violence	Stay Silent
Prone to Violence	Keep Killing	2, 1 "War of attrition" (Violent keep killing, but people take action against violence.)	4, 2 "Least preferred" (Violent keep killing, and people remain cowed.)
	Reduce Violence	1, 3 "2nd most preferred" (Violent less overt in the face of people's reaction against violence.)	3, 4 "Most preferred" (Violent less overt to avoid retribution, and people let go of the past.)

- The first number in each grid square is payoff to those prone to violence; the second number in each square represents payoff to the people at large. Number 4 represents the maximum payoff, and number 1 the minimum payoff.
- The "most preferred" circumstance for society as a whole is for the violence to be reduced while the people stay silent, not having to expend any resources and remaining in safe obscurity. Since that scenario would allow the violent to retain a dominant position while also reducing their chance of being accountable for bad behavior, it is the second best condition for them. Though it would be an improved state for the people at large, it does carry some risk. As a result, the "second most preferred" condition—reduced violence while the people become proactive—offers a strong payoff to the people who enjoy reduced violence but the worst payoff to the violent, who surrender their dominant, violence-sustained position amid people expending resources to combat the violence. The "war of attrition" category sees the violent continuing to kill among a people proactive against the violence. Since the people at large are exposing themselves to retribution, this category offers the least payoff for them while the killers too have diminished payoff in face of opposition to their bad behavior. Equilibrium is found in the "least preferred" category, where the violent enjoy the biggest payoff from their dominant position as the people experience at least some payoff through silence and safe obscurity—precisely the condition prevailing in the piney-woods region.
- Since an impartial and effective system of criminal justice is a public good benefiting nearly everyone, the challenge for residents centers on finding a credible enforcement mechanism for cooperation to achieve the "most preferred" category. Cooperation, though, is costly and difficult. Lacking the incentive to incur risk and expend resources to produce such cooperation, the residents persist in low-level equilibrium, the "least preferred" outcome, since no group has an incentive to expend the resources necessary for change.

someone puts their own interests at visible risk in order to break the cycle. As the residents of southeast Louisiana advanced into the twentieth century, no evidence of disruption in the cycle proved evident.[3]

As previously noted, similar conditions prevailed in some other regions of the South, but that they endured with such intensity in the Florida parishes should not be surprising. Since first European contact, the region had endured multiple ethnic overlords who issued conflicting land claims and promoted contrasting cultural priorities. Every major European power that intruded into the North American wilderness exercised control over the region at some period, as intrigue and manipulation of the legal system became a way of life. During the Spanish period especially, army deserters, outlaws of all stripes, former British loyalists, and anyone else hostile to American annexation had been offered safe haven. The colonial period closed in 1810 with a successful armed insurrection against the Spanish government that included a nasty civil war within the West Florida Revolt. At the onset of the American period, overt resistance to an ordered society remained evident among some residents, who resented the expectations of citizenship, such as political participation and jury service. Actions of the state legislature furthered the prevailing uncertainty. In 1823 a measure that sought to separate the Florida parishes from the state of Louisiana failed by one vote in the Louisiana state senate. The political upheaval of the 1840s–1850s, followed by the tumultuous conditions of the Civil War and Reconstruction, highlighted the Florida parishes as a society under stress, just as the bloody chaos of the 1880s–1890s confirmed the region's reputation as a dangerous place for residents and visitors alike. It is little wonder that residents of the Florida parishes accepted things as they were, and even less so that the killing continued.[4]

In a scathing 1909 demand for the restoration of order in the piney-woods parishes, the New Orleans *Picayune* offered a list of all the reasons the re-

3. Hodding Carter, "Not Much of a Man if He Had'nt," *Southern Legacy* (Baton Rouge, 1950), 48–63; Dixit and Nalebuff, *Thinking Strategically*, 143–46.

4. Samuel C. Hyde, Jr., "Consolidating the Revolution: Factionalism and Finesse in the West Florida Revolt, 1810," *Louisiana History*, LI (2010), 261–80; Cody Scallions, "The Rise and Fall of the Original Lone Star State: Infant American Imperialism Ascendant in West Florida," and William S. Belko, "The Origins of the Monroe Doctrine Revisited: The Madison Administration, the West Florida Revolt, and the No Transfer Policy," both in *Florida Historical Quarterly*, XC (2011), 157–220; William C. Davis, *The Rogue Republic: How Would-Be Patriots Waged the Shortest Revolution in American History* (New York, 2011); *Senate Journal*, 1st. Sess., 1823, pp. 13–14, 17–18; Baker to Hamilton, January 21, 1823, in Hamilton Papers.

gion, and especially Tangipahoa Parish, should be a model of progress. The list concluded, "these would seem to be highly civilizing instruments and influences, and yet cowardly assassination and savage human slaughter are as rife there as when the country was densely covered with pine forests and modern development was unknown. The question is naturally asked why this is so and it presses for an answer." The same paper noted that if the majority of the people were not peaceable, "it would be the duty of state authorities to go into that region with sufficient force and subdue its savage people into a condition of civilization and order. What then is the matter?" Grimly answering its own queries, the *Picayune* bemoaned the region's future. "Even if the lawless element is in the minority it is able to so terrorize the balance of the community to such a degree, that the bloody outlaws work their will while everybody submits. As to the courts apparently they punish none of the worst criminals, if indeed they ever get possession of them, but the defaults of the criminal courts are wholly chargeable to the juries." The paper concluded that jurors were either in sympathy with, or terrorized by, the killers, and refused to convict—essential components of the prevailing equilibrium.[5]

The generational challenge of an inept legal system had long undergirded the absence of stability in the piney-woods parishes, and its weakness provided perfect conditions for the violence to flourish. Even in the first decades of the twentieth century, reports submitted to the attorney general by the district attorneys from the various judicial districts across Louisiana remained erratic and limited. Existing records nonetheless demonstrate the leading role the piney-woods parishes of southeast Louisiana played concerning homicide in a violent state. In 1900, of the Florida parishes, only East Baton Rouge submitted a report to the attorney general. Reports submitted from 1902–1912 in two-year intervals per state law do nevertheless reveal a pattern of prosecutorial action. Of the 97 homicide cases that came to court in the two judicial districts of the western plantation parishes, including the city of Baton Rouge, 73 percent resulted in convictions. Of the remaining cases, 22.6 percent resulted in acquittals and 4.4 percent were nol-prossed—the charges against the defendants were dropped. Though the specifics of each case are not available for individual scrutiny, the numbers do suggest an efficiently functioning legal system.[6]

Analysis of the numbers for the eastern piney-woods parishes proves more

5. New Orleans *Picayune*, February 28, 1909.
6. "Report of the Attorney General to the General Assembly of the State of Louisiana," 1900–1902, 1902–1904, 1904–1906, 1906–1908, 1908–1910, 1910–1912.

challenging. By the first decade of the twentieth century, the former Sixteenth Judicial District had been divided into two districts. St. Helena, Livingston, and Tangipahoa Parishes were included in the new Twenty-Fifth Judicial District, while Washington and St. Tammany comprised the Twenty-Sixth District. For the period 1904–1906, the Twenty-Fifth District submitted no report. In his own report to the legislature, an exasperated attorney general Walter Guion complained that he had made repeated written requests for the Twenty-Fifth District report but had received no response. Existing numbers from the two piney-woods districts nonetheless reveal that in the period 1902–1912, 174 homicide cases were brought to court. An additional 23 murder cases were pending in the Twenty-Fifth District, and new district attorney W. H. McClendon added a contemptuous note asserting that ten of that number were known murderers who had never been arrested. Of the cases that actually went to court, 48 percent resulted in convictions, and almost 42 percent were acquitted. Fully 10 percent of the cases that grand juries sent forward for trial were nol-prossed. A startling 76.4 percent of the nol-prossed cases and 60.8 percent of the acquittals came from Tangipahoa.[7]

The vast chasm separating conviction and nol-prossed rates between the plantation and piney-woods parishes does not necessarily confirm the superior performance of the system of justice in one region over the other. It does, however, offer additional evidence of the weakness of the system in the piney-woods region and highlights Tangipahoa Parish's role as the epicenter of the trouble. The same pattern continued over the course of the next two decades. In 1920, though all the plantation parishes reported marked reductions in prosecutions for homicidal behavior, the district attorney for the Twenty-Fifth Judicial District, Matthew Allen, reported 4 convictions, 19 acquittals, and 33 cases pending, all for murder and attempted murder. A whopping 50 of the 56 cases were concentrated in Tangipahoa. Washington Parish followed closely among the piney-woods parishes. District Attorney J. Vol Brock reported 20 convictions, 8 acquittals, 2 nol-prossed, and 2 cases pending, all for murder and attempted murder. St. Tammany Parish filed no report that year. By 1929, the Twenty-Fifth and Twenty-Sixth Judicial Districts had become the Twenty-First and Twenty-Second Districts, respectively. District Attorney Amos L. Ponder of the Twenty-First District reported only convictions, noting that 16 of the 19 for murder or attempted murder occurred in Tangipahoa Parish. Sidney Frederick, district attorney

7. Ibid.

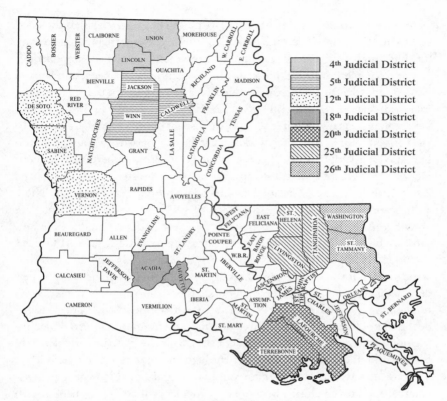

	4th Judicial District
	5th Judicial District
	12th Judicial District
	18th Judicial District
	20th Judicial District
	25th Judicial District
	26th Judicial District

Judicial Districts of Louisiana in the Early Twentieth Century
Map by Mary Lee Eggart

in the Twenty-Second District, reported 18 convictions, 2 acquittals, and 2 nol-prossed cases for the same crimes, with 17 of the 22 total cases occurring in Washington Parish.[8]

Other regions of Louisiana shared in the violence, but few compared to the eastern Florida parishes (see Table 13). In the same 1902–1912 time frame, the Fourth Judicial District, which included Lincoln and Union Parishes in north-central Louisiana, accounted for 55 murders. Of those cases, 49 percent resulted in convictions, 47 percent acquittals, and 3 percent

8. "Report of the Attorney General to the General Assembly of the State of Louisiana, 1918–1920" (New Orleans, 1920); "Statistical Report of the Attorney General to the Governor and the Legislature of the State of Louisiana, 1928–1930" (New Orleans, 1930).

were nol-prossed. In the neighboring Fifth Judicial District, which included Caldwell, Winn, and Jackson Parishes, 52 murder cases were brought to trial. Of that number, 59 percent resulted in conviction, 35 percent were acquitted, and 6 percent were nol-prossed. The Twelfth Judicial District, in the old borderlands territory along the Sabine River in the western part of the state, included Vernon, Sabine, and DeSoto Parishes. Historically known as a troubled region in its own right, the Twelfth District exhibits numbers closest to the figures found in the piney woods of the Florida parishes, though they too remained markedly lower. Of the 101 homicide cases, 56 percent were convictions, 28 percent acquittals, and 16 percent nol-prossed. In Acadiana, the Eighteenth Judicial District included Acadia and Lafayette Parishes, where 54 homicides were tried in the same period. Of those cases, 51 percent were convictions, 42 percent were acquittals, and just under 7 percent were nol-prossed. Finally, in the deep Delta country, the Twentieth Judicial District included Lafourche and Terrebonne Parishes. The 37 homicide cases that went to trial in the sample period resulted in 64 percent convictions, 21 percent acquittals, and 15 percent nol-prossed. For the 1920 reporting period, no reports were filed from the Fourth and Twelfth Districts, but prosecutions declined notably in the other three districts and a similar pattern of declining homicide cases coming to court continued for the Fourth, Fifth, Twelfth, Eighteenth, and Twentieth Districts through the 1929 reporting period.[9]

To be effective, a legal system requires a complicated blend of specific elements that proved elusive in the piney-woods parishes. Justice begins with the people who enforce it: competent officials committed to the performance of their duties must be present from the sheriff's office to the judge's chamber. A single corrupt sheriff's deputy or, worse, a district attorney partisan to certain factions or families can compromise the integrity of the entire system. Even with reliable officials in place, their labors matter little if the people do not provide sufficient financial support and, most important, virtuous jury service. Finally, an effective system requires adequate facilities to incarcerate and effectively punish those in violation of the law.

Every element necessary for competent dispensation of justice was lacking or marginalized in the piney-woods parishes. To begin with, the jails in the region were so notoriously decrepit and ill prepared for service that many convicted criminals had little to fear. Alvin Carter, who shot and killed

9. "Report of the Attorney General to the General Assembly of the State of Louisiana," 1900–1902, 1902–1904, 1904–1906, 1906–1908, 1908–1910, 1910–1912, 1918–1920, 1928–1930; Vandal, *Rethinking Southern Violence*.

Table 13. Recorded Homicides in Sample Judicial Districts, 1902–1912

Judicial District	Parishes Included	District Population 1900	1910	Reported Homicides (1902–12)	% Conviction	% Acquittal	% Nol-Prossed
Fourth	Lincoln Union	34,48	38,936	55	49	47	3
Fifth	Caldwell Winn Jackson	25,684	40,768	52	59	35	6
Twelfth	Vernon Sabine DeSoto	50,811	64,947	101	56	28	16
Eighteenth	Acadia Lafayette	46,308	60,580	54	51	42	7
Twentieth	Lafourche Terrebonne	53,346	61,431	37	64	21	15
Twenty-Fifth	Tangipahoa Livingston St. Helena	34,204	48,959	131*	38	46	16
Twenty-Sixth	St. Tammany Washington	22,963	37,803	53	69	27	4

*Includes the ten "known murders" wherein the perpetrator had never been arrested as reported by the district attorney.

Sources: United States Census Compendium, 1900 and 1910; "Report of the Attorney General to the General Assembly of the State of Louisiana," 1900–1902, 1902–1904, 1904–1906, 1906–1908, 1908–1910, 1910–1912.

his brother-in-law David Wall at Line Creek Church in 1903, was jailed in Amite City for only three months before "picking his way" through the wall and fleeing to South America. In an article noting that five prisoners had escaped from the same jail on November 22, 1912, the Amite City *Florida Parishes* complained that it was the fourth jailbreak in less than a year. That same year, four black prisoners charged with minor offenses escaped. The Kentwood *Commercial* expressed little surprise, noting that they had escaped the same way Will Varnado, who murdered Jeff Amacker, escaped several years earlier, "the bars on the window having never been repaired." Varnado, described as a vicious character who had murdered several others prior to Amacker, had sawed through the bars and let himself down the wall by use of a blanket to a waiting buggy, his mother having allegedly provided the saw. Only a few months later, Hines Hughes, charged with attempted murder, escaped with two others in precisely the same manner. After barely holding back a lynch mob in January 1909, Tangipahoa sheriff John Saal transferred three of the most dangerous men incarcerated in the "rickety parish jail" to New Orleans for safekeeping. The ever-growing list of escapes from the Tangipahoa Parish jail prompted an outraged Judge Steven Ellis in the spring of 1913 to order the parish grand jury to complete a survey of the prison and suggest security improvements. Inadequate prison facilities were not unique to Tangipahoa Parish. In the fall of 1907, three prisoners boldly broke out of the Washington Parish jail at Franklinton before amazed onlookers. A mass jailbreak in the fall of 1899 similarly occurred at the St. Tammany Parish jail in Covington. In a disturbing assessment of the suspect nature of the pursuit of justice in the region, the Franklinton *Era Leader*, reporting on a 1918 escape that included an accused rapist, noted that since the criminals were not locals it was believed they had made good their escape and no pursuit would be offered.[10]

Just how vigorously criminals would be pursued remained at the discretion of local law enforcement, which in turn depended on the level of competence and virtue evident among the people. Accounts published in the regional press along with official reports regularly noted incidents of juries dismissed due to improper paperwork or illegal tampering with criminal dockets. In one incident, the custodian of the Livingston Parish courthouse informed Judge Robert Reid that someone had broken into the courthouse and stolen every indictment. Attorneys joined members of the public in regularly attempting to influence the system of justice behind the scenes, requesting lists of jurors to be bribed or intimidated, or suggesting favors in exchange for acquittal of their client. In an article titled "Growing Plentiful Crops of Murderers," the *Picayune* condemned juries in the piney-woods parishes, arguing, "murderers are confident that no jury will hang a white man and that any term of imprisonment will be brought to an end quickly by political influence." Grand juries too frequently sought safe obscurity, or accepted the "he had it coming" defense and failed to indict guilty parties. In the spring of 1908,

10. Amite City *Florida Parishes*, October 29, 1910, November 23, 1912, June 21, 1913; Kentwood *Commercial*, April 25, 1912; Franklinton *New Era*, September 5, 1907; Amite City *Sun*, March 21, 1913; Twenty-Fifth Judicial District Court, Indictment and Appearances Bonds File, 1909, "State of Louisiana vs. Hines Hughes," docket no. 1472, Tangipahoa Parish Clerk of Court Archives; *St. Tammany Farmer*, October 28, 1899; Franklinton *Era Leader*, January 31, 1918; Baton Rouge *States*, June 24, 1910; New Orleans *Picayune*, June 20, 1899, January 24, 26, 1909, February 11, 1913.

the *St. Tammany Farmer* called for correction in the abuses of the grand jury system, urging the governor to instruct the attorney general to file a bill of information in cases where the grand jury failed to indict. That same year Governor Newton Blanchard chastised the prevailing grand jury system, noting, "a man can only be tried in a capital crime by presentment of a grand jury, if the grand jury will not indict, the state is denied its day in court to vindicate its own laws."[11]

Reflecting the same limitations evident in those serving on juries, regional sheriffs and their deputies varied widely in terms of both their effectiveness and their commitment to justice. In April 1905, the Amite City *Florida Parishes* lamented the condition of the sheriff's office in Tangipahoa: "The conduct of the sheriff's office in this parish in the past has left very much to be desired." In the summer of 1908, a chorus of voices urged the legislature to significantly raise the salaries of regional sheriffs in order to better attract competent men. A good example of the need for competence emerged in Livingston Parish when a deputy sheriff brought a friend along to make an arrest on a minor charge. After securing the fugitive, the deputy left him in the car with the friend, who permitted the accused to enter a café for a cup of coffee. When the man tried to flee, the friend shot him twice in the back and killed him. In November 1900, the Livingston Parish judicial system was thrown into near chaos when Sheriff L. D. Allen was arrested for shooting with intent to commit murder. Coroner J. B. Odom was called upon by the court to serve as acting sheriff until Allen was later released by a grand jury. In neighboring Tangipahoa Parish, Sheriff John Ballard was forced to resign when three thousand dollars turned up missing from his account. The former sheriff avoided jail time in an agreement to pay back the money. Hammond city marshal Oscar Joiner was charged with three separate murders of respected citizens. In the most outrageous case, he shot and killed prominent physician J. A. Cannon, who had rebuked him for beating a boy

11. Kentwood *Commercial*, January 15, 1908; A. W. Kinchen to Robert Reid, November 2, 1897, M. Cooper to Reid, February 9, 1899, Benjamin Miller to Reid, July 29, 1898, W. F. Kernan to Joe Reid, January 30, 1891, all in Reid Papers, CSLS; New Orleans *Picayune*, May 16, June 20, 1899; Ponchatoula *Enterprise*, June 16, 1922; Amite City *Tangipahoa Parish News*, May 20, 1926; "Cases Argued and Determined in the Supreme Court of Louisiana, November 1906," *Louisiana Reports*, LXVIII, Appeal of Defendants Bud Caron and Hines Hughes for Murder of Eugene McClendon, August 11, 1906 (St. Paul, Minn., 1907), 349–60; New Orleans *Picayune*, October 30, 1901; *St. Tammany Farmer*, May 16, 1908; "Message of the Governor to the General Assembly of the State of Louisiana," *Louisiana Documents*, I (Baton Rouge, 1908), 58–60.

Joiner accused of telling authorities he had killed squirrels out of season. In a dramatic demonstration of the prevailing ill-defined concept of justice, the *Tangipahoa Parish News* published an article titled "Oscar Joiner Must Hang" that closed with the assertion, "we do not advocate lynch law, but it looks like a good invitation to the people to inaugurate the system if this man is not effectively checked." With such examples being set by the presiding legal officers, it is not surprising that the courtroom itself sometimes descended to the realm of a cage fight. During a simple hearing concerning a peace bond in the Tangipahoa courthouse, John Dunnington, Sr., along with his son John, Jr., and Elmer Dunnington, attacked Ed Bickford and his brother George. Before order was restored, the Dunningtons had bitten off one of Ed Bickford's ears and ripped two handfuls of hair from his head.[12]

A particularly ludicrous example of law enforcement incompetence occurred in Amite City on Mardi Gras Day of 1902. Tangipahoa parish deputies allowed William Perry, who was an inmate in the parish jail, to go outside and watch the "magnificent Carnival Club parade" that was processing through the streets of the town. Perry promptly started a fight that resulted in a shootout. In the aftermath, two people lay dead—sixty-five-year-old Mrs. Faraba Russell and Perry.[13]

The enduring pattern of social equilibrium that facilitated the continuing culture of violence was summed up by Amite City attorney W. H. McClendon in a 1926 article titled "Why the Criminal Laws Are Not Enforced." McClendon laid blame for the ongoing violence squarely at the feet of the people, identifying as corrupting factors ever-present sympathy for the accused, the avoidance of jury service by good people, adherence to personal sensibilities rather than evidence in making decisions as jurors, and the gullibility of religious folk who believed the guilty when they said they had changed. Such succinct assessments of prevailing conditions failed to satisfy some residents. A particularly despicable murder in the spring of 1927 provoked Amite City newspaperman Lee Lanier to call for outside intervention. In May of that year, the body of young Henry Forest had been found along a pathway leading to the main highway between Springfield and Ponchatoula. Forest had been beaten and shot once in the head. The killer had laid his body out neatly

12. *St. Tammany Farmer*, June 13, 1908; Amite City *Florida Parishes*, April 29, 1905, August 3, 1907; Hammond *Vindicator*, October 11, 1929; Twenty-First Judicial District Court, Division A and B, Minute Books, No. 2, November 20, 1900, 185, Livingston Parish Courthouse; Amite City *Tangipahoa Parish News*, October 17, 24, 1925; Ponchatoula *Enterprise*, February 10, 17, 1922; Amite City *Florida Parish Times*, May 3, 31, 1924.
13. *St. Tammany Farmer*, February 15, 1902.

with his hands folded on his chest. Forest, who was scheduled to be married the next day, had just left his fiancée's home and was known to be carrying a large sum of money for the planned wedding and honeymoon. The case remained unresolved for nearly two years until an outraged Lanier called upon his friend, Chicago detective A. R. Osborn, who had broken the famed Leopold and Loeb case, to assist in the investigation. Within days of Osborn's arrival, the murderer was apprehended. Lanier later founded a separate paper whose title line read "Devoted to the Restoration of Orderly Government," seemingly wishful thinking in the troubled eastern Florida parishes.[14]

In the prevailing chaotic circumstances, criminal behavior flourished. Through the first three decades of the twentieth century the violence continued at an unrelenting pace, though its character had changed in some regards. To begin with, the violence that had been overwhelmingly concentrated in the rolling hill country of central and northern St. Helena, Washington, and especially Tangipahoa Parish began to shift south. In the late nineteenth century, approximately four of every five homicides occurred north of a dividing line equivalent to the northern border of Livingston Parish (see map 2). By 1920 the same uplands region accounted for two of every four murders. Although the environs about the towns of Amite City, Tangipahoa, and Franklinton continued to endure abundant violence, they were now being rivaled by the areas around Hammond, Springfield, and Covington. The societal equilibrium concerning accountability, personal responsibility, and the limitations of the system of justice was expanding to previously less affected regions of the eastern parishes as the limits of that system became ever more apparent.[15]

Another change in the character of the violence resulted from a demographic shift. In the late nineteenth and early twentieth centuries, as scores of Italian and Hungarian immigrants flocked to the region, Tangipahoa and Livingston Parishes became home to the largest rural Italian and Hungarian

14. Amite City *Tangipahoa Parish News*, May 26, June 30, 1927; Amite City *Lanier's Digest*, August 9, 1929.

15. Sixteenth Judicial District Court Minute Books, Nos. 4–7, Twenty-Fifth Judicial District Court Minute Book, No. 1, both in Tangipahoa Parish Clerk of Court Archives; Twenty-First Judicial District Court Minute Books, Nos. 2–7, Twenty-Fifth Judicial District Court Minute Book No. 3, both in Livingston Parish Courthouse; New Orleans *Picayune*, June 15, July 12, 1897, October 9, 10, 1899, February 7, 1901, February 28, 1909; Kentwood *Commercial*, March 27, 1897; Amite City *Florida Parishes*, November 22, 1913, March 18, 1922; Amite City *Florida Parish Times*, March 5, 1922, February 10, 1923, March 8, 1924; Ponchatoula *Enterprise*, January 20, 1921, January 27, February 10, 17, March 3, 24, April 14, May 19, 1922; Baton Rouge *States*, February 21, 1901; Franklinton *Era Leader*, September 3, November 5, 1925.

communities respectively in the nation. The Italians, many of them Sicilian, thrived in the booming truck farming industry that paralleled the Illinois Central Railroad line in Tangipahoa Parish, while the Hungarians set up logging communities in neighboring Livingston. The Hungarians lived a mostly peaceful existence, cutting timber and raising crops. Many Italians, by contrast, continued their Old World traditions that included personal feuds and vendettas. Those traditions fit perfectly with conditions in Tangipahoa Parish, exacerbating the violence.[16]

Upon learning that his brother-in-law Andrea Anato had allegedly "been too familiar" with his sixteen-year-old wife a few days before their wedding, Angelo Giurlando returned to Independence from his new home in Rockford, Illinois. Giurlando visited with his wife's family and then invited Anato to go with him into town, all the while showing no anger. Once in the village of Independence, he led Anato to the main street before pulling a pistol and shooting the young man five times as he begged for his life. Giurlando then advised the stunned onlookers that he had killed Anato in town "so that all would see and know it had been necessary," and that his only regret was that he had not killed Anato sooner. After surviving a gunshot wound inflicted by his brother-in-law Joe Cascio a month earlier, Joe Fasulo tracked Cascio down and engaged in a "spectacular shooting" with him in the streets of Amite City that left Cascio dead. The dead man's brother John was arrested the following day for threatening to kill Fasulo's wife and children in revenge.[17]

In some communities, such as Amite City and Independence, the Italians were warmly received; in others, they were treated with open hostility. The *Feliciana Record* echoed the disdain that some residents in the Felicianas held for Italians, calling them "the scum of Europe who will stop in New Orleans sell fruit and be voted by the New Orleans bosses for the Ring ticket and destroy the country votes." Some areas were proactive in their persecution of the new arrivals. After a crime was allegedly committed by Italians in another portion of the parish, the city marshal in Ponchatoula stopped a suspicious-looking man and asked his nationality. The marshal told the Ponchatoula *Enterprise* that when the man responded "French," it sounded like "wop lingo" so he arrested him. The *Enterprise* continued, "Italians are scarce

16. Victoria Mocsary, "Hungarian Settlement, 1896–2012: A Synthesis," *Southeast Louisiana Review,* IV (2012), 69–94; John Baiamonte, Jr., "Community Life in the Italian Colonies of Tangipahoa Parish, Louisiana, 1890–1950," *Louisiana History,* XXX (1989), 365–97; Amite City *Advocate,* April 4, 1907.

17. Amite City *Florida Parish Times,* December 17, 1921, January 14, 1922; Amite City *Florida Parishes,* April 1, May 6, 27, 1922.

in this particular portion of the parish so it is easy to catch them. Most of the Italians to the north of us know that they are not wanted in this community and stay out." A couple of weeks later, the same paper added, "mighty few Italians venture into Ponchatoula knowing as they do that they are persona non grata, and in a way it was easy for the marshal to spot the wop when he came."[18]

By the summer of 1921, it was becoming unsafe for enterprising Italians to even visit Ponchatoula. In July, 1921, Marshal Ed Tucker arrested two Italians for "illegally" selling bananas from a truck. The local paper vented, "just why these Italians summoned up enough nerve to come to Ponchatoula when they know they are not wanted here is not known, but they lost no time getting out of town as soon as they were released from custody and it is probably a good thing they did as a large number of citizens were beginning to congregate, and just what might have happened is hard to tell."[19]

Ponchatoula was not the only community to exhibit hostility to Italian immigrants. At the northern end of Tangipahoa Parish, something akin to ethnic cleansing was taking place. In the winter of 1908, a mass meeting in Kentwood produced a demand from local residents that all Italians leave the town by the following Saturday night. Approximately 160 Italians resided in the community, most employed at the lumber mills. When a series of layoffs created economic stress in the town, a committee of twelve white men visited the Italian quarter of Kentwood, telling residents that if they did not leave they would be "blown up in their houses with dynamite." The *Florida Parishes* reported that twenty Italian families quickly fled to New Orleans, but that Sheriff John Saal was urging others to stay. Harassment of the remaining Italian residents nonetheless continued. In March of the same year, Company I, First Regiment Louisiana State Militia, was deployed to Kentwood to assist hard-pressed local officials in protecting the Italian community. Sheriff Saal and a detachment of soldiers arrested six men for intimidation. As late as the fall of 1921, Italian merchants and laborers in Kentwood continued to receive threatening letters advising them to get out of town.[20]

The growing Italian community contributed to the emergence of a revived Ku Klux Klan in the region that included many prominent individuals. In a charged judicial race in the spring of 1923, Robert Ellis and Columbus Reid each claimed that the other was a member of the Klan. The sniping

18. Jackson *Feliciana Record*, July 31, 1909; Ponchatoula *Enterprise*, May 13, 27, 1921.
19. Ponchatoula *Enterprise*, July 15, 1921.
20. Amite City *Florida Parishes*, February 29, 1908; New Orleans *Picayune*, March 2, 1908; Amite City *Florida Parish Times*, October 8, 1921.

between Ellis and Reid led H. F. Brunot of Baton Rouge to enter the race as an avowed anti-Klan candidate. The *Florida Parish Times* noted that support, or lack thereof, of the KKK was the only division evident in the election. Emphasizing the depth of Klan influence, the same paper added mockingly, "if the Klan were to confront authorities in Tangipahoa they would have to march up to the front door, prop up the hood and mask on a broomstick and then run around through the back and open the front door to receive the delegation." More than twenty thousand people attended a mass Klan rally at Hammond in September 1923, where more than one thousand were initiated, or "naturalized," around a fiery cross. The Kentwood *Commercial* called for the formation of a Klan chapter in Kentwood, reminding readers that the KKK swept the carpetbaggers from power during Reconstruction. In Ponchatoula, the Klan announced its arrival when five robed members interrupted a service at the Baptist church and silently presented the pastor with a sealed envelope containing one hundred dollars "to be used for advancing the cause of Christianity in Ponchatoula."[21]

Klan support for Christianity did not extend to the Catholic Church. Indeed, Klan activity provoked a rare statement on the prevailing violence and intimidation practices from a regional religious community that otherwise seemed completely cowed by or uninterested in the troubled circumstances. Four prominent members of the St. Helena Catholic Church at Amite City penned a letter to a local newspaper disputing rumors that a prominent candidate for judge was no friend of the Catholic Church, only to disavow the letter the following week after the Klan endorsed the same candidate. Some church officials may have remembered that an elderly minister was nearly beaten to death when he spoke out against the violence in 1897, or that their relationship to the Lord's work offered no protection as evidenced by the murder of itinerant preacher S. B. Mullen. Others may have believed the prevailing circumstances remained God's will or that conditions were better addressed through prayer. Regardless of motive, the deafening silence from the religious community did little to confront the growing bigotry and intimidation.[22]

Ethnic bigotry was not the only change in the face of the violence. Many

21. Amite City *Florida Parish Times*, January 13, 20, March 3, 17, 24, 31, April 7, 28, July 21, August 25, September 28, 1923; Kentwood *Commercial*, August 6, 1920; Ponchatoula *Enterprise*, July 28, 1922.

22. Amite City *Florida Parish Times*, March 24, 31, 1923; *St. Helena Echo*, December 17, 1897; New Orleans *Times Democrat*, July 11, 14, 15, 19, August 3, December 13, 14, 25, 1897; Kentwood *Commercial*, December 18, 1897.

of the most visible individuals connected with the large-scale feuds had retreated from public view. Members of the Lanier and Kirby families, survivors of the bloody Tanner-Kirby feud in Livingston and St. Helena Parishes,
relocated away from one another to allow passions to subside. A similar "distance apart keeps the peace" pattern was followed among survivors of the
Jolly-Cousin feud in St. Tammany. High-profile members of the Branch men,
prominent in so many homicides in Tangipahoa and Washington Parishes
and the subject of numerous spectacular trials and controversies, sought to
recast their image. After killing another prominent member of a large family,
specifically Dewitt Varnado during a card game in Washington Parish, Otto
Bamber, who news accounts referenced as a man "who has figured conspic-
uously in Tangipahoa Parish feuds," became a self-styled preacher. Bamber's
newfound relationship with the Lord failed to protect him; he was murdered
in Cleveland, Mississippi, in 1912. One of the Gill brothers also became a
country preacher, yet he too found forgiveness for the past elusive. In October
1913 at a bank in McComb, Mississippi, he attempted to apologize for his role
in Sam Hyde's murder to one of Hyde's sons. He barely escaped with his life
by crawling out a back window of the bank and fleeing into a nearby swamp.[23]

As the older feuds diminished, new ones took their place, but they proved
less organized and more prone to happenchance violence. When John Stewart encountered Henry Hurst along a roadway in St. Helena Parish in December 1906, Stewart shot him multiple times with a shotgun, an "old feud
having existed between them." In a strikingly similar case, Ras Rogers encountered another man named Stewart on a road just west of Tickfaw in Tangipahoa Parish. When Rogers told Stewart that he "had lived long enough,"
Stewart beat him to the draw and settled their old feud by killing him. Ben
Lindsey and William Oliphant met to settle a long-running feud that had
spread to their children. The two residents of Pine Grove in St. Helena Parish
exchanged shotgun blasts that killed Lindsey outright and sent Oliphant to
the hospital in critical condition. Frank Allison and Marshall Magee killed

23. Baton Rouge *Capitolian Advocate*, May 22, 24, 1883; Magnolia *Gazette*, May 31, 1883;
"Biennial Report of the Attorney General to the General Assembly of Louisiana, 1888–1889,"
Louisiana Legislative Documents, 1890, p. 80; New Orleans *Picayune*, March 27, November 22,
27, 1897; Kentwood *Commercial*, December 4, 1897; undated newspaper clipping from *St. Hel-
ena Echo*, in Reid Papers, CSLS; Franklinton *Era Leader*, May 10, 30, 1912; E. Russ Williams,
Jr., *History of Washington Parish, Louisiana, 1798–1992* (Monroe, La., 1994); Baton Rouge
States, February 21, 1901; Interviews of Eugene Watson, R. A. Kent, Jr., and Samuel C. Hyde,
Sr., December 1980, August 1991, and July 1990; Bankston and Allen, "Rural Social Areas
and Patterns of Homicide," 223–37.

each other in a similar duel near Talisheek campground in Washington Parish. Through the fall and into the winter of 1929, the Sharp and Holden families exchanged gunfire near their residences along Big Chappapeela Creek. The feud subsided with the death of Calvin Holden and the arrest of Wilson Sharp.[24]

Other feuds emerged and terminated in a single day. On a spring morning in 1924, Wheat Rogers and John Johnson got into an argument that led both men to publicly announce that they had it in for the other. When the two men encountered each other later that day, Johnson shot and killed Rogers, then calmly turned himself in claiming justifiable homicide. Simon Oliphant was bushwhacked on his way to a religious service near Covington, two loads of buckshot and three pistol shots ensuring his death. Oliphant had challenged his brother-in-law Reddick Joiner to fight earlier in the day, and many believed the humiliation Joiner suffered led to Oliphant's death. Similarly, after a dispute earlier in the day Meyer Willie and Collier Fairburn bushwhacked and killed Charles Bossier on an isolated road northwest of Covington. Bossier's uncle William Bossier was similarly killed in an afternoon shootout in Covington that followed a morning argument.[25]

Some murders arose from affronts to honor, particularly in defense of the "fairer sex." Tobias Thornhill was shot trying to protect a friend who had inadvertently torn a girl's dress at a church picnic along the state line south of Magnolia, Mississippi. The shooter, Sam Brumfield, cared little that it had been an accident. In a similar case, Kentwood resident Ike Tate killed a man named Newman for using "insulting language" in front of his home in the presence of his wife. Protecting women and coveting their affection seemed to walk hand in hand. Finley Ballard joined his brother Willie in beating Noel West to death with a pine knot in a jealous rage over a girl both Willie and Noel had dated. Jealousy claimed other lives. Hattie Leroux, "an attractive widow of Tangipahoa," was murdered by a man who insisted that if he could not have her no one could. Leroux was killed in her bed; the baby who was sleeping with her was found playing in its mother's blood when the body was discovered. Two young male cousins who were sleeping in another room said they did not rise when they heard the shot as it was not uncommon to hear shooting in Tangipahoa. In other cases, women proved the aggressors.

24. Amite City *Florida Parishes*, December 22, 1906; Amite City *Florida Parish Times*, September 29, 1923, February 2, 1924; Amite City *Lanier's Digest*, October 18, November 8, 1929; *St. Tammany Farmer*, September 19, 1903.

25. Amite City *Florida Parish Times*, May 3, 1924; *St. Tammany Farmer*, December 23, 1899; New Orleans *Picayune*, July 18, 19, 25, August 1, 8, September 11, October 7, 1899.

In the summer of 1913, the Amite City *Florida Parishes* bemoaned the lack of justice meted out to female killers: "It appears practically impossible to convict a woman in Louisiana if she has committed no greater crime than killing a man. Law and evidence are swept aside and an unwritten law is used as a subterfuge to override justice."[26]

Other homicides occurred in connection with criminal behavior. In the summer of 1907, after Mrs. Charles Nelson was found murdered with her "face almost blown to bits" in her front yard in Hammond, neighbors accused a would-be thief of the crime. Joe Amato, who had been briefly jailed for "crimes against his daughter," was bushwhacked and killed near Tickfaw on a road in plain view of four houses. B. F. Scarborough's accusation that Dobb Davis had stolen some of his hogs from his farm near Slidell provoked bad blood for years. The trouble climaxed when Davis along with two of his sons was arrested for shooting and wounding Scarborough and murdering his three-year-old daughter. In perhaps one of the last acts involving this particular crime nationally, Ike Starns was shot and killed in the streets of Hammond as he attempted to murder Dr. S. L. Newsom, whom Starns and his brothers had tarred and feathered in Livingston Parish four years earlier.[27]

Stories connected to some victims of murderous criminal activity are lost to the historical record. In the spring of 1927, the mutilated body of a young man identified only by tattoos bearing a skull and a dragon was found crammed under a bridge along a parish road near Tickfaw. Though the victim had been shot four times in the back, no one in the area had heard shots or witnessed anything. Four months later, Lonnie Moak was found floating face down in Bogalusa Creek with a twenty-pound weight tied to his neck. Moak had been accused of theft, but no one had any information concerning his death or the whereabouts of the stolen funds. When the bullet-riddled body of a man some believed to be a merchant named Cambert was found below Denham Springs in Livingston Parish, a story circulated that he had been killed by a fellow merchant. No one came forward to substantiate the story, and the limited press coverage of the crime quickly ceased.[28]

26. Amite City *Florida Parishes*, July 23, 1910, April 22, 1922, August 16, 1913; St. *Tammany Farmer*, December 7, 1901; New Orleans *Picayune*, November 3, 1901; Amite City *Florida Parish Times*, January 7, 1922.

27. Amite City *Florida Parishes*, August 10, 1907; Amite City *Florida Parish Times*, January 14, 1922; Ponchatoula *Enterprise*, January 20, 1921; New Orleans *Picayune*, December 26, 1899; Baton Rouge *State Times*, November 15, 1934.

28. Amite City *Tangipahoa Parish News*, March 17, July 21, 1927; Baton Rouge *States*, June 21, 1910.

The major criminal activity that provoked violence remained bootlegging whiskey. The Kentwood *Commercial* argued that "hard drink" was responsible for four-fifths of all violent crime in the state. It was also very lucrative; notorious bootlegger Comer Rogers was said to have boasted that he turned a $75,000 profit on his bootlegging operation. The Hood Bill, passed by the Louisiana Legislature in 1921 as the state law complement to the federal Volstead Act, motivated local authorities to move aggressively against the plethora of stills and bootlegging operations in the region. By the winter of 1921, Livingston Parish sheriff L. R. Kimball was making weekly raids and arrests. Similarly, by the fall of 1929 in neighboring Tangipahoa Parish, Sheriff Frank M. Edwards and his deputies averaged six raids per week including some in the depths of the Manchac Swamp, which some bootleggers believed to be impenetrable. As the law cracked down, profits went up, and the work for all involved became far more dangerous. In one of the worst examples of bootlegging violence, two moonshiners ambushed and murdered Washington Parish deputies Wiley Pierce and Wesley Crain, concealing their bodies in a swamp south of Franklinton. The two perpetrators were quickly arrested, and a resulting crackdown netted thirteen more Washington Parish bootleggers in the spring of 1923.[29]

Other murders occurred under almost incomprehensible circumstances. S. J. Hart, foreman of the Cline Farm at Arcola, killed a man who showed up late for work and then argued with Hart when he sought to chastise him. Sidney Kinchen, a prominent strawberry farmer, was assassinated west of Hammond by his friend Charles Hagan, who blamed Kinchen for a fall from a horse Hagan suffered while riding drunk. Several friends tried to dissuade Hagan from killing Kinchen—who left nine children behind—as he waited in ambush along an isolated road. After his arrest, some believed Hagan would never be convicted for the crime since he was a physically small man and Kinchen, who weighed more than two hundred pounds, was alleged to have abused him in the past.[30]

A singularly common issue in each case was the challenge to secure justice

29. Kentwood *Commercial*, February 23, 1906, December 11, 1925; Amite City *Florida Parishes*, June 3, 1922, May 26, 1905; Amite City *Florida Parish Times*, December 24, 31, 1921, March 10, 24, May 12, October 27, 1923; Sixteen Judicial District Court, Parish of Tangipahoa, Minute Book 6, docket nos. 104, 113, 114, pp. 290–91, 293, 299; Franklinton *New Era*, March 22, 1906; Hammond *Vindicator*, March 15, 29, October 11, 1929; Independence *News*, April 9, 1926; Amite City *Tangipahoa Parish News*, April 8, 1926; Ponchatoula *Enterprise*, June 9, 16, 1922; Franklinton *Era Leader*, April 30, 1925.

30. Amite City *Florida Parish Times*, February 18, 25, March 25, June 17, 1922; Ponchatoula *Enterprise*, March 24, 1922.

for the victims. A case originating in the fall of 1925 illustrated the continuing convoluted challenges for regional justice. On a cool fall afternoon, Earl Bankston and Hatton Naretto were walking on a road near Loranger in central Tangipahoa Parish when a car driven by Adolph Willie, accompanied by William Toney and several others, approached. Bankston asked for a ride, but Willie insisted the vehicle was already too full. When an incensed Bankston confronted Willie, the two men proceeded to fight, with Willie getting the best of the affray. Sometime later a second car, containing Bankston, Naretto, and Breed Dunnington, caught up to Willie's party. What happened next remained in dispute, the only certainty being that Adolph Willie and William Toney were both dead.[31]

At the trial a number of witnesses affirmed the testimony of Ella Felder, sister to one victim and ex-wife of the other. Felder, who was in Willie's car along with her baby, testified that after the fist fight the car carrying the accused caught up to them and that Bankston murdered both men. Felder alleged that she fled to a nearby house with her baby after she heard one of the accused saying the men were dead before hearing yet another shot. James Willie and Vernon Hano testified that they too fled the victim's car when the shooting started. Both James, who was allegedly stabbed by Naretto, and Vernon, who was shot in the arm and shoulder as he ran, corroborated Felder's version of events. John Muret testified that Bankston and Naretto came to his house and borrowed a shotgun, claiming they had been robbed by five men. For their part, the accused, whom press accounts noted "are all well connected," claimed self-defense, insisting that they intended only to take Willie to jail for assaulting Bankston and stealing his wallet. Press reports noted that although Bankston claimed he had fired in self-defense, Willie had been shot in the back of the head. Bankston's cousin Ivy Brown testified as a surprise witness. Brown alleged that he happened to be riding a horse nearby and witnessed Willie and Toney attack Bankston with a "tire spring" as Bankston sought to retrieve his stolen wallet, forcing him to fire in self-defense. Following a host of character witnesses, including the president of the parish police jury and a former sheriff, all of whom testified to Bankston's good reputation, the case went to the jury.[32]

31. Amite City *Tangipahoa Parish News*, November 7, 1925, January 14, 28, 1926; Twenty-First Judicial District Court, Parish of Tangipahoa, Minute Books, No. 25, State of Louisiana vs. Earl Bankston, Hatton Naretto, and Breed Dunnington, p. 68; see also Coroner's Inquest Testimony in "Indictment and Appearance Bonds File," docket no. 254, October 27, 1926, both in Tangipahoa Parish Clerk of Court Archives.

32. See sources cited in note 31.

After barely ninety minutes' deliberation, the jury returned not-guilty verdicts against all of the accused. The vindicated men rushed to shake the hands of the jurors while the audience clapped. What actually happened the day of the shootings may never be known. But lingering doubts clearly remained concerning the veracity of the jury's decision. The same incident provoked at least two more trials as the prosecution continued to seek some semblance of justice for the victims.[33]

The Bankston case and scores of others like it underscored the prevailing societal equilibrium concerning the system of justice. Such failings of justice remained common in the early-twentieth-century South. Several far more dramatic cases from the same era serve to illustrate that the troubled conditions in the eastern Florida parishes were anything but normal. A series of dramatic incidents of violence in early 1909 climaxed with what some reports called the "most horrible and most diabolical crime that was ever perpetuated" in Tangipahoa Parish. Like many of the "troubles" occurring in the region, this series of events originated in a perceived affront to honor. The problems began several years earlier in a battle of words pitting the Everette brothers—Joe, John, and Walter—against Livingston Parish patriarch Ben Kinchen. Though they passed for white and moved in the circles of white society, the Everettes had long endured accusations that they were of mixed race. Whether true or not, such an accusation in the early twentieth century carried grave social and economic consequences. Word had been passed to the Everette brothers that Ben Kinchen regularly referenced them with a common racial slur. Kinchen was alleged to have stated he would not allow his daughter to attend school with blacks, and the reference was said to be directed at the Everettes.[34]

The two sides taunted each other and traded accusations for months. At one point Kinchen sent word for the Everettes to meet him at a prearranged point, but they, perhaps wisely, did not show at what they likely considered to be a bushwhacking. The feud reached a head in January 1909 when Kinchen encountered the Everettes at a funeral in the New Zion Cemetery near the Little River community west of Tickfaw. As bystanders sought to keep the peace, Joe Everette attacked Kinchen with a shovel, prompting Kinchen to draw a concealed pistol, shoot, and kill him. As the other Everettes scrambled to arm themselves, Kinchen shot and wounded them both before fleeing the scene. A warrant was issued for Kinchen's arrest, but he remained

33. See sources cited in note 31.
34. Opelousas St. Landry Clarion, January 30, 1909.

at large as he negotiated his surrender with Tangipahoa Parish authorities. With one Everette dead and the other two wounded, few assumed this would be the end of the matter. Of particular concern to Kinchen and his friends was one J. O. "Buzzy" Breland, whose fifteen-year-old stepdaughter was the newly made widow of Joe Everette and a witness against Ben Kinchen in the recent shooting of her husband.[35]

Three days after the New Zion Cemetery shootings, Breland and his wife Eliza traveled to collect his stepdaughter and her three-month-old baby from the farm where she had resided with Joe Everette. As the Breland family began their sad journey, two other principals to the case approached the same area. Ben Kinchen had been hiding out in the same region since the Everette killing. He had made arrangements to meet with an attorney in Amite City to discuss terms for his surrender. Ben's brother Garfield Kinchen, along with his friend Avery Blount, were also in the area to accompany Ben to Amite City. Reports indicated both men had been drinking heavily. As the two men departed Tickfaw heading north to pick up Ben Kinchen, about 7:00 P.M. they passed the Breland party heading south without incident. Breland was on foot, leading a cow ahead of a wagon carrying the two women, Mrs. Everette's baby, and a pig. As they moved through Tickfaw, Breland stopped at a store and purchased cheese and crackers for the family as they continued on to the Breland home.[36]

Less than half a mile from the store, two figures emerged from the brush and shot Breland point-blank with a load of buckshot from a ten-gauge shotgun. The scene then entered the realms of horror seldom approached even in the violent environs of Tangipahoa Parish. The killers now turned to the women, who begged for their lives and for the life of the baby. One of the killers grabbed the babe from its mother's arms and placed the child on the ground near the side of the road. The killer then shot Eliza Breland in the chest with a load of buckshot before turning on the young widow and blowing the top of her head off with the same weapon. Before departing, one of the killers knelt down and looked Breland directly in his face to confirm he was dead, giving the still-breathing Breland a clear view of one, but not both, of his killers. He lived just long enough to identify Avery Blount as one assassin and to state his belief that Garfield Kinchen was the other.[37]

35. New Orleans *Picayune*, January 24, 25, 30, February 2, November 18, 1909; Twenty-First Judicial District Court Parish of Tangipahoa, Minute Books, No. 12, "State of Louisiana vs. Ben Kinchen," docket nos. 1619, 1620, 1621, pp. 1, 3.

36. See sources cited in note 35.

37. See sources cited in note 35.

The Breland killings outraged and embarrassed residents of Tangipahoa Parish. Utter dismay at the savagery of prevailing conditions dominated news stories about the murders. The *St. Landry Clarion* revealed the prevailing contempt for circumstances in Tangipahoa under the headline "Bloody Tangipahoa Runs with the Blood of Women," suggesting that the parish had descended to a new level of barbarism. A group of young people who first encountered the murder scene rescued the baby from a slow death by exposure, but the plight of the child only stoked the outrage. Avery Blount, who was himself a Tangipahoa Parish constable, foolishly returned to the scene, only to be arrested as one of the killers. Blount and the Kinchens were known troublemakers in the eyes of many, and a mass meeting that was called to demand justice for the Brelands nearly turned into a lynch mob. Advised of the public reaction, Garfield Kinchen fled into the swamps of Livingston Parish, where he would remain in hiding for many months sustained by family and friends. Ben Kinchen, implicated as the mastermind behind the killings, was arrested and convicted in an initial trial only to have his conviction overturned in a second trial. It fell to Avery Blount to pay the ultimate price for the crimes. He was convicted in a jury trial and later hanged at the courthouse in Amite City on October 14, 1909.[38]

The outrage surrounding the Breland killings did provoke temporary activism among some residents, who considered a mass murder that included women simply unacceptable. A "Law and Order League" formed in Tangipahoa Parish that included numerous prominent individuals, largely from the southern end of the parish. The Law and Order League made a substantial presence at the trial of Avery Blount, yet it too offered no credible commitment for incentive to change the prevailing societal equilibrium. By the time Ben Kinchen came to trial, the League had fizzled out. In an article titled "Where Is the Law and Order League?" the Amite City *Florida Parishes* complained about a motion for bail for Kinchen—who faced four charges for murder, two charges for shooting with intent to kill, and one for carrying concealed weapons. "Now if a man charged with all this is entitled to bail, why not turn loose men with only one charge against them on their own

38. Opelousas *St. Landry Clarion*, January 30, 1909; New Orleans *Picayune*, May 8, 1900, January 24–26, May 8, November 4, 1909, June 21, July 16, 1910, May 20, 1912; Proclamation Offering $500 Reward for the Arrest of Garfield Kinchen, repr. Baton Rouge *New Advocate*, March 12, 1909; Twenty-First Judicial District Court, Parish of Livingston, Minute Book 2, pp. 181, 697, No. 3, pp. 5, 26, 29–30, 91–92, 155, 174, Livingston Parish Courthouse; Twenty-First Judicial District Court, Minute Book 12, "State of Louisiana vs. Avery Blount," docket no. 1602, pp. 4, 11–13, 15–20, 22–23.

honor to appear for trial. We believe in treating all people alike." Sensationalism and moral righteousness apparently impacted levels of virtue and courage only so much in Tangipahoa.[39]

Neighboring Washington Parish likewise endured sensational cases that may have impacted popular attitudes. Although the region was dotted with lumber mills, brickyards, fruit-processing plants, and the like, labor disputes remained almost nonexistent. A determined five-week-long strike at the Gullett Gin Company in Amite City in 1925 concluded peacefully with a negotiated settlement that both workers and management readily accepted. The positive result at Gullett may have been advanced by the ferocity with which a 1919 strike in Bogalusa concluded.[40]

Bogalusa originated for the sole purpose of exploiting the vast virgin pine forests of Washington Parish and environs. In the aftermath of World War I, the Great Southern Lumber Company at Bogalusa operated as the largest lumber mill in the world, employing more than 2,400 workers at its primary mill and subsidiary industries. With strikes and other labor troubles affecting industries across the nation, the company sought to discourage unionization of workers by raising wages and improving conditions. The Great Southern had nevertheless become too big to go unnoticed. In late 1919, William Donnels, a general organizer of the United Brotherhood of Carpenters and Joiners of America, came to Bogalusa accompanied by Sol Dacus, a black union organizer. The success the union organizers enjoyed created dismay among the business elite of the town, who responded by forming the Self Preservation and Loyalty League, essentially a vigilante group backed by legal sanction. At the same time, William H. Sullivan, who was both mayor of the town and general manager of the Great Southern, increased the local police force from eighteen to over one hundred with many recruited directly from the Loyalty League. Following a series of "accidents" that shut down the Great Southern and cut off both electricity and water to the town (since the Great Southern controlled both services), tensions reached a fever pitch as police and Loyal League members harassed union men and stopped trains entering Bogalusa, searching for agitators.[41]

On November 20, 1919, the troubles climaxed in a series of events that dramatically challenged perceptions of justice and racial order in the early-

39. Amite City *Florida Parishes*, May 8, 1909; Baton Rouge *States*, June 21, 1910; New Orleans *Picayune*, January 26, November 4, 1909.

40. Amite City *Tangipahoa Parish News*, October 17, November 7, 1925.

41. Quick, "The History of Bogalusa," 73–190; Hyman, "The Great Southern Lumber Company," 17–20; New Orleans *Picayune*, November 22, 23, 25, 1919.

twentieth-century South. Amid the previous day's union-busting activities, Bogalusa officials had ordered Dacus to leave town and looted his home as he hid in a nearby swamp. Instead of fleeing as ordered, the following morning Dacus boldly walked through the business district of Bogalusa protected by two white men, Peter Bouchillon and S. J. O'Rourke, both of whom carried shotguns. The sight was more than the company and their hirelings could take: the Great Southern blew its "riot whistle" to alert the town that an armed clash was underway. A mob gathered and proceeded to the garage of union organizer "Lum" Williams, where Dacus and the others sought refuge. When Williams refused a demand to turn over Dacus, the men surrounding the garage opened fire, killing Williams, Bouchillon, O'Rourke, and one other union man. One member of the attacking party was slightly wounded. During the melee, Dacus made good his escape. In a scene seldom repeated in the early-twentieth-century South, four white men had laid down their lives to ensure the safety of one black man.[42]

With the exception of the racial cooperation, the events at Bogalusa conformed to the standard pattern evident in the eastern Florida parishes. Violent resolution of disputes was accepted as a legitimate means to an end. Judge Prentiss B. Carter called for the parish grand jury to investigate the actions of those responsible for the deaths of the union men. Scores of prominent Washington Parish citizens joined as signatories on the accused men's bonds. The appearance of Donnels and Dacus at the grand jury hearing in Franklinton in December, 1919, provoked some excitement, but it did not dissuade District Attorney J. Vol Brock from reporting that the grand jury failed to find cause for indictment. A second effort to secure an indictment initiated by Lum Williams's brother in May, 1920, similarly failed to move the grand jury to return a true bill. In the end the unions seemed cowed, racial cooperation was discouraged, another episode of violence was socially accepted, and life continued in the piney-woods parishes.[43]

Still another violent episode, one that captured international attention, resulted in the hanging of six men for one crime and highlighted continuing challenges for the legal system. In the spring of 1921, six Italian immigrants, most of them new arrivals to New Orleans, received word that a country bank recently visited by an acquaintance offered "easy money" for the pickings. After a cartoonlike journey of wrong turns and automobile mishaps,

42. See sources cited in note 41.

43. Bogalusa *Enterprise and American*, November 25, December 4, 1919; Franklinton *Era Leader*, April 30, 1925; Quick, "The History of Bogalusa," 135–36; John N. Gallaspy, *The City That Refused to Die: Bogalusa's First Hundred Years* (New Orleans, 2014), 104–109.

the group arrived in Independence, site of a large concentration of residents of Italian ancestry and the veritable epicenter of "bloody" Tangipahoa Parish. The plan to rob the Farmers and Merchants Bank misfired from the start—but the noise the men made in the process awakened Independence merchant Dallas Calmes and his wife, who were sleeping in a back room of their restaurant located near the bank. When Calmes came out to confront what he suspected was a chicken thief, he was shot and killed by one of the would-be bank robbers. The gang attempted to flee but were soon rounded up and placed in the jail at Amite City. A grand jury quickly indicted all six for the murder of Calmes despite their profession of innocence.[44]

The case resulted in two trials with two convictions, appeals to the U.S. Supreme Court, and international outrage at the "nativism" supposedly behind the arrests and calls for blood. In his comprehensive study of the case, sociologist John Baiamonte makes no apologies for the accused, but he does link their fate both to anti-Italian sentiment and to the culture of violence that prevailed in the eastern Florida parishes. Abundant evidence supports Baiamonte's perspective. In more than one instance, lynch mobs menaced the accused. Their threats to storm the courthouse came close to provoking a crisis with the Italian government and led defense attorney Chandler Luzenburg to demand that federal troops be deployed in Amite City. An international incident was avoided only by direct intervention of Governor John Parker and federal officials. Adding to the mob's rage was the alleged discovery of dynamite that had been concealed in the roof of the car used in the Calmes murder. The car had subsequently been purchased by Tangipahoa Parish tax assessor Norman Vernon. The accused were reported to have frequently seen the car in use by Vernon, his wife, and young daughter, but they never warned the Vernons about the dynamite.[45]

Among the extreme precautions taken on the day of the executions were the deployment of state militia and the construction of a veritable rampart about the courthouse. The victim's wife had received threatening letters, addressed to "Mrs. Bloodthirsty" and sealed with the "Black Hand" of the Mafia, warning that she would be killed if the men were hanged. The threats against Mrs. Calmes, Judge Robert Ellis, and even Governor Parker stoked

44. Twenty-First Judicial District Court, Parish of Tangipahoa, Minute Book 21, State of Louisiana vs. Joseph Reni et al., docket nos. 4925, 4926, pp. 54–55; Ponchatoula *Enterprise*, May 13, 27, July 1, 1921; John V. Baiamonte, Jr., *Spirit of Vengeance: Nativism and Louisiana Justice, 1921–1924* (Baton Rouge, 1986).

45. Amite City *Florida Parishes*, May 13, 20, 27, 1922, March 3, 1923; Amite City *Florida Parish Times*, July 9, November 19, 1921, January 7, 1922, April 14, 1923.

the anger of the local population, necessitating the enhanced security, as did the size of the crowd. Special trains helped augment what the *Florida Parish Times* called the largest crowd ever to assemble in Amite City. Two of the condemned men attempted to cheat the hangman with suicide, and one offered a confession in hopes of saving the others, but the executions occurred as scheduled.[46]

While some believed that justice had been served, the process of securing convictions and the ultimate executions of the accused men diminished, rather than advanced, the standing of the legal system. The New Orleans press set the tone by casting suspicion on the system of justice in Tangipahoa. The New Orleans *Item* argued that the men had no chance for a fair trial because of the "mob mentality" that prevailed in Tangipahoa. Lending credence to such concerns, the parish jail had been deemed so insecure that the accused were moved to New Orleans, which outraged local residents. Many people believed the last-minute confession had not been made voluntarily and that it was reported only to justify the executions. Sheriff Lem Bowden engaged in a public fight with one of the defense attorneys, and there were rampant accusations of jury tampering. Juror W. C. O'Brian alleged that he had voted to acquit but had been intimidated into voting guilty by the other jurors and threats from the crowd. Bootlegger Comer Rogers claimed that the defense attorneys offered him five thousand dollars to bribe two jurors in the case. One of the allegedly bribed jurors was O'Brian, who was promptly arrested and confessed that he had received two thousand dollars from defense attorneys to vote for acquittal. The other, W. W. Varnado, fled the state before he could be arrested and was reported to have fled when a deputy sheriff approached him in Osyka, Mississippi. For his part, Rogers was mysteriously released from jail "through some court error" before standing trial for bootlegging.[47]

The two defense attorneys accused of bribing the jurors, William B. Kemp and W. A. Haughton, argued that feelings were so strong against them because they had served as part of the defense team. The accusations of jury tampering and public fighting between the police and legal teams nonetheless cast an aura of doubt over the whole process, highlighting the sordid history of the Tangipahoa Parish legal system that seemed to have changed little, if at all, from the darkest days of the feud violence. The *Florida Parish Times* speculated as to why the courts proved so effective in punishing the

46. Amite City *Florida Parish Times*, May 10, 1924; Baiamonte, *Spirit of Vengeance*.

47. Amite City *Florida Parish Times*, January 7, June 10, 17, 1922; Amite City *Florida Parishes*, May 20, 1922; Ponchatoula *Enterprise*, June 16, 30, 1922.

Calmes murderers when they failed so many local victims seeking justice. The paper argued that since the Calmes murder involved a bank and threatened people's savings, the prosecution had the support of the moneyed powers of the parish: "This combined public power forced the administration of justice in Tangipahoa, it took other legal talent than the state affords, but the machinery was made to function." The paper concluded that Tangipahoa must elect courageous officials who would administer justice in all situations without fear or favor, thereby acknowledging that a weakness existed in the court system.[48]

Other observers placed blame for the prevailing circumstances squarely on regional residents and the culture they embraced. One report concluded that people in the region "let malice rule them," arguing that residents were so quick to take offense and respond violently that it was nearly impossible to have peaceful gatherings. The report ended with the hopeful observation that some were beginning to see "the enormous futility of mere force." Such optimistic assessments were typically little more than appeals to reason. Expectations that enhanced contact with the outside world, increased local opportunities, and sweeping technological innovations would change the character of life were misplaced in a culture of violence at equilibrium, one where tragedy begets tragedy. Friends and family mourned when David Sanders was shot and killed by his first cousin and best friend, a boy of eighteen years referenced only as "young Davidson." Sanders, only twenty-eight years old, left a "broken hearted widow and several young children." His tragic demise occurred when he teased Davidson that he was lazy, provoking the young man to demonstrate otherwise by fetching a weapon and killing his friend and cousin. The killer turned out to be the brother of Will Davidson, who was murdered in St. Helena Parish two years earlier and, like his brother, one of the children left fatherless when Bill Davidson was murdered in 1896, initiating one of Tangipahoa Parish's bloodiest feuds.[49]

In November, 1913, on the death of Tangipahoa sheriff John Saal, whose second and final term of office concluded in 1912, a local newspaper praised Saal for "having rescued Tangipahoa's name from the obloquy to which it had been consigned." The report asserted that Saal's formula "for eradicating the evil that stifled progress in the parish" included three reforms. Specifically, he demanded fearlessness from his deputies, personally supervised the work of "talisman" to screen and secure competent jurors, and assisted the prose-

48. Ponchatoula *Enterprise*, June 16, 30, 1922; Amite City *Florida Parish Times*, June 10, 17, 1922, February 10, 1923.
49. Ponchatoula *Enterprise*, April 14, 1922; New Orleans *Picayune*, May 28, 1908.

cution to expose witnesses "who were willing to testify to anything in order to rescue friends from the clutches of the law." Despite this noble obituary, subsequent events would reveal that whatever reforms Saal initiated failed to produce enduring results. In the piney woods of the Florida parishes, credible commitment for change proved elusive; and the violence continued.[50]

•

On December 7, 1935, Burke, Walter, and Alton "Rags" Hughes entered the recently opened Lanier beer parlor and dance hall in Tangipahoa, Louisiana. At least one of the brothers had been involved in an altercation at the same establishment over the preceding Thanksgiving weekend. Each of the three had served time in a state penitentiary for various crimes, yet they remained fiercely devoted to each other, having lost their mother at a tender age. Shortly before 9:00 P.M., a shootout began that left each of the brothers dead from multiple gunshot wounds inflicted by the barroom owner, George Lanier, and his teenage son. Even though they admitted to repeatedly shooting the brothers—some of the shots even entering their backs as the victims tried to flee the scene—the Laniers were quickly exonerated by a "secret" coroner's inquest after Sheriff Frank Edwards demurred and declared it a coroner's case. Coroner L. L. Ricks complained that Edwards was "passing the buck" to him because the sheriff was in a tight reelection race and wanted to avoid controversy. The brothers' bodies remained where they had fallen when their surviving brother, Wilson, arrived. As he viewed the bodies, the grieving youngest brother was said to have shouted, "someone should shoot me too." Wilson Hughes likely realized that his brothers had been killed barely 150 yards from where their father, Hines Hughes, had been shot and killed twenty years earlier. Whether he knew that the bodies lay less than 200 yards from where Avery Draughon had been murdered fifteen years before that remains uncertain. In each case, no one served time for taking the life of another. The killing had passed to yet another generation; life, and death, in Tangipahoa continued much as it had for the past seventy-five years.[51]

Distance from the hard times of war and Reconstruction, along with a modernizing infrastructure and economy, failed to change the fundamental

50. Amite City *Florida Parishes*, November 22, 1913.

51. New Orleans *Picayune*, December 8–10, 1935; Baton Rouge *Morning Advocate*, December 8, 10, 1935; Amite City *Lanier's Digest*, October 18, 1929; Mayor's Court Ledger, 1923, multiple arrest warrants for Ben Wilkerson and others signed by Tangipahoa mayor John Lambert, and unsigned letter to Robert Ellis, August 29, 1931, all in John W. Lambert Papers.

character and culture of the piney-woods region. Instead, the prevailing equilibrium endured. As the region entered the hard times of the Great Depression, many hoped that as in the chaotic times of the Civil War, society might pull together, but the incentive to change remained elusive. In the spring of 1929, a crowd of more than one thousand converged on Amite City to join in events surrounding the hanging of Lige Wall. The man had been condemned for the murder of seventeen-year-old Percy Roberts, who was scheduled to testify against one of Wall's relatives in an arson case in Mississippi. Wall met his death with the stoic indifference characteristic of a lifelong resident of the piney woods of the Florida parishes. Between puffs on a "strong cigar," Wall looked at his jailers and admonished, "Boys, don't look so glum, I was just born to die this way!"[52]

52. Hammond *Vindicator*, March 8, 1929.

Epilogue: Securing a Credible Commitment for Change

From a period of territorial chaos that served as a magnet for desperadoes and other suspect characters, Louisiana's Florida parishes secured a measure of stability under the direction of a powerful planter elite. The catastrophe of war and the violence of Reconstruction shattered the prevailing order that benefited some to the detriment of others. As the planter hierarchy returned to power in the western plantation parishes, the piney-woods parishes endured a power vacuum that stimulated numerous feuds and the creation of a culture of violence. A suspect legal system furthered a warped impression of rights and responsibility among many residents, contributing to the emergence of a state of undesirable equilibrium where violence was both expected and tolerated that continued deep into the twentieth century. Assuming that it is human nature to desire peace and security, how then does the region secure credible commitment for change?

The Florida parishes provide a physical model of breathtaking beauty and diversity. Numerous clear running streams that traverse vast pine forests feed deepwater rivers, offering accessibility and entertainment to residents and visitors alike. The rolling hills in the upcountry region provide some of the highest ground in the state, while the swamplands to the south offer exotic plant and animal species rarely found anywhere else in the nation. The Mississippi River, at its mightiest, provides one border to the territory, and a series of interconnected lakes, which the first European observer, Pierre LeMoyne d'Iberville, described as "one of the prettiest spots I have seen," provide another. The region is also home to a complex and turbulent pattern of development that for generations challenged scholars to interpret without offending. As such, it has long remained a backwater of Louisiana history, though it arguably offers the most colorful and convoluted pattern of development found in the state. The generational residents, long-term families, are similar in many ways to other residents of the South, but there are some meaningful distinctions. The singularity that exists is not an issue of race, ethnicity, or socioeconomic status, but instead of a collectively endured history that more often than not has been unpleasant. As outlined in this study, the people who settled the area understood that life is full not simply of challenge, but also of risk. Their expectations of life, like the hazards that remained ever close, passed from one generation to the next, continuing from the early nineteenth century into the early twentieth century and beyond. It has simply been "the way things are" for those who call the region home. This study posits that up to the eve of World War II a manner of social equilibrium prevailed that witnessed development amid inordinate rates of rural homicide.[1]

In 1996 the Federal Bureau of Investigation released criminal statistics revealing the United States' status at the forefront of violence among industrialized nations. The South led in rates of violent crime among the various regions, contributing disproportionately to the national homicide rate of 7.4 per 100,000 deaths. Not surprisingly, Louisiana led the nation with a rate of 17.5 per 100,000 deaths, which contrasted sharply with last-place South Dakota's 1.2 per 100,000. FBI statistical reports for 2012 indicated a reduction in the rates of homicide, yet confirmed Louisiana's leadership in national rates at 10.8 per 100,000 deaths over second-ranked South Carolina at 6.8. When those statistics are broken down by parish in state reports to the FBI, the eastern Florida parishes continue as leaders in rural homicide in the Bayou State. Statistical analysis included in the 2013 Louisiana Supreme Court Annual Report further demonstrates that the Twenty-First Judicial District (Livingston, St. Helena, and Tangipahoa Parishes) led the Florida parishes in per capita criminal cases filed. The Twenty-Second District (St. Tammany and Washington Parishes) was second, with about 2,000 fewer criminal cases filed despite a similar total population to the Twenty-First District. The significantly less populated Twentieth District in the western plantation parishes (East and West Feliciana) continued a pattern of significantly fewer criminal cases filed than in their piney-woods neighbors. A recent report designed for popular consumption and less grounded in scholarly analysis listed Amite City first, Hammond third, Bogalusa ninth, and Denham Springs tenth, among the most dangerous places in Louisiana.[2]

1. *The Journals of Pierre Le Moyne d'Iberville and Jean-Jacques-Blaise d'Abbadie* (Lafayette, La., 1979).
2. FBI homicide statistics reprinted in Fox Butterfield, "Why the South's Homicide Rate Is So High," New York *Times*, July 26, 1998; Federal Bureau of Investigation, Uniform Crime Report, 2012 and 2015, and 2006–2007 Louisiana Commission on Law Enforcement, "Louisiana

The troubled pattern of historical development and the statistical analysis of current conditions suggest an ominous future for the region. Yet hope remains. Population growth and accompanying opportunity, occasioned significantly by flight from New Orleans and Baton Rouge, has dramatically expanded the tax base and workforce of the rural parishes. Today, St. Tammany and Livingston count among the fastest-growing parishes in the state with Tangipahoa not far behind. Technology-driven industries such as the River Bend Nuclear Power Plant in West Feliciana Parish, and the Laser Interferometer Gravitational-Wave Observatory (supercollider) in Livingston, offer higher-paying skilled employment that contributes to a ripple effect for an improved quality of life in the area. Southeastern Louisiana University now boasts the third-largest student body among higher educational institutions in the state, annually producing scores of new teachers, nurses, scientists, and the like to service the needs of the region. Two interstate highway systems, completed in the mid and late twentieth century, converge near the center of the Florida parishes and serve as sustained engines for growth. In short, the development that began in the early twentieth century has steadily accelerated, qualified only by a lingering frontier mentality in some of the residents that has continued to affect the orderly dispensation of justice. Credible commitment for change in that regard has remained elusive.

Analysis of the undesirable equilibrium prevailing in the piney-woods parishes not only advances understanding of the past, but may also offer a blueprint for combating similar challenges in current society. The presence of violence-prone criminals protecting their status and turf by killing any who challenge them and intimidating witnesses and potential jurors into tolerating such behavior by embracing safe obscurity, describes the piney-woods parishes of the recent past just as it describes many urban communities today. Instead of Whitecap gangs and feudists preying on a cowed population, drug lords and crime bosses exact the same societal misery. Considering the methods to overcome the challenge in one region, whether past or present, may offer guidance to combat similar challenges in the other.

Effective leadership always affects the quality of life in any region. In 2014

Index Crimes Reported to the FBI Through the Louisiana Uniform Crime Report"; Center for Disease Control, "Louisiana Homicide Death Rate, 1999–2014," Louisiana Life Expectancy Report, 2015; Supreme Court of Louisiana of the Judicial Council of the Supreme Court, "Annual Report, 2013," pp. 44–47; New Orleans Picayune, September 27, 2016; Nick James, "The Ten Most Dangerous Places in Louisiana," Roadsnacks, July, 2015.

Scott Perrilloux was elected to a fourth term as district attorney of the historically troubled Twenty-First Judicial District, which continues to include Livingston, St. Helena, and Tangipahoa Parishes. A determined-looking man with an air of confidence about him, Perrilloux first secured office by defeating three-term incumbent Duncan Kemp, grandson of the man of the same name who served as district attorney during the height of the large-scale feud-related troubles. Perrilloux ironically rose in standing, especially in the north end of the district, when the incumbent sought to label him a "brawler" who engaged in fist fights and the like. Whether true or not, many apparently believed that was precisely what the office needed. Perrilloux rose from obscurity to defeat the incumbent decisively. During a recent interview, Perrilloux admitted that he was not fully aware of the region's troubled history when he first ran for office, though he offered that he has seen elements of it appear in certain cases. He acknowledged the individual efforts to influence how his office pursues a case, noting that appeals to get someone out of jail or show leniency, even in murder cases, remain a "weekly" occurrence. "People in general want to be tough on crime until it comes to their family," he said.[3]

Perrilloux pointed with pride to the success of his office in prosecuting perpetrators of violent crime. The more than two hundred successful prosecutions for homicide secured in his twenty years in office stands in sharp contrast with statistics from the late nineteenth and early twentieth centuries. Despite such accomplishments, he nonetheless noted some enduring dilemmas. He acknowledged that even in a region long accustomed to violence, people have a tendency to sympathize with the family of a convicted criminal for the suffering they endure, and that impacts certain cases. Protecting the public and showing mercy are often difficult to coordinate; a great deal of responsibility rests with jurors. When asked if he has faith in the jury system after more than twenty years as a prosecutor in a violence-prone region, he responded, "I do, I have to. And I do." Yet he confessed frustration in certain cases that may advance understanding of why some cases resulted as they did in the past. He referenced one case where a murderer was acquitted only to walk from the courthouse and immediately, before the press, admit that he was indeed the killer. That case, like many others today, involved a drug deal gone bad. Perrilloux believes that juries tend to be less sympathetic to victims who were engaged in bad behavior themselves and are thus less likely to make the hard decision to lock someone away for years when the victim

3. Interview of District Attorney Scott Perrilloux, September 6, 2016.

may have, at least partially, brought it on themselves. It seems likely, if not probable, that some juries released guilty parties involved in feud-related violence because their victims participated in the same business.[4]

When asked how we may be able to secure a more effective, and respected, system of justice, the district attorney stressed the need for ongoing reform. One necessary reform centered on professionalism in the prosecutor's office. Perrilloux noted that historically the district attorney's office relied on part-time prosecutors who received a fixed monthly paycheck. Human nature typically dictates that one's private practice, where the more you work the more you earn, accordingly receives the lion's share of any assistant's attention. With financial help from the parish governments, particularly Tangipahoa, the district attorney converted the majority of prosecutors in his office to full-time assistants, which he argues vastly improved the quality of prosecution. Other obstacles to justice have proven more challenging. Perrilloux noted that police agencies typically have a culture about them—some demand virtuous performance from their employees, while others operate more like a good-old-boy network. The treatment of evidence often reflects the culture of the department; he noted that some departments require precision handling of evidence, while in others you may find a key piece of evidence riding around in someone's truck for two years. Moreover, some police are influenced by their own personal prejudices. Perrilloux stressed enhanced accountability as key to overcoming the culture of a police agency as well as advancing public confidence in the system of justice.

Another challenge in his effort to secure justice for the victims and fairness for the accused is the discretion his office enjoys. District attorneys in Louisiana are offered a great deal of discretion, leading Perrilloux to conclude, "the good thing about the job is the discretion, the discretion that you have, the bad thing about the job is the discretion you have." In the wrong hands—or, as he noted, in the hands of someone who has trouble saying "no"—discretion can compromise the administration of justice and undermine public confidence. The history of the region is replete with examples precisely reflecting this dilemma.

Two other components remain critical for creating a more efficient and effective system of justice. The first is education. It is naïve to think that because someone is elected sheriff, chief of police, or even justice of the peace, they must possess the experience and intelligence to effectively administer a policing agency. Louisiana requires very little mandated training for police

4. *Ibid.*

officials. The primary arbiter of an individual's qualifications often extends little beyond the voters, who frequently have a limited understanding of the complexities of the office. Police are often thrown into dangerous, emotionally challenging, and life-determining situations with little realistic training. Even good-intentioned efforts can lead to mishandling of evidence, violent confrontations, or other circumstances that diminish the effectiveness of the system of justice in the popular imagination. Enhanced education in all phases of the system of justice seems certain to produce greater confidence in every regard among police agencies and the general public.

The final component, and one that may offer the best evidence of a credible commitment to overcoming the high rates of violence undergirding the undesirable equilibrium, is resources. The people of southeast Louisiana desire peace and security, but they remain overwhelmingly hostile to paying the taxes necessary to sustain the effective administration of justice. Perrilloux refers to it as the "eyeball test." Parishes enjoying enough revenue to effectively administer justice typically have cutting-edge equipment, flashy patrol cars, and modern, efficiently organized courthouses. He compared Livingston Parish, where voters approved a designated sales tax in support of the sheriff's department, with resource-starved St. Helena Parish. The stark contrast in equipment, number of deputies, and courthouse facilities between the two parishes more effectively highlights the critical role resources play in supporting the effective pursuit of justice when one realizes that between 1996 and 2007, three St. Helena Parish sheriffs in a row were arrested and sent to federal prison. Incredibly, five different men served as sheriff during one normal term.[5]

One need only be reminded of the popular pleas to increase the salaries of sheriffs in the first decade of the twentieth century, as outlined in this study, to understand that adequate financial support has long been synonymous with quality. Yet resources committed refer to more than just money. It requires of the public an investment of time and courage. Though burdens few enjoy, there must be commitment for regular jury service from all quarters of the community and a willingness to testify honestly when interrogated concerning a crime. Since credible commitment to change requires participants to embrace risk as part of an incentive to alter the status quo, that risk may

5. Baton Rouge *Advocate*, April 22, 23, 1998, March 5, 2005; Hammond *Daily Star*, April 22, 1998, February 25, 2005; *Livingston Parish News*, April 23, 1998; *St. Helena Echo*, April 29, 1998; Matthew Lee and Graham Ousey, "Reconsidering the Culture and Violence Connection: Strategies of Action in the Rural South," *Journal of Interpersonal Violence*, XXVI (2011), 899–929.

be in the form of resources, including adequate financial support, time devoted to jury service, and courage to support law enforcement officials when needed. With increased emphasis on education, accountability, and resources (EAR), residents of the long troubled regions of the Florida parishes may be able to overcome a dark chapter in their history. The components included in the EAR formulation have long been identified as tools for combating criminal activity. The troubled history of southeast Louisiana nonetheless reveals that, when applied in unison, the EAR formulation may offer the best hope for a citizenry embracing credible commitment for change to assume a proactive role in improving their quality of life. The same may apply in distressed inner-city neighborhoods where peace-loving citizens and the system of justice confront similar challenges.

Peace and prosperity come with a price, a necessary component of credible commitment for change. When one considers the slowly changing attitudes of residents, departures from stereotypes of the past, dramatic demographic changes of the past twenty years, it may be that the process has already begun. Change, when confronting deeply entrenched historical truths, remains a work ever in progress that demands constant nurturing and vigilance. Where the residents of the Florida parishes, and other regions with similar troubled pasts, find themselves in the next millennium, may very well serve as a statement on the power of tradition, or of the benefits reaped from credible commitment for change.

BIBLIOGRAPHY

Federal Government Documents

American State Papers: Legislative Documents of the Congress of the United States in Relation to Public Lands. 19th Cong., 1st Sess., Nos. 455–57.

Center for Disease Control. "Louisiana Homicide Death Rate, 1999–2014." Louisiana Life Expectancy Report, 2015.

Civil War Naval Chronology, 1861–1865. Washington, D.C., 1966.

Federal Bureau of Investigation. Uniform Crime Reports. "Louisiana Index Crimes Reported to the FBI Through the Louisiana Uniform Crime Report," 2006, 2007, 2012, 2015.

Historical Records Survey. Works Progress Administration, Louisiana Parish Archives Inventory, No. 46, St. Helena Parish.

Historical Statistics of the United States, Colonial Times to 1970. 2 vols. Washington, D.C., 1975.

United States Census Bureau. *Third Census, 1810.* Compendium.

———. *Fourth Census, 1820.* Compendium.

———. *Fifth Census, 1830.* Compendium.

———. *Sixth Census, 1840.* Compendium.

———. *Seventh Census, 1850.* Compendium, Agriculture, and Manuscript Rolls.

———. *Eighth Census, 1860.* Compendium, Agriculture, Manufactures, and Manuscript Rolls.

———. *Ninth Census, 1870.* Compendium, Agriculture, Manufactures, and Manuscript Rolls.

———. *Tenth Census, 1880.* Compendium, Agriculture, Manufactures, and Manuscript Rolls.

———. *Eleventh Census, 1890.* Compendium.

———. *Twelfth Census, 1900.* Compendium, Agriculture, Manufactures, and Manuscript Rolls.

———. *Thirteenth Census, 1910.* Compendium.

United States Congress, *House Documents.* 25th Cong., 2nd Sess., Misc. Doc., No. 463.

————. 40th Cong., 2nd Sess., Exec. Doc., No. 291 (1343), 1867–68.

————. 44th Cong., 2nd Sess., Misc. Doc., No. 34, Vol. V, Pt. 3.

————. "Report of the Commissioner of Agriculture." 40th Cong., 2nd Sess., Exec. Doc., 1867.

————. "Report of the Commissioner of Patents for the Year 1850." 31st Cong., 2nd Sess., Exec. Doc., No. 34, Pt. 2, pp. 257–61.

————. "Report of the Special Congressional Investigating Committee of Three." 43rd Cong., 2nd Sess., No. 101 (1657), Pt. 1, 1875.

————. "Sub-Committee Investigating Elections in Louisiana." *Congressional Hearing Supplement,* House Committee on Elections, 41st Cong., 2nd Sess., No. 1, 1869.

————. "Testimony Taken by the Select Committee on Alleged Frauds in the Presidential Election of 1876." 45th Cong., 3rd Sess., Misc. Doc., No. 31, Pt. 1, 1878.

————. "Testimony Taken by the Select Committee on Alleged Frauds in the Presidential Election of 1876." 45th Cong., 3rd Sess., Misc. Doc., No. 31, Pt. 3, 1879.

————. "Testimony Taken by the Select Committee on the Recent Election in Louisiana." 44th Cong., 2nd Sess., Misc. Doc. No. 34, Pt. 2, 1877.

————. "Testimony Taken by the Select Committee to Investigate the Condition of Affairs in Louisiana." 42nd Cong., 2nd Sess., Misc. Doc. No. 211.

United States Department of Agriculture. *Forest Atlas of the South.* U.S. Forest Service Publication. Washington, D.C. 1969.

————. *Forest of Louisiana.* Forest Service Release No. 75. Washington, D.C. 1955.

————. *Preliminary Report upon the Florida Parishes of East Louisiana and the Bluff, Prairie, and Hill Lands of Southwest Louisiana.* U.S. Geological Survey Series, 1896, Pts. 1–4.

————. *Report of the Chief of the Bureau of Soils for 1905.* Washington, D.C., 1905.

United States Department of Justice. "Letters Received by the Department of Justice from the State of Louisiana, 1871–1884." Doc. F-167.

The War of the Rebellion: A Compilation of the Official Records of the Union and Confederate Armies. 130 vols. Washington, D.C., 1880–1901.

Manuscript Collections

Alabama State Archives, Montgomery, Ala.
    Attorney General Reports, 1884, 1887, 1894.
Arkansas History Commission–State Archives, Little Rock
    Governor J. B. Berry Correspondence.
    Governor Daniel W. Jones Correspondence.
Calvin McClung Historical Collection, Knoxville, Tenn.
    J. C. Houck Papers.
Center for Political and Governmental History, Baton Rouge
    Foster, Murphy J. Papers
Center for Southeast Louisiana Studies, Southeastern Louisiana University, Hammond

Dunn, Velmarae. Collection.
Lambert, John W. Papers.
Magee, Zuma. Collection
Reid, Robert R. Papers.
Tangipahoa Parish Courthouse Collection.
Tangipahoa Parish Tung Oil Collection.
Wands, James B. Papers.
Hessen-Nassau Hauptstadt Archiven, Wiesbaden, Germany
Zwei Bericht von New Orleans aus F. N. Freudenthal, Konsul, Hessen-Brunswick,
aus New Orleans.
Howard-Tilton Memorial Library, Tulane University, New Orleans
Department of Manuscripts and Rare Books
Everett Family Papers.
Farrar, Lee. Collection.
Kuntz Family Collection.
Young, Duncan Francis. Scrapbooks.
Louisiana and Lower Mississippi Valley Collections, Louisiana State University,
Baton Rouge
Allen, William M. Letters.
Alley, Mary. Scrapbooks.
Amacker, O. P. Papers.
Amite Navigation Company. Document, 1818.
Amite River Academy. Circular, 1879.
Anderson, John Q. Papers.
Andrews, James M. Papers.
Anonymous Civil War Letters Collections.
Aswell, James B. Papers.
Barrow, Robert. Letter.
Barrow, W. M. Family Papers.
Bass, John H. Diary.
Batchelor, Albert. Papers.
Batchelor, Ruth Ker. Papers.
Bell, William R. Papers.
Benson Family Papers.
Bond, Priscilla M. Diary.
Bond, William. Papers.
Bonner, Samuel C. Family Papers.
Bonny, P. L. Papers.
Bowman, James P. Family Papers.
Boyd, David F. Papers.
Bradley, James E., and Family. Papers.
Bringier, Louis. Papers.
Burke, E. A. Papers.

Burruss, John C. Papers.

Butler Family Papers.

Butler, Thomas. Papers.

Capell, Eli J. Papers.

Carpenter, George H. Family Papers.

Carruth, Elizabeth. Papers.

Cartwright, Samuel. Family Papers.

Causey, R. J. Correspondence.

Clinton-Port Hudson Railroad Company. Records.

Clouet, Alexander de. Papers.

Collins, O. L. Account Book.

Connor, Lemuel. Family Papers.

Corbin, Robert A. Papers.

Democratic Party. Handbill, 1876.

Dixon, William Y. Papers.

Draughon, S. B., and Company. Account Book.

Durnin, Henry. Notebook.

Durnin, James, and John Durnin. Papers.

East Baton Rouge Parish Volunteer Fund. Letter.

East Feliciana Parish Archives Collection.

Edwards, James Wiley. Papers.

Ellis Family Papers.

Embree, Joseph. Papers.

Evans, Nathaniel. Family Papers.

Flanders, Benjamin F. Papers.

Fluker, David J. Papers.

Fuqua, James O. Papers.

Garig, W. W. Papers.

Gayarre, Charles. Collection.

Gayle, W. O. Record Book.

George, John Thomas. Papers.

Gurley, John W. Papers.

Hamilton, William S. Papers.

Hardin, J. Fair. Letters.

Harris, John A. Letters.

Harrower, G. T. Letters.

Hayden, S. A. Letter.

Haynes, Bythell. Letter.

Hennen-Jennings Papers.

Hephzibah Church. Books.

Herrin, Edmund. Papers.

Hulin, Aaron. Letter.

Hunter-Taylor Family Papers.
Hursey, Asa H. Family Papers.
Johnson, Charles James. Letters.
Kellogg, William P. Papers.
Kemp, John. Papers.
Kendall, John Irwin. Biography.
Kendrick, Benjamin. Papers.
Kent, Amos. Papers.
Kilbourne, James Gilliam. Correspondence.
Kilbourne, J. G. Family Papers.
Killian and Harry. Account Book.
Knighton, Josiah. Family Papers.
Knights of Honor. Books.
Koch, Christian D. Papers.
Ku Klux Klan. Items.
Lambert, John W. Papers.
Lambert, Samuel. Military History.
Lea, Lemanda. Papers.
Leake, W. W. Letter.
Lebret, Peter. Account Books.
Livingston Parish Papers Collection.
Louisiana Broadside Collection.
Louisiana State Executive Department. Governor's Correspondence Collection.
Lusher, Robert M. Papers.
Lyons, Mary E. Notebook.
Marston, Henry W. Family Papers.
McBeth. Letter, 1864.
McCollam, Andrew and Ellen E. Papers.
McGee, Zuma F. Collection.
McGehee, James Stewart. Papers.
McGehee, John Burruss. Papes.
McKinney, Jeptha. Papers.
McKowen, John C. Papers.
Miscellaneous File.
Newsom, Maston S. Papers.
Nichols, Francis T. Papers.
Norsworthy, W. F. Letter.
Norwood, Abel John. Papers.
Patrick, Robert W. Family Papers.
Pike, George A. Scrapbook.
Pugh, Alex. Diaries.
Pugh, Josephine. Papers.

Raoul, W. Greene. Papers.

Redhead, Joseph. Diary.

Reid, Robert R. Papers.

Reminiscences of Jane McCausland Chinn.

Richardson, Hardy. Papers.

Richardson, Henry. Papers.

Roxborough, Charles A. Letter.

Ruggles, Daniel. Confederate Military Report.

Russell, J. Letter.

Scott, M. J. Letter.

Sherman, Thomas W. Letter.

Sherman, William T. Letters.

Slauson, Daniel D. Notebook.

Smith, Annabel. Diary.

Smith, Richard H. Correspondence.

Snell, S. F. Letter.

Southern Watchman. Mailing List.

Stevens, Charles E. Letters.

Stewart, William, and Walter Stewart. Papers.

St. Helena Parish. Records.

Stirling, Lewis. Family Papers.

Stokes, Joel A. Papers.

Taylor, Calvin. Papers.

Taylor, Margaret A. Papers.

Taylor, Sereno. Papers.

Tyson, Robert A. Diary.

Vinet, John B. Letters.

Warmoth, Henry Clay. Papers.

Warner, Thomas E. Family Papers.

Washington Hall Hotel. Ledger.

Watson, William. Sheriff's Fee Book.

Wells, J. Madison. Papers.

West Feliciana Parish Military Board. Minute Book.

Wilkinson, Micajah. Papers.

WPA Louisiana Parish Police Jury Minutes Collection.

Mississippi State Archives, Jackson

East Fork Baptist Church. Records.

Military Annals of Mississippi.

New Orleans-Jackson and Great Northern Railroad. Collection.

Ruggles, Daniel. Papers.

Terry, Joseph S. Papers.

WPA Mississippi County Board of Police Minutes Collection.
National Archives, Washington, D.C.
  Johnson, Andrew. Papers.
  Records of the Assistant Commissioner for the State of Louisiana Bureau of Refugees, Freedmen, and Abandoned Lands, Record Group 105.
  Records of the Louisiana State Government, 1850–88, War Department Collection of Confederate Records, Doc. F-75.
Newberry Library, Chicago.
  Francis, W. M., and E. D. Frost. Out Letters Collection.
  Illinois Central Railroad. Collection; Overflow Reports.
  Sheridan, General Philip H. Letter.
  Skene, E. P. Outletters.
  West Feliciana Railroad. Collection.
Southern Historical Collection, University of North Carolina, Chapel Hill.
  Warmoth, Henry Clay. Papers.

Other Unpublished Materials

Amite City Council. Minute Books. Amite City Hall, Amite City, La.
Hyde, Samuel C. Papers. In possession of Margaret Hyde Quin, Amite City, La.
Livingston, St. Helena, and St. Tammany Elected Officials Collection. In possession of Clark Forrest, Holden, La.
Pike County, Mississippi, Circuit Court. Minutes. Books A, B. Pike County Courthouse, Magnolia, Miss.
St. Tammany Parish. Clerk of Court Archives. Covington, La.
Sixteenth Judicial District Court. Minute Books, Nos. 2, 4–7. Tangipahoa Parish Clerk of Court Archives, Amite City, La.
Twenty-First Judicial District. Minute Books, Division A and B, No. 2, 12. Livingston Parish Clerk of Court. Livingston, La.
Twenty-Fifth Judicial District Court. Minutes (Successions Records). Tangipahoa Parish Clerk of Court Archives, Amite City, La.

Newspapers

Amite City

Daily Wanderer, 1864–65.
Democrat, 1874–76.
Florida Parishes, 1890–97, 1904–1922.
Florida Parish Times, 1922–24.
Gazette, 1887–90.
Independent, 1874, 1879, 1882–83, 1887.
Lanier's Digest, 1929.

Louisiana Star, 1880.
News Digest, 1959, 1975, 1976.
Progress, 1934, 1936, 1937, 1945, 1940.
Sun, 1913.
Sunday Wanderer, 1865.
Tangipahoa Advocate, 1867.
Tangipahoa Democrat, 1872–75.
Tangipahoa Parish News, 1926–27.
Times, 1867, 1915.
Tri-Weekly Wanderer, 1865.
True Democrat, 1875.

Baton Rouge

Capitolian-Advocate, 1883, 1888.
Daily Advocate, 1854–1901, 1998.
Daily Comet, 1852.
Gazette, 1830–34, 1852.
States, 1901–1912.
Tri-Weekly Advocate, 1868.
Weekly Advocate, 1855–68.

Bayou Sara

Ledger, 1861, 1876.

Birmingham, Ala.

Age Herald, 1893.

Bogalusa

Enterprise and American, 1919.

Chicago, Ill.

Chronicle, 1897.
Tribune, 1872.

Clinton

American Patriot, 1855.
East Feliciana Patriot, 1866–70.
Feliciana Democrat, 1855–67.
Feliciana Whig, 1842.
Louisiana Floridian, 1846.

Patriot-Democrat, 1880, 1887–90.
Semi-Weekly Patriot Democrat, 1888–90.

Covington

St. Tammany Farmer, 1899–1904.
Wanderer, 1862, 1864.

Denham Springs

Livingston Parish News, 1998.

Fort Adams, Miss.

Item, 1854.

Franklin, Tenn.

Southern Lumberman, 1911.

Franklinton

Era Leader, 1925.
New Era, 1887–88, 1896, 1898–99, 1904–1909, 1917.

Greensburg

Gazette, 1882.
Imperial, 1857–61.
Journal, 1866.
St. Helena Echo, 1866–98, 1910, 1998.
Weekly Star and Journal, 1867.

Hammond

Daily Herald, 1909.
Daily Star, 1998, 2005.
Louisiana Sun, 1913.
Vindicator, 1929.

Independence

Independence News, 1926.

Jackson, La.

Feliciana Record, 1909.

Jackson, Miss.

Daily Southern Crisis, 1863.
Mississippian, 1863.

Kentwood

Commercial, 1895–1919.

Liberty, Miss.

Southern Herald, 1883–84.

Magnolia, Miss.

Gazette, 1882–83.
Grand Trunk, 1862.

New Orleans

Bee, 1840, 1859–61.
Bulletin, 1885.
Daily Crescent, 1856–57.
Daily Delta, 1845, 1854–61.
Daily Picayune, 1852–1909, 1928.
Price Current and Commercial Intelligencer, 1859–60.
Republican, 1869–70, 1873.
Times, 1873.
Times Democrat, 1888, 1890, 1894–1901.
Tribune, 1867.
Weekly Courier, 1856–66.
Weekly Pelican, 1887.
Weekly Picayune, 1894–97.

New York

Times, 1998

Opelousas

St. Landry Clarion, 1909.

Osyka, Miss.

Two States, 1888.

Pocahontas, Ark.

Randolph Herald, 1893.

Ponchatoula

Enterprise, 1921–1922.

Port Vincent

Livingstonian, 1879.
Triune, 1873.

Roseland

Herald, 1894.

Springfield

Livingston Times, 1906–07.

St. Francisville

Asylum and Feliciana Advertiser, 1822–24.
Feliciana Sentinel, 1889.
Louisiana Journal, 1824–26.
Louisianian, 1819–20.

Wesson, Miss.

Southern Industry, 1885.

Woodville, Miss.

Republican, 1872.
Sentinel, 1871.
Wilkinson Gazette, 1861.

Interviews by Author

Davidson, Orin. Arcola, La., June 1988.
Dyson, Luther. Amite, La., September, 1990.
Forrest, Clark. Holden, La., November, 2014
Hart, Herbert. Kentwood, La., February 2, 1991.
Hyde, Samuel C., Sr., Amite, La., July 1990.
Kent, R. A., Jr., Fluker, La., August 1, 1991.

Lambert, Norma. Tangipahoa, La., July 26, 1988.
Perrilloux, Scott. Hammond, La., September, 2016.
Ricks, Junie. Franklinton, La., June 21, July, August, 1988, February 3, 1996.
Watson, Eugene B., Fluker, La., December 27, 1980.

Published Sources

Books

American Institute of Homeopathy. *Official Report of the Homeopathic Yellow Fever Commission*. New Orleans, 1879.
Arthur, Stanley C. *The Story of the West Florida Rebellion*. St. Francisville, La., 1935.
Ash, Stephen V. *Middle Tennessee Society Transformed, 1860–1870: War and Peace in the Upper South*. Baton Rouge, 1988.
Asseff, Emmett. *The History of the Government of Louisiana*. Baton Rouge, 1964.
Bacon, Edward. *Among the Cotton Thieves*. Detriot, 1867.
Baiamonte, John V., Jr. *Immigrants in Rural America: A Study of the Italians of Tangipahoa Parish, Louisiana*. New York, 1990.
———. *Spirit of Vengeance: Nativism and Louisiana Justice, 1921–1924*. Baton Rouge, 1986.
Barnes, Kenneth C. *Who Killed John Clayton? Political Violence and the Emergence of the New South, 1861–1893*. Durham, N.C., 1998.
Bertrand, Alvin L. *The Many Louisianas: Rural Social Areas and Cultural Islands*. Baton Rouge, 1955.
Bettersworth, John. *Confederate Mississippi: The People and Politics of a Cotton State in Wartime*. Baton Rouge, 1943.
Binmore, Ken. *Essays on the Foundations of Game Theory*. Cambridge, Mass., 1990.
Booth, Andrew. *Records of Louisiana Confederate Soldiers and Louisiana Confederate Commands*. 3 vols. Spartanburg, S.C., 1984.
Brackenridge, H. M. *Views of Louisiana: Together with a Journal of a Voyage up the Missouri River, in 1811*. Pittsburgh, 1814.
Burton, Orville V. *In My Father's House There Are Many Mansions: Family and Community in Edgefield, South Caroline*. Chapel Hill, N. C., 1985.
Caldwell, Erskine. *Tobacco Road*. New York, 1932.
Carlton, Mark T. *River Capital: An Illustrated History of Baton Rouge*. New York, 1981.
Carter, Howell. *A Cavalryman's Reminiscences of the Civil War*. New Orleans, 1900.
Casey, Powell. *The Story of Camp Moore*. New Orleans, 1985.
Cash, Wilbur J. *The Mind of the South*. New York, 1941.
Chambers, Henry. *A History of Louisiana, Wilderness—Colony—Province—Territory—State – People*. New York, 1925.
Claille, S. E. *Intimidation and the Number of White and Colored Voters in Louisiana in 1876 as Shown by Statistical Data Derived from Republican Official Reports*. New Orleans, 1877.

Cooper, William J., Jr. *Liberty and Slavery: Southern Politics to 1860*. New York, 1983.

Cresswell, Stephen. *Mormons, Cowboys, Moonshiners, and Klansmen: Federal Law Enforcement in the South and West*. Tuscaloosa, Ala., 1992.

Darby, William. *Geographical Description of the State of Louisiana . . . with an Account of the Characters and Manners of the Inhabitants*. Philadelphia, 1816.

Davis, Edwin A., ed. *Diary of Bennett H. Barrow: Plantation Life in the Florida Parishes of Louisiana, 1836–1846, as Reflected in the Diary of Bennett Barrow*. New York, 1943.

Davis, Thomas H. *The Whitecaps: A History of the Organization in Sevier County*. Knoxville, 1899.

Davis, William C. *The Rogue Republic: How Would-Be Patriots Waged the Shortest Revolution in American History*. New York, 2011.

Dawson, Joseph G., III. *Army Generals and Reconstruction: Louisiana, 1862–1877*. Baton Rouge, 1982.

Dawson, Sara Morgan. *A Confederate Girl's Diary*. New York, 1913.

De Bow, J. D. B. *The Industrial Resources, Etc., of the Southern and Western State: Embracing a View of their Commerce, Agriculture, Manufacturers . . . with an Appendix*. 2 vols. New Orleans, 1853.

Dennett, Daniel. *Louisiana as It Is: Its Topography and Material Resources . . . Climate and People of the State*. New Orleans, 1879.

Dixit, Avinash K., and Barry J. Nalebuff. *Thinking Strategically: The Competitive Edge in Business, Politics, and Everyday Life*. New York, 1991.

Donald, David H. *The Politics of Reconstruction, 1863–1867*. Baton Rouge, 1965.

Donnell, E. J. *Chronological and Statistical History of Cotton*. New York, 1872.

Dorris, Jonathan. *Pardon and Amnesty Under Lincoln and Johnson: The Restoration of the Confederates to Their Rights and Privileges*. Chapel Hill, N.C., 1953.

Durrill, Wayne. *War of Another Kind: A Southern Community in the Great Rebellion*. New York, 1990.

Duval, Mary V. *History of Mississippi . . . with an Appendix Containing the Constitution of Mississippi, Adopted November 1, 1890*. Louisville, 1890.

Evans, William M. *Ballots and Fence Rails: Reconstruction in the Lower Cape Fear*. Chapel Hill, N.C., 1967.

Faust, Drew Gilpin, ed. *The Ideology of Slavery: Proslavery Thought in the Antebellum South, 1830–1860*. Baton Rouge, 1981.

Fellman, Michael. *Inside War: The Guerrilla Conflict in Missouri During the American Civil War*. New York, 1989.

Fleming, Walter L. *The Reconstruction of the Seceded States*. Albany, N.Y., 1905.

Flint, Timothy. *Recollections of the Last Ten Years in the Valley of the Mississippi*. Carbondale, Ill., 1968.

Foner, Eric. *Reconstruction: America's Unfinished Revolution, 1863–1877*. New York, 1988.

Ford, Lacy. *Origins of Southern Radicalism: The South Carolina Upcountry, 1800–1860.* New York, 1988.

Gallaspy, John N. *The City That Refused to Die: Bogalusa's First Hundred Years.* New Orleans, 2014.

Garcia, Celine F. *Celine Remembering Louisiana, 1850–1871.* Ed. Patrick Geary. Athens, Ga., 1987.

Goodyear, C. W. *Bogalusa Story.* New York, 1950.

Gray, Lewis C. *History of Agriculture in the Southern United States to 1860.* 2 vols. New York, 1941–58.

Griffith, Francis Williams. *True Life Story of Will Purvis.* Purvis, Miss., 1935.

Hahn, Steven. *The Roots of Southern Populism: Yeoman Farmers and the Transformation of the Georgia Upcountry, 1850–1890.* New York, 1983.

Hair, William Ivy. *Bourbonism and Agrarian Protest: Louisiana Politics, 1877–1900.* Baton Rouge, 1969.

Hansell, F. F., ed. *Commercial and Statistical Almanac: Containing a History of the Epidemic of 1878.* New Orleans, 1879.

Harris, J. William. *Plain Folk and Gentry in a Slave Society: White Liberty and Black Slavery in Augusta's Hinterlands.* Middletown, Conn., 1985.

Harris, Ronald. *We Hail Thee Now Southeastern: Remembering the First Seventy-Five Years of Southeastern Louisiana University.* Hammond, La., 2000.

Hernando, Matthew. *Faces like Devils: The Bald Knobber Vigilantes in the Ozarks.* Columbia, Mo., 2014.

Hilliard, Sam B. *Hog Meat and Hoecake: Food Supply in the Old South, 1840–1860.* Carbondale, Ill., 1972.

Howard, Perry. *Political Tendencies in Louisiana, 1812–1952.* Baton Rouge, 1957.

Hyde, Sarah. *Schooling in the Antebellum South: The Rise of Public and Private Education in Louisiana, Mississippi, and Alabama.* Baton Rouge, 2016.

Hyman, Michael. *The Anti-Redeemers: Hill-Country Political Dissenters in the Lower South from Redemption to Populism.* Baton Rouge, 1990.

Illinois Central Railroad Company. *Where to Locate New Factories in the States of Kentucky, Tennessee, Mississippi, Louisiana, on the Line of the Southern Division of the Illinois Central Railroad.* Cedar Rapids, Iowa, 1892.

Ingalls, Robert P. *Urban Vigilantes in the New South: Tampa, 1882–1936.* Knoxville, 1988.

Inscoe, John. *Mountain Masters, Slavery, and the Sectional Crisis in Western North Carolina.* Knoxville, 1989.

Jeffery, E. T. *Remarks of E. T. Jeffery, General Manager, Illinois Central Railroad, Before the New Orleans City Council.* New Orleans, 1888.

Jones, Virgil. *Gray Ghosts and Rebel Raiders.* New York, 1956.

Kirby, Jack T. *Rural Worlds Lost: The American South, 1920–1960.* Baton Rouge, 1987.

Kousser, J. M., and James McPherson, eds. *Region, Race, and Reconstruction: Essays in Honor of C. Vann Woodward.* New York, 1982.

Lester, J. C., and D. L. Wilson. *Ku Klux Klan: Its Origin, Growth, and Disbandment.* New York, 1905.

Lonn, Ella. *Salt as a Factor in the Confederacy.* Birmingham, Ala., 1965.

Louisiana Folklife Program. *Folklife in the Florida Parishes.* Baton Rouge, 1989.

McWhiney, Grady. *Cracker Culture: Celtic Ways in the Old South.* Tuscaloosa, Ala., 1988.

Meyers, Marvin. *The Jacksonian Persuasion: Politics and Belief.* Stanford, 1957.

Moore, John Hebron. *The Emergence of the Cotton Kingdom in the Old Southwest: Mississippi, 1770–1860.* Baton Rouge, 1988.

Morris, Peter. *Introduction to Game Theory.* New York, 1994.

Mutzenberg, Charles. *Kentucky's Famous Feuds and Tragedies.* New York, 1917.

Napier, John Hawkins, III. *Lower Pearl River's Piney Woods: Its Land and People.* Oxford, Miss., 1985.

Newton, Milton B. *Atlas of Louisiana: A Guide for Students.* Baton Rouge, 1972.

Oakes, James. *The Ruling Race: A History of American Slaveholders.* New York, 1982.

Olmsted, Frederick L. *The Cotton Kingdom: A Traveller's Observations on Cotton and Slavery in the American Slave States.* Edited by Arthur M. Schlesinger. New York, 1953.

———. *A Journey in the Backcountry.* New York, 1863.

Owen, Guillermo. *Game Theory.* 2nd ed. New York, 1982.

Owsley, Frank Lawrence. *Plain Folk of the Old South.* Baton Rouge, 1949.

Polk, Noel, ed. *Mississippi's Piney Woods: A Human Perspective.* Jackson, Miss., 1986.

Rable, George. *But There Was No Peace: The Role of Violence in the Politics of Reconstruction.* Athens, Ga., 1984.

Reed, Merl. *New Orleans and the Railroads: The Struggle for Commercial Empire, 1830–1860.* Baton Rouge, 1966.

Roark, James L. *Masters Without Slaves: Southern Planters in the Civil War and Reconstruction.* New York, 1977.

Rowland, Dunbar. *Military History of Mississippi, 1803–1898.* Spartanburg, S.C., 1978.

———, ed. *Official Letter Books of W. C. C. Claiborne, 1801–1816.* 6 vols. Jackson, Miss., 1917.

Rowland, Eron, ed. *Life, Letters, and Papers of William Dunbar of Elgin, Morayshire, Scotland, and Natchez, Mississippi: Pioneer Scientist of the Southern United States.* Jackson, Miss., 1930.

Russell, Sir William Howard. *My Diary, North and South.* New York, 1954.

Savitt, Todd, and James Young. *Disease and Distinctiveness in the American South.* Knoxville, 1988.

Shaw, Arthur Marvin. *Centenary College Goes to War in 1861.* Shreveport, La., 1940.

Shugg, Roger W. *Origins of Class Struggle in Louisiana: A Social History of White Farmers and Laborers During Slavery and After, 1840–1875.* Baton Rouge, 1939.

Sifakis, Stewart. *Compendium of the Confederate Armies: Florida and Arkansas.* New York, 1992.

Stampp, Kenneth. *Era of Reconstruction, 1865–1877*. New York, 1965.

Taylor, F. J., ed. *Reluctant Rebel: The Secret Diary of Robert Patrick, 1861–1865*. Baton Rouge, 1959.

Taylor, Joe Gray. *Louisiana Reconstructed, 1863–1877*. Baton Rouge, 1974.

Thornton, J. Mills, III. *Politics and Power in a Slave Society: Alabama, 1800–1860*. Baton Rouge, 1978.

Tunnell, Ted. *Crucible of Reconstruction: War, Radicalism, and Race in Louisiana, 1862–1877*. Baton Rouge, 1984.

———, ed. *Carpetbagger from Vermont: The Autobiography of Marshall Harvey Twitchell*. Baton Rouge, 1989.

Vandal, Gilles. *Rethinking Southern Violence: Homicides in Post–Civil War Louisiana, 1866–1884*. Columbus, Ohio, 2000.

Waldrep, Christopher. *Nightriders: Defending Community in the Black Patch, 1890–1915*. Durham, N.C.. 1993.

Waller, Altina. *Feud: Hatfields, McCoys, and Social Change in Appalachia, 1860–1900*. Chapel Hill, N.C., 1988.

White, Howard A. *The Freedmen's Bureau in Louisiana*. Baton Rouge, 1970.

Wiebe, Robert H. *The Search for Order, 1877–1920*. New York, 1967.

Wiener, Jonathan M. *Social Origins of the New South: Alabama, 1860–1885*. Baton Rouge, 1978.

Williams, E. Russ, Jr. *History of Washington Parish, Louisiana, 1798–1992*. Monroe, La., 1994.

Winters, John D. *The Civil War in Louisiana*. Baton Rouge, 1963.

Wood, Frank E. *Industrial Directory of Louisiana, 1925–1926*. New Orleans, 1926.

Woodman, Harold D. *King Cotton & His Retainers: Financing & Marketing the Cotton Crop of the South, 1800–1925*. Lexington, 1968.

Wright, Gavin. *The Political Economy of the Cotton South: Households, Markets, and Wealth in the Nineteenth Century*. New York, 1978.

Wyatt-Brown, Bertram. *Honor and Violence in the Old South*. New York, 1986.

Articles and Essays

Baiamonte, John, Jr. "Community Life in the Italian Colonies of Tangipahoa Parish, Louisiana, 1890–1950." *Louisiana History*, XXX (1989), 365–97.

Bankston, William B., and David H. Allen. "Rural Social Areas and Patterns of Homicide: An Analysis of Lethal Violence in Louisiana." *Rural Sociology*, XLV (1987), 223–37.

Baxter, Robert J. "Cattle Raising in Early Mississippi." *Mississippi Folklore Register*, X (1976), 1–25.

Belko, William S. "The Origins of the Monroe Doctrine Revisited: The Madison Administration, the West Florida Revolt, and the No Transfer Policy." *Florida Historical Quarterly*, XC (2011), 157–92.

Bridges, Kenneth. "The Tucker Parnell Feud." *Encyclopedia of Arkansas History and Culture*, 2009.

Carter, Hodding. "Not Much of a Man if He Hadn't." In Hodding Carter, *Southern Legacy*. Baton Rouge, 1966.

Casey, Powell. "Military Roads in the Florida Parishes of Louisiana." *Louisiana History*, XV (1974), 229–42.

Claiborne, J. F. H. "A Trip Through the Piney Woods." *Publications of the Mississippi Historical Society*, IX (1906), 491–534.

Dart, Henry, ed. "Documents Covering a Royal Land Grant and Other Transactions on the Mississippi and Amite Rivers During the English Rule." *Louisiana Historical Quarterly*, XII (1929), 630–44.

Davis, Donald W. "Ratification of the Constitution of 1868—Record of Votes." *Louisiana History*, VI (1965), 301–305.

Dew, C. [Charles?], ed. "Slavery in the Virginia Legislature." *De Bow's Review*, XX (1856), 468–87.

Dew, Charles B. "Who Won the Secession Election in Louisiana?" *Journal of Southern History*, XXXVI (1970), 18–32.

Din, Gilbert. "Early Spanish Colonization Efforts in Louisiana." *Louisiana Studies*, XI (1972), 31–49.

Duval, Margaret L. "Legends of Wilkinson County and the Surrounding Area." *Louisiana Folklore Miscellany*, III (1975), 47–64.

Eisterhold, John. "Lumber and Trade in the Lower Mississippi Valley and New Orleans, 1800–1860." *Louisiana History*, XIII (1972), 71–92.

Estaville, Lawrence, Jr. "A Strategic Railroad: The New Orleans-Jackson and Great Northern in the Civil War." *Louisiana History*, XIV (1973), 117–36.

Evans, Harry H. "James Robb, Banker and Pioneer Railroad Builder." *Louisiana Historical Quarterly*, XXIII (1940), 170–256.

Galambos, Louis. "The Emerging Organizational Synthesis in Modern American History." *Business History Review*, XLIV (1970), 279–90.

———. "Technology, Political Economy, and Professionalism: Central Themes of the Organizational Synthesis." *Business History Review*, LVII (1983), 471–93.

Greer, James K. "Louisiana Politics, 1845–1861." *Louisiana Historical Quarterly*, XII (1929), 383–425.

Hackett, Derek. "Vote Early! Beware of Fraud! A Note on Voter Turnout in Presidential and Gubernatorial Elections in Louisiana, 1828–1844." *Louisiana Studies*, XIV (1975), 179–88.

Haskin, Ralph. "Planter and Cotton Factor in the Old South: Some Areas of Friction." *Agricultural History*, XXIX (1955), 1–14.

Holmes, Jack D. L. "Indigo in Colonial Louisiana and the Floridas." *Louisiana History*, VIII (1967), 329–50.

Holmes, William F. "Whitecapping: Agrarian Violence in Mississippi, 1902–1906." *Journal of Southern History*, XXXV (1969), 165–85.

Hyde, Samuel C., Jr. "Consolidating the Revolution: Factionalism and Finesse in the West Florida Revolt, 1810." *Louisiana History*, LI (2010), 261–80.

Hyman, Owen. "The Great Southern Lumber Company in Bogalusa, Louisiana, 1902–1935." *Southeast Louisiana Review*, IV (2012), 6–36.

Kendall, John S. "Recollections of a Confederate Officer." *Louisiana Historical Quarterly*, XXIX (1946), 1055–70.

———, ed. "Muster Rolls of the Fourth Louisiana Regiment of Volunteers, Confederate States Army." *Louisiana Historical Quarterly*, XXX (1947), 481–522.

Lee, Matthew, and Graham Ousey. "Reconsidering the Culture and Violence Connection: Strategies of Action in the Rural South." *Journal of Interpersonal Violence*, XXVI (2011), 899–929.

Lestage, Oscar. "The White League in Louisiana." *Louisiana Historical Quarterly*, XVIII (1935), 617–93.

McDonald, Forrest, and Grady McWhiney. "The Antebellum Southern Herdsman: A Reinterpretation." *Journal of Southern History*, XLI (1975), 147–66.

McMillen, Sally. "Southern Women and the Sunday School Movement, 1865–1915." In Samuel C. Hyde, Jr., ed., *Plain Folk of the South Revisited*. Baton Rouge, 1997.

Mencken, H. L. "The Sahara of the Bozart." *Prejudices, Second Series*, New York, 1920.

Mobley, James William. "The Academy Movement in Louisiana." *Louisiana Historical Quarterly*, XXX (1947), 821–31.

Mocsary, Victoria. "Hungarian Settlement, 1896–1912: A Synthesis." *Southeast Louisiana Review*, IV (2012), 69–94.

Padgett, James A. "The Constitution of the West Florida Republic." *Louisiana Historical Quarterly*, XX (1937), 881–94.

Peacock, James. "Historical and Statistical Sketches of Louisiana." *De Bow's Review*, XI (1851), 264–65.

Prichard, Walter, ed. "Minutes of the Police Jury of St. Helena Parish, August 16–19, 1813." *Louisiana Historical Quarterly*, XXIII (1940), 405–27.

Quick, Amy. "The History of Bogalusa, the Magic City of Louisiana." *Louisiana Historical Quarterly*, XXIX (1946), 73–190.

Rickels, Milton. "Thomas Bands Thorpe in the Felicianas, 1836–1842." *Louisiana Historical Quarterly*, XXXIX (1956), 169–97.

Romero, Ginger. "Hungarian Folklife: The Sweet Taste of Yesterday." *Florida Parishes of Southeast Louisiana Series*, III (1987), 1–26.

Romero, Sidney. "The Political Career of Murphy J. Foster." *Louisiana Historical Quarterly*, XXVIII (1945), 1129–1237.

Ruffin, Minnie, and Lilla McClure. "General Soloman Weathersby Downs, Democratic Leader of North Louisiana, 1840–1854." *Louisiana Historical Quarterly*, XVII (1934), 5–43.

Scallions, Cody. "The Rise and Fall of the Original Lone Star State: Infant American

Imperialism Ascendant in West Florida." *Florida Historical Quarterly*, XC (2011), 193–220.

Shugg, Roger. "Suffrage and Representation in Antebellum Louisiana." *Louisiana Historical Quarterly*, XIX (1936), 390–406.

Smith, Henry L. "Southwestern Railroad Convention at New Orleans." *De Bow's Review*, X (1851), 690–94.

Suarez, Raleigh. "Bargains, Bills, and Bankruptcies: Business Activity in Rural Antebellum Louisiana." *Louisiana History*, VII (1966), 189–206.

"Train Fired Upon." *Lumber Trade Journal*, January 15, 1911, p. 26.

"Train Is Attacked." *Southern Lumberman*, January 14, 1911, p. 28.

Turner, Arthur. "Turkey Drives: South Mississippi, Greene County." *Mississippi Folklore Register*, III (1969), 30–42.

Vincent, Charles. "Negro Leadership and Programs in the Constitutional Convention of 1868." *Louisiana History*, X (1969), 339–51.

Waldrep, Christopher. "Planters and the Planters Protective Association in Kentucky and Tennessee." *Journal of Southern History*, LII (1986), 565–88.

State Government Documents

Annual Report of the Adjutant General of the State of Louisiana for the Year Ending December 31, 1896. Baton Rouge, 1897.

Biennial Report of the Louisiana State Board of Health to the Legislature of the State of Louisiana. New Orleans, 1919, 1927.

Cases Argued and Determined in the Supreme Court of Louisiana, November, 1906. *Louisiana Reports*, Vol. 118, St. Paul, Minn., 1907, 349–60.

Constitution of Form of Government of the State of Louisiana. New Orleans, 1812.

Constitution of the State of Louisiana Adopted in Convention at the City of New Orleans, May 12, 1898. New Orleans, 1898.

Journal of the Convention Called for the Purpose of Re-Adopting, Amending, or Changing the Constitution of the State of Louisiana. New Orleans, 1845.

Journal of the Proceedings of the Convention of the State of Louisiana, 1861–1862; microfilm rpr. New Haven, 1970.

Journal of the State Convention to Form a New Constitution for Louisiana, 1852. New Orleans, 1852.

Louisiana Constitutional Convention, 1844–1845, Official Report of Constitutional Debates. New Orleans, 1845.

Louisiana House Journal. 1812–99.

Louisiana Legislative Documents. 1812–1906.

Louisiana Senate Journal. 1812–1920.

Louisiana State Board of Registration. *Instructions to Supervisors of Registration with a Transcript of the Constitutional, Naturalization, and Other Laws Pertaining to Qualification of Electors*. New Orleans, 1868.

Louisiana State Secession Debates. New Haven, 1970.

Message of Governor Newton C. Blanchard to the General Assembly, 1908. Baton Rouge, 1908.

A New Digest of the Statute Laws of the State of Louisiana, from the Change of Government to the Year 1841, Inclusive. New Orleans, 1842.

Official Journal of the Proceedings of the Convention for Framing a Constitution for the State of Louisiana, 1867–1868. New Orleans, 1868.

Police Jury Code for the Parish of East Feliciana, Louisiana, Containing a Digest of the State Laws Relative to Police Juries, and also a Digest of the Ordinances of East Feliciana Having the Force of Laws up to May 1, 1859. Clinton, La., 1859.

Report of the Attorney General to the General Assembly of Louisiana, 1895–1898. New Orleans, 1898.

Report of the Attorney General to the General Assembly of Louisiana, 1898–1900. New Orleans, 1900.

Report of the Attorney General to the General Assembly of Louisiana, 1900, 1902, 1904, 1906, 1908, 1910, 1912, 1920, 1930. New Orleans, 1902, 1904, 1906, 1908, 1910, 1912, 1920, 1930.

Report of the Board of Returning Officers, Session 1876, to the General Assembly of the State of Louisiana, Relating to the Election Held November 7, 1876. New Orleans, 1877.

Report of the Commissioner of Labor and Industrial Statistics to the General Assembly of the State of Louisiana. New Orleans, 1916.

Report of the Joint Committee of the General Assembly of Louisiana on the Conduct of the Late Elections and the Condition of Peace and Order in the State. Baton Rouge, 1869.

Report of the Returning Board of the State of Louisiana to the General Assembly, 1875 Session. New Orleans, 1876.

Reports of Cases Argued and Determined in the Supreme Court of Louisiana. Vol. XXV. New Orleans, 1873.

Supreme Court of Louisiana of the Judicial Council of the Supreme Court, "Annual Report, 2013."

Theses and Dissertations

Singletary, Otis A. "The Negro Militia Movement During Radical Reconstruction." Ph.D. dissertation, Louisiana State University, 1949.

Tregle, Joseph G. "Louisiana in the Age of Jackson: A Study in Ego Politics." Ph.D. dissertation, University of Pennsylvania, 1954.

Index

Nash equilibrium, 312–16
Natchez, Miss., 129
New Orleans: 2, 5, 7, 9, 30, 31, 34, 36, 37, 38, 49, 58, 74, 116, 123, 132, 173, 184, 248, 253; voting patterns in, 47–48; and railroads, 77–81; and yellow fever, 83–85; strategic significance of, 108; capture of, 110; race riot in, 161, 293–94, 296, 301, 327
New Orleans and Mississippi Valley Railroad, 289
New Orleans-Jackson Railroad: 145, 191; influencing elections, 73; relevance of, 77–82, 85–87, 109, 112; destruction of, 119, 121, 147, 293
New Zion Cemetery, 334–35
Newsham, J. P., 171
Newsom, Maston, 175
Nickerson, Arthur, 272
Nightriders, 208–209, 211, 212
North Carolina, 9
Norwood, Abel John, 36

Oak Lawn Plantation, 31
Odom, J. B., 323
Offley, Maj. James, 162–63
Olive Branch, La., 170
Osband, Col. E. D., 137
Osborn, A. R., 325
Osyka, Miss., 85, 122, 136, 138, 152, 169, 234–35
Overton, Bill, 241
Overton, Tom, 241

Packard, Stephen, 189
Paine, Gen. Halbert, 128
Parker, John, 339
Parker, Julius, 252–53, 254, 258, 266
Parker, Linus, 140, 152
Partisans, 111, 127–28, 133–34
Patrick, Robert, 10, 131, 308
Pearl River: 2, 9, 25, 29, 37; fighting near, 113, 135; deserters near, 126
Peck, Maj. Frank, 113
Penn, Abraham, 40
Perrilloux, Scott, 347
Perry, Dr. James, 29

Pharr, John, 244
Pike County, Miss.: 25, 193; violence in, 235
Pinckneyville, Miss., 20, 40, 188
Pipes, John, 166
Pitkins, Annabelle, 118
Plain folk: 1, 7, 12, 13, 14, 15, 17, 18, 28, 30, 88–90, 139; and slaves, 32, 35–36; economic exploitation of, 41, 43–44, 46; expanding power of, 58; political exploitation of, 67–71, 76; and railroads, 80–87; challenging planters, 152, 180–81, 190–91, 229, 261
Plains Store, La., 128
Planters: 1, 10, 14–18, 28–29; purchasing goods, 30–31, 32; economic dominance of, 35–37, 41–44, 46; newspapers as tool of, 53; political dominance of, 59–72, 76, 151–53, 180–81, 190; and railroads, 78–82, 86, 88–90; decline of, 201, 203, 212, 228, 232, 261; suppressing outlaws, 235, 243
Pleasant, Ruffin G., 306
Pleasant Hill Plantation, 147
Plessy vs. Ferguson case, 274
Ponchatoula, La.: 85, 118–19; destruction of, 119–20, 121; deprivation in, 124, 299, 310, 326–28
Pond, Preston, 72–74
Ponder, Amos L., 318
Populist party, 236, 238, 246, 264–65
Populist-Republican Fusion party, 238, 244, 246
Port Hudson, La.: 7, 83, 108, 117; battle near, 119, 127–28, 129, 133, 296
Port Vincent, La., 3, 183
Powers, Col. Frank, 133
Preston, E. V., 266
Privatization, 38–43
Protestants, 2, 6
Pugh, Josephine, 131
Pulver, Maj. Martin, 127
Purser, Iona, 306
Purvis, Will, 209, 237

Railroads, 11. See also Illinois Central Railroad; New Orleans-Jackson Railroad
Raoul, W. Greene, 134